THE WHO'S BUYING SERIES
BY THE NEW STRATEGIST EDITORS

Who's Buying

Groceries

11th EDITION

New Strategist Press, LLC.
P.O. Box 635, Amityville, New York 11701
800/848-0842; 631-608-8795
www.newstrategist.com

© 2014. NEW STRATEGIST PRESS, LLC.

ISBN 978-1-940308-63-0 (paper)
ISBN 978-1-940308-64-7 (e-book)

Printed in the United States of America.

Contents

Household Spending on Groceries by Product Category, 2012

About the Data in *Who's Buying Groceries*

Introduction

The spending data in *Who's Buying Groceries* are based on the Bureau of Labor Statistics' Consumer Expenditure Survey, an ongoing, nationwide survey of household spending. The Consumer Expenditure Survey is a complete accounting of household expenditures. It includes everything from big-ticket items, such as homes and cars, to small purchases like laundry detergent and videos. The survey does not include expenditures by government, business, or institutions. The data in this report are from the 2012 Consumer Expenditure Survey, unless otherwise noted.

To produce this report, New Strategist Press analyzed the Consumer Expenditure Survey's average household spending data in a variety of ways, calculating household spending indexes, aggregate (or total) household spending, and market shares. This report shows spending data by age, household income, household type, race, Hispanic origin, region of residence, and education. These analyses are presented in two formats—for all product categories by demographic characteristic and for all demographic characteristics by product category.

Definition of Consumer Unit

The Consumer Expenditure Survey uses the consumer unit rather than the household as the sampling unit. The term "household" is used interchangeably with the term "consumer unit" in this report for convenience, although they are not exactly the same. Some households contain more than one consumer unit.

The Bureau of Labor Statistics defines consumer units as either: (1) members of a household who are related by blood, marriage, adoption, or other legal arrangements; (2) a person living alone or sharing a household with others or living as a roomer in a private home or lodging house or in permanent living quarters in a hotel or motel, but who is financially independent; or (3) two or more persons living together who pool their income to make joint expenditure decisions. The bureau defines financial independence in terms of "the three major expense categories: housing, food, and other living expenses. To be considered financially independent, at least two of the three major expense categories have to be provided by the respondent."

The Census Bureau uses the household as its sampling unit in the decennial census and in the monthly Current Population Survey. The Census Bureau's household "consists of all persons who occupy a housing unit. A house, an apartment or other groups of rooms, or a single room is regarded as a housing unit when it is occupied or intended for occupancy as separate living quarters; that is, when the occupants do not live and eat with any other persons in the structure and there is direct access from the outside or through a common hall."

The definition goes on to specify that "a household includes the related family members and all the unrelated persons, if any, such as lodgers, foster children, wards, or employees who share the housing unit. A person living alone in a housing unit or a group of unrelated persons sharing a housing unit as partners is also counted as a household. The count of households excludes group quarters."

Because there can be more than one consumer unit in a household, consumer units outnumber households by several million. Young adults under age 25 head most of the additional consumer units.

How to Use the Tables in This Report

The starting point for all calculations are the unpublished, detailed average household spending data collected by the Consumer Expenditure Survey. These numbers are shown on the report's average spending tables and on each of the product-specific tables. New Strategist's editors calculated the other figures in the report based on the average figures. The indexed spending tables and the indexed spending column (Best Customers) on the product-specific tables reveal whether spending by households in a given segment is above or below the average for all households and by how much. The total (or aggregate) spending tables show the overall size of the market. The market share tables and market share column (Biggest Customers) on the product-specific tables reveal how much spending each household segment controls. These analyses are described in detail below.

• **Average Spending.** The average spending figures show the average annual spending of households on groceries in 2012. The Consumer Expenditure Survey produces average spending data for all households in a segment, e.g., all households with a householder aged 25 to 34, not just for those who purchased the item. When examining spending data, it is important to remember that by including both purchasers and nonpurchasers in the calculation, the average is less than the amount spent on the item by buyers. (See Table 1 for the percentage of households that spent on groceries in 2012 and how much the purchasers spent.)

Because average spending figures include both buyers and nonbuyers, they reveal spending patterns by demographic characteristic. By knowing who is most likely to spend on an item, marketers can target their advertising and promotions more efficiently, and businesses can determine the market potential of a product or service in a city or neighborhood. By multiplying the average amount households spend on fresh fish by the number of households in an area, for example, a retailer can estimate the potential size of the local market for fresh fish.

• **Indexed Spending (Best Customers).** The indexed spending figures compare the spending of each household segment with that of the average household. To compute the indexes, New Strategist divides the average amount each household segment spends on an item by average household spending and multiplies the resulting figure by 100.

An index of 100 is the average for all households. An index of 125 means the spending of a household segment is 25 percent above average (100 plus 25). An index of 75 indicates spending that is 25 percent below the average for all households (100 minus 25). Indexed spending figures identify the best customers for a product or service. Households with an index of 178 for coffee, for example, are a strong market for this product. Those with an index below 100 are a weak market.

Spending indexes can reveal hidden markets—household segments with a high propensity to buy a particular product or service but which are overshadowed by household segments that account for a larger share of the market. Hispanic householders, for example, account for only 15 percent of the market for baby food versus the 79 percent share accounted for by non-Hispanic white householders, but a look at the indexed spending figures reveals that, in fact, Hispanics are better customers. Hispanics spend 21 percent more than average (index of 121) on baby food, while non-Hispanic whites spend just 5 percent more than average (index of 105). Grocery stores can use this type of information to craft advertising and promotions to appeal to their best customers.

Note that because of sampling errors, small differences in index values may be insignificant. But the broader patterns revealed by indexes can guide marketers to the best customers.

• **Total (Aggregate) Spending.** To produce the total (aggregate) spending figures, New Strategist multiplies average spending by the number of households in a segment. The result is the dollar size of the total household market and of each market segment. All totals are shown in thousands of dollars. To convert the numbers in the total spending tables to dollars, you must append "000" to the number. For example, households headed by people aged 35 to 44 spent approximately $2.5 billion ($2,516,167,000) on cereal in 2012.

When comparing the total spending figures in this report with total spending estimates from the Bureau of Economic Analysis, other government agencies, or trade associations, keep in mind that the Consumer Expenditure Survey includes only household spending, not spending by businesses or institutions. Sales data also differ from household spending totals because sales figures for consumer products include the value of goods sold to industries, government, and foreign markets, which may be a significant proportion of sales.

• **Market Shares (Biggest Customers).** New Strategist produces market share figures by converting total (aggregate) spending data into percentages. To calculate the percentage of total spending on an item that is controlled by each demographic segment—i.e., its market share—each segment's total spending on an item is divided by aggregate household spending on the item.

Market shares reveal the biggest customers—the demographic segments that account for the largest share of spending on a particular product or service. In 2012, for example, householders aged 45 or older accounted for nearly 70 percent of spending on coffee. By targeting only older adults, the coffee industry could reach well more than half its customers. There is a danger here, however. By single-mindedly targeting the biggest customers, businesses cannot nurture potential growth markets. With competition for customers more heated than ever, targeting potential markets is increasingly important to business survival.

• **Product-Specific Tables.** The product-specific tables reveal at a glance the demographic characteristics of spending by individual product category. These tables show average spending, indexed spending (Best Customers), and market shares (Biggest Customers) by age, income, household type, race and Hispanic origin, region of residence, and education. If you want to see the spending pattern for an individual product at a glance, these are the tables for you.

History and Methodology of the Consumer Expenditure Survey

The Consumer Expenditure Survey is an ongoing study of the day-to-day spending of American households. In taking the survey, government interviewers collect spending data on products and services as well as the amount and sources of household income, changes in saving and debt, and demographic and economic characteristics of household members. The Bureau of the Census collects data for the Consumer Expenditure Survey under contract with the Bureau of Labor Statistics, which is responsible for analysis and release of the survey data.

Since the late 19th century, the federal government has conducted expenditure surveys about every 10 years. Although the results have been used for a variety of purposes, their primary application is to track consumer prices. In 1980, the Consumer Expenditure Survey became continuous with annual release of data. The survey is used to update prices for the market basket of products and services used in calculating the Consumer Price Index.

The Consumer Expenditure Survey consists of two separate surveys: an interview survey and a diary survey. In the interview portion of the survey, respondents are asked each quarter for five consecutive quarters to report their expenditures for the previous three months. The interview survey records purchases of big-ticket items such as houses, cars, and major appliances, and recurring expenses such as insurance premiums, utility payments, and rent. The interview component covers about 95 percent of all expenditures.

The diary survey records expenditures on small, frequently purchased items during a two-week period. These detailed records include expenses for food and beverages purchased in grocery stores and at restaurants, as well as other items such as tobacco, housekeeping supplies, nonprescription drugs, and personal care products and services. The diary survey is intended to capture expenditures respondents are likely to forget or recall incorrectly over longer periods of time.

Two separate, nationally representative samples are used for the interview and diary surveys. For the interview survey, about 7,000 consumer units are interviewed on a rotating panel basis each quarter for five consecutive quarters. Another 7,000 consumer units kept weekly diaries of spending for two consecutive weeks. Data collection is carried out in 91 areas of the country.

The Bureau of Labor Statistics reviews, audits, and cleanses the data, then weights them to reflect the number and characteristics of all U.S. consumer units. Like any sample survey, the Consumer Expenditure Survey is subject to two major types of error. Nonsampling error occurs when respondents misinterpret questions or interviewers are inconsistent in the way they ask questions or record answers. Respondents may forget items, recall expenses incorrectly, or deliberately give wrong answers. A respondent may remember how much he or she spent at the grocery store but forget the items picked up at a local convenience store. Mistakes during the various stages of data processing and refinement can also cause nonsampling error.

Sampling error occurs when a sample does not accurately represent the population it is supposed to represent. This kind of error is present in every sample-based survey and is minimized by using a proper sampling procedure. Standard error tables documenting the extent of sampling error in the Consumer Expenditure Survey are available from the Bureau of Labor Statistics at http://www.bls.gov/cex/csxcombined.htm.

Although the Consumer Expenditure Survey is the best source of information about the spending behavior of American households, it should be treated with caution because of the above problems.

For More Information

To find out more about the Consumer Expenditure Survey, contact the specialists at the Bureau of Labor Statistics at (202) 691-6900, or visit the Consumer Expenditure Survey home page at http://www.bls.gov/cex/. The web site includes news releases, technical documentation, and current and historical summary-level data. The detailed average spending data shown in this report are available from the Bureau of Labor Statistics only by special request.

For a comprehensive look at detailed household spending data for all products and services, see the 19th edition of *Household Spending: Who Spends How Much on What*. New Strategist's books are available in hardcopy or as downloads with links to the Excel version of each table. Find out more by visiting http://www .newstrategist.com or by calling 1-800-848-0842.

Table 1. Percent reporting expenditure and amount spent, average week, 2012

(percent of consumer units reporting expenditure and amount spent by purchasers during the average week, 2012)

	average week	
	percent reporting expenditure	amount spent by purchasers
GROCERIES	**81.2%**	**$91.64**
Cereals and bakery products	**69.3**	**14.92**
Cereals and cereal products	45.1	7.76
Flour	4.4	4.09
Prepared flour mixes	8.2	3.79
Ready-to-eat and cooked cereals	30.3	6.01
Rice	9.2	5.13
Pasta, cornmeal, and other cereal products	18.5	3.84
Bakery products	63.6	10.75
Bread	45.2	4.47
White bread	31.4	2.68
Bread, other than white	38.3	3.08
Crackers and cookies	30.2	5.59
Cookies	20.7	4.68
Crackers	16.8	4.22
Frozen and refrigerated bakery products	11.2	4.89
Other bakery products	37.3	6.92
Biscuits and rolls	24.4	4.11
Cakes and cupcakes	10.7	6.85
Bread and cracker products	4.0	3.49
Sweetrolls, coffee cakes, doughnuts	10.1	4.54
Pies, tarts, turnovers	5.1	5.06
Meats, poultry, fish, and eggs	**64.4**	**25.43**
Beef	31.4	13.86
Ground beef	21.0	8.59
Roast	5.2	12.62
Steak	11.7	13.04
Other beef	3.9	9.51
Pork	30.0	10.64
Bacon	10.6	5.87
Pork chops	6.9	7.88
Ham	8.4	7.64
Sausage	10.9	5.68
Other pork	7.6	10.08
Other meats	30.5	7.72
Frankfurters	10.0	4.79
Lunch meats (cold cuts)	24.6	6.83
Lamb, organ meats, and others	1.7	11.83
Poultry	29.9	10.23
Fresh and frozen chicken	25.9	9.38
Other poultry	8.5	7.39
Fish and seafood	20.7	11.69
Canned fish and seafood	7.2	4.86
Fresh fish and shellfish	9.4	12.99
Frozen fish and shellfish	8.1	10.44
Eggs	30.6	3.33

	average week	
	percent reporting expenditure	**amount spent by purchasers**
Dairy products	**66.2%**	**$12.18**
Fresh milk and cream	53.1	5.49
Fresh milk, all types	49.9	4.95
Cream	13.2	3.42
Other dairy products	51.7	9.95
Butter	11.7	4.20
Cheese	37.4	6.76
Ice cream and related products	18.6	5.90
Miscellaneous dairy products	20.4	4.95
Fruits and vegetables	**69.5**	**20.23**
Fresh fruits	53.9	9.31
Apples	17.7	4.52
Bananas	33.6	2.50
Oranges	10.8	4.74
Citrus fruits, excl. oranges	21.7	3.55
Other fresh fruits	36.1	5.82
Fresh vegetables	53.3	8.17
Potatoes	19.0	3.91
Lettuce	19.8	3.13
Tomatoes	22.3	3.42
Other fresh vegetables	44.0	5.07
Processed fruits	35.4	6.19
Frozen fruits and fruit juices	4.3	5.65
Frozen orange juice	1.5	3.95
Frozen fruits	2.0	6.86
Frozen fruit juices, excluding orange	1.3	3.79
Canned fruits	10.0	3.89
Dried fruits	4.2	4.10
Fresh fruit juice	7.6	4.35
Canned and bottled fruit juice	22.2	4.77
Processed vegetables	37.3	6.71
Frozen vegetables	15.6	4.63
Canned and dried vegetables and juices	30.8	5.74
Canned beans	10.7	3.45
Canned corn	5.8	3.28
Canned miscellaneous vegetables	13.5	3.64
Dried peas	0.3	3.23
Dried beans	2.5	3.67
Dried miscellaneous vegetables	5.5	4.16
Dried processed vegetables	0.2	5.26
Frozen vegetable juices	0.4	2.27
Fresh and canned vegetable juices	9.6	3.77
Sugar and other sweets	**40.0**	**7.06**
Candy and chewing gum	28.9	5.85
Sugar	11.0	4.27
Artificial sweeteners	1.7	5.33
Jams, preserves, other sweets	12.7	4.48
Fats and oils	**32.3**	**6.78**
Margarine	4.6	3.66
Fats and oils	11.3	6.29
Salad dressings	13.4	4.47
Nondairy cream and imitation milk	8.4	4.28
Peanut butter	7.1	5.06

	average week	
	percent reporting expenditure	amount spent by purchasers
Miscellaneous foods	**67.0%**	**$20.08**
Frozen prepared foods	25.4	9.94
Frozen meals	14.0	8.38
Other frozen prepared foods	17.4	7.78
Canned and packaged soups	18.6	4.79
Potato chips, nuts, and other snacks	40.7	7.28
Potato chips and other snacks	36.6	5.88
Nuts	11.9	6.81
Condiments and seasonings	41.2	6.61
Salt, spices, and other seasonings	19.3	3.83
Olives, pickles, relishes	8.2	4.14
Sauces and gravies	27.1	4.28
Baking needs and miscellaneous products	10.7	4.47
Other canned/packaged prepared foods	43.1	10.12
Prepared salads	14.0	4.79
Prepared desserts	7.0	3.84
Baby food	2.4	19.83
Miscellaneous prepared foods	34.5	8.22
Nonalcoholic beverages	**56.5**	**12.60**
Cola	29.3	4.89
Other carbonated drinks	27.5	4.55
Tea	12.2	4.77
Coffee	16.8	9.89
Noncarbonated fruit-flavored drinks	9.3	5.39
Other nonalcoholic beverages and ice	6.1	4.94
Bottled water	19.1	5.71
Sports drinks	4.9	5.98

Source: Calculations by New Strategist based on the 2012 Consumer Expenditure Survey

Household Spending Trends, 2000 to 2012

Household spending declined during the Great Recession and its aftermath, bottoming out in 2010. Then things began to get better. Between 2010 and 2012, average annual household spending climbed 1.6 percent to $51,442, after adjusting for inflation. The 2012 figure was still 6.7 percent below the 2006 peak, however, when the average household spent $55,119.

Although household spending is growing again, the average household is spending less than it did in 2006 on most items. Spending on alcoholic beverages is an example. Although the average household spent 4 percent more on alcoholic beverages in 2012 ($451) than in 2010 ($434), the 2012 figure is 20 percent below the 2006 figure ($566). Many categories show a similar pattern. The average household spent 5 percent more on furniture in 2012 ($391) than in 2010 ($374), but the amount spent by the average household on furniture in 2012 was 26 percent below the spending of 2006 ($527). Spending on new cars and trucks increased by a substantial 28 percent between 2010 and 2012, but the 2012 figure was still 20 percent below the level of 2006.

Other categories continued their decline in the 2010-to-2012 time period, despite the overall spending recovery. Average household spending on mortgage interest fell 13 percent between 2010 and 2012, after adjusting for inflation, as more Americans chose to rent rather than buy a home. Spending on apparel continued its long-term decline. Conversely, a handful of spending categories have grown steadily despite the Great Recession, including health insurance, medical services, education, and the category "pets, toys, and playground equipment" (dominated by pet spending).

Although household spending is beginning to recover from the Great Recession, the recovery is slow and spending on many categories continues to decline. But those who have been eagerly awaiting good economic news should take heart at the spending boost for items such as new cars and trucks, household textiles, reading material, footwear, personal care products and services, cash contributions, and gifts for people in other households. Americans may be starting to open their wallets, at least a bit.

Households are spending more, but still less than they once did

(percent change in spending by the average household on selected products and services, 2006, 2010, and 2012; in 2012 dollars)

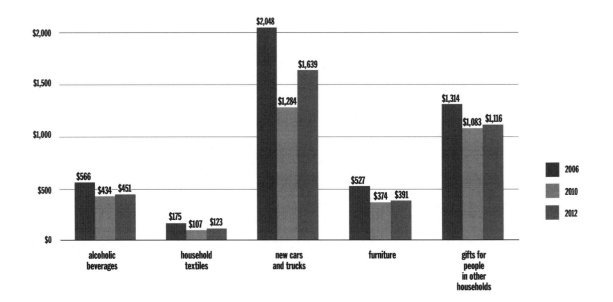

Table 2. Household spending trends, 2000 to 2012

(average annual spending of total consumer units, 2000, 2006, 2010, and 2012; percent change, 2000–06, 2006–12, and 2010–12; in 2012 dollars)

	average annual household spending (in 2012$)				percent change		
	2012	2010	2006	2000	2010–12	2006–12	2000–06
Number of consumer units (in 000s)	124,416	121,107	118,843	109,367	2.7%	4.7%	8.7%
Average annual spending of consumer units	$51,442	$50,655	$55,118	$50,725	1.6	–6.7	8.7
FOOD	**6,599**	**6,453**	**6,960**	**6,877**	**2.3**	**–5.2**	**1.2**
Food at home	**3,921**	**3,816**	**3,891**	**4,028**	**2.8**	**0.8**	**–3.4**
Cereals and bakery products	538	529	508	604	1.8	5.9	–15.9
Cereals and cereal products	182	174	163	208	4.8	11.8	–21.7
Bakery products	356	355	346	396	0.3	2.8	–12.6
Meats, poultry, fish, and eggs	852	825	908	1,060	3.2	–6.1	–14.4
Beef	226	228	269	317	–1.1	–15.9	–15.3
Pork	166	157	179	223	5.8	–7.2	–19.7
Other meats	122	123	120	135	–1.0	2.0	–11.2
Poultry	159	145	161	193	9.4	–1.0	–16.9
Fish and seafood	126	123	139	147	2.3	–9.3	–5.3
Eggs	53	48	42	45	9.4	25.8	–7.0
Dairy products	419	400	419	433	4.7	0.0	–3.3
Fresh milk and cream	152	148	159	175	2.4	–4.7	–8.7
Other dairy products	267	253	260	257	5.7	2.8	0.9
Fruits and vegetables	731	715	674	695	2.2	8.4	–2.9
Fresh fruits	261	244	222	217	6.8	17.5	2.2
Fresh vegetables	226	221	220	212	2.2	2.8	3.7
Processed fruits	114	119	124	153	–4.2	–8.2	–19.0
Processed vegetables	130	131	108	112	–0.4	20.2	–3.4
Other food at home	1,380	1,346	1,380	1,236	2.6	0.0	11.7
Sugar and other sweets	147	139	142	156	5.8	3.3	–8.7
Fats and oils	114	108	98	111	5.1	16.4	–11.5
Miscellaneous foods	699	702	714	583	–0.5	–2.1	22.6
Nonalcoholic beverages	370	351	378	333	5.5	–2.1	13.4
Food prepared by consumer unit on trips	50	45	49	53	10.4	2.1	–8.2
Food away from home	**2,678**	**2,638**	**3,068**	**2,849**	**1.5**	**–12.7**	**7.7**
ALCOHOLIC BEVERAGES	**451**	**434**	**566**	**496**	**4.0**	**–20.3**	**14.1**
HOUSING	**16,887**	**17,433**	**18,639**	**16,425**	**–3.1**	**–9.4**	**13.5**
Shelter	**9,891**	**10,331**	**11,016**	**9,485**	**–4.3**	**–10.2**	**16.1**
Owned dwellings	6,056	6,609	7,421	6,136	–8.4	–18.4	20.9
Mortgage interest and charges	3,067	3,528	4,274	3,519	–13.1	–28.2	21.5
Property taxes	1,836	1,910	1,878	1,519	–3.9	–2.2	23.7
Maintenance, repair, insurance, other expenses	1,153	1,171	1,270	1,100	–1.5	–9.2	15.4
Rented dwellings	3,186	3,053	2,950	2,712	4.3	8.0	8.8
Other lodging	649	669	646	637	–2.9	0.5	1.3
Utilities, fuels, and public services	**3,648**	**3,854**	**3,869**	**3,319**	**–5.3**	**–5.7**	**16.6**
Natural gas	359	463	580	409	–22.5	–38.1	41.6
Electricity	1,388	1,488	1,442	1,215	–6.7	–3.7	18.7
Fuel oil and other fuels	137	147	157	129	–7.1	–12.8	21.5
Telephone services	1,239	1,240	1,238	1,169	–0.1	0.1	5.9
Water and other public services	525	515	452	395	2.0	16.1	14.6
Household services	**1,159**	**1,060**	**1,080**	**912**	**9.3**	**7.4**	**18.4**
Personal services	368	358	448	435	2.8	–17.8	3.0
Other household services	791	702	632	477	12.6	25.1	32.4
Housekeeping supplies	**610**	**644**	**729**	**643**	**–5.3**	**–16.3**	**13.4**
Laundry and cleaning supplies	155	158	172	175	–1.9	–9.9	–1.5
Other household products	319	346	376	301	–7.9	–15.1	24.7
Postage and stationery	136	139	181	168	–2.1	–24.9	7.8
Household furnishings and equipment	**1,580**	**1,545**	**1,945**	**2,065**	**2.3**	**–18.8**	**–5.8**
Household textiles	123	107	175	141	14.5	–29.9	24.1
Furniture	391	374	527	521	4.6	–25.8	1.1
Floor coverings	16	38	55	59	–57.8	–70.7	–6.8
Major appliances	197	220	274	252	–10.5	–28.2	8.9
Small appliances and miscellaneous housewares	98	113	124	116	–13.0	–21.1	7.0
Miscellaneous household equipment	754	692	789	975	9.0	–4.5	–19.0

	average annual household spending (in 2012$)				percent change		
	2012	2010	2006	2000	2010–12	2006–12	2000–06
APPAREL AND RELATED SERVICES	**$1,736**	**$1,790**	**$2,134**	**$2,475**	**–3.0%**	**–18.7%**	**–13.8%**
Men and boys	**408**	**402**	**506**	**587**	**1.4**	**–19.3**	**–13.8**
Men, aged 16 or older	320	320	402	459	0.0	–20.4	–12.3
Boys, aged 2 to 15	88	82	104	128	7.1	–15.1	–19.0
Women and girls	**688**	**698**	**855**	**967**	**–1.4**	**–19.6**	**–11.5**
Women, aged 16 or older	573	592	716	809	–3.2	–20.0	–11.5
Girls, aged 2 to 15	116	106	139	157	9.1	–16.5	–11.7
Children under age 2	**63**	**96**	**109**	**109**	**–34.2**	**–42.4**	**0.0**
Footwear	**347**	**319**	**346**	**457**	**8.8**	**0.2**	**–24.3**
Other apparel products and services	**230**	**275**	**319**	**355**	**–16.3**	**–27.9**	**–10.1**
TRANSPORTATION	**8,998**	**8,083**	**9,689**	**9,889**	**11.3**	**–7.1**	**–2.0**
Vehicle purchases	**3,210**	**2,725**	**3,896**	**4,557**	**17.8**	**–17.6**	**–14.5**
Cars and trucks, new	1,639	1,284	2,048	2,140	27.7	–20.0	–4.3
Cars and trucks, used	1,516	1,388	1,786	2,360	9.2	–15.1	–24.3
Gasoline and motor oil	**2,756**	**2,245**	**2,536**	**1,721**	**22.8**	**8.7**	**47.3**
Other vehicle expenses	**2,490**	**2,594**	**2,682**	**3,041**	**–4.0**	**–7.2**	**–11.8**
Vehicle finance charges	223	256	339	437	–12.8	–34.3	–22.4
Maintenance and repairs	814	829	784	832	–1.8	3.9	–5.8
Vehicle insurance	1,018	1,063	1,009	1,037	–4.3	0.9	–2.7
Vehicle rentals, leases, licenses, other charges	434	445	549	735	–2.6	–20.9	–25.3
Public transportation	**542**	**519**	**575**	**569**	**4.4**	**–5.8**	**1.0**
HEALTH CARE	**3,556**	**3,324**	**3,150**	**2,755**	**7.0**	**12.9**	**14.4**
Health insurance	2,061	1,928	1,668	1,311	6.9	23.5	27.3
Medical services	839	760	763	757	10.4	10.0	0.8
Drugs	515	511	585	555	0.8	–12.0	5.5
Medical supplies	142	125	133	132	13.3	6.6	0.9
ENTERTAINMENT	**2,605**	**2,637**	**2,706**	**2,484**	**–1.2**	**–3.7**	**8.9**
Fees and admissions	614	612	690	687	0.4	–11.0	0.5
Audio and visual equipment and services	979	1,004	1,032	829	–2.5	–5.1	24.4
Pets, toys, and playground equipment	648	638	469	445	1.6	38.1	5.4
Other entertainment products and services	363	383	514	524	–5.3	–29.3	–2.0
PERSONAL CARE PRODUCTS AND SERVICES	**628**	**613**	**666**	**752**	**2.5**	**–5.7**	**–11.4**
READING	**109**	**105**	**133**	**195**	**3.5**	**–18.2**	**–31.5**
EDUCATION	**1,207**	**1,131**	**1,011**	**843**	**6.7**	**19.4**	**20.0**
TOBACCO PRODUCTS AND SMOKING SUPPLIES	**332**	**381**	**372**	**425**	**–12.9**	**–10.9**	**–12.4**
MISCELLANEOUS	**829**	**894**	**963**	**1,035**	**–7.3**	**–14.0**	**–6.9**
CASH CONTRIBUTIONS	**1,913**	**1,719**	**2,129**	**1,589**	**11.3**	**–10.1**	**33.9**
PERSONAL INSURANCE AND PENSIONS	**5,591**	**5,657**	**6,002**	**4,487**	**–1.2**	**–6.8**	**33.8**
Life and other personal insurance	353	335	367	532	5.4	–3.7	–31.1
Pensions and Social Security*	5,238	5,321	5,635	3,955	–1.6	–7.0	*
PERSONAL TAXES	**2,226**	**1,863**	**2,770**	**4,156**	**19.5**	**–19.6**	**–33.4**
Federal income taxes	1,568	1,196	1,949	3,212	31.1	–19.5	–39.3
State and local income taxes	526	508	591	749	3.6	–11.0	–21.1
Other taxes	132	159	230	195	–17.0	–42.6	18.2
GIFTS FOR PEOPLE IN OTHER HOUSEHOLDS	**1,116**	**1,083**	**1,314**	**1,444**	**3.0**	**–15.1**	**–9.0**

*Recent spending on pensions and Social Security is not comparable with 2000 because of changes in methodology.
Note: Spending by category does not add to total spending because gift spending is also included in the preceding product and service categories and personal taxes are not included in the total.
Source: Bureau of Labor Statistics, 2000, 2006, 2010, and 2012 Consumer Expenditure Surveys, Internet site http://www.bls.gov/cex/; calculations by New Strategist

Household Spending on Groceries, 2000 to 2012

Groceries are one of the largest household expense categories. In 2012, the average household spent $3,921 on groceries—about $100 less than in 2000, after adjusting for inflation. Spending on groceries fell 3 percent between 2000 and 2006 (the year when overall household spending peaked), as households ate out more often. Grocery spending fell another 2 percent between 2006 and 2010 (the year when overall household spending bottomed out) as shoppers substituted private labels for branded products and bought less expensive items in an attempt to cut costs because of the Great Recession. Between 2010 and 2012 average household spending on groceries registered a 3 percent rise.

Fresh fruit and fresh vegetables are the two grocery items on which the average household spends the most, with spending on each category amounting to more than $200 annually in 2012. Prepared food—such as food from the supermarket deli—ranks third as busy households look for convenience. Carbonated drinks rank fourth in spending, followed by cheese and milk. Chicken, potato chips and other snacks, cereal, and ground beef round out the top-10 grocery list.

During the average week of 2012, 81 percent of households shopped for groceries. The shoppers spent an average of $92 on groceries during the week. Grocery spending is largely driven by household size, and larger households spend more than smaller ones on most items. Average household spending on groceries may decline in the years ahead as boomers become empty-nesters and household size falls. On the other hand, though, some grocery items have experienced steep increases recently as grocery stores compete—sometimes successfully—with restaurants. In the end, household demographic characteristics, shifting food preferences, and nutritional claims will continue to affect spending patterns—patterns that will determine the future success of grocery retailers and food manufacturers.

Table 3. Spending on groceries, 2000–2012

(average annual and percent distribution of household spending on groceries by category, 2000 to 2012; percent change in spending and percentage point change in distribution, 2000–06, 2006–12, and 2010–12; in 2012 dollars; ranked by amount spent)

	average annual household spending (in 2012$)				percent change		
	2012	2010	2006	2000	2010–12	2006–12	2000–06
Average household spending on groceries	**$3,920.65**	**$3,815.80**	**$3,891.32**	**$4,027.89**	**2.7%**	**0.8%**	**–3.4%**
Fruit, fresh (apples, bananas, and citrus also shown separately)	261.29	244.53	222.58	217.55	6.9	17.4	2.3
Vegetables, fresh (potatoes, tomatoes, and lettuce also shown separately)	226.14	221.61	220.10	211.62	2.0	2.7	4.0
Prepared food (except salads, desserts, and frozen meals)	147.81	154.53	151.10	98.54	–4.3	–2.2	53.3
Carbonated drinks	139.74	139.67	153.23	179.17	0.1	–8.8	–14.5
Cheese	131.47	121.54	126.13	127.94	8.2	4.2	–1.4
Milk, fresh	128.28	127.43	141.75	159.48	0.7	–9.5	–11.1
Chicken, fresh and frozen	126.52	116.08	127.68	152.57	9.0	–0.9	–16.3
Potato chips and other snacks	111.59	104.58	108.44	95.56	6.7	2.9	13.5
Cereal, ready-to-eat and cooked	94.82	87.21	96.50	115.84	8.7	–1.7	–16.7
Ground beef	93.50	89.15	102.73	117.01	4.9	–9.0	–12.2
Candy and chewing gum	87.86	81.43	90.12	101.73	7.9	–2.5	–11.4
Lunch meats (cold cuts)	87.23	86.13	86.12	90.65	1.3	1.3	–5.0
Coffee	86.50	63.44	56.82	55.80	36.4	52.2	1.8
Steak	79.44	86.62	96.47	126.02	–8.3	–17.7	–23.4
Prepared food, frozen (except meals)	70.22	74.94	76.92	82.26	–6.3	–8.7	–6.5
Fish and shellfish, fresh	63.29	58.17	70.99	89.09	8.8	–10.8	–20.3
Bread, other than white	61.60	62.88	61.76	63.22	–2.0	–0.3	–2.3
Prepared meals, frozen	60.61	64.18	78.63	38.00	–5.6	–22.9	106.9
Sauces and gravies	60.27	55.21	54.95	49.64	9.2	9.7	10.7
Ice cream and related products	57.37	57.13	70.18	75.41	0.4	–18.2	–6.9
Water, bottled	56.80	54.79	62.90	–	3.7	–9.7	–
Fruit juice, canned and bottled	54.92	54.72	62.97	74.94	0.4	–12.8	–16.0
Vegetables, canned	54.59	55.29	43.73	49.89	–1.3	24.8	–12.3
Eggs	53.08	48.74	41.76	45.95	8.9	27.1	–9.1
Dairy products (except butter, cheese, eggs, ice cream, and milk)	52.67	49.28	42.78	31.85	6.9	23.1	34.3
Biscuits and rolls	51.85	51.42	47.65	51.37	0.8	8.8	–7.2
Cookies	50.56	48.33	50.54	63.61	4.6	0.0	–20.5
Soup, canned and packaged	46.30	44.54	48.04	47.39	4.0	–3.6	1.4
Fish and shellfish, frozen	44.27	43.87	48.80	36.87	0.9	–9.3	32.4
Bananas	43.81	43.04	32.81	42.27	1.8	33.5	–22.4
Bread, white	43.52	41.94	36.18	48.83	3.8	20.3	–25.9
Nuts	42.35	35.43	36.99	27.77	19.5	14.5	33.2
Apples	41.61	39.27	38.64	39.32	5.9	7.7	–1.7
Pork (except bacon, frankfurters, ham, chops, and sausage)	39.99	37.48	44.62	51.76	6.7	–10.4	–13.8
Citrus fruit, fresh (other than oranges)	39.95	33.08	19.20	19.08	20.8	108.1	0.6
Tomatoes, fresh	39.35	41.36	41.75	39.37	–4.9	–5.7	6.0
Salt, spices, and other seasonings	38.72	34.21	28.86	27.53	13.2	34.2	4.8
Potatoes, fresh	38.44	38.02	35.60	37.43	1.1	8.0	–4.9
Cakes and cupcakes	37.94	37.17	39.88	51.23	2.1	–4.9	–22.1
Vegetables, frozen	37.50	38.07	34.78	35.23	–1.5	7.8	–1.3
Crackers	37.17	38.18	36.25	31.09	–2.6	2.5	16.6
Pasta, cornmeal, and other cereal products	36.98	35.71	27.59	38.19	3.5	34.0	–27.7
Fats and oils	36.79	33.16	32.30	31.13	11.0	13.9	3.7

	average annual household spending (in 2012$)				percent change		
	2012	**2010**	**2006**	**2000**	**2010–12**	**2006–12**	**2000–06**
Salads, prepared	$35.09	$37.30	$36.80	$24.73	−5.9%	−4.6%	48.8%
Roast beef	34.02	31.03	45.59	53.12	9.6	−25.4	−14.2
Ham	33.42	33.57	38.74	48.35	−0.4	−13.7	−19.9
Poultry (except chicken)	32.84	29.33	32.34	40.97	12.0	1.5	−21.1
Lettuce	32.33	31.66	28.86	27.67	2.1	12.0	4.3
Bacon	32.18	33.28	31.15	34.73	−3.3	3.3	−10.3
Sausage	32.14	27.51	29.37	33.65	16.8	9.4	−12.7
Salad dressings	31.29	30.29	29.76	36.24	3.3	5.1	−17.9
Tea	30.36	30.75	29.96	20.91	−1.3	1.3	43.3
Jams, preserves, other sweets	29.61	27.89	26.24	26.48	6.2	12.8	−0.9
Bakery products, frozen and refrigerated	28.77	26.52	29.15	32.71	8.5	−1.3	−10.9
Pork chops	28.04	25.03	35.18	54.09	12.0	−20.3	−35.0
Oranges	26.74	26.03	25.33	25.24	2.7	5.6	0.4
Fruit-flavored drinks, noncarbonated	25.83	25.53	20.21	25.89	1.2	27.8	−21.9
Butter	25.56	24.25	20.86	22.67	5.4	22.5	−8.0
Baby food	25.05	34.20	38.32	43.01	−26.8	−34.6	−10.9
Baking needs and miscellaneous products	24.95	27.57	26.15	22.61	−9.5	−4.6	15.6
Frankfurters	24.71	25.81	22.99	27.57	−4.3	7.5	−16.6
Rice	24.65	26.03	19.94	26.07	−5.3	23.6	−23.5
Sugar	24.38	23.96	18.84	22.40	1.7	29.4	−15.9
Sweetrolls, coffee cakes, and doughnuts	23.73	23.46	23.70	30.24	1.2	0.1	−21.6
Cream	23.58	20.93	17.89	15.48	12.7	31.8	15.6
Fruit, canned	20.35	21.62	20.98	20.64	−5.9	−3.0	1.6
Beef other than ground, roast, steak	19.35	21.35	24.26	21.44	−9.4	−20.2	13.1
Vegetable juice, fresh and canned	18.98	15.94	13.83	12.40	19.1	37.3	11.5
Peanut butter	18.68	16.28	12.81	15.75	14.8	45.8	−18.6
Nondairy cream and imitation milk	18.59	17.86	14.58	12.20	4.1	27.5	19.5
Vegetables, dried	18.22	19.22	13.43	14.00	−5.2	35.7	−4.1
Fish and seafood, canned	18.18	21.23	18.78	20.89	−14.4	−3.2	−10.1
Olives, pickles, and relishes	17.46	15.65	14.55	13.03	11.6	20.0	11.7
Fruit juice, fresh	17.06	20.17	19.85	31.25	−15.4	−14.1	−36.5
Flour, prepared mixes	16.18	16.06	12.85	17.80	0.8	26.0	−27.8
Other noncarbonated beverages and ice	15.36	15.92	–	–	−3.5	–	–
Sports drinks	15.12	20.12	–	–	−24.9	–	–
Desserts, prepared	14.29	17.40	13.69	12.41	−17.9	4.4	10.3
Pies, tarts, and turnovers	13.41	17.16	15.86	17.71	−21.9	−15.5	−10.4
Lamb, organ meats, and other meat	10.19	11.46	10.34	15.83	−11.0	−1.5	−34.7
Flour	9.36	8.31	5.64	10.64	12.7	66.0	−47.0
Margarine	8.74	10.44	8.31	15.48	−16.3	5.1	−46.3
Fruit, dried	8.71	8.63	10.20	7.33	0.9	−14.6	39.2
Bread and cracker products	7.31	7.88	4.95	5.88	−7.2	47.6	−15.7
Fruit, frozen	7.16	7.14	4.64	4.83	0.3	54.5	−4.0
Fruit juice, frozen	5.55	6.43	5.75	14.32	−13.7	−3.5	−59.8
Artificial sweeteners	4.91	5.69	6.61	5.59	−13.6	−25.7	18.2

PERCENT DISTRIBUTION OF SPENDING ON GROCERIES	2012	2010	2006	2000	percentage point change		
					2010–12	2006–12	2000–06
Average household spending on groceries	**100.0%**	**100.0%**	**100.0%**	**100.0%**	–	–	–
Fruit, fresh (apples, bananas, and citrus also shown separately)	6.7	6.4	5.7	5.4	0.3	0.9	0.3
Vegetables, fresh (potatoes, tomatoes, and lettuce also shown separately)	5.8	5.8	5.7	5.3	0.0	0.1	0.4
Prepared food (except salads, desserts, and frozen meals)	3.8	4.0	3.9	2.4	–0.3	–0.1	1.4
Carbonated drinks	3.6	3.7	3.9	4.4	–0.1	–0.4	–0.5
Cheese	3.4	3.2	3.2	3.2	0.2	0.1	0.1
Milk, fresh	3.3	3.3	3.6	4.0	–0.1	–0.4	–0.3
Chicken, fresh and frozen	3.2	3.0	3.3	3.8	0.2	–0.1	–0.5
Potato chips and other snacks	2.8	2.7	2.8	2.4	0.1	0.1	0.4
Cereal, ready-to-eat and cooked	2.4	2.3	2.5	2.9	0.1	–0.1	–0.4
Ground beef	2.4	2.3	2.6	2.9	0.0	–0.3	–0.3
Candy and chewing gum	2.2	2.1	2.3	2.5	0.1	–0.1	–0.2
Lunch meats (cold cuts)	2.2	2.3	2.2	2.3	0.0	0.0	0.0
Coffee	2.2	1.7	1.5	1.4	0.5	0.7	0.1
Steak	2.0	2.3	2.5	3.1	–0.2	–0.5	–0.6
Prepared food, frozen (except meals)	1.8	2.0	2.0	2.0	–0.2	–0.2	–0.1
Fish and shellfish, fresh	1.6	1.5	1.8	2.2	0.1	–0.2	–0.4
Bread, other than white	1.6	1.6	1.6	1.6	–0.1	0.0	0.0
Prepared meals, frozen	1.5	1.7	2.0	0.9	–0.1	–0.5	1.1
Sauces and gravies	1.5	1.4	1.4	1.2	0.1	0.1	0.2
Ice cream and related products	1.5	1.5	1.8	1.9	0.0	–0.3	–0.1
Water, bottled	1.4	1.4	1.6	–	0.0	–0.2	–
Fruit juice, canned and bottled	1.4	1.4	1.6	1.9	0.0	–0.2	–0.2
Vegetables, canned	1.4	1.4	1.1	1.2	–0.1	0.3	–0.1
Eggs	1.4	1.3	1.1	1.1	0.1	0.3	–0.1
Dairy products (except butter, cheese, eggs, ice cream, and milk)	1.3	1.3	1.1	0.8	0.1	0.2	0.3
Biscuits and rolls	1.3	1.3	1.2	1.3	0.0	0.1	–0.1
Cookies	1.3	1.3	1.3	1.6	0.0	0.0	–0.3
Soup, canned and packaged	1.2	1.2	1.2	1.2	0.0	–0.1	0.1
Fish and shellfish, frozen	1.1	1.1	1.3	0.9	0.0	–0.1	0.3
Bananas	1.1	1.1	0.8	1.0	0.0	0.3	–0.2
Bread, white	1.1	1.1	0.9	1.2	0.0	0.2	–0.3
Nuts	1.1	0.9	1.0	0.7	0.2	0.1	0.3
Apples	1.1	1.0	1.0	1.0	0.0	0.1	0.0
Pork (except bacon, frankfurters, ham, chops, and sausage)	1.0	1.0	1.1	1.3	0.0	–0.1	–0.1
Citrus fruit, fresh (other than oranges)	1.0	0.9	0.5	0.5	0.2	0.5	0.0
Tomatoes, fresh	1.0	1.1	1.1	1.0	–0.1	–0.1	0.1
Salt, spices, and other seasonings	1.0	0.9	0.7	0.7	0.1	0.2	0.1
Potatoes, fresh	1.0	1.0	0.9	0.9	0.0	0.1	0.0
Cakes and cupcakes	1.0	1.0	1.0	1.3	0.0	–0.1	–0.2
Vegetables, frozen	1.0	1.0	0.9	0.9	0.0	0.1	0.0
Crackers	0.9	1.0	0.9	0.8	–0.1	0.0	0.2
Pasta, cornmeal, and other cereal products	0.9	0.9	0.7	0.9	0.0	0.2	–0.2
Fats and oils	0.9	0.9	0.8	0.8	0.1	0.1	0.1
Salads, prepared	0.9	1.0	0.9	0.6	–0.1	–0.1	0.3
Roast beef	0.9	0.8	1.2	1.3	0.1	–0.3	–0.1
Ham	0.9	0.9	1.0	1.2	0.0	–0.1	–0.2
Poultry (except chicken)	0.8	0.8	0.8	1.0	0.1	0.0	–0.2

PERCENT DISTRIBUTION OF SPENDING ON GROCERIES	2012	2010	2006	2000	percentage point change 2010–12	2006–12	2000–06
Lettuce	0.8%	0.8%	0.7%	0.7%	0.0	0.1	0.1
Bacon	0.8	0.9	0.8	0.9	−0.1	0.0	−0.1
Sausage	0.8	0.7	0.8	0.8	0.1	0.1	−0.1
Salad dressings	0.8	0.8	0.8	0.9	0.0	0.0	−0.1
Tea	0.8	0.8	0.8	0.5	0.0	0.0	0.3
Jams, preserves, other sweets	0.8	0.7	0.7	0.7	0.0	0.1	0.0
Bakery products, frozen and refrigerated	0.7	0.7	0.7	0.8	0.0	0.0	−0.1
Pork chops	0.7	0.7	0.9	1.3	0.1	−0.2	−0.4
Oranges	0.7	0.7	0.7	0.6	0.0	0.0	0.0
Fruit-flavored drinks, noncarbonated	0.7	0.7	0.5	0.6	0.0	0.1	−0.1
Butter	0.7	0.6	0.5	0.6	0.0	0.1	0.0
Baby food	0.6	0.9	1.0	1.1	−0.3	−0.3	−0.1
Baking needs and miscellaneous products	0.6	0.7	0.7	0.6	−0.1	0.0	0.1
Frankfurters	0.6	0.7	0.6	0.7	0.0	0.0	−0.1
Rice	0.6	0.7	0.5	0.6	−0.1	0.1	−0.1
Sugar	0.6	0.6	0.5	0.6	0.0	0.1	−0.1
Sweetrolls, coffee cakes, and doughnuts	0.6	0.6	0.6	0.8	0.0	0.0	−0.1
Cream	0.6	0.5	0.5	0.4	0.1	0.1	0.1
Fruit, canned	0.5	0.6	0.5	0.5	0.0	0.0	0.0
Beef other than ground, roast, steak	0.5	0.6	0.6	0.5	−0.1	−0.1	0.1
Vegetable juice, fresh and canned	0.5	0.4	0.4	0.3	0.1	0.1	0.0
Peanut butter	0.5	0.4	0.3	0.4	0.0	0.1	−0.1
Nondairy cream and imitation milk	0.5	0.5	0.4	0.3	0.0	0.1	0.1
Vegetables, dried	0.5	0.5	0.3	0.3	0.0	0.1	0.0
Fish and seafood, canned	0.5	0.6	0.5	0.5	−0.1	0.0	0.0
Olives, pickles, and relishes	0.4	0.4	0.4	0.3	0.0	0.1	0.1
Fruit juice, fresh	0.4	0.5	0.5	0.8	−0.1	−0.1	−0.3
Flour, prepared mixes	0.4	0.4	0.3	0.4	0.0	0.1	−0.1
Other noncarbonated beverages and ice	0.4	0.4	–	–	0.0	–	–
Sports drinks	0.4	0.5	–	–	−0.1	–	–
Desserts, prepared	0.4	0.5	0.4	0.3	−0.1	0.0	0.0
Pies, tarts, and turnovers	0.3	0.4	0.4	0.4	−0.1	−0.1	0.0
Lamb, organ meats, and other meat	0.3	0.3	0.3	0.4	0.0	0.0	−0.1
Flour	0.2	0.2	0.1	0.3	0.0	0.1	−0.1
Margarine	0.2	0.3	0.2	0.4	−0.1	0.0	−0.2
Fruit, dried	0.2	0.2	0.3	0.2	0.0	0.0	0.1
Bread and cracker products	0.2	0.2	0.1	0.1	0.0	0.1	0.0
Fruit, frozen	0.2	0.2	0.1	0.1	0.0	0.1	0.0
Fruit juice, frozen	0.1	0.2	0.1	0.4	0.0	0.0	−0.2
Artificial sweeteners	0.1	0.1	0.2	0.1	0.0	0.0	0.0

Note: Numbers do not add to total because apples, bananas, and citirus fruit are shown separately and are included in the fresh fruit total; lettuce, potatoes, and tomatoes are shown separately and are included in the fresh vegetable total; and not all categories are shown. Percentage point change calculations are based on unrounded figures. "–" means not applicable or data are unavailable.
Source: Bureau of Labor Statistics, 2000, 2006, 2010, and 2012 Consumer Expenditure Surveys; calculations by New Strategist

Household Spending on Groceries by Demographic Characteristic, 2012

Spending by Age

The largest households spend the most on groceries. Households headed by people aged 35 to 54, the largest households, spend 15 to 20 percent more than average on groceries. Householders aged 35 to 44 are particularly big spenders on the foods preferred by children. They devote 23 percent more than the average household to cereal, 27 percent more to milk, 29 percent more to potato chips and other snacks, and 57 percent more to sports drinks.

Spending by Household Income

The most affluent households spend the most at the grocery store. In 2012, households with incomes of $100,000 or more spent 55 percent more than the average household on groceries. In general, spending on groceries is above average for households with incomes of $70,000 or more, and below average for those with incomes below $50,000. Household size accounts for some of these spending differences, the number of people per household rising parallel with income.

Spending by Household Type

Spending on groceries is highest among married couples with school-aged or older children at home because their households are the largest. Those couples spend 52 to 55 percent more than the average household on groceries. Married couples with school-aged children spend 93 percent more than average on potato chips and other snacks, 77 percent more on cereal, and 66 percent more on milk. Households with preschoolers spend 54 percent more on milk than the average household, while households that include adult children spend 42 percent more than average on cereal. People who live alone spend one-half the average on groceries. Because there are many millions of single-person households, however, they account for a significant share of the grocery market. They account for 22 percent of the market for frozen meals.

Spending by Race and Hispanic Origin

The food preferences of racial and ethnic minorities are of paramount importance to the grocery industry not only because Asians, blacks, and Hispanics control a significant share of the market but also because the general population increasingly enjoys ethnic foods. Households headed by Asians spend 11 percent more on groceries than the average household—$4,367 in 2012 and more than any other racial or ethnic group. Asians spend more because their households have the highest incomes. Asian householders spend over three-and-one-half times the average on rice and more than double the average on fish and seafood. Black households spend 24 percent less than the average household on groceries overall, but they spend 39 percent more than average on pork chops, 20 percent more than average on sausage, and 19 percent more than average on chicken. Hispanics, who have the largest households, are big spenders on beef (29 percent more than average), dried vegetables (70 percent more), rice (65 percent more), chicken (46 percent more than average), and noncarbonated fruit-flavored drinks (34 percent more) among others.

Spending by Region

Households in the West spend 9 percent more than average on groceries, while those in the South spend 7 percent less than average. Northeastern and Midwestern households spend about an average amount on groceries. Householders in the Northeast are big spenders on fresh fruit juice, fresh fish and shellfish, butter, and tea among other items. Households in the South spend 32 percent more than average on artificial sweeteners; they spend 23 percent more than average on pork chops and account for 46 percent of the market. Households in the West spend the most on fresh vegetables, and the Midwest spends the most on peanut butter.

Spending by Education

Spending on groceries rises with education because educated householders have higher incomes. College graduates spend 15 percent more than the average household on groceries, while those with a high school diploma and no further education spend 9 percent less than average. On some products, however, college graduates spend less than high school graduates. Their spending on ground beef is 16 percent below average, for example, while householders who went no further than high school spend 18 percent more than average on this item. College graduates spend 24 percent less than average on sugar, while high school graduates spend 26 percent more. College graduates spend 24 percent more than the average household on fruits and vegetables, but less than average on bacon and carbonated drinks among others.

Table 4. Groceries: Average spending by age, 2012

(average annual spending of consumer units on groceries, by age of consumer unit reference person, 2012)

	total consumer units	under 25	25 to 34	35 to 44	45 to 54	55 to 64	65 to 74	75+
Number of consumer units (in 000s)	124,416	8,159	20,112	21,598	24,624	22,770	14,993	12,161
Number of persons per consumer unit	2.5	2.0	2.8	3.4	2.7	2.1	1.8	1.5
Average before-tax income of consumer units	$65,596.00	$36,639.00	$58,832.00	$78,169.00	$81,704.00	$77,507.00	$53,521.00	$33,853.00
Average spending of consumer units, total	51,441.87	31,411.08	49,543.74	58,069.31	62,102.54	55,636.31	45,967.87	33,529.54
GROCERIES	3,920.65	2,529.03	3,679.69	4,490.39	4,706.91	4,012.27	3,719.16	2,715.64
Cereals and bakery products	537.85	354.54	511.61	631.77	633.05	527.50	489.96	420.91
Cereals and cereal products	181.98	143.16	186.86	222.67	227.92	158.84	142.82	122.12
Flour	9.36	6.15	9.95	9.82	11.47	10.01	7.24	6.77
Prepared flour mixes	16.18	9.40	13.60	18.61	21.09	16.27	15.09	11.93
Ready-to-eat and cooked cereals	94.82	75.05	99.18	116.50	115.79	82.67	76.06	63.54
Rice	24.65	25.33	27.06	31.53	33.08	17.86	15.39	13.88
Pasta, cornmeal, and other cereal products	36.98	27.23	37.07	46.21	46.48	32.02	29.04	25.98
Bakery products	355.87	211.38	324.75	409.10	405.13	368.66	347.14	298.79
Bread	105.12	58.75	96.38	118.44	122.10	113.57	100.19	83.71
White bread	43.52	26.38	42.02	51.89	49.56	45.14	38.46	33.51
Bread other than white	61.60	32.37	54.36	66.54	72.53	68.43	61.73	50.20
Crackers and cookies	87.73	57.89	80.63	96.49	101.82	89.01	89.18	71.53
Cookies	50.56	34.75	45.30	54.98	56.65	52.60	52.56	43.81
Crackers	37.17	23.14	35.33	41.52	45.17	36.42	36.62	27.71
Frozen and refrigerated bakery products	28.77	19.96	30.63	38.74	30.74	26.60	22.91	20.66
Other bakery products	134.25	74.78	117.11	155.43	150.48	139.47	134.85	122.89
Biscuits and rolls	51.85	27.14	44.52	63.28	57.59	57.18	50.52	40.81
Cakes and cupcakes	37.94	21.02	38.61	41.93	40.92	37.60	35.39	39.11
Bread and cracker products	7.31	6.03	7.31	8.09	8.78	6.55	7.03	5.48
Sweetrolls, coffee cakes, doughnuts	23.73	13.82	17.24	25.89	26.69	25.65	25.10	26.62
Pies, tarts, turnovers	13.41	6.78	9.43	16.23	16.50	12.49	16.81	10.87
Meats, poultry, fish, and eggs	852.41	572.56	755.39	998.85	1,047.35	887.08	803.71	538.55
Beef	226.32	160.04	192.35	263.80	287.50	241.22	202.46	137.46
Ground beef	93.50	64.24	90.01	108.48	112.67	101.04	80.44	54.95
Roast	34.02	25.04	23.42	35.62	45.64	37.18	33.02	27.01
Chuck roast	9.42	14.87	6.42	10.88	9.67	11.32	7.85	5.90
Round roast	6.63	1.02	4.51	10.28	10.21	5.33	4.96	4.59
Other roast	17.97	9.15	12.49	14.46	25.75	20.53	20.21	16.51
Steak	79.44	59.84	64.13	97.02	99.24	85.36	71.22	45.30
Round steak	16.91	12.18	13.44	24.73	20.03	15.89	14.79	9.86
Sirloin steak	21.76	16.57	20.73	23.69	26.48	25.56	19.25	9.85
Other steak	40.77	31.08	29.97	48.61	52.73	43.91	37.18	25.59
Other beef	19.35	10.92	14.79	22.68	29.96	17.63	17.78	10.20
Pork	165.77	109.61	144.98	197.85	195.25	174.76	167.01	102.69
Bacon	32.18	21.70	29.13	34.40	38.76	36.79	29.31	22.12
Pork chops	28.04	17.04	26.29	34.46	31.32	29.11	28.65	17.45
Ham	33.42	20.85	28.37	39.99	39.72	33.92	35.39	22.45
Ham, not canned	32.19	19.82	28.00	39.51	36.73	32.60	33.95	22.26
Canned ham	1.23	1.04	0.37	0.48	2.99	1.32	1.44	0.19
Sausage	32.14	24.19	26.89	38.36	39.67	30.27	35.54	18.91
Other pork	39.99	25.82	34.29	50.64	45.78	44.67	38.12	21.77
Other meats	122.13	76.85	111.04	147.52	143.67	120.84	121.94	84.36
Frankfurters	24.71	19.14	23.50	32.33	27.55	26.11	19.86	14.19
Lunch meats (cold cuts)	87.23	49.46	79.71	110.73	104.25	86.42	80.49	58.13
Bologna, liverwurst, salami	25.65	13.25	25.02	32.89	31.19	23.88	22.47	17.91
Other lunch meats	61.58	36.20	54.69	77.85	73.06	62.54	58.02	40.21
Lamb, organ meats, and others	10.19	8.25	7.83	4.46	11.88	8.31	21.60	12.04

	total consumer units	under 25	25 to 34	35 to 44	45 to 54	55 to 64	65 to 74	75+
Poultry	$159.36	$114.39	$163.37	$179.62	$207.36	$159.41	$122.75	$92.47
Fresh and frozen chicken	126.52	95.41	133.05	145.33	163.66	122.15	97.45	69.52
Fresh and frozen whole chicken	37.82	29.21	41.07	43.22	50.99	33.14	27.09	22.97
Fresh and frozen chicken parts	88.70	66.20	91.97	102.11	112.67	89.00	70.36	46.55
Other poultry	32.84	18.97	30.32	34.29	43.69	37.26	25.30	22.95
Fish and seafood	125.74	72.99	93.19	149.60	153.72	137.76	137.23	80.55
Canned fish and seafood	18.18	7.79	13.49	20.22	18.55	21.34	22.46	17.97
Fresh fish and shellfish	63.29	23.78	49.93	72.84	79.94	77.24	64.79	34.34
Frozen fish and shellfish	44.27	41.42	29.77	56.55	55.23	39.18	49.98	28.24
Eggs	53.08	38.69	50.47	60.46	59.86	53.10	52.32	41.01
Dairy products	**418.93**	**251.49**	**393.87**	**497.06**	**497.96**	**433.02**	**384.63**	**288.86**
Fresh milk and cream	151.86	99.91	149.59	189.92	181.64	142.12	125.82	110.96
Fresh milk, all types	128.28	88.89	129.01	162.73	152.50	117.35	101.83	94.21
Cream	23.58	11.01	20.58	27.20	29.14	24.77	23.98	16.76
Other dairy products	267.07	151.58	244.27	307.14	316.31	290.90	258.82	177.90
Butter	25.56	10.47	22.68	26.08	30.25	30.30	25.04	22.35
Cheese	131.47	67.10	123.26	154.60	152.14	146.85	128.43	80.72
Ice cream and related products	57.37	36.91	46.19	62.96	69.27	62.34	61.75	41.48
Miscellaneous dairy products	52.67	37.11	52.14	63.50	64.65	51.41	43.60	33.35
Fruits and vegetables	**730.98**	**456.45**	**683.38**	**807.76**	**871.91**	**732.93**	**722.90**	**580.08**
Fresh fruits	261.29	162.19	236.97	296.71	308.31	257.81	259.75	219.11
Apples	41.61	32.09	40.38	52.08	48.45	38.33	35.26	30.93
Bananas	43.81	27.94	39.98	48.55	53.35	43.12	39.00	40.44
Oranges	26.74	19.10	21.41	34.47	32.91	25.19	26.34	17.61
Citrus fruits, except oranges	39.95	24.06	37.88	44.65	49.50	39.51	36.82	30.97
Other fresh fruits	109.19	59.00	97.32	116.96	124.10	111.66	122.32	99.15
Fresh vegetables	226.14	128.49	208.36	243.26	269.33	234.43	242.22	169.44
Potatoes	38.44	25.57	33.70	41.84	45.52	40.69	40.33	28.20
Lettuce	32.33	18.93	29.73	36.22	37.38	32.37	34.24	26.24
Tomatoes	39.35	25.26	38.04	43.71	48.87	37.92	37.09	29.30
Other fresh vegetables	116.01	58.73	106.89	121.48	137.55	123.45	130.57	85.69
Processed fruits	113.76	76.80	111.93	124.07	134.90	110.91	99.56	103.20
Frozen fruits and fruit juices	12.71	7.31	11.19	13.18	18.44	11.12	11.37	11.04
Frozen fruits	7.16	2.65	4.70	7.47	11.86	7.24	6.92	4.44
Frozen fruit juices	5.55	4.65	6.49	5.70	6.58	3.88	4.45	6.60
Canned fruits	20.35	10.34	19.21	22.41	24.12	18.78	19.96	21.27
Dried fruits	8.71	3.29	10.52	7.53	8.52	8.86	10.39	9.69
Fresh fruit juice	17.06	10.35	14.40	21.68	21.28	17.69	13.28	12.66
Canned and bottled fruit juice	54.92	45.51	56.60	59.27	62.55	54.46	44.56	48.54
Processed vegetables	129.80	88.98	126.13	143.73	159.37	129.79	121.37	88.33
Frozen vegetables	37.50	18.91	39.02	43.03	44.50	37.42	35.27	26.22
Canned and dried vegetables and juices	92.30	70.07	87.11	100.70	114.87	92.37	86.10	62.12
Canned vegetables	54.59	43.97	50.31	59.42	62.30	58.39	53.57	38.78
Dried vegetables	18.22	10.44	16.34	19.43	26.16	16.95	18.86	9.88
Fresh and canned vegetable juices	18.98	15.50	19.99	21.26	25.58	16.47	13.40	13.33
Sugar and other sweets	**146.77**	**90.64**	**134.90**	**170.33**	**162.74**	**159.56**	**140.89**	**113.92**
Candy and chewing gum	87.86	49.30	82.87	101.13	98.40	96.90	87.26	61.37
Sugar	24.38	21.22	23.80	30.30	26.51	23.60	21.72	17.07
Artificial sweeteners	4.91	2.30	2.84	4.35	4.32	8.34	5.62	5.31
Jams, preserves, other sweets	29.61	17.82	25.39	34.55	33.52	30.72	26.29	30.17
Fats and oils	**114.09**	**81.53**	**97.87**	**133.08**	**137.34**	**113.21**	**109.10**	**89.70**
Margarine	8.74	7.40	6.40	9.96	8.38	8.60	10.01	10.95
Fats and oils	36.79	31.44	32.70	45.27	44.33	33.40	31.56	29.09
Salad dressings	31.29	19.27	26.81	32.90	36.28	34.81	33.97	24.33
Nondairy cream and imitation milk	18.59	12.06	15.84	19.98	24.73	19.43	16.82	13.29
Peanut butter	18.68	11.37	16.10	24.97	23.62	16.98	16.74	12.04

	total consumer units	under 25	25 to 34	35 to 44	45 to 54	55 to 64	65 to 74	75+
Miscellaneous foods	**$699.27**	**$441.20**	**$731.69**	**$785.75**	**$834.82**	**$711.16**	**$649.57**	**$424.07**
Frozen prepared foods	130.83	99.04	146.52	138.18	165.10	124.00	106.83	83.92
Frozen meals	60.61	37.28	60.48	59.38	79.08	58.72	58.06	47.97
Other frozen prepared foods	70.22	61.76	86.04	78.80	86.02	65.28	48.77	35.96
Canned and packaged soups	46.30	29.63	38.40	47.59	56.21	45.27	54.07	41.05
Potato chips, nuts, and other snacks	153.94	95.16	146.31	183.86	193.60	156.69	144.48	77.57
Potato chips and other snacks	111.59	71.79	116.07	144.29	142.52	107.56	84.13	48.88
Nuts	42.35	23.37	30.24	39.57	51.08	49.13	60.36	28.69
Condiments and seasonings	141.39	84.54	136.44	161.51	176.08	144.27	132.46	86.73
Salt, spices, and other seasonings	38.72	27.05	36.62	44.68	48.40	38.58	36.27	22.77
Olives, pickles, relishes	17.46	9.32	13.70	17.73	20.84	21.12	19.26	13.11
Sauces and gravies	60.27	35.37	59.78	72.31	75.54	60.60	50.91	35.78
Baking needs and miscellaneous products	24.95	12.80	26.34	26.79	31.29	23.97	26.01	15.07
Other canned/packaged prepared foods	226.81	132.82	264.02	254.60	243.83	240.93	211.73	134.79
Prepared salads	35.09	15.95	30.86	37.07	41.07	38.02	41.87	25.99
Prepared desserts	14.29	11.74	12.17	14.90	14.98	14.14	15.82	15.64
Baby food	25.05	21.05	65.77	36.66	18.70	8.37	5.29	4.78
Miscellaneous prepared foods	147.81	82.31	152.41	163.54	163.81	170.26	142.81	88.38
Nonalcoholic beverages	**370.13**	**272.26**	**331.48**	**418.75**	**455.33**	**383.65**	**353.20**	**235.11**
Carbonated drinks	139.74	112.25	130.56	161.92	171.16	148.37	122.32	74.19
Tea	30.36	19.86	28.98	32.82	35.48	33.73	29.98	19.21
Coffee	86.50	45.53	63.79	78.12	106.55	99.16	108.29	78.06
Noncarbonated fruit-flavored drinks	25.83	29.14	23.60	33.70	31.11	19.62	20.92	19.47
Other nonalcoholic beverages and ice	15.36	12.33	13.36	20.59	20.03	14.33	11.72	8.02
Bottled water	56.80	42.01	54.25	67.82	73.49	55.05	49.54	28.87
Sports drinks	15.12	11.13	16.96	23.78	16.84	12.35	10.00	6.74
Food prepared by consumer unit on trips	**50.23**	**8.36**	**39.51**	**47.04**	**66.42**	**64.15**	**65.21**	**24.43**

Source: Bureau of Labor Statistics, unpublished tables from the 2012 Consumer Expenditure Survey

Table 5. Groceries: Indexed spending by age, 2012

(indexed average annual spending of consumer units on groceries, by age of consumer unit reference person, 2012; index definition: an index of 100 is the average for all consumer units; an index of 125 means that spending by consumer units in that group is 25 percent above the average for all consumer units; an index of 75 indicates spending that is 25 percent below the average for all consumer units)

	total consumer units	under 25	25 to 34	35 to 44	45 to 54	55 to 64	65 to 74	75+
Average spending of consumer units, total	$51,442	$31,411	$49,544	$58,069	$62,103	$55,636	$45,968	$33,530
Average spending of consumer units, index	100	61	96	113	121	108	89	65
GROCERIES	100	65	94	115	120	102	95	69
Cereals and bakery products	100	66	95	117	118	98	91	78
Cereals and cereal products	100	79	103	122	125	87	78	67
Flour	100	66	106	105	123	107	77	72
Prepared flour mixes	100	58	84	115	130	101	93	74
Ready-to-eat and cooked cereals	100	79	105	123	122	87	80	67
Rice	100	103	110	128	134	72	62	56
Pasta, cornmeal, and other cereal products	100	74	100	125	126	87	79	70
Bakery products	100	59	91	115	114	104	98	84
Bread	100	56	92	113	116	108	95	80
White bread	100	61	97	119	114	104	88	77
Bread other than white	100	53	88	108	118	111	100	81
Crackers and cookies	100	66	92	110	116	101	102	82
Cookies	100	69	90	109	112	104	104	87
Crackers	100	62	95	112	122	98	99	75
Frozen and refrigerated bakery products	100	69	106	135	107	92	80	72
Other bakery products	100	56	87	116	112	104	100	92
Biscuits and rolls	100	52	86	122	111	110	97	79
Cakes and cupcakes	100	55	102	111	108	99	93	103
Bread and cracker products	100	82	100	111	120	90	96	75
Sweetrolls, coffee cakes, doughnuts	100	58	73	109	112	108	106	112
Pies, tarts, turnovers	100	51	70	121	123	93	125	81
Meats, poultry, fish, and eggs	100	67	89	117	123	104	94	63
Beef	100	71	85	117	127	107	89	61
Ground beef	100	69	96	116	121	108	86	59
Roast	100	74	69	105	134	109	97	79
Chuck roast	100	158	68	115	103	120	83	63
Round roast	100	15	68	155	154	80	75	69
Other roast	100	51	70	80	143	114	112	92
Steak	100	75	81	122	125	107	90	57
Round steak	100	72	79	146	118	94	87	58
Sirloin steak	100	76	95	109	122	117	88	45
Other steak	100	76	74	119	129	108	91	63
Other beef	100	56	76	117	155	91	92	53
Pork	100	66	87	119	118	105	101	62
Bacon	100	67	91	107	120	114	91	69
Pork chops	100	61	94	123	112	104	102	62
Ham	100	62	85	120	119	101	106	67
Ham, not canned	100	62	87	123	114	101	105	69
Canned ham	100	85	30	39	243	107	117	15
Sausage	100	75	84	119	123	94	111	59
Other pork	100	65	86	127	114	112	95	54
Other meats	100	63	91	121	118	99	100	69
Frankfurters	100	77	95	131	111	106	80	57
Lunch meats (cold cuts)	100	57	91	127	120	99	92	67
Bologna, liverwurst, salami	100	52	98	128	122	93	88	70
Other lunch meats	100	59	89	126	119	102	94	65
Lamb, organ meats, and others	100	81	77	44	117	82	212	118

	total consumer units	under 25	25 to 34	35 to 44	45 to 54	55 to 64	65 to 74	75+
Poultry	100	72	103	113	130	100	77	58
Fresh and frozen chicken	100	75	105	115	129	97	77	55
Fresh and frozen whole chicken	100	77	109	114	135	88	72	61
Fresh and frozen chicken parts	100	75	104	115	127	100	79	52
Other poultry	100	58	92	104	133	113	77	70
Fish and seafood	100	58	74	119	122	110	109	64
Canned fish and seafood	100	43	74	111	102	117	124	99
Fresh fish and shellfish	100	38	79	115	126	122	102	54
Frozen fish and shellfish	100	94	67	128	125	89	113	64
Eggs	100	73	95	114	113	100	99	77
Dairy products	**100**	**60**	**94**	**119**	**119**	**103**	**92**	**69**
Fresh milk and cream	100	66	99	125	120	94	83	73
Fresh milk, all types	100	69	101	127	119	91	79	73
Cream	100	47	87	115	124	105	102	71
Other dairy products	100	57	91	115	118	109	97	67
Butter	100	41	89	102	118	119	98	87
Cheese	100	51	94	118	116	112	98	61
Ice cream and related products	100	64	81	110	121	109	108	72
Miscellaneous dairy products	100	70	99	121	123	98	83	63
Fruits and vegetables	**100**	**62**	**93**	**111**	**119**	**100**	**99**	**79**
Fresh fruits	100	62	91	114	118	99	99	84
Apples	100	77	97	125	116	92	85	74
Bananas	100	64	91	111	122	98	89	92
Oranges	100	71	80	129	123	94	99	66
Citrus fruits, except oranges	100	60	95	112	124	99	92	78
Other fresh fruits	100	54	89	107	114	102	112	91
Fresh vegetables	100	57	92	108	119	104	107	75
Potatoes	100	67	88	109	118	106	105	73
Lettuce	100	59	92	112	116	100	106	81
Tomatoes	100	64	97	111	124	96	94	74
Other fresh vegetables	100	51	92	105	119	106	113	74
Processed fruits	100	68	98	109	119	97	88	91
Frozen fruits and fruit juices	100	58	88	104	145	87	89	87
Frozen fruits	100	37	66	104	166	101	97	62
Frozen fruit juices	100	84	117	103	119	70	80	119
Canned fruits	100	51	94	110	119	92	98	105
Dried fruits	100	38	121	86	98	102	119	111
Fresh fruit juice	100	61	84	127	125	104	78	74
Canned and bottled fruit juice	100	83	103	108	114	99	81	88
Processed vegetables	100	69	97	111	123	100	94	68
Frozen vegetables	100	50	104	115	119	100	94	70
Canned and dried vegetables and juices	100	76	94	109	124	100	93	67
Canned vegetables	100	81	92	109	114	107	98	71
Dried vegetables	100	57	90	107	144	93	104	54
Fresh and canned vegetable juices	100	82	105	112	135	87	71	70
Sugar and other sweets	**100**	**62**	**92**	**116**	**111**	**109**	**96**	**78**
Candy and chewing gum	100	56	94	115	112	110	99	70
Sugar	100	87	98	124	109	97	89	70
Artificial sweeteners	100	47	58	89	88	170	114	108
Jams, preserves, other sweets	100	60	86	117	113	104	89	102
Fats and oils	**100**	**71**	**86**	**117**	**120**	**99**	**96**	**79**
Margarine	100	85	73	114	96	98	115	125
Fats and oils	100	85	89	123	120	91	86	79
Salad dressings	100	62	86	105	116	111	109	78
Nondairy cream and imitation milk	100	65	85	107	133	105	90	71
Peanut butter	100	61	86	134	126	91	90	64

	total consumer units	under 25	25 to 34	35 to 44	45 to 54	55 to 64	65 to 74	75+
Miscellaneous foods	**100**	**63**	**105**	**112**	**119**	**102**	**93**	**61**
Frozen prepared foods	100	76	112	106	126	95	82	64
Frozen meals	100	62	100	98	130	97	96	79
Other frozen prepared foods	100	88	123	112	123	93	69	51
Canned and packaged soups	100	64	83	103	121	98	117	89
Potato chips, nuts, and other snacks	100	62	95	119	126	102	94	50
Potato chips and other snacks	100	64	104	129	128	96	75	44
Nuts	100	55	71	93	121	116	143	68
Condiments and seasonings	100	60	96	114	125	102	94	61
Salt, spices, and other seasonings	100	70	95	115	125	100	94	59
Olives, pickles, relishes	100	53	78	102	119	121	110	75
Sauces and gravies	100	59	99	120	125	101	84	59
Baking needs and miscellaneous products	100	51	106	107	125	96	104	60
Other canned/packaged prepared foods	100	59	116	112	108	106	93	59
Prepared salads	100	45	88	106	117	108	119	74
Prepared desserts	100	82	85	104	105	99	111	109
Baby food	100	84	263	146	75	33	21	19
Miscellaneous prepared foods	100	56	103	111	111	115	97	60
Nonalcoholic beverages	**100**	**74**	**90**	**113**	**123**	**104**	**95**	**64**
Carbonated drinks	100	80	93	116	122	106	88	53
Tea	100	65	95	108	117	111	99	63
Coffee	100	53	74	90	123	115	125	90
Noncarbonated fruit-flavored drinks	100	113	91	130	120	76	81	75
Other nonalcoholic beverages and ice	100	80	87	134	130	93	76	52
Bottled water	100	74	96	119	129	97	87	51
Sports drinks	100	74	112	157	111	82	66	45
Food prepared by consumer unit on trips	**100**	**17**	**79**	**94**	**132**	**128**	**130**	**49**

Source: Calculations by New Strategist based on the Bureau of Labor Statistics' 2012 Consumer Expenditure Survey

Table 6. Groceries: Total spending by age, 2012

(total annual spending on groceries, by consumer unit age groups, 2012; consumer units and dollars in thousands)

	total consumer units	under 25	25 to 34	35 to 44	45 to 54	55 to 64	65 to 74	75+
Number of consumer units	124,416	8,159	20,112	21,598	24,624	22,770	14,993	12,161
Total spending of all consumer units	$6,400,191,698	$256,283,002	$996,423,699	$1,254,180,957	$1,529,212,945	$1,266,838,779	$689,196,275	$407,752,736
GROCERIES	487,791,590	20,634,356	74,005,925	96,983,443	115,902,952	91,359,388	55,761,366	33,024,898
Cereals and bakery products	66,917,146	2,892,692	10,289,500	13,644,968	15,588,223	12,011,175	7,345,970	5,118,687
Cereals and cereal products	22,641,224	1,168,042	3,758,128	4,809,227	5,612,302	3,616,787	2,141,300	1,485,101
Flour	1,164,534	50,178	200,114	212,092	282,437	227,928	108,549	82,330
Prepared flour mixes	2,013,051	76,695	273,523	401,939	519,320	370,468	226,244	145,081
Ready-to-eat and cooked cereals	11,797,125	612,333	1,994,708	2,516,167	2,851,213	1,882,396	1,140,368	772,710
Rice	3,066,854	206,667	544,231	680,985	814,562	406,672	230,742	168,795
Pasta, cornmeal, and other cereal products	4,600,904	222,170	745,552	998,044	1,144,524	729,095	435,397	315,943
Bakery products	44,275,922	1,724,649	6,531,372	8,835,742	9,975,921	8,394,388	5,204,670	3,633,585
Bread	13,078,610	479,341	1,938,395	2,558,067	3,006,590	2,585,989	1,502,149	1,017,997
White bread	5,414,584	215,234	845,106	1,120,720	1,220,365	1,027,838	576,631	407,515
Bread other than white	7,664,026	264,107	1,093,288	1,437,131	1,785,979	1,558,151	925,518	610,482
Crackers and cookies	10,915,016	472,325	1,621,631	2,083,991	2,507,216	2,026,758	1,337,076	869,876
Cookies	6,290,473	283,525	911,074	1,187,458	1,394,950	1,197,702	788,032	532,773
Crackers	4,624,543	188,799	710,557	896,749	1,112,266	829,283	549,044	336,981
Frozen and refrigerated bakery products	3,579,448	162,854	616,031	836,707	756,942	605,682	343,490	251,246
Other bakery products	16,702,848	610,130	2,355,316	3,356,977	3,705,420	3,175,732	2,021,806	1,494,465
Biscuits and rolls	6,450,970	221,435	895,386	1,366,721	1,418,096	1,301,989	757,446	496,290
Cakes and cupcakes	4,720,343	171,502	776,524	905,604	1,007,614	856,152	530,602	475,617
Bread and cracker products	909,481	49,199	147,019	174,728	216,199	149,144	105,401	66,642
Sweetrolls, coffee cakes, doughnuts	2,952,392	112,757	346,731	559,172	657,215	584,051	376,324	323,726
Pies, tarts, turnovers	1,668,419	55,318	189,656	350,536	406,296	284,397	252,032	132,190
Meats, poultry, fish, and eggs	106,053,443	4,671,517	15,192,404	21,573,162	25,789,946	20,198,812	12,050,024	6,549,307
Beef	28,157,829	1,305,766	3,868,543	5,697,552	7,079,400	5,492,579	3,035,483	1,671,651
Ground beef	11,632,896	524,134	1,810,281	2,342,951	2,774,386	2,300,681	1,206,037	668,247
Roast	4,232,632	204,301	471,023	769,321	1,123,839	846,589	495,069	328,469
Chuck roast	1,171,999	121,324	129,119	234,986	238,114	257,756	117,695	71,750
Round roast	824,878	8,322	90,705	222,027	251,411	121,364	74,365	55,819
Other roast	2,235,756	74,655	251,199	312,307	634,068	467,468	303,009	200,778
Steak	9,883,607	488,235	1,289,783	2,095,438	2,443,686	1,943,647	1,067,801	550,893
Round steak	2,103,875	99,377	270,305	534,119	493,219	361,815	221,746	119,907
Sirloin steak	2,707,292	135,195	416,922	511,657	652,044	582,001	288,615	119,786
Other steak	5,072,440	253,582	602,757	1,049,879	1,298,424	999,831	557,440	311,200
Other beef	2,407,450	89,096	297,456	489,843	737,735	401,435	266,576	124,042
Pork	20,624,440	894,308	2,915,838	4,273,164	4,807,836	3,979,285	2,503,981	1,248,813
Bacon	4,003,707	177,050	585,863	742,971	954,426	837,708	439,445	269,001
Pork chops	3,488,625	139,029	528,744	744,267	771,224	662,835	429,549	212,209
Ham	4,157,983	170,115	570,577	863,704	978,065	772,358	530,602	273,014
Ham, not canned	4,004,951	161,711	563,136	853,337	904,440	742,302	509,012	270,704
Canned ham	153,032	8,485	7,441	10,367	73,626	30,056	21,590	2,311
Sausage	3,998,730	197,366	540,812	828,499	976,834	689,248	532,851	229,965
Other pork	4,975,396	210,665	689,640	1,093,723	1,127,287	1,017,136	571,533	264,745
Other meats	15,194,926	627,019	2,233,236	3,186,137	3,537,730	2,751,527	1,828,246	1,025,902
Frankfurters	3,074,319	156,163	472,632	698,263	678,391	594,525	297,761	172,565
Lunch meats (cold cuts)	10,852,808	403,544	1,603,128	2,391,547	2,567,052	1,967,783	1,206,787	706,919
Bologna, liverwurst, salami	3,191,270	108,107	503,202	710,358	768,023	543,748	336,893	217,804
Other lunch meats	7,661,537	295,356	1,099,925	1,681,404	1,799,029	1,424,036	869,894	488,994
Lamb, organ meats, and others	1,267,799	67,312	157,477	96,327	292,533	189,219	323,849	146,418

	total consumer units	under 25	25 to 34	35 to 44	45 to 54	55 to 64	65 to 74	75+
Poultry	$19,826,934	$933,308	$3,285,697	$3,879,433	$5,106,033	$3,629,766	$1,840,391	$1,124,528
Fresh and frozen chicken	15,741,112	778,450	2,675,902	3,138,837	4,029,964	2,781,356	1,461,068	845,433
Fresh and frozen whole chicken	4,705,413	238,324	826,000	933,466	1,255,578	754,598	406,160	279,338
Fresh and frozen chicken parts	11,035,699	540,126	1,849,701	2,205,372	2,774,386	2,026,530	1,054,907	566,095
Other poultry	4,085,821	154,776	609,796	740,595	1,075,823	848,410	379,323	279,095
Fish and seafood	15,644,068	595,525	1,874,237	3,231,061	3,785,201	3,136,795	2,057,489	979,569
Canned fish and seafood	2,261,883	63,559	271,311	436,712	456,775	485,912	336,743	218,533
Fresh fish and shellfish	7,874,289	194,021	1,004,192	1,573,198	1,968,443	1,758,755	971,396	417,609
Frozen fish and shellfish	5,507,896	337,946	598,734	1,221,367	1,359,984	892,129	749,350	343,427
Eggs	6,604,001	315,672	1,015,053	1,305,815	1,473,993	1,209,087	784,434	498,723
Dairy products	**52,121,595**	**2,051,907**	**7,921,513**	**10,735,502**	**12,261,767**	**9,859,865**	**5,766,758**	**3,512,826**
Fresh milk and cream	18,893,814	815,166	3,008,554	4,101,892	4,472,703	3,236,072	1,886,419	1,349,385
Fresh milk, all types	15,960,084	725,254	2,594,649	3,514,643	3,755,160	2,672,060	1,526,737	1,145,688
Cream	2,933,729	89,831	413,905	587,466	717,543	564,013	359,532	203,818
Other dairy products	33,227,781	1,236,741	4,912,758	6,633,610	7,788,817	6,623,793	3,880,488	2,163,442
Butter	3,180,073	85,425	456,140	563,276	744,876	689,931	375,425	271,798
Cheese	16,356,972	547,469	2,479,005	3,339,051	3,746,295	3,343,775	1,925,551	981,636
Ice cream and related products	7,137,746	301,149	928,973	1,359,810	1,705,704	1,419,482	925,818	504,438
Miscellaneous dairy products	6,552,991	302,780	1,048,640	1,371,473	1,591,942	1,170,606	653,695	405,569
Fruits and vegetables	**90,945,608**	**3,724,176**	**13,744,139**	**17,446,000**	**21,469,912**	**16,688,816**	**10,838,440**	**7,054,353**
Fresh fruits	32,508,657	1,323,308	4,765,941	6,408,343	7,591,825	5,870,334	3,894,432	2,664,597
Apples	5,176,950	261,822	812,123	1,124,824	1,193,033	872,774	528,653	376,140
Bananas	5,450,665	227,962	804,078	1,048,583	1,313,690	981,842	584,727	491,791
Oranges	3,326,884	155,837	430,598	744,483	810,376	573,576	394,916	214,155
Citrus fruits, except oranges	4,970,419	196,306	761,843	964,351	1,218,888	899,643	552,042	376,626
Other fresh fruits	13,584,983	481,381	1,957,300	2,526,102	3,055,838	2,542,498	1,833,944	1,205,763
Fresh vegetables	28,135,434	1,048,350	4,190,536	5,253,929	6,631,982	5,337,971	3,631,604	2,060,560
Potatoes	4,782,551	208,626	677,774	903,660	1,120,884	926,511	604,668	342,940
Lettuce	4,022,369	154,450	597,930	782,280	920,445	737,065	513,360	319,105
Tomatoes	4,895,770	206,096	765,060	944,049	1,203,375	863,438	556,090	356,317
Other fresh vegetables	14,433,500	479,178	2,149,772	2,623,725	3,387,031	2,810,957	1,957,636	1,042,076
Processed fruits	14,153,564	626,611	2,251,136	2,679,664	3,321,778	2,525,421	1,492,703	1,255,015
Frozen fruits and fruit juices	1,581,327	59,642	225,053	284,662	454,067	253,202	170,470	134,257
Frozen fruits	890,819	21,621	94,526	161,337	292,041	164,855	103,752	53,995
Frozen fruit juices	690,509	37,939	130,527	123,109	162,026	88,348	66,719	80,263
Canned fruits	2,531,866	84,364	386,352	484,011	593,931	427,621	299,260	258,664
Dried fruits	1,083,663	26,843	211,578	162,633	209,796	201,742	155,777	117,840
Fresh fruit juice	2,122,537	84,446	289,613	468,245	523,999	402,801	199,107	153,958
Canned and bottled fruit juice	6,832,927	371,316	1,138,339	1,280,113	1,540,231	1,240,054	668,088	590,295
Processed vegetables	16,149,197	725,988	2,536,727	3,104,281	3,924,327	2,955,318	1,819,700	1,074,181
Frozen vegetables	4,665,600	154,287	784,770	929,362	1,095,768	852,053	528,803	318,861
Canned and dried vegetables and juices	11,483,597	571,701	1,751,956	2,174,919	2,828,559	2,103,265	1,290,897	755,441
Canned vegetables	6,791,869	358,751	1,011,835	1,283,353	1,534,075	1,329,540	803,175	471,604
Dried vegetables	2,266,860	85,180	328,630	419,649	644,164	385,952	282,768	120,151
Fresh and canned vegetable juices	2,361,416	126,465	402,039	459,173	629,882	375,022	200,906	162,106
Sugar and other sweets	**18,260,536**	**739,532**	**2,713,109**	**3,678,787**	**4,007,310**	**3,633,181**	**2,112,364**	**1,385,381**
Candy and chewing gum	10,931,190	402,239	1,666,681	2,184,206	2,423,002	2,206,413	1,308,289	746,321
Sugar	3,033,262	173,134	478,666	654,419	652,782	537,372	325,648	207,588
Artificial sweeteners	610,883	18,766	57,118	93,951	106,376	189,902	84,261	64,575
Jams, preserves, other sweets	3,683,958	145,393	510,644	746,211	825,396	699,494	394,166	366,897
Fats and oils	**14,194,621**	**665,203**	**1,968,361**	**2,874,262**	**3,381,860**	**2,577,792**	**1,635,736**	**1,090,842**
Margarine	1,087,396	60,377	128,717	215,116	206,349	195,822	150,080	133,163
Fats and oils	4,577,265	256,519	657,662	977,741	1,091,582	760,518	473,179	353,763
Salad dressings	3,892,977	157,224	539,203	710,574	893,359	792,624	509,312	295,877
Nondairy cream and imitation milk	2,312,893	98,398	318,574	431,528	608,952	442,421	252,182	161,620
Peanut butter	2,324,091	92,768	323,803	539,302	581,619	386,635	250,983	146,418

	total consumer units	under 25	25 to 34	35 to 44	45 to 54	55 to 64	65 to 74	75+
Miscellaneous foods	**$87,000,376**	**$3,599,751**	**$14,715,749**	**$16,970,629**	**$20,556,608**	**$16,193,113**	**$9,739,003**	**$5,157,115**
Frozen prepared foods	16,277,345	808,067	2,946,810	2,984,412	4,065,422	2,823,480	1,601,702	1,020,551
Frozen meals	7,540,854	304,168	1,216,374	1,282,489	1,947,266	1,337,054	870,494	583,363
Other frozen prepared foods	8,736,492	503,900	1,730,436	1,701,922	2,118,156	1,486,426	731,209	437,310
Canned and packaged soups	5,760,461	241,751	772,301	1,027,849	1,384,115	1,030,798	810,672	499,209
Potato chips, nuts, and other snacks	19,152,599	776,410	2,942,587	3,971,008	4,767,206	3,567,831	2,166,189	943,329
Potato chips and other snacks	13,883,581	585,735	2,334,400	3,116,375	3,509,412	2,449,141	1,261,361	594,430
Nuts	5,269,018	190,676	608,187	854,633	1,257,794	1,118,690	904,977	348,899
Condiments and seasonings	17,591,178	689,762	2,744,081	3,488,293	4,335,794	3,285,028	1,985,973	1,054,724
Salt, spices, and other seasonings	4,817,388	220,701	736,501	964,999	1,191,802	878,467	543,796	276,906
Olives, pickles, relishes	2,172,303	76,042	275,534	382,933	513,164	480,902	288,765	159,431
Sauces and gravies	7,498,552	288,584	1,202,295	1,561,751	1,860,097	1,379,862	763,294	435,121
Baking needs and miscellaneous products	3,104,179	104,435	529,750	578,610	770,485	545,797	389,968	183,266
Other canned/packaged prepared foods	28,218,793	1,083,678	5,309,970	5,498,851	6,004,070	5,485,976	3,174,468	1,639,181
Prepared salads	4,365,757	130,136	620,656	800,638	1,011,308	865,715	627,757	316,064
Prepared desserts	1,777,905	95,787	244,763	321,810	368,868	321,968	237,189	190,198
Baby food	3,116,621	171,747	1,322,766	791,783	460,469	190,585	79,313	58,130
Miscellaneous prepared foods	18,389,929	671,567	3,065,270	3,532,137	4,033,657	3,876,820	2,141,150	1,074,789
Nonalcoholic beverages	**46,050,094**	**2,221,369**	**6,666,726**	**9,044,163**	**11,212,046**	**8,735,711**	**5,295,528**	**2,859,173**
Carbonated drinks	17,385,892	915,848	2,625,823	3,497,148	4,214,644	3,378,385	1,833,944	902,225
Tea	3,777,270	162,038	582,846	708,846	873,660	768,032	449,490	233,613
Coffee	10,761,984	371,479	1,282,944	1,687,236	2,623,687	2,257,873	1,623,592	949,288
Noncarbonated fruit-flavored drinks	3,213,665	237,753	474,643	727,853	766,053	446,747	313,654	236,775
Other nonalcoholic beverages and ice	1,911,030	100,600	268,696	444,703	493,219	326,294	175,718	97,531
Bottled water	7,066,829	342,760	1,091,076	1,464,776	1,809,618	1,253,489	742,753	351,088
Sports drinks	1,881,170	90,810	341,100	513,600	414,668	281,210	149,930	81,965
Food prepared by consumer unit on trips	**6,249,416**	**68,209**	**794,625**	**1,015,970**	**1,635,526**	**1,460,696**	**977,694**	**297,093**

Note: Numbers may not add to total because of rounding.
Source: Calculations by New Strategist based on the Bureau of Labor Statistics' 2012 Consumer Expenditure Survey

Table 7. Groceries: Market shares by age, 2012

(percentage of total annual spending on groceries accounted for by consumer unit age groups, 2012)

	total consumer units	under 25	25 to 34	35 to 44	45 to 54	55 to 64	65 to 74	75+
Share of total consumer units	100.0%	6.6%	16.2%	17.4%	19.8%	18.3%	12.1%	9.8%
Share of total before-tax income	100.0	3.7	14.5	20.7	24.7	21.6	9.8	5.0
Share of total spending	100.0	4.0	15.6	19.6	23.9	19.8	10.8	6.4
GROCERIES	100.0	4.2	15.2	19.9	23.8	18.7	11.4	6.8
Cereals and bakery products	100.0	4.3	15.4	20.4	23.3	17.9	11.0	7.6
Cereals and cereal products	100.0	5.2	16.6	21.2	24.8	16.0	9.5	6.6
Flour	100.0	4.3	17.2	18.2	24.3	19.6	9.3	7.1
Prepared flour mixes	100.0	3.8	13.6	20.0	25.8	18.4	11.2	7.2
Ready-to-eat and cooked cereals	100.0	5.2	16.9	21.3	24.2	16.0	9.7	6.5
Rice	100.0	6.7	17.7	22.2	26.6	13.3	7.5	5.5
Pasta, cornmeal, and other cereal products	100.0	4.8	16.2	21.7	24.9	15.8	9.5	6.9
Bakery products	100.0	3.9	14.8	20.0	22.5	19.0	11.8	8.2
Bread	100.0	3.7	14.8	19.6	23.0	19.8	11.5	7.8
White bread	100.0	4.0	15.6	20.7	22.5	19.0	10.6	7.5
Bread other than white	100.0	3.4	14.3	18.8	23.3	20.3	12.1	8.0
Crackers and cookies	100.0	4.3	14.9	19.1	23.0	18.6	12.2	8.0
Cookies	100.0	4.5	14.5	18.9	22.2	19.0	12.5	8.5
Crackers	100.0	4.1	15.4	19.4	24.1	17.9	11.9	7.3
Frozen and refrigerated bakery products	100.0	4.5	17.2	23.4	21.1	16.9	9.6	7.0
Other bakery products	100.0	3.7	14.1	20.1	22.2	19.0	12.1	8.9
Biscuits and rolls	100.0	3.4	13.9	21.2	22.0	20.2	11.7	7.7
Cakes and cupcakes	100.0	3.6	16.5	19.2	21.3	18.1	11.2	10.1
Bread and cracker products	100.0	5.4	16.2	19.2	23.8	16.4	11.6	7.3
Sweetrolls, coffee cakes, doughnuts	100.0	3.8	11.7	18.9	22.3	19.8	12.7	11.0
Pies, tarts, turnovers	100.0	3.3	11.4	21.0	24.4	17.0	15.1	7.9
Meats, poultry, fish, and eggs	100.0	4.4	14.3	20.3	24.3	19.0	11.4	6.2
Beef	100.0	4.6	13.7	20.2	25.1	19.5	10.8	5.9
Ground beef	100.0	4.5	15.6	20.1	23.8	19.8	10.4	5.7
Roast	100.0	4.8	11.1	18.2	26.6	20.0	11.7	7.8
Chuck roast	100.0	10.4	11.0	20.1	20.3	22.0	10.0	6.1
Round roast	100.0	1.0	11.0	26.9	30.5	14.7	9.0	6.8
Other roast	100.0	3.3	11.2	14.0	28.4	20.9	13.6	9.0
Steak	100.0	4.9	13.0	21.2	24.7	19.7	10.8	5.6
Round steak	100.0	4.7	12.8	25.4	23.4	17.2	10.5	5.7
Sirloin steak	100.0	5.0	15.4	18.9	24.1	21.5	10.7	4.4
Other steak	100.0	5.0	11.9	20.7	25.6	19.7	11.0	6.1
Other beef	100.0	3.7	12.4	20.3	30.6	16.7	11.1	5.2
Pork	100.0	4.3	14.1	20.7	23.3	19.3	12.1	6.1
Bacon	100.0	4.4	14.6	18.6	23.8	20.9	11.0	6.7
Pork chops	100.0	4.0	15.2	21.3	22.1	19.0	12.3	6.1
Ham	100.0	4.1	13.7	20.8	23.5	18.6	12.8	6.6
Ham, not canned	100.0	4.0	14.1	21.3	22.6	18.5	12.7	6.8
Canned ham	100.0	5.5	4.9	6.8	48.1	19.6	14.1	1.5
Sausage	100.0	4.9	13.5	20.7	24.4	17.2	13.3	5.8
Other pork	100.0	4.2	13.9	22.0	22.7	20.4	11.5	5.3
Other meats	100.0	4.1	14.7	21.0	23.3	18.1	12.0	6.8
Frankfurters	100.0	5.1	15.4	22.7	22.1	19.3	9.7	5.6
Lunch meats (cold cuts)	100.0	3.7	14.8	22.0	23.7	18.1	11.1	6.5
Bologna, liverwurst, salami	100.0	3.4	15.8	22.3	24.1	17.0	10.6	6.8
Other lunch meats	100.0	3.9	14.4	21.9	23.5	18.6	11.4	6.4
Lamb, organ meats, and others	100.0	5.3	12.4	7.6	23.1	14.9	25.5	11.5

	total consumer units	under 25	25 to 34	35 to 44	45 to 54	55 to 64	65 to 74	75+
Poultry	100.0%	4.7%	16.6%	19.6%	25.8%	18.3%	9.3%	5.7%
Fresh and frozen chicken	100.0	4.9	17.0	19.9	25.6	17.7	9.3	5.4
Fresh and frozen whole chicken	100.0	5.1	17.6	19.8	26.7	16.0	8.6	5.9
Fresh and frozen chicken parts	100.0	4.9	16.8	20.0	25.1	18.4	9.6	5.1
Other poultry	100.0	3.8	14.9	18.1	26.3	20.8	9.3	6.8
Fish and seafood	100.0	3.8	12.0	20.7	24.2	20.1	13.2	6.3
Canned fish and seafood	100.0	2.8	12.0	19.3	20.2	21.5	14.9	9.7
Fresh fish and shellfish	100.0	2.5	12.8	20.0	25.0	22.3	12.3	5.3
Frozen fish and shellfish	100.0	6.1	10.9	22.2	24.7	16.2	13.6	6.2
Eggs	100.0	4.8	15.4	19.8	22.3	18.3	11.9	7.6
Dairy products	**100.0**	**3.9**	**15.2**	**20.6**	**23.5**	**18.9**	**11.1**	**6.7**
Fresh milk and cream	100.0	4.3	15.9	21.7	23.7	17.1	10.0	7.1
Fresh milk, all types	100.0	4.5	16.3	22.0	23.5	16.7	9.6	7.2
Cream	100.0	3.1	14.1	20.0	24.5	19.2	12.3	6.9
Other dairy products	100.0	3.7	14.8	20.0	23.4	19.9	11.7	6.5
Butter	100.0	2.7	14.3	17.7	23.4	21.7	11.8	8.5
Cheese	100.0	3.3	15.2	20.4	22.9	20.4	11.8	6.0
Ice cream and related products	100.0	4.2	13.0	19.1	23.9	19.9	13.0	7.1
Miscellaneous dairy products	100.0	4.6	16.0	20.9	24.3	17.9	10.0	6.2
Fruits and vegetables	**100.0**	**4.1**	**15.1**	**19.2**	**23.6**	**18.4**	**11.9**	**7.8**
Fresh fruits	100.0	4.1	14.7	19.7	23.4	18.1	12.0	8.2
Apples	100.0	5.1	15.7	21.7	23.0	16.9	10.2	7.3
Bananas	100.0	4.2	14.8	19.2	24.1	18.0	10.7	9.0
Oranges	100.0	4.7	12.9	22.4	24.4	17.2	11.9	6.4
Citrus fruits, except oranges	100.0	3.9	15.3	19.4	24.5	18.1	11.1	7.6
Other fresh fruits	100.0	3.5	14.4	18.6	22.5	18.7	13.5	8.9
Fresh vegetables	100.0	3.7	14.9	18.7	23.6	19.0	12.9	7.3
Potatoes	100.0	4.4	14.2	18.9	23.4	19.4	12.6	7.2
Lettuce	100.0	3.8	14.9	19.4	22.9	18.3	12.8	7.9
Tomatoes	100.0	4.2	15.6	19.3	24.6	17.6	11.4	7.3
Other fresh vegetables	100.0	3.3	14.9	18.2	23.5	19.5	13.6	7.2
Processed fruits	100.0	4.4	15.9	18.9	23.5	17.8	10.5	8.9
Frozen fruits and fruit juices	100.0	3.8	14.2	18.0	28.7	16.0	10.8	8.5
Frozen fruits	100.0	2.4	10.6	18.1	32.8	18.5	11.6	6.1
Frozen fruit juices	100.0	5.5	18.9	17.8	23.5	12.8	9.7	11.6
Canned fruits	100.0	3.3	15.3	19.1	23.5	16.9	11.8	10.2
Dried fruits	100.0	2.5	19.5	15.0	19.4	18.6	14.4	10.9
Fresh fruit juice	100.0	4.0	13.6	22.1	24.7	19.0	9.4	7.3
Canned and bottled fruit juice	100.0	5.4	16.7	18.7	22.5	18.1	9.8	8.6
Processed vegetables	100.0	4.5	15.7	19.2	24.3	18.3	11.3	6.7
Frozen vegetables	100.0	3.3	16.8	19.9	23.5	18.3	11.3	6.8
Canned and dried vegetables and juices	100.0	5.0	15.3	18.9	24.6	18.3	11.2	6.6
Canned vegetables	100.0	5.3	14.9	18.9	22.6	19.6	11.8	6.9
Dried vegetables	100.0	3.8	14.5	18.5	28.4	17.0	12.5	5.3
Fresh and canned vegetable juices	100.0	5.4	17.0	19.4	26.7	15.9	8.5	6.9
Sugar and other sweets	**100.0**	**4.0**	**14.9**	**20.1**	**21.9**	**19.9**	**11.6**	**7.6**
Candy and chewing gum	100.0	3.7	15.2	20.0	22.2	20.2	12.0	6.8
Sugar	100.0	5.7	15.8	21.6	21.5	17.7	10.7	6.8
Artificial sweeteners	100.0	3.1	9.4	15.4	17.4	31.1	13.8	10.6
Jams, preserves, other sweets	100.0	3.9	13.9	20.3	22.4	19.0	10.7	10.0
Fats and oils	**100.0**	**4.7**	**13.9**	**20.2**	**23.8**	**18.2**	**11.5**	**7.7**
Margarine	100.0	5.6	11.8	19.8	19.0	18.0	13.8	12.2
Fats and oils	100.0	5.6	14.4	21.4	23.8	16.6	10.3	7.7
Salad dressings	100.0	4.0	13.9	18.3	22.9	20.4	13.1	7.6
Nondairy cream and imitation milk	100.0	4.3	13.8	18.7	26.3	19.1	10.9	7.0
Peanut butter	100.0	4.0	13.9	23.2	25.0	16.6	10.8	6.3

	total consumer units	under 25	25 to 34	35 to 44	45 to 54	55 to 64	65 to 74	75+
Miscellaneous foods	100.0%	4.1%	16.9%	19.5%	23.6%	18.6%	11.2%	5.9%
Frozen prepared foods	100.0	5.0	18.1	18.3	25.0	17.3	9.8	6.3
Frozen meals	100.0	4.0	16.1	17.0	25.8	17.7	11.5	7.7
Other frozen prepared foods	100.0	5.8	19.8	19.5	24.2	17.0	8.4	5.0
Canned and packaged soups	100.0	4.2	13.4	17.8	24.0	17.9	14.1	8.7
Potato chips, nuts, and other snacks	100.0	4.1	15.4	20.7	24.9	18.6	11.3	4.9
Potato chips and other snacks	100.0	4.2	16.8	22.4	25.3	17.6	9.1	4.3
Nuts	100.0	3.6	11.5	16.2	23.9	21.2	17.2	6.6
Condiments and seasonings	100.0	3.9	15.6	19.8	24.6	18.7	11.3	6.0
Salt, spices, and other seasonings	100.0	4.6	15.3	20.0	24.7	18.2	11.3	5.7
Olives, pickles, relishes	100.0	3.5	12.7	17.6	23.6	22.1	13.3	7.3
Sauces and gravies	100.0	3.8	16.0	20.8	24.8	18.4	10.2	5.8
Baking needs and miscellaneous products	100.0	3.4	17.1	18.6	24.8	17.6	12.6	5.9
Other canned/packaged prepared foods	100.0	3.8	18.8	19.5	21.3	19.4	11.2	5.8
Prepared salads	100.0	3.0	14.2	18.3	23.2	19.8	14.4	7.2
Prepared desserts	100.0	5.4	13.8	18.1	20.7	18.1	13.3	10.7
Baby food	100.0	5.5	42.4	25.4	14.8	6.1	2.5	1.9
Miscellaneous prepared foods	100.0	3.7	16.7	19.2	21.9	21.1	11.6	5.8
Nonalcoholic beverages	100.0	4.8	14.5	19.6	24.3	19.0	11.5	6.2
Carbonated drinks	100.0	5.3	15.1	20.1	24.2	19.4	10.5	5.2
Tea	100.0	4.3	15.4	18.8	23.1	20.3	11.9	6.2
Coffee	100.0	3.5	11.9	15.7	24.4	21.0	15.1	8.8
Noncarbonated fruit-flavored drinks	100.0	7.4	14.8	22.6	23.8	13.9	9.8	7.4
Other nonalcoholic beverages and ice	100.0	5.3	14.1	23.3	25.8	17.1	9.2	5.1
Bottled water	100.0	4.9	15.4	20.7	25.6	17.7	10.5	5.0
Sports drinks	100.0	4.8	18.1	27.3	22.0	14.9	8.0	4.4
Food prepared by consumer unit on trips	100.0	1.1	12.7	16.3	26.2	23.4	15.6	4.8

Note: Numbers may not add to total because of rounding.
Source: Calculations by New Strategist based on the Bureau of Labor Statistics' 2012 Consumer Expenditure Survey

Table 8. Groceries: Average spending by income, 2012

(average annual spending on groceries, by before-tax income of consumer units, 2012)

	total consumer units	under $20,000	$20,000–$39,999	$40,000–$49,999	$50,000–$69,999	$70,000–$79,999	$80,000–$99,999	$100,000 or more
Number of consumer units (in 000s)	124,416	26,177	28,041	11,010	17,972	6,946	10,977	23,293
Number of persons per consumer unit	2.5	1.8	2.2	2.5	2.6	2.8	2.9	3.2
Average before-tax income of consumer units	$65,596.00	$10,445.26	$29,593.01	$44,759.00	$59,283.00	$74,689.00	$88,974.00	$171,910.00
Average spending of consumer units, total	51,441.87	22,404.57	33,454.51	41,567.34	49,981.57	59,984.14	67,417.91	101,422.59
GROCERIES	3,920.65	2,411.60	3,040.52	3,621.44	3,910.30	4,944.59	4,865.08	6,060.39
Cereals and bakery products	537.85	337.83	410.01	520.99	548.81	668.71	664.27	813.81
Cereals and cereal products	181.98	116.99	138.99	176.31	176.99	233.54	227.97	275.62
Flour	9.36	6.58	7.04	12.19	8.96	8.95	10.01	13.77
Prepared flour mixes	16.18	9.55	12.54	18.11	12.41	20.54	23.19	25.11
Ready-to-eat and cooked cereals	94.82	57.41	70.70	92.91	97.37	123.96	120.22	143.75
Rice	24.65	19.26	20.54	23.51	24.41	28.31	26.39	34.54
Pasta, cornmeal, and other cereal products	36.98	24.19	28.20	29.59	33.85	51.79	48.17	58.45
Bakery products	355.87	220.84	271.02	344.68	371.82	435.18	436.30	538.18
Bread	105.12	68.98	88.20	96.97	107.07	130.80	129.11	148.73
White bread	43.52	30.36	37.75	44.42	43.81	52.64	52.62	57.07
Bread other than white	61.60	38.61	50.45	52.54	63.26	78.15	76.49	91.67
Crackers and cookies	87.73	53.02	64.34	80.85	90.83	100.40	107.93	141.82
Cookies	50.56	31.18	37.88	44.58	56.01	55.56	60.72	79.30
Crackers	37.17	21.84	26.46	36.28	34.82	44.84	47.21	62.51
Frozen and refrigerated bakery products	28.77	17.02	22.13	24.90	29.77	42.11	35.05	43.87
Other bakery products	134.25	81.82	96.36	141.96	144.16	161.87	164.22	203.77
Biscuits and rolls	51.85	29.73	38.23	46.16	51.65	64.20	62.26	86.94
Cakes and cupcakes	37.94	24.41	22.68	52.60	36.58	50.24	49.28	55.98
Bread and cracker products	7.31	3.97	5.75	9.16	7.74	8.78	8.77	10.51
Sweetrolls, coffee cakes, doughnuts	23.73	15.33	18.26	24.09	31.33	21.12	24.79	33.85
Pies, tarts, turnovers	13.41	8.38	11.44	9.95	16.86	17.52	19.11	16.49
Meats, poultry, fish, and eggs	852.41	552.29	686.69	790.64	825.31	1,073.94	1,086.35	1,263.93
Beef	226.32	130.78	180.56	230.92	222.13	271.62	285.25	347.35
Ground beef	93.50	66.31	83.23	92.15	97.80	117.76	119.62	114.03
Roast	34.02	14.38	25.32	35.36	29.95	41.72	41.24	62.99
Chuck roast	9.42	4.08	6.14	10.70	7.42	8.32	18.64	16.49
Round roast	6.63	1.96	5.01	3.98	5.93	6.38	4.45	16.62
Other roast	17.97	8.35	14.16	20.68	16.60	27.03	18.14	29.88
Steak	79.44	41.25	55.01	87.59	75.30	95.43	87.30	141.19
Round steak	16.91	7.42	11.17	20.48	15.73	19.22	18.67	31.70
Sirloin steak	21.76	12.04	13.59	24.43	20.00	28.12	23.74	39.58
Other steak	40.77	21.78	30.25	42.68	39.58	48.08	44.89	69.91
Other beef	19.35	8.83	17.00	15.82	19.07	16.71	37.09	29.14
Pork	165.77	119.03	137.07	145.07	168.05	217.47	211.70	225.54
Bacon	32.18	23.55	24.29	31.85	31.40	37.95	45.65	44.17
Pork chops	28.04	20.67	27.26	25.06	29.23	35.73	33.64	32.34
Ham	33.42	24.94	27.78	27.06	34.55	50.17	42.01	43.34
Ham, not canned	32.19	23.69	27.16	26.59	33.91	42.57	41.23	42.43
Canned ham	1.23	1.25	0.62	0.48	0.64	7.60	0.78	0.92
Sausage	32.14	23.69	25.34	26.28	34.27	41.48	40.21	45.24
Other pork	39.99	26.18	32.39	34.83	38.61	52.13	50.19	60.45
Other meats	122.13	73.35	104.39	116.57	116.66	156.41	144.71	183.08
Frankfurters	24.71	17.49	23.46	23.15	22.16	31.45	29.14	32.52
Lunch meats (cold cuts)	87.23	50.30	68.36	82.60	86.92	117.67	107.16	134.29
Bologna, liverwurst, salami	25.65	16.55	21.21	24.30	25.28	33.15	31.45	36.99
Other lunch meats	61.58	33.75	47.16	58.30	61.64	84.51	75.71	97.31
Lamb, organ meats, and others	10.19	5.56	12.57	10.81	7.58	7.29	8.41	16.26

	total consumer units	under $20,000	$20,000–$39,999	$40,000–$49,999	$50,000–$69,999	$70,000–$79,999	$80,000–$99,999	$100,000 or mor
Poultry	$159.36	$106.82	$129.17	$149.23	$152.47	$207.77	$200.44	$230.95
Fresh and frozen chicken	126.52	87.31	108.10	123.10	119.74	169.16	154.48	173.54
Fresh and frozen whole chicken	37.82	24.85	34.62	40.76	33.52	46.15	43.04	52.86
Fresh and frozen chicken parts	88.70	62.46	73.48	82.34	86.22	123.01	111.44	120.67
Other poultry	32.84	19.51	21.07	26.13	32.73	38.61	45.96	57.42
Fish and seafood	125.74	82.49	89.21	99.27	115.33	156.71	182.98	204.66
Canned fish and seafood	18.18	13.07	15.03	15.96	18.65	23.81	25.14	23.50
Fresh fish and shellfish	63.29	41.39	41.79	48.04	54.48	78.67	90.83	111.68
Frozen fish and shellfish	44.27	28.03	32.39	35.26	42.20	54.23	67.02	69.47
Eggs	53.08	39.83	46.30	49.58	50.68	63.96	61.27	72.35
Dairy products	**418.93**	**242.21**	**317.24**	**373.92**	**414.11**	**541.43**	**532.70**	**672.64**
Fresh milk and cream	151.86	101.12	126.56	141.81	151.57	192.88	184.64	215.44
Fresh milk, all types	128.28	87.93	108.80	118.36	128.43	164.55	157.02	176.59
Cream	23.58	13.19	17.76	23.45	23.14	28.33	27.62	38.84
Other dairy products	267.07	141.09	190.68	232.11	262.54	348.55	348.06	457.20
Butter	25.56	13.58	18.24	24.65	27.65	33.06	31.12	41.21
Cheese	131.47	68.50	93.61	117.19	125.86	169.54	167.23	230.47
Ice cream and related products	57.37	34.85	42.28	46.75	57.06	75.09	77.64	91.07
Miscellaneous dairy products	52.67	24.17	36.54	43.53	51.97	70.86	72.08	94.45
Fruits and vegetables	**730.98**	**437.34**	**566.07**	**655.17**	**719.48**	**877.99**	**906.09**	**1,175.88**
Fresh fruits	261.29	141.93	186.03	232.87	261.43	306.16	332.65	451.13
Apples	41.61	21.70	27.89	36.47	41.39	47.82	52.27	76.07
Bananas	43.81	26.51	34.35	45.47	47.47	49.25	56.11	63.14
Oranges	26.74	12.93	20.45	21.82	27.92	30.32	38.57	44.47
Citrus fruits, except oranges	39.95	22.06	30.61	34.30	42.04	44.43	48.36	66.95
Other fresh fruits	109.19	58.73	72.72	94.80	102.61	134.34	137.34	200.49
Fresh vegetables	226.14	135.71	176.11	209.28	216.96	267.51	272.62	367.96
Potatoes	38.44	26.09	31.23	37.51	39.93	45.03	45.66	54.66
Lettuce	32.33	19.16	23.71	28.46	33.91	45.37	37.49	51.53
Tomatoes	39.35	24.11	33.15	38.41	36.83	45.89	43.83	61.51
Other fresh vegetables	116.01	66.34	88.02	104.90	106.29	131.22	145.64	200.26
Processed fruits	113.76	68.92	95.35	95.05	113.30	149.66	140.62	172.75
Frozen fruits and fruit juices	12.71	7.14	9.56	8.57	14.51	19.84	17.28	19.25
Frozen fruits	7.16	2.87	4.87	4.40	7.29	11.97	11.40	12.73
Frozen fruit juices	5.55	4.27	4.69	4.17	7.21	7.87	5.88	6.52
Canned fruits	20.35	12.44	19.16	13.60	21.43	23.79	27.38	29.10
Dried fruits	8.71	3.38	7.32	7.11	9.83	9.02	10.12	15.37
Fresh fruit juice	17.06	10.03	13.67	14.42	16.19	18.13	22.68	28.12
Canned and bottled fruit juice	54.92	35.94	45.64	51.34	51.34	78.87	63.16	80.91
Processed vegetables	129.80	90.78	108.59	117.98	127.80	154.66	160.20	184.04
Frozen vegetables	37.50	26.03	28.85	28.07	38.32	47.20	53.59	54.59
Canned and dried vegetables and juices	92.30	64.75	79.74	89.91	89.48	107.46	106.61	129.45
Canned vegetables	54.59	36.02	45.84	51.82	53.91	63.31	64.30	80.13
Dried vegetables	18.22	–	17.07	16.86	18.37	21.11	17.95	22.23
Fresh and canned vegetable juices	18.98	12.90	16.36	20.87	16.46	22.09	23.72	26.72
Sugar and other sweets	**146.77**	**89.48**	**113.26**	**131.41**	**152.08**	**195.06**	**166.31**	**228.81**
Candy and chewing gum	87.86	46.60	66.73	74.22	88.48	128.02	98.54	147.18
Sugar	24.38	20.53	21.26	26.56	30.66	26.68	22.45	26.28
Artificial sweeteners	4.91	4.28	3.54	5.06	3.89	7.87	5.36	6.66
Jams, preserves, other sweets	29.61	18.06	21.73	25.57	29.05	32.50	39.96	48.70
Fats and oils	**114.09**	**77.10**	**94.42**	**114.03**	**114.63**	**140.63**	**128.24**	**163.46**
Margarine	8.74	7.35	7.73	6.28	10.45	11.54	9.23	10.42
Fats and oils	36.79	27.13	32.88	34.91	31.23	43.50	44.50	51.86
Salad dressings	31.29	20.70	23.65	32.66	34.15	37.20	37.97	44.53
Nondairy cream and imitation milk	18.59	12.05	14.57	21.85	20.34	23.83	18.27	26.10
Peanut butter	18.68	9.87	15.59	18.32	18.45	24.56	18.27	30.54

	total consumer units	under $20,000	$20,000– $39,999	$40,000– $49,999	$50,000– $69,999	$70,000– $79,999	$80,000– $99,999	$100,000 or mor
Miscellaneous foods	**$699.27**	**$426.43**	**$527.58**	**$653.80**	**$705.82**	**$877.26**	**$869.43**	**$1,095.17**
Frozen prepared foods	130.83	91.32	105.28	129.19	144.73	161.28	143.94	179.26
Frozen meals	60.61	46.02	46.60	52.37	63.59	75.42	65.91	88.98
Other frozen prepared foods	70.22	45.31	58.69	76.82	81.13	85.86	78.03	90.28
Canned and packaged soups	46.30	31.45	38.13	43.47	46.27	47.49	58.13	68.17
Potato chips, nuts, and other snacks	153.94	80.39	105.97	140.96	154.49	207.81	208.11	258.65
Potato chips and other snacks	111.59	61.11	78.84	101.06	115.60	149.57	147.79	181.87
Nuts	42.35	19.28	27.13	39.90	38.89	58.24	60.32	76.78
Condiments and seasonings	141.39	81.03	108.79	125.81	142.31	179.26	177.00	226.97
Salt, spices, and other seasonings	38.72	24.53	29.16	35.40	34.21	47.04	47.57	64.84
Olives, pickles, relishes	17.46	9.55	13.07	13.67	19.63	24.52	24.37	26.43
Sauces and gravies	60.27	33.43	47.05	51.82	63.25	80.16	76.92	94.19
Baking needs and miscellaneous products	24.95	13.52	19.51	24.92	25.22	27.54	28.13	41.51
Other canned/packaged prepared foods	226.81	142.25	169.39	214.37	218.02	281.42	282.25	362.12
Prepared salads	35.09	20.16	27.13	29.97	34.45	41.64	40.44	59.95
Prepared desserts	14.29	8.49	12.08	12.01	16.74	14.92	17.74	20.82
Baby food	25.05	14.72	18.76	38.02	25.55	28.68	26.85	35.73
Miscellaneous prepared foods	147.81	96.39	107.96	131.05	137.25	179.92	188.87	241.24
Nonalcoholic beverages	**370.13**	**233.43**	**297.34**	**348.42**	**386.92**	**501.87**	**432.26**	**535.94**
Carbonated drinks	139.74	94.08	123.52	138.48	145.14	190.44	151.96	184.03
Tea	30.36	19.06	22.02	31.96	33.76	52.19	33.02	41.28
Coffee	86.50	50.50	59.27	73.50	85.90	118.64	106.42	146.71
Noncarbonated fruit-flavored drinks	25.83	16.61	23.66	23.85	32.09	31.65	31.01	30.63
Other nonalcoholic beverages and ice	15.36	8.31	12.10	14.05	17.00	21.19	18.19	23.02
Bottled water	56.80	37.34	44.69	54.20	56.22	69.45	75.20	82.32
Sports drinks	15.12	7.54	10.92	12.38	16.81	16.57	16.46	27.65
Food prepared by consumer unit on trips	**50.23**	**15.50**	**27.90**	**33.07**	**43.13**	**67.71**	**79.43**	**110.76**

Note: "–" means sample is too small to make a reliable estimate.
Source: Bureau of Labor Statistics, unpublished tables from the 2012 Consumer Expenditure Survey

Table 9. Groceries: Indexed spending by income, 2012

(indexed average annual spending of consumer units on groceries by before-tax income of consumer unit, 2012; index definition: an index of 100 is the average for all consumer units; an index of 125 means that spending by consumer units in that group is 25 percent above the average for all consumer units; an index of 75 indicates spending that is 25 percent below the average for all consumer units)

	total consumer units	under $20,000	$20,000–$39,999	$40,000–$49,999	$50,000–$69,999	$70,000–$79,999	$80,000–$99,999	$100,000 or more
Average spending of consumer units, total	$51,442	$22,405	$33,455	$41,567	$49,982	$59,984	$67,418	$101,423
Average spending of consumer units, index	100	44	65	81	97	117	131	197
GROCERIES	**100**	**62**	**78**	**92**	**100**	**126**	**124**	**155**
Cereals and bakery products	**100**	**63**	**76**	**97**	**102**	**124**	**124**	**151**
Cereals and cereal products	100	64	76	97	97	128	125	151
Flour	100	70	75	130	96	96	107	147
Prepared flour mixes	100	59	77	112	77	127	143	155
Ready-to-eat and cooked cereals	100	61	75	98	103	131	127	152
Rice	100	78	83	95	99	115	107	140
Pasta, cornmeal, and other cereal products	100	65	76	80	92	140	130	158
Bakery products	100	62	76	97	104	122	123	151
Bread	100	66	84	92	102	124	123	141
White bread	100	70	87	102	101	121	121	131
Bread other than white	100	63	82	85	103	127	124	149
Crackers and cookies	100	60	73	92	104	114	123	162
Cookies	100	62	75	88	111	110	120	157
Crackers	100	59	71	98	94	121	127	168
Frozen and refrigerated bakery products	100	59	77	87	103	146	122	152
Other bakery products	100	61	72	106	107	121	122	152
Biscuits and rolls	100	57	74	89	100	124	120	168
Cakes and cupcakes	100	64	60	139	96	132	130	148
Bread and cracker products	100	54	79	125	106	120	120	144
Sweetrolls, coffee cakes, doughnuts	100	65	77	102	132	89	104	143
Pies, tarts, turnovers	100	62	85	74	126	131	143	123
Meats, poultry, fish, and eggs	**100**	**65**	**81**	**93**	**97**	**126**	**127**	**148**
Beef	100	58	80	102	98	120	126	153
Ground beef	100	71	89	99	105	126	128	122
Roast	100	42	74	104	88	123	121	185
Chuck roast	100	43	65	114	79	88	198	175
Round roast	100	30	76	60	89	96	67	251
Other roast	100	46	79	115	92	150	101	166
Steak	100	52	69	110	95	120	110	178
Round steak	100	44	66	121	93	114	110	187
Sirloin steak	100	55	62	112	92	129	109	182
Other steak	100	53	74	105	97	118	110	171
Other beef	100	46	88	82	99	86	192	151
Pork	100	72	83	88	101	131	128	136
Bacon	100	73	75	99	98	118	142	137
Pork chops	100	74	97	89	104	127	120	115
Ham	100	75	83	81	103	150	126	130
Ham, not canned	100	74	84	83	105	132	128	132
Canned ham	100	101	51	39	52	618	63	75
Sausage	100	74	79	82	107	129	125	141
Other pork	100	65	81	87	97	130	126	151
Other meats	100	60	85	95	96	128	118	150
Frankfurters	100	71	95	94	90	127	118	132
Lunch meats (cold cuts)	100	58	78	95	100	135	123	154
Bologna, liverwurst, salami	100	65	83	95	99	129	123	144
Other lunch meats	100	55	77	95	100	137	123	158
Lamb, organ meats, and others	100	55	123	106	74	72	83	160

	total consumer units	under $20,000	$20,000–$39,999	$40,000–$49,999	$50,000–$69,999	$70,000–$79,999	$80,000–$99,999	$100,000 or more
Poultry	100	67	81	94	96	130	126	145
Fresh and frozen chicken	100	69	85	97	95	134	122	137
Fresh and frozen whole chicken	100	66	92	108	89	122	114	140
Fresh and frozen chicken parts	100	70	83	93	97	139	126	136
Other poultry	100	59	64	80	100	118	140	175
Fish and seafood	100	66	71	79	92	125	146	163
Canned fish and seafood	100	72	83	88	103	131	138	129
Fresh fish and shellfish	100	65	66	76	86	124	144	176
Frozen fish and shellfish	100	63	73	80	95	122	151	157
Eggs	100	75	87	93	95	120	115	136
Dairy products	**100**	**58**	**76**	**89**	**99**	**129**	**127**	**161**
Fresh milk and cream	100	67	83	93	100	127	122	142
Fresh milk, all types	100	69	85	92	100	128	122	138
Cream	100	56	75	99	98	120	117	165
Other dairy products	100	53	71	87	98	131	130	171
Butter	100	53	71	96	108	129	122	161
Cheese	100	52	71	89	96	129	127	175
Ice cream and related products	100	61	74	81	99	131	135	159
Miscellaneous dairy products	100	46	69	83	99	135	137	179
Fruits and vegetables	**100**	**60**	**77**	**90**	**98**	**120**	**124**	**161**
Fresh fruits	100	54	71	89	100	117	127	173
Apples	100	52	67	88	99	115	126	183
Bananas	100	61	78	104	108	112	128	144
Oranges	100	48	76	82	104	113	144	166
Citrus fruits, except oranges	100	55	77	86	105	111	121	168
Other fresh fruits	100	54	67	87	94	123	126	184
Fresh vegetables	100	60	78	93	96	118	121	163
Potatoes	100	68	81	98	104	117	119	142
Lettuce	100	59	73	88	105	140	116	159
Tomatoes	100	61	84	98	94	117	111	156
Other fresh vegetables	100	57	76	90	92	113	126	173
Processed fruits	100	61	84	84	100	132	124	152
Frozen fruits and fruit juices	100	56	75	67	114	156	136	151
Frozen fruits	100	40	68	61	102	167	159	178
Frozen fruit juices	100	77	85	75	130	142	106	117
Canned fruits	100	61	94	67	105	117	135	143
Dried fruits	100	39	84	82	113	104	116	176
Fresh fruit juice	100	59	80	85	95	106	133	165
Canned and bottled fruit juice	100	65	83	93	93	144	115	147
Processed vegetables	100	70	84	91	98	119	123	142
Frozen vegetables	100	69	77	75	102	126	143	146
Canned and dried vegetables and juices	100	70	86	97	97	116	116	140
Canned vegetables	100	66	84	95	99	116	118	147
Dried vegetables	100	–	94	93	101	116	99	122
Fresh and canned vegetable juices	100	68	86	110	87	116	125	141
Sugar and other sweets	**100**	**61**	**77**	**90**	**104**	**133**	**113**	**156**
Candy and chewing gum	100	53	76	84	101	146	112	168
Sugar	100	84	87	109	126	109	92	108
Artificial sweeteners	100	87	72	103	79	160	109	136
Jams, preserves, other sweets	100	61	73	86	98	110	135	164
Fats and oils	**100**	**68**	**83**	**100**	**100**	**123**	**112**	**143**
Margarine	100	84	88	72	120	132	106	119
Fats and oils	100	74	89	95	85	118	121	141
Salad dressings	100	66	76	104	109	119	121	142
Nondairy cream and imitation milk	100	65	78	118	109	128	98	140
Peanut butter	100	53	83	98	99	131	98	163

	total consumer units	under $20,000	$20,000– $39,999	$40,000– $49,999	$50,000– $69,999	$70,000– $79,999	$80,000– $99,999	$100,000 or more
Miscellaneous foods	**100**	**61**	**75**	**93**	**101**	**125**	**124**	**157**
Frozen prepared foods	100	70	80	99	111	123	110	137
Frozen meals	100	76	77	86	105	124	109	147
Other frozen prepared foods	100	65	84	109	116	122	111	129
Canned and packaged soups	100	68	82	94	100	103	126	147
Potato chips, nuts, and other snacks	100	52	69	92	100	135	135	168
Potato chips and other snacks	100	55	71	91	104	134	132	163
Nuts	100	46	64	94	92	138	142	181
Condiments and seasonings	100	57	77	89	101	127	125	161
Salt, spices, and other seasonings	100	63	75	91	88	121	123	167
Olives, pickles, relishes	100	55	75	78	112	140	140	151
Sauces and gravies	100	55	78	86	105	133	128	156
Baking needs and miscellaneous products	100	54	78	100	101	110	113	166
Other canned/packaged prepared foods	100	63	75	95	96	124	124	160
Prepared salads	100	57	77	85	98	119	115	171
Prepared desserts	100	59	85	84	117	104	124	146
Baby food	100	59	75	152	102	114	107	143
Miscellaneous prepared foods	100	65	73	89	93	122	128	163
Nonalcoholic beverages	**100**	**63**	**80**	**94**	**105**	**136**	**117**	**145**
Carbonated drinks	100	67	88	99	104	136	109	132
Tea	100	63	73	105	111	172	109	136
Coffee	100	58	69	85	99	137	123	170
Noncarbonated fruit-flavored drinks	100	64	92	92	124	123	120	119
Other nonalcoholic beverages and ice	100	54	79	91	111	138	118	150
Bottled water	100	66	79	95	99	122	132	145
Sports drinks	100	50	72	82	111	110	109	183
Food prepared by consumer unit on trips	**100**	**31**	**56**	**66**	**86**	**135**	**158**	**221**

Note: "–" means sample is too small to make a reliable estimate.
Source: Calculations by New Strategist based on the Bureau of Labor Statistics' 2012 Consumer Expenditure Survey

Table 10. Groceries: Total spending by income, 2012

(total annual spending on groceries, by before-tax income group of consumer units, 2012; consumer units and dollars in thousands)

	total consumer units	under $20,000	$20,000–$39,999	$40,000–$49,999	$50,000–$69,999	$70,000–$79,999	$80,000–$99,999	$100,000 or more
Number of consumer units	124,416	26,177	28,041	11,010	17,972	6,946	10,977	23,293
Total spending of all consumer units	$6,400,191,698	$586,484,559	$938,098,035	$457,656,413	$898,268,776	$416,649,836	$740,046,398	$2,362,436,389
GROCERIES	487,791,590	63,128,454	85,259,169	39,872,054	70,275,912	34,345,122	53,403,983	141,164,664
Cereals and bakery products	66,917,146	8,843,289	11,497,131	5,736,100	9,863,213	4,644,860	7,291,692	18,956,076
Cereals and cereal products	22,641,224	3,062,456	3,897,394	1,941,173	3,180,864	1,622,169	2,502,427	6,420,017
Flour	1,164,534	172,249	197,293	134,212	161,029	62,167	109,880	320,745
Prepared flour mixes	2,013,051	250,034	351,538	199,391	223,033	142,671	254,557	584,887
Ready-to-eat and cooked cereals	11,797,125	1,502,768	1,982,502	1,022,939	1,749,934	861,026	1,319,655	3,348,369
Rice	3,066,854	504,257	575,837	258,845	438,697	196,641	289,683	804,540
Pasta, cornmeal, and other cereal products	4,600,904	633,228	790,649	325,786	608,352	359,733	528,762	1,361,476
Bakery products	44,275,922	5,780,833	7,599,601	3,794,927	6,682,349	3,022,760	4,789,265	12,535,827
Bread	13,078,610	1,805,705	2,473,207	1,067,640	1,924,262	908,537	1,417,240	3,464,368
White bread	5,414,584	794,863	1,058,506	489,064	787,353	365,637	577,610	1,329,332
Bread other than white	7,664,026	1,010,810	1,414,701	578,465	1,136,909	542,830	839,631	2,135,269
Crackers and cookies	10,915,016	1,387,873	1,804,179	890,159	1,632,397	697,378	1,184,748	3,303,413
Cookies	6,290,473	816,265	1,062,211	490,826	1,006,612	385,920	666,523	1,847,135
Crackers	4,624,543	571,607	741,968	399,443	625,785	311,459	518,224	1,456,045
Frozen and refrigerated bakery products	3,579,448	445,500	620,432	274,149	535,026	292,496	384,744	1,021,864
Other bakery products	16,702,848	2,141,755	2,701,928	1,562,980	2,590,844	1,124,349	1,802,643	4,746,415
Biscuits and rolls	6,450,970	778,112	1,072,041	508,222	928,254	445,933	683,428	2,025,093
Cakes and cupcakes	4,720,343	638,925	636,008	579,126	657,416	348,967	540,947	1,303,942
Bread and cracker products	909,481	103,968	161,101	100,852	139,103	60,986	96,268	244,809
Sweetrolls, coffee cakes, doughnuts	2,952,392	401,310	511,916	265,231	563,063	146,700	272,120	788,468
Pies, tarts, turnovers	1,668,419	219,359	320,717	109,550	303,008	121,694	209,770	384,102
Meats, poultry, fish, and eggs	106,053,443	14,457,290	19,255,484	8,704,946	14,832,471	7,459,587	11,924,864	29,440,721
Beef	28,157,829	3,423,420	5,063,029	2,542,429	3,992,120	1,886,673	3,131,189	8,090,824
Ground beef	11,632,896	1,735,907	2,333,845	1,014,572	1,757,662	817,961	1,313,069	2,656,101
Roast	4,232,632	376,473	709,909	389,314	538,261	289,787	452,691	1,467,226
Chuck roast	1,171,999	106,736	172,225	117,807	133,352	57,791	204,611	384,102
Round roast	824,878	51,289	140,601	43,820	106,574	44,315	48,848	387,130
Other roast	2,235,756	218,448	396,937	227,687	298,335	187,750	199,123	695,995
Steak	9,883,607	1,079,673	1,542,503	964,366	1,353,292	662,857	958,292	3,288,739
Round steak	2,103,875	194,293	313,208	225,485	282,700	133,502	204,941	738,388
Sirloin steak	2,707,292	315,230	380,984	268,974	359,440	195,322	260,594	921,937
Other steak	5,072,440	570,070	848,311	469,907	711,332	333,964	492,758	1,628,414
Other beef	2,407,450	231,207	476,772	174,178	342,726	116,068	407,137	678,758
Pork	20,624,440	3,115,911	3,843,443	1,597,221	3,020,195	1,510,547	2,323,831	5,253,503
Bacon	4,003,707	616,581	681,100	350,669	564,321	263,601	501,100	1,028,852
Pork chops	3,488,625	541,067	764,339	275,911	525,322	248,181	369,266	753,296
Ham	4,157,983	652,963	779,079	297,931	620,933	348,481	461,144	1,009,519
Ham, not canned	4,004,951	620,259	761,611	292,756	609,431	295,691	452,582	988,322
Canned ham	153,032	32,653	17,468	5,285	11,502	52,790	8,562	21,430
Sausage	3,998,730	620,020	710,582	289,343	615,900	288,120	441,385	1,053,775
Other pork	4,975,396	685,230	908,343	383,478	693,899	362,095	550,936	1,408,062
Other meats	15,194,926	1,919,974	2,927,244	1,283,436	2,096,614	1,086,424	1,588,482	4,264,482
Frankfurters	3,074,319	457,953	657,917	254,882	398,260	218,452	319,870	757,488
Lunch meats (cold cuts)	10,852,808	1,316,644	1,916,973	909,426	1,562,126	817,336	1,176,295	3,128,017
Bologna, liverwurst, salami	3,191,270	433,108	594,655	267,543	454,332	230,260	345,227	861,608
Other lunch meats	7,661,537	883,456	1,322,318	641,883	1,107,794	587,006	831,069	2,266,642
Lamb, organ meats, and others	1,267,799	145,426	352,354	119,018	136,228	50,636	92,317	378,744

	total consumer units	under $20,000	$20,000– $39,999	$40,000– $49,999	$50,000– $69,999	$70,000– $79,999	$80,000– $99,999	$100,000 or more
Poultry	$19,826,934	$2,796,287	$3,621,995	$1,643,022	$2,740,191	$1,443,170	$2,200,230	$5,379,518
Fresh and frozen chicken	15,741,112	2,285,636	3,031,260	1,355,331	2,151,967	1,174,985	1,695,727	4,042,267
Fresh and frozen whole chicken	4,705,413	650,468	970,702	448,768	602,421	320,558	472,450	1,231,268
Fresh and frozen chicken parts	11,035,699	1,635,120	2,060,423	906,563	1,549,546	854,427	1,223,277	2,810,766
Other poultry	4,085,821	510,598	590,735	287,691	588,224	268,185	504,503	1,337,484
Fish and seafood	15,644,068	2,159,232	2,501,605	1,092,963	2,072,711	1,088,508	2,008,571	4,767,145
Canned fish and seafood	2,261,883	342,142	421,549	175,720	335,178	165,384	275,962	547,386
Fresh fish and shellfish	7,874,289	1,083,482	1,171,798	528,920	979,115	546,442	997,041	2,601,362
Frozen fish and shellfish	5,507,896	733,636	908,269	388,213	758,418	376,682	735,679	1,618,165
Eggs	6,604,001	1,042,568	1,298,169	545,876	910,821	444,266	672,561	1,685,249
Dairy products	**52,121,595**	**6,340,250**	**8,895,806**	**4,116,859**	**7,442,385**	**3,760,773**	**5,847,448**	**15,667,804**
Fresh milk and cream	18,893,814	2,646,933	3,548,764	1,561,328	2,724,016	1,339,744	2,026,793	5,018,244
Fresh milk, all types	15,960,084	2,301,632	3,050,927	1,303,144	2,308,144	1,142,964	1,723,609	4,113,311
Cream	2,933,729	345,402	498,117	258,185	415,872	196,780	303,185	904,700
Other dairy products	33,227,781	3,693,266	5,346,761	2,555,531	4,718,369	2,421,028	3,820,655	10,649,560
Butter	3,180,073	355,523	511,477	271,397	496,926	229,635	341,604	959,905
Cheese	16,356,972	1,793,014	2,624,874	1,290,262	2,261,956	1,177,625	1,835,684	5,368,338
Ice cream and related products	7,137,746	912,179	1,185,708	514,718	1,025,482	521,575	852,254	2,121,294
Miscellaneous dairy products	6,552,991	632,602	1,024,557	479,265	934,005	492,194	791,222	2,200,024
Fruits and vegetables	**90,945,608**	**11,448,122**	**15,873,276**	**7,213,422**	**12,930,495**	**6,098,519**	**9,946,150**	**27,389,773**
Fresh fruits	32,508,657	3,715,273	5,216,405	2,563,899	4,698,420	2,126,587	3,651,499	10,508,171
Apples	5,176,950	567,968	782,177	401,535	743,861	332,158	573,768	1,771,899
Bananas	5,450,665	694,038	963,258	500,625	853,131	342,091	615,919	1,470,720
Oranges	3,326,884	338,565	573,506	240,238	501,778	210,603	423,383	1,035,840
Citrus fruits, except oranges	4,970,419	577,349	858,312	377,643	755,543	308,611	530,848	1,559,466
Other fresh fruits	13,584,983	1,537,430	2,039,016	1,043,748	1,844,107	933,126	1,507,581	4,670,014
Fresh vegetables	28,135,434	3,552,350	4,938,169	2,304,173	3,899,205	1,858,124	2,992,550	8,570,892
Potatoes	4,782,551	683,021	875,759	412,985	717,622	312,778	501,210	1,273,195
Lettuce	4,022,369	501,625	664,830	313,345	609,431	315,140	411,528	1,200,288
Tomatoes	4,895,770	630,997	929,592	422,894	661,909	318,752	481,122	1,432,752
Other fresh vegetables	14,433,500	1,736,626	2,468,124	1,154,949	1,910,244	911,454	1,598,690	4,664,656
Processed fruits	14,153,564	1,804,024	2,673,586	1,046,501	2,036,228	1,039,538	1,543,586	4,023,866
Frozen fruits and fruit juices	1,581,327	186,901	268,009	94,356	260,774	137,809	189,683	448,390
Frozen fruits	890,819	75,056	136,477	48,444	131,016	83,144	125,138	296,520
Frozen fruit juices	690,509	111,897	131,532	45,912	129,578	54,665	64,545	151,870
Canned fruits	2,531,866	325,654	537,298	149,736	385,140	165,245	300,550	677,826
Dried fruits	1,083,663	88,446	205,214	78,281	176,665	62,653	111,087	358,013
Fresh fruit juice	2,122,537	262,504	383,403	158,764	290,967	125,931	248,958	654,999
Canned and bottled fruit juice	6,832,927	940,810	1,279,661	565,253	922,682	547,831	693,307	1,884,637
Processed vegetables	16,149,197	2,376,398	3,044,981	1,298,960	2,296,822	1,074,268	1,758,515	4,286,844
Frozen vegetables	4,665,600	681,442	809,116	309,051	688,687	327,851	588,257	1,271,565
Canned and dried vegetables and juices	11,483,597	1,694,955	2,236,000	989,909	1,608,135	746,417	1,170,258	3,015,279
Canned vegetables	6,791,869	942,889	1,285,402	570,538	968,871	439,751	705,821	1,866,468
Dried vegetables	2,266,860	–	478,763	185,629	330,146	146,630	197,037	517,803
Fresh and canned vegetable juices	2,361,416	337,710	458,709	229,779	295,819	153,437	260,374	622,389
Sugar and other sweets	**18,260,536**	**2,342,273**	**3,175,813**	**1,446,824**	**2,733,182**	**1,354,887**	**1,825,585**	**5,329,671**
Candy and chewing gum	10,931,190	1,219,900	1,871,056	817,162	1,590,163	889,227	1,081,674	3,428,264
Sugar	3,033,262	537,382	596,156	292,426	551,022	185,319	246,434	612,140
Artificial sweeteners	610,883	112,118	99,166	55,711	69,911	54,665	58,837	155,131
Jams, preserves, other sweets	3,683,958	472,842	609,436	281,526	522,087	225,745	438,641	1,134,369
Fats and oils	**14,194,621**	**2,018,197**	**2,647,745**	**1,255,470**	**2,060,130**	**976,816**	**1,407,690**	**3,807,474**
Margarine	1,087,396	192,440	216,840	69,143	187,807	80,157	101,318	242,713
Fats and oils	4,577,265	710,083	921,912	384,359	561,266	302,151	488,477	1,207,975
Salad dressings	3,892,977	541,739	663,227	359,587	613,744	258,391	416,797	1,037,237
Nondairy cream and imitation milk	2,312,893	315,524	408,579	240,569	365,550	165,523	200,550	607,947
Peanut butter	2,324,091	258,412	437,187	201,703	331,583	170,594	200,550	711,368

	total consumer units	under $20,000	$20,000–$39,999	$40,000–$49,999	$50,000–$69,999	$70,000–$79,999	$80,000–$99,999	$100,000 or more
Miscellaneous foods	**$87,000,376**	**$11,162,766**	**$14,793,881**	**$7,198,338**	**$12,684,997**	**$6,093,448**	**$9,543,733**	**$25,509,795**
Frozen prepared foods	16,277,345	2,390,477	2,952,198	1,422,382	2,601,088	1,120,251	1,580,029	4,175,503
Frozen meals	7,540,854	1,204,543	1,306,850	576,594	1,142,839	523,867	723,494	2,072,611
Other frozen prepared foods	8,736,492	1,186,015	1,645,629	845,788	1,458,068	596,384	856,535	2,102,892
Canned and packaged soups	5,760,461	823,140	1,069,307	478,605	831,564	329,866	638,093	1,587,884
Potato chips, nuts, and other snacks	19,152,599	2,104,416	2,971,637	1,551,970	2,776,494	1,443,448	2,284,423	6,024,734
Potato chips and other snacks	13,883,581	1,599,741	2,210,824	1,112,671	2,077,563	1,038,913	1,622,291	4,236,298
Nuts	5,269,018	504,595	760,813	439,299	698,931	404,535	662,133	1,788,437
Condiments and seasonings	17,591,178	2,121,057	3,050,600	1,385,168	2,557,595	1,245,140	1,942,929	5,286,812
Salt, spices, and other seasonings	4,817,388	642,216	817,740	389,754	614,822	326,740	522,176	1,510,318
Olives, pickles, relishes	2,172,303	249,917	366,575	150,507	352,790	170,316	267,509	615,634
Sauces and gravies	7,498,552	874,985	1,319,396	570,538	1,136,729	556,791	844,351	2,193,968
Baking needs and miscellaneous products	3,104,179	353,938	547,024	274,369	453,254	191,293	308,783	966,892
Other canned/packaged prepared foods	28,218,793	3,723,575	4,749,859	2,360,214	3,918,255	1,954,743	3,098,258	8,434,861
Prepared salads	4,365,757	527,794	760,843	329,970	619,135	289,231	443,910	1,396,415
Prepared desserts	1,777,905	222,173	338,860	132,230	300,851	103,634	194,732	484,960
Baby food	3,116,621	385,415	526,032	418,600	459,185	199,211	294,732	832,259
Miscellaneous prepared foods	18,389,929	2,523,202	3,027,269	1,442,861	2,466,657	1,249,724	2,073,226	5,619,203
Nonalcoholic beverages	**46,050,094**	**6,110,495**	**8,337,720**	**3,836,104**	**6,953,726**	**3,485,989**	**4,744,918**	**12,483,650**
Carbonated drinks	17,385,892	2,462,675	3,463,493	1,524,665	2,608,456	1,322,796	1,668,065	4,286,611
Tea	3,777,270	498,870	617,581	351,880	606,735	362,512	362,461	961,535
Coffee	10,761,984	1,322,023	1,661,972	809,235	1,543,795	824,073	1,168,172	3,417,316
Noncarbonated fruit-flavored drinks	3,213,665	434,705	663,382	262,589	576,721	219,841	340,397	713,465
Other nonalcoholic beverages and ice	1,911,030	217,607	339,287	154,691	305,524	147,186	199,672	536,205
Bottled water	7,066,829	977,417	1,253,193	596,742	1,010,386	482,400	825,470	1,917,480
Sports drinks	1,881,170	197,330	306,298	136,304	302,109	115,095	180,681	644,051
Food prepared by consumer unit on trips	**6,249,416**	**405,771**	**782,448**	**364,101**	**775,132**	**470,314**	**871,903**	**2,579,933**

Note: Numbers may not add to total because of rounding. "–" means sample is too small to make a reliable estimate.
Source: Calculations by New Strategist based on the Bureau of Labor Statistics' 2012 Consumer Expenditure Survey

Table 11. Groceries: Market shares by income, 2012

(percentage of total annual spending on groceries accounted for by before-tax income group of consumer units, 2012)

	total consumer units	under $20,000	$20,000–$39,999	$40,000–$49,999	$50,000–$69,999	$70,000–$79,999	$80,000–$99,999	$100,000 or more
Share of total consumer units	100.0%	21.0%	22.5%	8.8%	14.4%	5.6%	8.8%	18.7%
Share of total before-tax income	100.0	3.4	10.2	6.0	13.1	6.4	12.0	49.1
Share of total spending	100.0	9.2	14.7	7.2	14.0	6.5	11.6	36.9
GROCERIES	100.0	12.9	17.5	8.2	14.4	7.0	10.9	28.9
Cereals and bakery products	100.0	13.2	17.2	8.6	14.7	6.9	10.9	28.3
Cereals and cereal products	100.0	13.5	17.2	8.6	14.0	7.2	11.1	28.4
Flour	100.0	14.8	16.9	11.5	13.8	5.3	9.4	27.5
Prepared flour mixes	100.0	12.4	17.5	9.9	11.1	7.1	12.6	29.1
Ready-to-eat and cooked cereals	100.0	12.7	16.8	8.7	14.8	7.3	11.2	28.4
Rice	100.0	16.4	18.8	8.4	14.3	6.4	9.4	26.2
Pasta, cornmeal, and other cereal products	100.0	13.8	17.2	7.1	13.2	7.8	11.5	29.6
Bakery products	100.0	13.1	17.2	8.6	15.1	6.8	10.8	28.3
Bread	100.0	13.8	18.9	8.2	14.7	6.9	10.8	26.5
White bread	100.0	14.7	19.5	9.0	14.5	6.8	10.7	24.6
Bread other than white	100.0	13.2	18.5	7.5	14.8	7.1	11.0	27.9
Crackers and cookies	100.0	12.7	16.5	8.2	15.0	6.4	10.9	30.3
Cookies	100.0	13.0	16.9	7.8	16.0	6.1	10.6	29.4
Crackers	100.0	12.4	16.0	8.6	13.5	6.7	11.2	31.5
Frozen and refrigerated bakery products	100.0	12.4	17.3	7.7	14.9	8.2	10.7	28.5
Other bakery products	100.0	12.8	16.2	9.4	15.5	6.7	10.8	28.4
Biscuits and rolls	100.0	12.1	16.6	7.9	14.4	6.9	10.6	31.4
Cakes and cupcakes	100.0	13.5	13.5	12.3	13.9	7.4	11.5	27.6
Bread and cracker products	100.0	11.4	17.7	11.1	15.3	6.7	10.6	26.9
Sweetrolls, coffee cakes, doughnuts	100.0	13.6	17.3	9.0	19.1	5.0	9.2	26.7
Pies, tarts, turnovers	100.0	13.1	19.2	6.6	18.2	7.3	12.6	23.0
Meats, poultry, fish, and eggs	100.0	13.6	18.2	8.2	14.0	7.0	11.2	27.8
Beef	100.0	12.2	18.0	9.0	14.2	6.7	11.1	28.7
Ground beef	100.0	14.9	20.1	8.7	15.1	7.0	11.3	22.8
Roast	100.0	8.9	16.8	9.2	12.7	6.8	10.7	34.7
Chuck roast	100.0	9.1	14.7	10.1	11.4	4.9	17.5	32.8
Round roast	100.0	6.2	17.0	5.3	12.9	5.4	5.9	46.9
Other roast	100.0	9.8	17.8	10.2	13.3	8.4	8.9	31.1
Steak	100.0	10.9	15.6	9.8	13.7	6.7	9.7	33.3
Round steak	100.0	9.2	14.9	10.7	13.4	6.3	9.7	35.1
Sirloin steak	100.0	11.6	14.1	9.9	13.3	7.2	9.6	34.1
Other steak	100.0	11.2	16.7	9.3	14.0	6.6	9.7	32.1
Other beef	100.0	9.6	19.8	7.2	14.2	4.8	16.9	28.2
Pork	100.0	15.1	18.6	7.7	14.6	7.3	11.3	25.5
Bacon	100.0	15.4	17.0	8.8	14.1	6.6	12.5	25.7
Pork chops	100.0	15.5	21.9	7.9	15.1	7.1	10.6	21.6
Ham	100.0	15.7	18.7	7.2	14.9	8.4	11.1	24.3
Ham, not canned	100.0	15.5	19.0	7.3	15.2	7.4	11.3	24.7
Canned ham	100.0	21.3	11.4	3.5	7.5	34.5	5.6	14.0
Sausage	100.0	15.5	17.8	7.2	15.4	7.2	11.0	26.4
Other pork	100.0	13.8	18.3	7.7	13.9	7.3	11.1	28.3
Other meats	100.0	12.6	19.3	8.4	13.8	7.1	10.5	28.1
Frankfurters	100.0	14.9	21.4	8.3	13.0	7.1	10.4	24.6
Lunch meats (cold cuts)	100.0	12.1	17.7	8.4	14.4	7.5	10.8	28.8
Bologna, liverwurst, salami	100.0	13.6	18.6	8.4	14.2	7.2	10.8	27.0
Other lunch meats	100.0	11.5	17.3	8.4	14.5	7.7	10.8	29.6
Lamb, organ meats, and others	100.0	11.5	27.8	9.4	10.7	4.0	7.3	29.9

	total consumer units	under $20,000	$20,000–$39,999	$40,000–$49,999	$50,000–$69,999	$70,000–$79,999	$80,000–$99,999	$100,000 or more
Poultry	100.0%	14.1%	18.3%	8.3%	13.8%	7.3%	11.1%	27.1%
Fresh and frozen chicken	100.0	14.5	19.3	8.6	13.7	7.5	10.8	25.7
Fresh and frozen whole chicken	100.0	13.8	20.6	9.5	12.8	6.8	10.0	26.2
Fresh and frozen chicken parts	100.0	14.8	18.7	8.2	14.0	7.7	11.1	25.5
Other poultry	100.0	12.5	14.5	7.0	14.4	6.6	12.3	32.7
Fish and seafood	100.0	13.8	16.0	7.0	13.2	7.0	12.8	30.5
Canned fish and seafood	100.0	15.1	18.6	7.8	14.8	7.3	12.2	24.2
Fresh fish and shellfish	100.0	13.8	14.9	6.7	12.4	6.9	12.7	33.0
Frozen fish and shellfish	100.0	13.3	16.5	7.0	13.8	6.8	13.4	29.4
Eggs	100.0	15.8	19.7	8.3	13.8	6.7	10.2	25.5
Dairy products	**100.0**	**12.2**	**17.1**	**7.9**	**14.3**	**7.2**	**11.2**	**30.1**
Fresh milk and cream	100.0	14.0	18.8	8.3	14.4	7.1	10.7	26.6
Fresh milk, all types	100.0	14.4	19.1	8.2	14.5	7.2	10.8	25.8
Cream	100.0	11.8	17.0	8.8	14.2	6.7	10.3	30.8
Other dairy products	100.0	11.1	16.1	7.7	14.2	7.3	11.5	32.1
Butter	100.0	11.2	16.1	8.5	15.6	7.2	10.7	30.2
Cheese	100.0	11.0	16.0	7.9	13.8	7.2	11.2	32.8
Ice cream and related products	100.0	12.8	16.6	7.2	14.4	7.3	11.9	29.7
Miscellaneous dairy products	100.0	9.7	15.6	7.3	14.3	7.5	12.1	33.6
Fruits and vegetables	**100.0**	**12.6**	**17.5**	**7.9**	**14.2**	**6.7**	**10.9**	**30.1**
Fresh fruits	100.0	11.4	16.0	7.9	14.5	6.5	11.2	32.3
Apples	100.0	11.0	15.1	7.8	14.4	6.4	11.1	34.2
Bananas	100.0	12.7	17.7	9.2	15.7	6.3	11.3	27.0
Oranges	100.0	10.2	17.2	7.2	15.1	6.3	12.7	31.1
Citrus fruits, except oranges	100.0	11.6	17.3	7.6	15.2	6.2	10.7	31.4
Other fresh fruits	100.0	11.3	15.0	7.7	13.6	6.9	11.1	34.4
Fresh vegetables	100.0	12.6	17.6	8.2	13.9	6.6	10.6	30.5
Potatoes	100.0	14.3	18.3	8.6	15.0	6.5	10.5	26.6
Lettuce	100.0	12.5	16.5	7.8	15.2	7.8	10.2	29.8
Tomatoes	100.0	12.9	19.0	8.6	13.5	6.5	9.8	29.3
Other fresh vegetables	100.0	12.0	17.1	8.0	13.2	6.3	11.1	32.3
Processed fruits	100.0	12.7	18.9	7.4	14.4	7.3	10.9	28.4
Frozen fruits and fruit juices	100.0	11.8	16.9	6.0	16.5	8.7	12.0	28.4
Frozen fruits	100.0	8.4	15.3	5.4	14.7	9.3	14.0	33.3
Frozen fruit juices	100.0	16.2	19.0	6.6	18.8	7.9	9.3	22.0
Canned fruits	100.0	12.9	21.2	5.9	15.2	6.5	11.9	26.8
Dried fruits	100.0	8.2	18.9	7.2	16.3	5.8	10.3	33.0
Fresh fruit juice	100.0	12.4	18.1	7.5	13.7	5.9	11.7	30.9
Canned and bottled fruit juice	100.0	13.8	18.7	8.3	13.5	8.0	10.1	27.6
Processed vegetables	100.0	14.7	18.9	8.0	14.2	6.7	10.9	26.5
Frozen vegetables	100.0	14.6	17.3	6.6	14.8	7.0	12.6	27.3
Canned and dried vegetables and juices	100.0	14.8	19.5	8.6	14.0	6.5	10.2	26.3
Canned vegetables	100.0	13.9	18.9	8.4	14.3	6.5	10.4	27.5
Dried vegetables	100.0	– 67	21.1	8.2	14.6	6.5	8.7	22.8
Fresh and canned vegetable juices	100.0	14.3	19.4	9.7	12.5	6.5	11.0	26.4
Sugar and other sweets	**100.0**	**12.8**	**17.4**	**7.9**	**15.0**	**7.4**	**10.0**	**29.2**
Candy and chewing gum	100.0	11.2	17.1	7.5	14.5	8.1	9.9	31.4
Sugar	100.0	17.7	19.7	9.6	18.2	6.1	8.1	20.2
Artificial sweeteners	100.0	18.4	16.2	9.1	11.4	8.9	9.6	25.4
Jams, preserves, other sweets	100.0	12.8	16.5	7.6	14.2	6.1	11.9	30.8
Fats and oils	**100.0**	**14.2**	**18.7**	**8.8**	**14.5**	**6.9**	**9.9**	**26.8**
Margarine	100.0	17.7	19.9	6.4	17.3	7.4	9.3	22.3
Fats and oils	100.0	15.5	20.1	8.4	12.3	6.6	10.7	26.4
Salad dressings	100.0	13.9	17.0	9.2	15.8	6.6	10.7	26.6
Nondairy cream and imitation milk	100.0	13.6	17.7	10.4	15.8	7.2	8.7	26.3
Peanut butter	100.0	11.1	18.8	8.7	14.3	7.3	8.6	30.6

	total consumer units	under $20,000	$20,000– $39,999	$40,000– $49,999	$50,000– $69,999	$70,000– $79,999	$80,000– $99,999	$100,000 or more
Miscellaneous foods	**100.0%**	**12.8%**	**17.0%**	**8.3%**	**14.6%**	**7.0%**	**11.0%**	**29.3%**
Frozen prepared foods	100.0	14.7	18.1	8.7	16.0	6.9	9.7	25.7
Frozen meals	100.0	16.0	17.3	7.6	15.2	6.9	9.6	27.5
Other frozen prepared foods	100.0	13.6	18.8	9.7	16.7	6.8	9.8	24.1
Canned and packaged soups	100.0	14.3	18.6	8.3	14.4	5.7	11.1	27.6
Potato chips, nuts, and other snacks	100.0	11.0	15.5	8.1	14.5	7.5	11.9	31.5
Potato chips and other snacks	100.0	11.5	15.9	8.0	15.0	7.5	11.7	30.5
Nuts	100.0	9.6	14.4	8.3	13.3	7.7	12.6	33.9
Condiments and seasonings	100.0	12.1	17.3	7.9	14.5	7.1	11.0	30.1
Salt, spices, and other seasonings	100.0	13.3	17.0	8.1	12.8	6.8	10.8	31.4
Olives, pickles, relishes	100.0	11.5	16.9	6.9	16.2	7.8	12.3	28.3
Sauces and gravies	100.0	11.7	17.6	7.6	15.2	7.4	11.3	29.3
Baking needs and miscellaneous products	100.0	11.4	17.6	8.8	14.6	6.2	9.9	31.1
Other canned/packaged prepared foods	100.0	13.2	16.8	8.4	13.9	6.9	11.0	29.9
Prepared salads	100.0	12.1	17.4	7.6	14.2	6.6	10.2	32.0
Prepared desserts	100.0	12.5	19.1	7.4	16.9	5.8	11.0	27.3
Baby food	100.0	12.4	16.9	13.4	14.7	6.4	9.5	26.7
Miscellaneous prepared foods	100.0	13.7	16.5	7.8	13.4	6.8	11.3	30.6
Nonalcoholic beverages	**100.0**	**13.3**	**18.1**	**8.3**	**15.1**	**7.6**	**10.3**	**27.1**
Carbonated drinks	100.0	14.2	19.9	8.8	15.0	7.6	9.6	24.7
Tea	100.0	13.2	16.3	9.3	16.1	9.6	9.6	25.5
Coffee	100.0	12.3	15.4	7.5	14.3	7.7	10.9	31.8
Noncarbonated fruit-flavored drinks	100.0	13.5	20.6	8.2	17.9	6.8	10.6	22.2
Other nonalcoholic beverages and ice	100.0	11.4	17.8	8.1	16.0	7.7	10.4	28.1
Bottled water	100.0	13.8	17.7	8.4	14.3	6.8	11.7	27.1
Sports drinks	100.0	10.5	16.3	7.2	16.1	6.1	9.6	34.2
Food prepared by consumer unit on trips	**100.0**	**6.5**	**12.5**	**5.8**	**12.4**	**7.5**	**14.0**	**41.3**

Note: Numbers may not add to total because of rounding. "–" means sample is too small to make a reliable estimate.
Source: Calculations by New Strategist based on the Bureau of Labor Statistics' 2012 Consumer Expenditure Survey

Table 12. Groceries: Average spending by high-income consumer units, 2012

(average annual spending on groceries, by before-tax income of consumer units with high incomes, 2012)

	total consumer units	$100,000 or more	$100,000–$119,999	$120,000–$149,999	$150,000 or more
Number of consumer units (in 000s)	124,416	23,293	7,183	6,947	9,162
Number of persons per consumer unit	2.5	3.2	3.1	3.2	3.2
Average before-tax income of consumer units	$65,596.00	$171,910.00	$108,977.00	$132,318.00	$251,270.00
Average spending of consumer units, total	51,441.87	101,422.59	77,965.87	89,521.33	129,211.07
GROCERIES	3,920.65	6,060.39	5,279.45	6,002.94	6,789.78
Cereals and bakery products	537.85	813.81	719.58	797.45	909.22
Cereals and cereal products	181.98	275.62	254.43	271.65	297.31
Flour	9.36	13.77	16.18	13.23	12.06
Prepared flour mixes	16.18	25.11	23.72	25.52	26.02
Ready-to-eat and cooked cereals	94.82	143.75	124.18	139.88	163.92
Rice	24.65	34.54	34.60	34.66	34.39
Pasta, cornmeal, and other cereal products	36.98	58.45	55.74	58.35	60.92
Bakery products	355.87	538.18	465.15	525.80	611.91
Bread	105.12	148.73	126.93	145.65	170.28
White bread	43.52	57.07	50.76	58.04	61.89
Bread other than white	61.60	91.67	76.17	87.61	108.39
Crackers and cookies	87.73	141.82	118.80	140.39	163.19
Cookies	50.56	79.30	66.55	78.89	90.85
Crackers	37.17	62.51	52.24	61.50	72.33
Frozen and refrigerated bakery products	28.77	43.87	42.94	41.19	46.70
Other bakery products	134.25	203.77	176.48	198.57	231.74
Biscuits and rolls	51.85	86.94	72.23	89.15	98.24
Cakes and cupcakes	37.94	55.98	45.36	51.37	68.82
Bread and cracker products	7.31	10.51	9.94	10.95	10.67
Sweetrolls, coffee cakes, doughnuts	23.73	33.85	33.44	28.52	38.25
Pies, tarts, turnovers	13.41	16.49	15.51	18.58	15.76
Meats, poultry, fish, and eggs	852.41	1,263.93	1,126.61	1,204.26	1,430.06
Beef	226.32	347.35	319.64	277.06	424.92
Ground beef	93.50	114.03	118.03	99.09	121.79
Roast	34.02	62.99	50.06	52.39	82.40
Chuck roast	9.42	16.49	26.25	11.99	11.28
Round roast	6.63	16.62	11.68	10.36	25.72
Other roast	17.97	29.88	12.13	30.05	45.40
Steak	79.44	141.19	126.51	101.23	184.34
Round steak	16.91	31.70	26.45	20.89	44.51
Sirloin steak	21.76	39.58	34.95	32.14	49.29
Other steak	40.77	69.91	65.11	48.20	90.55
Other beef	19.35	29.14	25.03	24.35	36.38
Pork	165.77	225.54	204.79	219.05	248.73
Bacon	32.18	44.17	33.57	44.46	53.28
Pork chops	28.04	32.34	28.66	27.77	39.04
Ham	33.42	43.34	40.92	39.02	48.75
Ham, not canned	32.19	42.43	40.82	38.61	46.73
Canned ham	1.23	0.92	0.10	0.41	2.02
Sausage	32.14	45.24	42.30	43.45	49.17
Other pork	39.99	60.45	59.33	64.35	58.48
Other meats	122.13	183.08	151.37	177.77	215.04
Frankfurters	24.71	32.52	25.44	34.50	37.28
Lunch meats (cold cuts)	87.23	134.29	116.37	119.06	161.61
Bologna, liverwurst, salami	25.65	36.99	29.68	35.06	44.89
Other lunch meats	61.58	97.31	86.69	84.01	116.72
Lamb, organ meats, and others	10.19	16.26	9.56	24.21	16.16

	total consumer units	$100,000 or more	$100,000– $119,999	$120,000– $149,999	$150,000 or more
Poultry	$159.36	$230.95	$192.91	$264.72	$238.95
Fresh and frozen chicken	126.52	173.54	148.19	203.77	173.01
Fresh and frozen whole chicken	37.82	52.86	44.55	66.31	50.02
Fresh and frozen chicken parts	88.70	120.67	103.64	137.47	122.99
Other poultry	32.84	57.42	44.72	60.94	65.94
Fish and seafood	125.74	204.66	190.02	192.66	226.63
Canned fish and seafood	18.18	23.50	23.02	24.57	23.12
Fresh fish and shellfish	63.29	111.68	108.04	85.54	134.67
Frozen fish and shellfish	44.27	69.47	58.96	82.56	68.85
Eggs	53.08	72.35	67.89	73.00	75.79
Dairy products	**418.93**	**672.64**	**581.14**	**654.28**	**767.14**
Fresh milk and cream	151.86	215.44	194.40	205.47	241.51
Fresh milk, all types	128.28	176.59	161.07	167.40	197.22
Cream	23.58	38.84	33.33	38.07	44.29
Other dairy products	267.07	457.20	386.74	448.81	525.64
Butter	25.56	41.21	37.56	39.39	45.79
Cheese	131.47	230.47	190.53	236.72	260.94
Ice cream and related products	57.37	91.07	80.98	91.02	100.00
Miscellaneous dairy products	52.67	94.45	77.67	81.68	118.90
Fruits and vegetables	**730.98**	**1,175.88**	**984.69**	**1,172.12**	**1,347.22**
Fresh fruits	261.29	451.13	363.32	456.59	524.39
Apples	41.61	76.07	58.89	79.70	88.47
Bananas	43.81	63.14	53.92	60.54	73.23
Oranges	26.74	44.47	35.88	44.85	51.76
Citrus fruits, except oranges	39.95	66.95	57.09	67.25	75.42
Other fresh fruits	109.19	200.49	157.53	204.24	235.51
Fresh vegetables	226.14	367.96	292.74	369.52	433.07
Potatoes	38.44	54.66	45.98	55.29	61.82
Lettuce	32.33	51.53	43.51	48.98	60.53
Tomatoes	39.35	61.51	56.70	62.33	65.15
Other fresh vegetables	116.01	200.26	146.55	202.92	245.57
Processed fruits	113.76	172.75	150.00	165.34	198.39
Frozen fruits and fruit juices	12.71	19.25	18.24	16.15	22.48
Frozen fruits	7.16	12.73	12.24	11.00	14.47
Frozen fruit juices	5.55	6.52	6.00	5.15	8.01
Canned fruits	20.35	29.10	25.53	31.23	30.63
Dried fruits	8.71	15.37	11.93	15.75	18.12
Fresh fruit juice	17.06	28.12	20.45	29.07	34.16
Canned and bottled fruit juice	54.92	80.91	73.85	73.14	93.01
Processed vegetables	129.80	184.04	178.63	180.68	191.36
Frozen vegetables	37.50	54.59	49.54	55.89	58.06
Canned and dried vegetables and juices	92.30	129.45	129.09	124.79	133.30
Canned vegetables	54.59	80.13	81.21	78.28	80.60
Dried vegetables	18.22	22.23	21.65	22.66	22.45
Fresh and canned vegetable juices	18.98	26.72	26.12	23.09	29.98
Sugar and other sweets	**146.77**	**228.81**	**198.50**	**225.56**	**257.98**
Candy and chewing gum	87.86	147.18	131.84	143.31	163.62
Sugar	24.38	26.28	25.07	24.88	28.39
Artificial sweeteners	4.91	6.66	5.12	5.64	8.79
Jams, preserves, other sweets	29.61	48.70	36.47	51.73	57.18
Fats and oils	**114.09**	**163.46**	**151.91**	**179.93**	**161.18**
Margarine	8.74	10.42	10.55	7.76	12.32
Fats and oils	36.79	51.86	52.37	62.40	43.45
Salad dressings	31.29	44.53	41.12	46.87	45.76
Nondairy cream and imitation milk	18.59	26.10	27.38	26.25	24.85
Peanut butter	18.68	30.54	20.48	36.64	34.80

	total consumer units	$100,000 or more	$100,000– $119,999	$120,000– $149,999	$150,000 or more
Miscellaneous foods	**$699.27**	**$1,095.17**	**$951.77**	**$1,129.02**	**$1,195.94**
Frozen prepared foods	130.83	179.26	160.80	197.35	181.86
Frozen meals	60.61	88.98	75.44	109.54	85.38
Other frozen prepared foods	70.22	90.28	85.36	87.81	96.48
Canned and packaged soups	46.30	68.17	54.89	71.40	77.43
Potato chips, nuts, and other snacks	153.94	258.65	227.68	256.01	287.93
Potato chips and other snacks	111.59	181.87	160.30	179.60	202.60
Nuts	42.35	76.78	67.38	76.40	85.33
Condiments and seasonings	141.39	226.97	191.42	233.64	253.26
Salt, spices, and other seasonings	38.72	64.84	50.37	79.36	66.61
Olives, pickles, relishes	17.46	26.43	21.11	25.76	31.62
Sauces and gravies	60.27	94.19	82.87	88.84	108.22
Baking needs and miscellaneous products	24.95	41.51	37.06	39.67	46.82
Other canned/packaged prepared foods	226.81	362.12	316.99	370.63	395.45
Prepared salads	35.09	59.95	54.57	56.05	67.63
Prepared desserts	14.29	20.82	20.11	26.00	17.54
Baby food	25.05	35.73	31.98	18.89	51.78
Miscellaneous prepared foods	147.81	241.24	204.96	266.33	254.23
Nonalcoholic beverages	**370.13**	**535.94**	**478.21**	**545.46**	**579.63**
Carbonated drinks	139.74	184.03	174.91	193.38	184.98
Tea	30.36	41.28	34.36	47.55	42.64
Coffee	86.50	146.71	126.00	141.46	168.92
Noncarbonated fruit-flavored drinks	25.83	30.63	28.66	28.29	34.14
Other nonalcoholic beverages and ice	15.36	23.02	14.18	26.64	28.07
Bottled water	56.80	82.32	73.37	81.17	91.08
Sports drinks	15.12	27.65	26.10	26.62	29.80
Food prepared by consumer unit on trips	**50.23**	**110.76**	**87.04**	**94.86**	**141.40**

Source: Bureau of Labor Statistics, unpublished tables from the 2012 Consumer Expenditure Survey

Table 13. Groceries: Indexed spending by high-income consumer units, 2012

(indexed average annual spending of consumer units with high incomes on groceries, by before-tax income of consumer unit, 2012; index definition: an index of 100 is the average for all consumer units; an index of 125 means that spending by consumer units in that group is 25 percent above the average for all consumer units; an index of 75 indicates spending that is 25 percent below the average for all consumer units)

	total consumer units	$100,000 or more	$100,000– $119,999	$120,000– $149,999	$150,000 or more
Average spending of consumer units, total	$51,442	$101,423	$77,966	$89,521	$129,211
Average spending of consumer units, index	100	197	152	174	251
GROCERIES	**100**	**155**	**135**	**153**	**173**
Cereals and bakery products	**100**	**151**	**134**	**148**	**169**
Cereals and cereal products	100	151	140	149	163
Flour	100	147	173	141	129
Prepared flour mixes	100	155	147	158	161
Ready-to-eat and cooked cereals	100	152	131	148	173
Rice	100	140	140	141	140
Pasta, cornmeal, and other cereal products	100	158	151	158	165
Bakery products	100	151	131	148	172
Bread	100	141	121	139	162
White bread	100	131	117	133	142
Bread other than white	100	149	124	142	176
Crackers and cookies	100	162	135	160	186
Cookies	100	157	132	156	180
Crackers	100	168	141	165	195
Frozen and refrigerated bakery products	100	152	149	143	162
Other bakery products	100	152	131	148	173
Biscuits and rolls	100	168	139	172	189
Cakes and cupcakes	100	148	120	135	181
Bread and cracker products	100	144	136	150	146
Sweetrolls, coffee cakes, doughnuts	100	143	141	120	161
Pies, tarts, turnovers	100	123	116	139	118
Meats, poultry, fish, and eggs	**100**	**148**	**132**	**141**	**168**
Beef	100	153	141	122	188
Ground beef	100	122	126	106	130
Roast	100	185	147	154	242
Chuck roast	100	175	279	127	120
Round roast	100	251	176	156	388
Other roast	100	166	68	167	253
Steak	100	178	159	127	232
Round steak	100	187	156	124	263
Sirloin steak	100	182	161	148	227
Other steak	100	171	160	118	222
Other beef	100	151	129	126	188
Pork	100	136	124	132	150
Bacon	100	137	104	138	166
Pork chops	100	115	102	99	139
Ham	100	130	122	117	146
Ham, not canned	100	132	127	120	145
Canned ham	100	75	8	33	164
Sausage	100	141	132	135	153
Other pork	100	151	148	161	146
Other meats	100	150	124	146	176
Frankfurters	100	132	103	140	151
Lunch meats (cold cuts)	100	154	133	136	185
Bologna, liverwurst, salami	100	144	116	137	175
Other lunch meats	100	158	141	136	190
Lamb, organ meats, and others	100	160	94	238	159

	total consumer units	$100,000 or more	$100,000–$119,999	$120,000–$149,999	$150,000 or more
Poultry	100	145	121	166	150
Fresh and frozen chicken	100	137	117	161	137
Fresh and frozen whole chicken	100	140	118	175	132
Fresh and frozen chicken parts	100	136	117	155	139
Other poultry	100	175	136	186	201
Fish and seafood	100	163	151	153	180
Canned fish and seafood	100	129	127	135	127
Fresh fish and shellfish	100	176	171	135	213
Frozen fish and shellfish	100	157	133	186	156
Eggs	100	136	128	138	143
Dairy products	**100**	**161**	**139**	**156**	**183**
Fresh milk and cream	100	142	128	135	159
Fresh milk, all types	100	138	126	130	154
Cream	100	165	141	161	188
Other dairy products	100	171	145	168	197
Butter	100	161	147	154	179
Cheese	100	175	145	180	198
Ice cream and related products	100	159	141	159	174
Miscellaneous dairy products	100	179	147	155	226
Fruits and vegetables	**100**	**161**	**135**	**160**	**184**
Fresh fruits	100	173	139	175	201
Apples	100	183	142	192	213
Bananas	100	144	123	138	167
Oranges	100	166	134	168	194
Citrus fruits, except oranges	100	168	143	168	189
Other fresh fruits	100	184	144	187	216
Fresh vegetables	100	163	129	163	192
Potatoes	100	142	120	144	161
Lettuce	100	159	135	152	187
Tomatoes	100	156	144	158	166
Other fresh vegetables	100	173	126	175	212
Processed fruits	100	152	132	145	174
Frozen fruits and fruit juices	100	151	144	127	177
Frozen fruits	100	178	171	154	202
Frozen fruit juices	100	117	108	93	144
Canned fruits	100	143	125	153	151
Dried fruits	100	176	137	181	208
Fresh fruit juice	100	165	120	170	200
Canned and bottled fruit juice	100	147	134	133	169
Processed vegetables	100	142	138	139	147
Frozen vegetables	100	146	132	149	155
Canned and dried vegetables and juices	100	140	140	135	144
Canned vegetables	100	147	149	143	148
Dried vegetables	100	122	119	124	123
Fresh and canned vegetable juices	100	141	138	122	158
Sugar and other sweets	**100**	**156**	**135**	**154**	**176**
Candy and chewing gum	100	168	150	163	186
Sugar	100	108	103	102	116
Artificial sweeteners	100	136	104	115	179
Jams, preserves, other sweets	100	164	123	175	193
Fats and oils	**100**	**143**	**133**	**158**	**141**
Margarine	100	119	121	89	141
Fats and oils	100	141	142	170	118
Salad dressings	100	142	131	150	146
Nondairy cream and imitation milk	100	140	147	141	134
Peanut butter	100	163	110	196	186

	total consumer units	$100,000 or more	$100,000– $119,999	$120,000– $149,999	$150,000 or more
Miscellaneous foods	**100**	**157**	**136**	**161**	**171**
Frozen prepared foods	100	137	123	151	139
Frozen meals	100	147	124	181	141
Other frozen prepared foods	100	129	122	125	137
Canned and packaged soups	100	147	119	154	167
Potato chips, nuts, and other snacks	100	168	148	166	187
Potato chips and other snacks	100	163	144	161	182
Nuts	100	181	159	180	201
Condiments and seasonings	100	161	135	165	179
Salt, spices, and other seasonings	100	167	130	205	172
Olives, pickles, relishes	100	151	121	148	181
Sauces and gravies	100	156	137	147	180
Baking needs and miscellaneous products	100	166	149	159	188
Other canned/packaged prepared foods	100	160	140	163	174
Prepared salads	100	171	156	160	193
Prepared desserts	100	146	141	182	123
Baby food	100	143	128	75	207
Miscellaneous prepared foods	100	163	139	180	172
Nonalcoholic beverages	**100**	**145**	**129**	**147**	**157**
Carbonated drinks	100	132	125	138	132
Tea	100	136	113	157	140
Coffee	100	170	146	164	195
Noncarbonated fruit-flavored drinks	100	119	111	110	132
Other nonalcoholic beverages and ice	100	150	92	173	183
Bottled water	100	145	129	143	160
Sports drinks	100	183	173	176	197
Food prepared by consumer unit on trips	**100**	**221**	**173**	**189**	**282**

Source: Calculations by New Strategist based on the Bureau of Labor Statistics' 2012 Consumer Expenditure Survey

Table 14. Groceries: Total spending by high-income consumer units, 2012

(total annual spending on groceries, by before-tax income group of consumer units with high incomes, 2012; consumer units and dollars in thousands)

	total consumer units	$100,000 or more	$100,000–$119,999	$120,000–$149,999	$150,000 or more
Number of consumer units	124,416	23,293	7,183	6,947	9,162
Total spending of all consumer units	$6,400,191,698	$2,362,436,389	$560,028,844	$621,904,680	$1,183,831,823
GROCERIES	487,791,590	141,164,664	37,922,289	41,702,424	62,207,964
Cereals and bakery products	66,917,146	18,956,076	5,168,743	5,539,885	8,330,274
Cereals and cereal products	22,641,224	6,420,017	1,827,571	1,887,153	2,723,954
Flour	1,164,534	320,745	116,221	91,909	110,494
Prepared flour mixes	2,013,051	584,887	170,381	177,287	238,395
Ready-to-eat and cooked cereals	11,797,125	3,348,369	891,985	971,746	1,501,835
Rice	3,066,854	804,540	248,532	240,783	315,081
Pasta, cornmeal, and other cereal products	4,600,904	1,361,476	400,380	405,357	558,149
Bakery products	44,275,922	12,535,827	3,341,172	3,652,733	5,606,319
Bread	13,078,610	3,464,368	911,738	1,011,831	1,560,105
White bread	5,414,584	1,329,332	364,609	403,204	567,036
Bread other than white	7,664,026	2,135,269	547,129	608,627	993,069
Crackers and cookies	10,915,016	3,303,413	853,340	975,289	1,495,147
Cookies	6,290,473	1,847,135	478,029	548,049	832,368
Crackers	4,624,543	1,456,045	375,240	427,241	662,687
Frozen and refrigerated bakery products	3,579,448	1,021,864	308,438	286,147	427,865
Other bakery products	16,702,848	4,746,415	1,267,656	1,379,466	2,123,202
Biscuits and rolls	6,450,970	2,025,093	518,828	619,325	900,075
Cakes and cupcakes	4,720,343	1,303,942	325,821	356,867	630,529
Bread and cracker products	909,481	244,809	71,399	76,070	97,759
Sweetrolls, coffee cakes, doughnuts	2,952,392	788,468	240,200	198,128	350,447
Pies, tarts, turnovers	1,668,419	384,102	111,408	129,075	144,393
Meats, poultry, fish, and eggs	106,053,443	29,440,721	8,092,440	8,365,994	13,102,210
Beef	28,157,829	8,090,824	2,295,974	1,924,736	3,893,117
Ground beef	11,632,896	2,656,101	847,809	688,378	1,115,840
Roast	4,232,632	1,467,226	359,581	363,953	754,949
Chuck roast	1,171,999	384,102	188,554	83,295	103,347
Round roast	824,878	387,130	83,897	71,971	235,647
Other roast	2,235,756	695,995	87,130	208,757	415,955
Steak	9,883,607	3,288,739	908,721	703,245	1,688,923
Round steak	2,103,875	738,388	189,990	145,123	407,801
Sirloin steak	2,707,292	921,937	251,046	223,277	451,595
Other steak	5,072,440	1,628,414	467,685	334,845	829,619
Other beef	2,407,450	678,758	179,790	169,159	333,314
Pork	20,624,440	5,253,503	1,471,007	1,521,740	2,278,864
Bacon	4,003,707	1,028,852	241,133	308,864	488,151
Pork chops	3,488,625	753,296	205,865	192,918	357,684
Ham	4,157,983	1,009,519	293,928	271,072	446,648
Ham, not canned	4,004,951	988,322	293,210	268,224	428,140
Canned ham	153,032	21,430	718	2,848	18,507
Sausage	3,998,730	1,053,775	303,841	301,847	450,496
Other pork	4,975,396	1,408,062	426,167	447,039	535,794
Other meats	15,194,926	4,264,482	1,087,291	1,234,968	1,970,196
Frankfurters	3,074,319	757,488	182,736	239,672	341,559
Lunch meats (cold cuts)	10,852,808	3,128,017	835,886	827,110	1,480,671
Bologna, liverwurst, salami	3,191,270	861,608	213,191	243,562	411,282
Other lunch meats	7,661,537	2,266,642	622,694	583,617	1,069,389
Lamb, organ meats, and others	1,267,799	378,744	68,669	168,187	148,058

	total consumer units	$100,000 or more	$100,000–$119,999	$120,000–$149,999	$150,000 or more
Poultry	$19,826,934	$5,379,518	$1,385,673	$1,839,010	$2,189,260
Fresh and frozen chicken	15,741,112	4,042,267	1,064,449	1,415,590	1,585,118
Fresh and frozen whole chicken	4,705,413	1,231,268	320,003	460,656	458,283
Fresh and frozen chicken parts	11,035,699	2,810,766	744,446	955,004	1,126,834
Other poultry	4,085,821	1,337,484	321,224	423,350	604,142
Fish and seafood	15,644,068	4,767,145	1,364,914	1,338,409	2,076,384
Canned fish and seafood	2,261,883	547,386	165,353	170,688	211,825
Fresh fish and shellfish	7,874,289	2,601,362	776,051	594,246	1,233,847
Frozen fish and shellfish	5,507,896	1,618,165	423,510	573,544	630,804
Eggs	6,604,001	1,685,249	487,654	507,131	694,388
Dairy products	**52,121,595**	**15,667,804**	**4,174,329**	**4,545,283**	**7,028,537**
Fresh milk and cream	18,893,814	5,018,244	1,396,375	1,427,400	2,212,715
Fresh milk, all types	15,960,084	4,113,311	1,156,966	1,162,928	1,806,930
Cream	2,933,729	904,700	239,409	264,472	405,785
Other dairy products	33,227,781	10,649,560	2,777,953	3,117,883	4,815,914
Butter	3,180,073	959,905	269,793	273,642	419,528
Cheese	16,356,972	5,368,338	1,368,577	1,644,494	2,390,732
Ice cream and related products	7,137,746	2,121,294	581,679	632,316	916,200
Miscellaneous dairy products	6,552,991	2,200,024	557,904	567,431	1,089,362
Fruits and vegetables	**90,945,608**	**27,389,773**	**7,073,028**	**8,142,718**	**12,343,230**
Fresh fruits	32,508,657	10,508,171	2,609,728	3,171,931	4,804,461
Apples	5,176,950	1,771,899	423,007	553,676	810,562
Bananas	5,450,665	1,470,720	387,307	420,571	670,933
Oranges	3,326,884	1,035,840	257,726	311,573	474,225
Citrus fruits, except oranges	4,970,419	1,559,466	410,077	467,186	690,998
Other fresh fruits	13,584,983	4,670,014	1,131,538	1,418,855	2,157,743
Fresh vegetables	28,135,434	8,570,892	2,102,751	2,567,055	3,967,787
Potatoes	4,782,551	1,273,195	330,274	384,100	566,395
Lettuce	4,022,369	1,200,288	312,532	340,264	554,576
Tomatoes	4,895,770	1,432,752	407,276	433,007	596,904
Other fresh vegetables	14,433,500	4,664,656	1,052,669	1,409,685	2,249,912
Processed fruits	14,153,564	4,023,866	1,077,450	1,148,617	1,817,649
Frozen fruits and fruit juices	1,581,327	448,390	131,018	112,194	205,962
Frozen fruits	890,819	296,520	87,920	76,417	132,574
Frozen fruit juices	690,509	151,870	43,098	35,777	73,388
Canned fruits	2,531,866	677,826	183,382	216,955	280,632
Dried fruits	1,083,663	358,013	85,693	109,415	166,015
Fresh fruit juice	2,122,537	654,999	146,892	201,949	312,974
Canned and bottled fruit juice	6,832,927	1,884,637	530,465	508,104	852,158
Processed vegetables	16,149,197	4,286,844	1,283,099	1,255,184	1,753,240
Frozen vegetables	4,665,600	1,271,565	355,846	388,268	531,946
Canned and dried vegetables and juices	11,483,597	3,015,279	927,253	866,916	1,221,295
Canned vegetables	6,791,869	1,866,468	583,331	543,811	738,457
Dried vegetables	2,266,860	517,803	155,512	157,419	205,687
Fresh and canned vegetable juices	2,361,416	622,389	187,620	160,406	274,677
Sugar and other sweets	**18,260,536**	**5,329,671**	**1,425,826**	**1,566,965**	**2,363,613**
Candy and chewing gum	10,931,190	3,428,264	947,007	995,575	1,499,086
Sugar	3,033,262	612,140	180,078	172,841	260,109
Artificial sweeteners	610,883	155,131	36,777	39,181	80,534
Jams, preserves, other sweets	3,683,958	1,134,369	261,964	359,368	523,883
Fats and oils	**14,194,621**	**3,807,474**	**1,091,170**	**1,249,974**	**1,476,731**
Margarine	1,087,396	242,713	75,781	53,909	112,876
Fats and oils	4,577,265	1,207,975	376,174	433,493	398,089
Salad dressings	3,892,977	1,037,237	295,365	325,606	419,253
Nondairy cream and imitation milk	2,312,893	607,947	196,671	182,359	227,676
Peanut butter	2,324,091	711,368	147,108	254,538	318,838

	total consumer units	$100,000 or more	$100,000– $119,999	$120,000– $149,999	$150,000 or more
Miscellaneous foods	**$87,000,376**	**$25,509,795**	**$6,836,564**	**$7,843,302**	**$10,957,202**
Frozen prepared foods	16,277,345	4,175,503	1,155,026	1,370,990	1,666,201
Frozen meals	7,540,854	2,072,611	541,886	760,974	782,252
Other frozen prepared foods	8,736,492	2,102,892	613,141	610,016	883,950
Canned and packaged soups	5,760,461	1,587,884	394,275	496,016	709,414
Potato chips, nuts, and other snacks	19,152,599	6,024,734	1,635,425	1,778,501	2,638,015
Potato chips and other snacks	13,883,581	4,236,298	1,151,435	1,247,681	1,856,221
Nuts	5,269,018	1,788,437	483,991	530,751	781,793
Condiments and seasonings	17,591,178	5,286,812	1,374,970	1,623,097	2,320,368
Salt, spices, and other seasonings	4,817,388	1,510,318	361,808	551,314	610,281
Olives, pickles, relishes	2,172,303	615,634	151,633	178,955	289,702
Sauces and gravies	7,498,552	2,193,968	595,255	617,171	991,512
Baking needs and miscellaneous products	3,104,179	966,892	266,202	275,587	428,965
Other canned/packaged prepared foods	28,218,793	8,434,861	2,276,939	2,574,767	3,623,113
Prepared salads	4,365,757	1,396,415	391,976	389,379	619,626
Prepared desserts	1,777,905	484,960	144,450	180,622	160,701
Baby food	3,116,621	832,259	229,712	131,229	474,408
Miscellaneous prepared foods	18,389,929	5,619,203	1,472,228	1,850,195	2,329,255
Nonalcoholic beverages	**46,050,094**	**12,483,650**	**3,434,982**	**3,789,311**	**5,310,570**
Carbonated drinks	17,385,892	4,286,611	1,256,379	1,343,411	1,694,787
Tea	3,777,270	961,535	246,808	330,330	390,668
Coffee	10,761,984	3,417,316	905,058	982,723	1,547,645
Noncarbonated fruit-flavored drinks	3,213,665	713,465	205,865	196,531	312,791
Other nonalcoholic beverages and ice	1,911,030	536,205	101,855	185,068	257,177
Bottled water	7,066,829	1,917,480	527,017	563,888	834,475
Sports drinks	1,881,170	644,051	187,476	184,929	273,028
Food prepared by consumer unit on trips	**6,249,416**	**2,579,933**	**625,208**	**658,992**	**1,295,507**

Note: Numbers may not add to total because of rounding.
Source: Calculations by New Strategist based on the Bureau of Labor Statistics' 2012 Consumer Expenditure Survey

Table 15. Groceries: Market shares by high-income consumer units, 2012

(percentage of total annual spending on groceries accounted for by before-tax income group of consumer units with high incomes, 2012)

	total consumer units	$100,000 or more	$100,000– $119,999	$120,000– $149,999	$150,000 or more
Share of total consumer units	100.0%	18.7%	5.8%	5.6%	7.4%
Share of total before-tax income	100.0	49.1	9.6	11.3	28.2
Share of total spending	100.0	36.9	8.8	9.7	18.5
GROCERIES	**100.0**	**28.9**	**7.8**	**8.5**	**12.8**
Cereals and bakery products	**100.0**	**28.3**	**7.7**	**8.3**	**12.4**
Cereals and cereal products	100.0	28.4	8.1	8.3	12.0
Flour	100.0	27.5	10.0	7.9	9.5
Prepared flour mixes	100.0	29.1	8.5	8.8	11.8
Ready-to-eat and cooked cereals	100.0	28.4	7.6	8.2	12.7
Rice	100.0	26.2	8.1	7.9	10.3
Pasta, cornmeal, and other cereal products	100.0	29.6	8.7	8.8	12.1
Bakery products	100.0	28.3	7.5	8.2	12.7
Bread	100.0	26.5	7.0	7.7	11.9
White bread	100.0	24.6	6.7	7.4	10.5
Bread other than white	100.0	27.9	7.1	7.9	13.0
Crackers and cookies	100.0	30.3	7.8	8.9	13.7
Cookies	100.0	29.4	7.6	8.7	13.2
Crackers	100.0	31.5	8.1	9.2	14.3
Frozen and refrigerated bakery products	100.0	28.5	8.6	8.0	12.0
Other bakery products	100.0	28.4	7.6	8.3	12.7
Biscuits and rolls	100.0	31.4	8.0	9.6	14.0
Cakes and cupcakes	100.0	27.6	6.9	7.6	13.4
Bread and cracker products	100.0	26.9	7.9	8.4	10.7
Sweetrolls, coffee cakes, doughnuts	100.0	26.7	8.1	6.7	11.9
Pies, tarts, turnovers	100.0	23.0	6.7	7.7	8.7
Meats, poultry, fish, and eggs	**100.0**	**27.8**	**7.6**	**7.9**	**12.4**
Beef	100.0	28.7	8.2	6.8	13.8
Ground beef	100.0	22.8	7.3	5.9	9.6
Roast	100.0	34.7	8.5	8.6	17.8
Chuck roast	100.0	32.8	16.1	7.1	8.8
Round roast	100.0	46.9	10.2	8.7	28.6
Other roast	100.0	31.1	3.9	9.3	18.6
Steak	100.0	33.3	9.2	7.1	17.1
Round steak	100.0	35.1	9.0	6.9	19.4
Sirloin steak	100.0	34.1	9.3	8.2	16.7
Other steak	100.0	32.1	9.2	6.6	16.4
Other beef	100.0	28.2	7.5	7.0	13.8
Pork	100.0	25.5	7.1	7.4	11.0
Bacon	100.0	25.7	6.0	7.7	12.2
Pork chops	100.0	21.6	5.9	5.5	10.3
Ham	100.0	24.3	7.1	6.5	10.7
Ham, not canned	100.0	24.7	7.3	6.7	10.7
Canned ham	100.0	14.0	0.5	1.9	12.1
Sausage	100.0	26.4	7.6	7.5	11.3
Other pork	100.0	28.3	8.6	9.0	10.8
Other meats	100.0	28.1	7.2	8.1	13.0
Frankfurters	100.0	24.6	5.9	7.8	11.1
Lunch meats (cold cuts)	100.0	28.8	7.7	7.6	13.6
Bologna, liverwurst, salami	100.0	27.0	6.7	7.6	12.9
Other lunch meats	100.0	29.6	8.1	7.6	14.0
Lamb, organ meats, and others	100.0	29.9	5.4	13.3	11.7

	total consumer units	$100,000 or more	$100,000–$119,999	$120,000–$149,999	$150,000 or more
Poultry	100.0%	27.1%	7.0%	9.3%	11.0%
Fresh and frozen chicken	100.0	25.7	6.8	9.0	10.1
Fresh and frozen whole chicken	100.0	26.2	6.8	9.8	9.7
Fresh and frozen chicken parts	100.0	25.5	6.7	8.7	10.2
Other poultry	100.0	32.7	7.9	10.4	14.8
Fish and seafood	100.0	30.5	8.7	8.6	13.3
Canned fish and seafood	100.0	24.2	7.3	7.5	9.4
Fresh fish and shellfish	100.0	33.0	9.9	7.5	15.7
Frozen fish and shellfish	100.0	29.4	7.7	10.4	11.5
Eggs	100.0	25.5	7.4	7.7	10.5
Dairy products	**100.0**	**30.1**	**8.0**	**8.7**	**13.5**
Fresh milk and cream	100.0	26.6	7.4	7.6	11.7
Fresh milk, all types	100.0	25.8	7.2	7.3	11.3
Cream	100.0	30.8	8.2	9.0	13.8
Other dairy products	100.0	32.1	8.4	9.4	14.5
Butter	100.0	30.2	8.5	8.6	13.2
Cheese	100.0	32.8	8.4	10.1	14.6
Ice cream and related products	100.0	29.7	8.1	8.9	12.8
Miscellaneous dairy products	100.0	33.6	8.5	8.7	16.6
Fruits and vegetables	**100.0**	**30.1**	**7.8**	**9.0**	**13.6**
Fresh fruits	100.0	32.3	8.0	9.8	14.8
Apples	100.0	34.2	8.2	10.7	15.7
Bananas	100.0	27.0	7.1	7.7	12.3
Oranges	100.0	31.1	7.7	9.4	14.3
Citrus fruits, except oranges	100.0	31.4	8.3	9.4	13.9
Other fresh fruits	100.0	34.4	8.3	10.4	15.9
Fresh vegetables	100.0	30.5	7.5	9.1	14.1
Potatoes	100.0	26.6	6.9	8.0	11.8
Lettuce	100.0	29.8	7.8	8.5	13.8
Tomatoes	100.0	29.3	8.3	8.8	12.2
Other fresh vegetables	100.0	32.3	7.3	9.8	15.6
Processed fruits	100.0	28.4	7.6	8.1	12.8
Frozen fruits and fruit juices	100.0	28.4	8.3	7.1	13.0
Frozen fruits	100.0	33.3	9.9	8.6	14.9
Frozen fruit juices	100.0	22.0	6.2	5.2	10.6
Canned fruits	100.0	26.8	7.2	8.6	11.1
Dried fruits	100.0	33.0	7.9	10.1	15.3
Fresh fruit juice	100.0	30.9	6.9	9.5	14.7
Canned and bottled fruit juice	100.0	27.6	7.8	7.4	12.5
Processed vegetables	100.0	26.5	7.9	7.8	10.9
Frozen vegetables	100.0	27.3	7.6	8.3	11.4
Canned and dried vegetables and juices	100.0	26.3	8.1	7.5	10.6
Canned vegetables	100.0	27.5	8.6	8.0	10.9
Dried vegetables	100.0	22.8	6.9	6.9	9.1
Fresh and canned vegetable juices	100.0	26.4	7.9	6.8	11.6
Sugar and other sweets	**100.0**	**29.2**	**7.8**	**8.6**	**12.9**
Candy and chewing gum	100.0	31.4	8.7	9.1	13.7
Sugar	100.0	20.2	5.9	5.7	8.6
Artificial sweeteners	100.0	25.4	6.0	6.4	13.2
Jams, preserves, other sweets	100.0	30.8	7.1	9.8	14.2
Fats and oils	**100.0**	**26.8**	**7.7**	**8.8**	**10.4**
Margarine	100.0	22.3	7.0	5.0	10.4
Fats and oils	100.0	26.4	8.2	9.5	8.7
Salad dressings	100.0	26.6	7.6	8.4	10.8
Nondairy cream and imitation milk	100.0	26.3	8.5	7.9	9.8
Peanut butter	100.0	30.6	6.3	11.0	13.7

	total consumer units	$100,000 or more	$100,000– $119,999	$120,000– $149,999	$150,000 or more
Miscellaneous foods	**100.0%**	**29.3%**	**7.9%**	**9.0%**	**12.6%**
Frozen prepared foods	100.0	25.7	7.1	8.4	10.2
Frozen meals	100.0	27.5	7.2	10.1	10.4
Other frozen prepared foods	100.0	24.1	7.0	7.0	10.1
Canned and packaged soups	100.0	27.6	6.8	8.6	12.3
Potato chips, nuts, and other snacks	100.0	31.5	8.5	9.3	13.8
Potato chips and other snacks	100.0	30.5	8.3	9.0	13.4
Nuts	100.0	33.9	9.2	10.1	14.8
Condiments and seasonings	100.0	30.1	7.8	9.2	13.2
Salt, spices, and other seasonings	100.0	31.4	7.5	11.4	12.7
Olives, pickles, relishes	100.0	28.3	7.0	8.2	13.3
Sauces and gravies	100.0	29.3	7.9	8.2	13.2
Baking needs and miscellaneous products	100.0	31.1	8.6	8.9	13.8
Other canned/packaged prepared foods	100.0	29.9	8.1	9.1	12.8
Prepared salads	100.0	32.0	9.0	8.9	14.2
Prepared desserts	100.0	27.3	8.1	10.2	9.0
Baby food	100.0	26.7	7.4	4.2	15.2
Miscellaneous prepared foods	100.0	30.6	8.0	10.1	12.7
Nonalcoholic beverages	**100.0**	**27.1**	**7.5**	**8.2**	**11.5**
Carbonated drinks	100.0	24.7	7.2	7.7	9.7
Tea	100.0	25.5	6.5	8.7	10.3
Coffee	100.0	31.8	8.4	9.1	14.4
Noncarbonated fruit-flavored drinks	100.0	22.2	6.4	6.1	9.7
Other nonalcoholic beverages and ice	100.0	28.1	5.3	9.7	13.5
Bottled water	100.0	27.1	7.5	8.0	11.8
Sports drinks	100.0	34.2	10.0	9.8	14.5
Food prepared by consumer unit on trips	**100.0**	**41.3**	**10.0**	**10.5**	**20.7**

Note: Numbers may not add to total because of rounding.
Source: Calculations by New Strategist based on the Bureau of Labor Statistics' 2012 Consumer Expenditure Survey

Table 16. Groceries: Average spending by household type, 2012

(average annual spending of consumer units on groceries, by type of consumer unit, 2012)

	total consumer units	total married couples	married couples, no children	married couples with children total	oldest child under age 6	oldest child aged 6 to 17	oldest child aged 18 or older	single parent, at least one child under age 18	single person
Number of consumer units (in 000s)	124,416	60,428	25,936	29,252	5,676	14,797	8,778	6,524	36,942
Number of persons per consumer unit	2.5	3.2	2.0	3.9	3.5	4.2	3.9	2.9	1.0
Average before-tax income of consumer units	$65,596.00	$90,393.00	$81,717.00	$98,104.00	$85,200.00	$100,698.00	$102,074.00	$34,194.00	$34,102.00
Average spending of consumer units, total	51,441.87	67,310.04	61,284.60	72,814.06	64,103.17	74,658.88	75,286.36	38,667.27	30,715.83
GROCERIES	**3,920.65**	**5,088.66**	**4,263.22**	**5,742.09**	**4,452.08**	**6,094.63**	**5,958.14**	**3,673.01**	**1,964.01**
Cereals and bakery products	**537.85**	**697.81**	**558.52**	**802.64**	**622.89**	**877.70**	**789.43**	**515.08**	**270.20**
Cereals and cereal products	181.98	233.88	175.38	277.99	205.97	310.43	268.73	181.95	84.46
Flour	9.36	12.76	10.90	15.13	9.16	16.36	16.81	7.40	3.65
Prepared flour mixes	16.18	22.44	16.72	27.50	22.04	30.09	26.59	13.92	6.35
Ready-to-eat and cooked cereals	94.82	122.89	93.96	147.53	112.48	168.24	134.83	97.55	43.12
Rice	24.65	28.68	18.18	33.42	21.79	36.94	34.81	30.62	11.64
Pasta, cornmeal, and other cereal products	36.98	47.11	35.63	54.39	40.51	58.81	55.69	32.45	19.70
Bakery products	355.87	463.93	383.14	524.65	416.91	567.27	520.70	333.13	185.74
Bread	105.12	133.54	116.12	146.37	111.79	155.53	152.65	113.50	57.70
White bread	43.52	53.77	45.20	60.20	42.24	65.36	62.79	51.24	24.28
Bread other than white	61.60	79.77	70.92	86.17	69.55	90.17	89.86	62.26	33.42
Crackers and cookies	87.73	114.74	93.87	131.74	115.07	140.67	127.22	75.87	45.53
Cookies	50.56	64.94	54.51	71.94	56.47	76.66	73.72	44.04	26.20
Crackers	37.17	49.80	39.36	59.79	58.59	64.01	53.51	31.82	19.33
Frozen and refrigerated bakery products	28.77	40.09	30.85	49.10	41.84	55.02	43.75	29.02	12.50
Other bakery products	134.25	175.56	142.30	197.44	148.21	216.05	197.08	114.75	70.01
Biscuits and rolls	51.85	69.57	56.64	79.85	61.71	89.56	74.97	45.05	25.61
Cakes and cupcakes	37.94	49.11	40.09	54.49	39.38	59.30	55.89	27.78	20.94
Bread and cracker products	7.31	9.75	7.58	11.65	11.16	10.42	14.00	6.33	3.00
Sweetrolls, coffee cakes, doughnuts	23.73	30.18	25.57	31.89	21.69	34.66	33.63	22.58	12.51
Pies, tarts, turnovers	13.41	16.95	12.41	19.55	14.27	22.10	18.59	13.01	7.95
Meats, poultry, fish, and eggs	**852.41**	**1,095.50**	**922.41**	**1,213.21**	**830.07**	**1,301.81**	**1,304.16**	**802.04**	**392.39**
Beef	226.32	292.18	239.89	322.61	188.34	338.66	379.51	194.31	91.77
Ground beef	93.50	118.02	90.36	135.03	86.42	145.44	147.95	86.75	39.20
Roast	34.02	45.41	37.09	49.43	20.74	47.20	71.01	22.11	13.47
Chuck roast	9.42	12.61	10.58	13.90	6.06	12.32	21.43	4.98	3.31
Round roast	6.63	8.43	5.66	11.06	4.23	10.17	16.80	2.87	3.07
Other roast	17.97	24.38	20.85	24.46	10.45	24.71	32.78	14.25	7.10
Steak	79.44	104.63	89.47	114.10	69.49	122.08	128.59	65.24	32.58
Round steak	16.91	21.87	15.79	25.19	10.40	26.22	32.67	15.11	6.11
Sirloin steak	21.76	29.27	26.33	30.83	16.35	33.44	35.51	17.21	9.05
Other steak	40.77	53.49	47.35	58.08	42.74	62.42	60.41	32.93	17.41
Other beef	19.35	24.12	22.97	24.06	11.68	23.94	31.95	20.21	6.53
Pork	165.77	210.60	179.12	233.58	168.08	251.22	244.95	170.34	76.62
Bacon	32.18	39.17	32.90	43.64	38.92	45.01	44.29	29.85	16.10
Pork chops	28.04	33.54	28.29	37.37	26.10	41.20	37.98	35.99	13.85
Ham	33.42	43.48	34.48	49.67	26.10	57.78	50.82	28.70	16.67
Ham, not canned	32.19	41.85	33.94	47.15	25.82	56.79	44.34	27.24	16.32
Canned ham	1.23	1.63	0.55	2.52	0.27	0.99	6.48	1.46	0.35
Sausage	32.14	40.82	34.61	45.91	35.99	47.40	49.59	34.86	15.01
Other pork	39.99	53.58	48.85	57.00	40.97	59.83	62.26	40.95	14.99
Other meats	122.13	160.42	129.92	184.15	140.87	195.36	192.41	120.59	61.20
Frankfurters	24.71	31.16	21.99	36.33	29.79	38.16	37.34	28.57	11.09
Lunch meats (cold cuts)	87.23	115.42	92.69	135.87	100.25	150.75	133.22	87.03	44.41
Bologna, liverwurst, salami	25.65	32.74	26.47	39.08	26.91	42.96	40.19	32.39	13.44
Other lunch meats	61.58	82.68	66.22	96.79	73.34	107.79	93.03	54.64	30.97
Lamb, organ meats, and others	10.19	13.84	15.24	11.96	10.84	6.45	21.84	4.99	5.70

	total consumer units	total married couples	married couples, no children	married couples with children				single parent, at least one child under age 18	single person
				total	oldest child under age 6	oldest child aged 6 to 17	oldest child aged 18 or older		
Poultry	$159.36	$199.90	$160.38	$228.14	$180.23	$242.90	$233.36	$166.00	$77.03
Fresh and frozen chicken	126.52	157.92	121.14	181.91	141.64	196.84	182.10	132.71	60.86
Fresh and frozen whole chicken	37.82	47.68	38.45	53.11	34.27	57.33	57.81	40.46	17.34
Fresh and frozen chicken parts	88.70	110.24	82.69	128.80	107.37	139.50	124.29	92.25	43.52
Other poultry	32.84	41.97	39.24	46.23	38.60	46.07	51.26	33.28	16.18
Fish and seafood	125.74	166.38	157.59	172.57	100.19	197.94	175.35	100.16	56.45
Canned fish and seafood	18.18	21.58	20.92	20.97	12.41	22.02	24.57	16.85	11.02
Fresh fish and shellfish	63.29	85.56	79.42	88.73	46.86	99.96	96.09	57.45	27.21
Frozen fish and shellfish	44.27	59.24	57.25	62.86	40.92	75.96	54.69	25.85	18.22
Eggs	53.08	66.03	55.51	72.17	52.36	75.71	78.59	50.64	29.31
Dairy products	**418.93**	**560.72**	**448.03**	**656.00**	**570.48**	**693.16**	**647.30**	**352.56**	**206.68**
Fresh milk and cream	151.86	198.38	145.59	240.43	224.52	248.49	236.91	145.49	75.30
Fresh milk, all types	128.28	166.88	120.59	203.11	197.74	212.58	190.65	124.72	65.23
Cream	23.58	31.51	25.00	37.32	26.78	35.91	46.26	20.77	10.07
Other dairy products	267.07	362.34	302.44	415.57	345.96	444.67	410.40	207.06	131.38
Butter	25.56	34.28	28.47	38.78	30.00	41.22	40.17	20.47	12.72
Cheese	131.47	180.88	154.46	205.27	172.10	214.87	209.93	94.63	65.00
Ice cream and related products	57.37	76.44	62.46	87.34	62.96	96.93	86.54	49.33	27.24
Miscellaneous dairy products	52.67	70.74	57.05	84.18	80.89	91.65	73.75	42.63	26.43
Fruits and vegetables	**730.98**	**953.42**	**824.84**	**1,059.70**	**858.02**	**1,099.91**	**1,118.30**	**676.15**	**383.60**
Fresh fruits	261.29	346.98	296.93	394.92	326.03	408.84	414.63	251.61	133.79
Apples	41.61	56.27	47.18	66.99	47.43	73.97	67.52	39.77	19.88
Bananas	43.81	54.68	45.56	60.48	49.45	62.29	64.34	51.78	22.82
Oranges	26.74	36.45	29.74	42.44	26.93	46.43	45.45	22.48	12.06
Citrus fruits, except oranges	39.95	52.21	42.70	60.90	50.42	58.78	70.98	41.84	20.24
Other fresh fruits	109.19	147.36	131.75	164.10	151.80	167.36	166.34	95.75	58.77
Fresh vegetables	226.14	298.36	272.08	317.32	260.26	329.64	332.34	176.69	118.25
Potatoes	38.44	48.85	41.94	53.59	40.51	56.38	57.06	37.56	18.44
Lettuce	32.33	41.99	37.73	44.94	37.67	44.85	49.60	24.25	17.54
Tomatoes	39.35	51.36	43.33	55.27	44.65	54.81	62.65	30.66	21.58
Other fresh vegetables	116.01	156.16	149.09	163.53	137.43	173.60	163.02	84.22	60.69
Processed fruits	113.76	146.73	122.23	166.79	141.63	175.83	167.40	110.88	64.13
Frozen fruits and fruit juices	12.71	18.44	18.44	19.88	7.25	23.13	22.32	9.73	5.88
Frozen fruits	7.16	11.18	11.48	11.96	2.06	13.34	15.84	4.11	3.41
Frozen fruit juices	5.55	7.25	6.95	7.91	5.19	9.79	6.48	5.62	2.47
Canned fruits	20.35	27.27	21.39	32.91	31.77	34.59	30.81	19.99	10.00
Dried fruits	8.71	12.18	11.78	12.12	17.20	11.73	9.62	6.29	4.55
Fresh fruit juice	17.06	21.31	16.66	25.24	22.50	26.72	24.47	14.73	10.33
Canned and bottled fruit juice	54.92	67.54	53.97	76.65	62.91	79.66	80.18	60.14	33.37
Processed vegetables	129.80	161.35	133.59	180.66	130.09	185.59	203.94	136.98	67.43
Frozen vegetables	37.50	47.95	39.99	54.74	34.83	55.99	65.06	42.01	19.54
Canned and dried vegetables and juices	92.30	113.39	93.60	125.92	95.26	129.61	138.88	94.97	47.89
Canned vegetables	54.59	68.11	60.47	73.08	55.65	75.67	79.62	52.86	28.68
Dried vegetables	18.22	21.84	16.40	24.27	15.53	24.31	29.68	18.86	8.79
Fresh and canned vegetable juices	18.98	22.84	16.09	27.97	23.83	28.99	28.84	23.01	10.06
Sugar and other sweets	**146.77**	**193.23**	**167.60**	**213.54**	**139.94**	**244.36**	**207.99**	**132.88**	**74.54**
Candy and chewing gum	87.86	116.90	100.91	129.44	75.99	156.60	117.42	79.01	46.24
Sugar	24.38	29.41	23.33	33.35	24.72	32.95	39.42	28.15	11.56
Artificial sweeteners	4.91	6.67	7.37	5.64	1.14	5.26	9.08	3.01	2.66
Jams, preserves, other sweets	29.61	40.24	35.99	45.11	38.09	49.56	42.07	22.71	14.09
Fats and oils	**114.09**	**145.18**	**120.97**	**162.61**	**122.45**	**167.21**	**179.97**	**108.52**	**58.50**
Margarine	8.74	10.19	10.07	10.07	5.99	12.88	7.91	11.24	4.41
Fats and oils	36.79	45.33	37.04	50.49	31.28	55.44	54.22	34.13	18.97
Salad dressings	31.29	41.85	38.34	42.94	36.80	42.04	48.26	24.14	16.01
Nondairy cream and imitation milk	18.59	23.03	19.07	26.43	22.93	23.51	33.48	17.25	9.40
Peanut butter	18.68	24.78	16.45	32.68	25.46	33.33	36.09	21.77	9.71

	total consumer units	total married couples	married couples, no children	married couples with children				single parent, at least one child under age 18	single person
				total	oldest child under age 6	oldest child aged 6 to 17	oldest child aged 18 or older		
Miscellaneous foods	**$699.27**	**$906.48**	**$734.79**	**$1,065.98**	**$928.55**	**$1,108.06**	**$1,081.43**	**$698.75**	**$354.31**
Frozen prepared foods	130.83	155.56	120.24	187.13	141.53	203.30	188.57	156.61	78.46
Frozen meals	60.61	70.15	61.49	75.65	63.62	73.57	86.63	74.39	44.23
Other frozen prepared foods	70.22	85.41	58.76	111.48	77.92	129.73	101.94	82.22	34.23
Canned and packaged soups	46.30	60.48	59.16	62.94	46.32	64.98	69.89	39.69	25.91
Potato chips, nuts, and other snacks	153.94	209.93	172.52	246.64	179.65	270.74	248.18	136.90	70.72
Potato chips and other snacks	111.59	150.71	106.62	191.88	136.74	214.89	187.84	113.87	47.68
Nuts	42.35	59.22	65.90	54.77	42.91	55.85	60.35	23.03	23.04
Condiments and seasonings	141.39	188.18	156.46	215.39	160.45	228.53	227.70	128.54	65.12
Salt, spices, and other seasonings	38.72	51.60	44.13	56.32	42.82	58.74	60.68	36.66	16.06
Olives, pickles, relishes	17.46	23.10	21.84	24.64	18.39	24.19	29.30	12.36	9.57
Sauces and gravies	60.27	80.06	64.47	93.37	69.58	101.97	93.84	56.56	27.60
Baking needs and miscellaneous products	24.95	33.42	26.03	41.05	29.66	43.62	43.87	22.96	11.89
Other canned/packaged prepared foods	226.81	292.33	226.41	353.89	400.59	340.52	347.09	237.01	114.09
Prepared salads	35.09	43.86	46.82	42.24	33.37	45.00	43.14	30.15	22.79
Prepared desserts	14.29	18.19	16.44	19.32	15.25	21.41	18.37	14.92	8.23
Baby food	25.05	33.32	6.97	55.70	196.42	32.04	7.49	59.87	3.69
Miscellaneous prepared foods	147.81	192.16	149.81	232.60	153.52	241.58	266.89	132.06	73.68
Nonalcoholic beverages	**370.13**	**462.23**	**396.83**	**502.38**	**334.44**	**524.52**	**570.11**	**360.98**	**200.02**
Carbonated drinks	139.74	173.24	144.39	187.07	139.84	189.33	212.76	139.71	72.43
Tea	30.36	38.76	34.07	41.42	24.79	45.15	45.54	34.43	14.49
Coffee	86.50	112.16	117.77	108.06	72.41	106.36	133.11	59.60	49.93
Noncarbonated fruit-flavored drinks	25.83	31.27	21.97	37.98	26.29	41.44	39.50	33.09	11.45
Other nonalcoholic beverages and ice	15.36	19.97	14.03	24.68	14.89	26.23	28.20	12.70	8.01
Bottled water	56.80	67.37	52.49	77.56	41.22	86.44	85.38	65.03	35.30
Sports drinks	15.12	19.12	11.64	25.36	14.99	29.57	24.79	16.43	7.49
Food prepared by consumer unit on trips	**50.23**	**74.10**	**89.21**	**66.03**	**45.26**	**77.90**	**59.45**	**26.05**	**23.77**

Source: Bureau of Labor Statistics, unpublished tables from the 2012 Consumer Expenditure Survey

Table 17. Groceries: Indexed spending by household type, 2012

(indexed average annual spending of consumer units on groceries, by type of consumer unit, 2012; index definition: an index of 100 is the average for all consumer units; an index of 125 means that spending by consumer units in that group is 25 percent above the average for all consumer units; an index of 75 indicates spending that is 25 percent below the average for all consumer units)

| | total consumer units | total married couples | married couples, no children | married couples with children | | | | single parent, at least one child under age 18 | single person |
				total	oldest child under age 6	oldest child aged 6 to 17	oldest child aged 18 or older		
Average spending of consumer units, total	$51,442	$67,310	$61,285	$72,814	$64,103	$74,659	$75,286	$38,667	$30,716
Average spending of consumer units, index	100	131	119	142	125	145	146	75	60
GROCERIES	100	130	109	146	114	155	152	94	50
Cereals and bakery products	100	130	104	149	116	163	147	96	50
Cereals and cereal products	100	129	96	153	113	171	148	100	46
Flour	100	136	116	162	98	175	180	79	39
Prepared flour mixes	100	139	103	170	136	186	164	86	39
Ready-to-eat and cooked cereals	100	130	99	156	119	177	142	103	45
Rice	100	116	74	136	88	150	141	124	47
Pasta, cornmeal, and other cereal products	100	127	96	147	110	159	151	88	53
Bakery products	100	130	108	147	117	159	146	94	52
Bread	100	127	110	139	106	148	145	108	55
White bread	100	124	104	138	97	150	144	118	56
Bread other than white	100	129	115	140	113	146	146	101	54
Crackers and cookies	100	131	107	150	131	160	145	86	52
Cookies	100	128	108	142	112	152	146	87	52
Crackers	100	134	106	161	158	172	144	86	52
Frozen and refrigerated bakery products	100	139	107	171	145	191	152	101	43
Other bakery products	100	131	106	147	110	161	147	85	52
Biscuits and rolls	100	134	109	154	119	173	145	87	49
Cakes and cupcakes	100	129	106	144	104	156	147	73	55
Bread and cracker products	100	133	104	159	153	143	192	87	41
Sweetrolls, coffee cakes, doughnuts	100	127	108	134	91	146	142	95	53
Pies, tarts, turnovers	100	126	93	146	106	165	139	97	59
Meats, poultry, fish, and eggs	100	129	108	142	97	153	153	94	46
Beef	100	129	106	143	83	150	168	86	41
Ground beef	100	126	97	144	92	156	158	93	42
Roast	100	133	109	145	61	139	209	65	40
Chuck roast	100	134	112	148	64	131	227	53	35
Round roast	100	127	85	167	64	153	253	43	46
Other roast	100	136	116	136	58	138	182	79	40
Steak	100	132	113	144	87	154	162	82	41
Round steak	100	129	93	149	62	155	193	89	36
Sirloin steak	100	135	121	142	75	154	163	79	42
Other steak	100	131	116	142	105	153	148	81	43
Other beef	100	125	119	124	60	124	165	104	34
Pork	100	127	108	141	101	152	148	103	46
Bacon	100	122	102	136	121	140	138	93	50
Pork chops	100	120	101	133	93	147	135	128	49
Ham	100	130	103	149	78	173	152	86	50
Ham, not canned	100	130	105	146	80	176	138	85	51
Canned ham	100	133	45	205	22	80	527	119	28
Sausage	100	127	108	143	112	147	154	108	47
Other pork	100	134	122	143	102	150	156	102	37
Other meats	100	131	106	151	115	160	158	99	50
Frankfurters	100	126	89	147	121	154	151	116	45
Lunch meats (cold cuts)	100	132	106	156	115	173	153	100	51
Bologna, liverwurst, salami	100	128	103	152	105	167	157	126	52
Other lunch meats	100	134	108	157	119	175	151	89	50
Lamb, organ meats, and others	100	136	150	117	106	63	214	49	56

	total consumer units	total married couples	married couples, no children	married couples with children				single parent, at least one child under age 18	single person
				total	oldest child under age 6	oldest child aged 6 to 17	oldest child aged 18 or older		
Poultry	100	125	101	143	113	152	146	104	48
Fresh and frozen chicken	100	125	96	144	112	156	144	105	48
Fresh and frozen whole chicken	100	126	102	140	91	152	153	107	46
Fresh and frozen chicken parts	100	124	93	145	121	157	140	104	49
Other poultry	100	128	119	141	118	140	156	101	49
Fish and seafood	100	132	125	137	80	157	139	80	45
Canned fish and seafood	100	119	115	115	68	121	135	93	61
Fresh fish and shellfish	100	135	125	140	74	158	152	91	43
Frozen fish and shellfish	100	134	129	142	92	172	124	58	41
Eggs	100	124	105	136	99	143	148	95	55
Dairy products	**100**	**134**	**107**	**157**	**136**	**165**	**155**	**84**	**49**
Fresh milk and cream	100	131	96	158	148	164	156	96	50
Fresh milk, all types	100	130	94	158	154	166	149	97	51
Cream	100	134	106	158	114	152	196	88	43
Other dairy products	100	136	113	156	130	166	154	78	49
Butter	100	134	111	152	117	161	157	80	50
Cheese	100	138	117	156	131	163	160	72	49
Ice cream and related products	100	133	109	152	110	169	151	86	47
Miscellaneous dairy products	100	134	108	160	154	174	140	81	50
Fruits and vegetables	**100**	**130**	**113**	**145**	**117**	**150**	**153**	**92**	**52**
Fresh fruits	100	133	114	151	125	156	159	96	51
Apples	100	135	113	161	114	178	162	96	48
Bananas	100	125	104	138	113	142	147	118	52
Oranges	100	136	111	159	101	174	170	84	45
Citrus fruits, except oranges	100	131	107	152	126	147	178	105	51
Other fresh fruits	100	135	121	150	139	153	152	88	54
Fresh vegetables	100	132	120	140	115	146	147	78	52
Potatoes	100	127	109	139	105	147	148	98	48
Lettuce	100	130	117	139	117	139	153	75	54
Tomatoes	100	131	110	140	113	139	159	78	55
Other fresh vegetables	100	135	129	141	118	150	141	73	52
Processed fruits	100	129	107	147	124	155	147	97	56
Frozen fruits and fruit juices	100	145	145	156	57	182	176	77	46
Frozen fruits	100	156	160	167	29	186	221	57	48
Frozen fruit juices	100	131	125	143	94	176	117	101	45
Canned fruits	100	134	105	162	156	170	151	98	49
Dried fruits	100	140	135	139	197	135	110	72	52
Fresh fruit juice	100	125	98	148	132	157	143	86	61
Canned and bottled fruit juice	100	123	98	140	115	145	146	110	61
Processed vegetables	100	124	103	139	100	143	157	106	52
Frozen vegetables	100	128	107	146	93	149	173	112	52
Canned and dried vegetables and juices	100	123	101	136	103	140	150	103	52
Canned vegetables	100	125	111	134	102	139	146	97	53
Dried vegetables	100	120	90	133	85	133	163	104	48
Fresh and canned vegetable juices	100	120	85	147	126	153	152	121	53
Sugar and other sweets	**100**	**132**	**114**	**145**	**95**	**166**	**142**	**91**	**51**
Candy and chewing gum	100	133	115	147	86	178	134	90	53
Sugar	100	121	96	137	101	135	162	115	47
Artificial sweeteners	100	136	150	115	23	107	185	61	54
Jams, preserves, other sweets	100	136	122	152	129	167	142	77	48
Fats and oils	**100**	**127**	**106**	**143**	**107**	**147**	**158**	**95**	**51**
Margarine	100	117	115	115	69	147	91	129	50
Fats and oils	100	123	101	137	85	151	147	93	52
Salad dressings	100	134	123	137	118	134	154	77	51
Nondairy cream and imitation milk	100	124	103	142	123	126	180	93	51
Peanut butter	100	133	88	175	136	178	193	117	52

	total consumer units	total married couples	married couples, no children	married couples with children				single parent, at least one child under age 18	single person
				total	oldest child under age 6	oldest child aged 6 to 17	oldest child aged 18 or older		
Miscellaneous foods	**100**	**130**	**105**	**152**	**133**	**158**	**155**	**100**	**51**
Frozen prepared foods	100	119	92	143	108	155	144	120	60
Frozen meals	100	116	101	125	105	121	143	123	73
Other frozen prepared foods	100	122	84	159	111	185	145	117	49
Canned and packaged soups	100	131	128	136	100	140	151	86	56
Potato chips, nuts, and other snacks	100	136	112	160	117	176	161	89	46
Potato chips and other snacks	100	135	96	172	123	193	168	102	43
Nuts	100	140	156	129	101	132	143	54	54
Condiments and seasonings	100	133	111	152	113	162	161	91	46
Salt, spices, and other seasonings	100	133	114	145	111	152	157	95	41
Olives, pickles, relishes	100	132	125	141	105	139	168	71	55
Sauces and gravies	100	133	107	155	115	169	156	94	46
Baking needs and miscellaneous products	100	134	104	165	119	175	176	92	48
Other canned/packaged prepared foods	100	129	100	156	177	150	153	104	50
Prepared salads	100	125	133	120	95	128	123	86	65
Prepared desserts	100	127	115	135	107	150	129	104	58
Baby food	100	133	28	222	784	128	30	239	15
Miscellaneous prepared foods	100	130	101	157	104	163	181	89	50
Nonalcoholic beverages	**100**	**125**	**107**	**136**	**90**	**142**	**154**	**98**	**54**
Carbonated drinks	100	124	103	134	100	135	152	100	52
Tea	100	128	112	136	82	149	150	113	48
Coffee	100	130	136	125	84	123	154	69	58
Noncarbonated fruit-flavored drinks	100	121	85	147	102	160	153	128	44
Other nonalcoholic beverages and ice	100	130	91	161	97	171	184	83	52
Bottled water	100	119	92	137	73	152	150	114	62
Sports drinks	100	126	77	168	99	196	164	109	50
Food prepared by consumer unit on trips	**100**	**148**	**178**	**131**	**90**	**155**	**118**	**52**	**47**

Source: Calculations by New Strategist based on the Bureau of Labor Statistics' 2012 Consumer Expenditure Survey

Table 18. Groceries: Total spending by household type, 2012

(total annual spending on groceries, by consumer unit type, 2012; consumer units and dollars in thousands)

	total consumer units	total married couples	married couples, no children	married couples with children				single parent, at least one child under age 18	single person
				total	oldest child under age 6	oldest child aged 6 to 17	oldest child aged 18 or older		
Number of consumer units	124,416	60,428	25,936	29,252	5,676	14,797	8,778	6,524	36,942
Total spending of all consumer units	$6,400,191,698	$4,067,411,097	$1,589,477,386	$2,129,956,883	$363,849,593	$1,104,727,447	$660,863,668	$252,265,269	$1,134,704,192
GROCERIES	487,791,590	307,497,546	110,570,874	167,967,617	25,270,006	90,182,240	52,300,553	23,962,717	72,554,457
Cereals and bakery products	66,917,146	42,167,263	14,485,775	23,478,825	3,535,524	12,987,327	6,929,617	3,360,382	9,981,728
Cereals and cereal products	22,641,224	14,132,901	4,548,656	8,131,763	1,169,086	4,593,433	2,358,912	1,187,042	3,120,121
Flour	1,164,534	771,061	282,702	442,583	51,992	242,079	147,558	48,278	134,838
Prepared flour mixes	2,013,051	1,356,004	433,650	804,430	125,099	445,242	233,407	90,814	234,582
Ready-to-eat and cooked cereals	11,797,125	7,425,997	2,436,947	4,315,548	638,436	2,489,447	1,183,538	636,416	1,592,939
Rice	3,066,854	1,733,075	471,516	977,602	123,680	546,601	305,562	199,765	430,005
Pasta, cornmeal, and other cereal products	4,600,904	2,846,763	924,100	1,591,016	229,935	870,212	488,847	211,704	727,757
Bakery products	44,275,922	28,034,362	9,937,119	15,347,062	2,366,381	8,393,894	4,570,705	2,173,340	6,861,607
Bread	13,078,610	8,069,555	3,011,688	4,281,615	634,520	2,301,377	1,339,962	740,474	2,131,553
White bread	5,414,584	3,249,214	1,172,307	1,760,970	239,754	967,132	551,171	334,290	896,952
Bread other than white	7,664,026	4,820,342	1,839,381	2,520,645	394,766	1,334,245	788,791	406,184	1,234,602
Crackers and cookies	10,915,016	6,933,509	2,434,612	3,853,658	653,137	2,081,494	1,116,737	494,976	1,681,969
Cookies	6,290,473	3,924,194	1,413,771	2,104,389	320,524	1,134,338	647,114	287,317	967,880
Crackers	4,624,543	3,009,314	1,020,841	1,748,977	332,557	947,156	469,711	207,594	714,089
Frozen and refrigerated bakery products	3,579,448	2,422,559	800,126	1,436,273	237,484	814,131	384,038	189,326	461,775
Other bakery products	16,702,848	10,608,740	3,690,693	5,775,515	841,240	3,196,892	1,729,968	748,629	2,586,309
Biscuits and rolls	6,450,970	4,203,976	1,469,015	2,335,772	350,266	1,325,219	658,087	293,906	946,085
Cakes and cupcakes	4,720,343	2,967,619	1,039,774	1,593,941	223,521	877,462	490,602	181,237	773,565
Bread and cracker products	909,481	589,173	196,595	340,786	63,344	154,185	122,892	41,297	110,826
Sweetrolls, coffee cakes, doughnuts	2,952,392	1,823,717	663,184	932,846	123,112	512,864	295,204	147,312	462,144
Pies, tarts, turnovers	1,668,419	1,024,255	321,866	571,877	80,997	327,014	163,183	84,877	293,689
Meats, poultry, fish, and eggs	106,053,443	66,198,874	23,923,626	35,488,819	4,711,477	19,262,883	11,447,916	5,232,509	14,495,671
Beef	28,157,829	17,655,853	6,221,787	9,436,988	1,069,018	5,011,152	3,331,339	1,267,678	3,390,167
Ground beef	11,632,896	7,131,713	2,343,577	3,949,898	490,520	2,152,076	1,298,705	565,957	1,448,126
Roast	4,232,632	2,744,035	961,966	1,445,926	117,720	698,418	623,326	144,246	497,609
Chuck roast	1,171,999	761,997	274,403	406,603	34,397	182,299	188,113	32,490	122,278
Round roast	824,878	509,408	146,798	323,527	24,009	150,485	147,470	18,724	113,412
Other roast	2,235,756	1,473,235	540,766	715,504	59,314	365,634	287,743	92,967	262,288
Steak	9,883,607	6,322,582	2,320,494	3,337,653	394,425	1,806,418	1,128,763	425,626	1,203,570
Round steak	2,103,875	1,321,560	409,529	736,858	59,030	387,977	286,777	98,578	225,716
Sirloin steak	2,707,292	1,768,728	682,895	901,839	92,803	494,812	311,707	112,278	334,325
Other steak	5,072,440	3,232,294	1,228,070	1,698,956	242,592	923,629	530,279	214,835	643,160
Other beef	2,407,450	1,457,523	595,750	703,803	66,296	354,240	280,457	131,850	241,231
Pork	20,624,440	12,726,137	4,645,656	6,832,682	954,022	3,717,302	2,150,171	1,111,298	2,830,496
Bacon	4,003,707	2,366,965	853,294	1,276,557	220,910	666,013	388,778	194,741	594,766
Pork chops	3,488,625	2,026,755	733,729	1,093,147	148,144	609,636	333,388	234,799	511,647
Ham	4,157,983	2,627,409	894,273	1,452,947	148,144	854,971	446,098	187,239	615,823
Ham, not canned	4,004,951	2,528,912	880,268	1,379,232	146,554	840,322	389,217	177,714	602,893
Canned ham	153,032	98,498	14,265	73,715	1,533	14,649	56,881	9,525	12,930
Sausage	3,998,730	2,466,671	897,645	1,342,959	204,279	701,378	435,301	227,427	554,499
Other pork	4,975,396	3,237,732	1,266,974	1,667,364	232,546	885,305	546,518	267,158	553,761
Other meats	15,194,926	9,693,860	3,369,605	5,386,756	799,578	2,890,742	1,688,975	786,729	2,260,850
Frankfurters	3,074,319	1,882,936	570,333	1,062,725	169,088	564,654	327,771	186,391	409,687
Lunch meats (cold cuts)	10,852,808	6,974,600	2,404,008	3,974,469	569,019	2,230,648	1,169,405	567,784	1,640,594
Bologna, liverwurst, salami	3,191,270	1,978,413	686,526	1,143,168	152,741	635,679	352,788	211,312	496,500
Other lunch meats	7,661,537	4,996,187	1,717,482	2,831,301	416,278	1,594,969	816,617	356,471	1,144,094
Lamb, organ meats, and others	1,267,799	836,324	395,265	349,854	61,528	95,441	191,712	32,555	210,569

	total consumer units	total married couples	married couples, no children	married couples with children				single parent, at least one child under age 18	single person
				total	oldest child under age 6	oldest child aged 6 to 17	oldest child aged 18 or older		
Poultry	$19,826,934	$12,079,557	$4,159,616	$6,673,551	$1,022,985	$3,594,191	$2,048,434	$1,082,984	$2,845,642
Fresh and frozen chicken	15,741,112	9,542,790	3,141,887	5,321,231	803,949	2,912,641	1,598,474	865,800	2,248,290
Fresh and frozen whole chicken	4,705,413	2,881,207	997,239	1,553,574	194,517	848,312	507,456	263,961	640,574
Fresh and frozen chicken parts	11,035,699	6,661,583	2,144,648	3,767,658	609,432	2,064,182	1,091,018	601,839	1,607,716
Other poultry	4,085,821	2,536,163	1,017,729	1,352,320	219,094	681,698	449,960	217,119	597,722
Fish and seafood	15,644,068	10,054,011	4,087,254	5,048,018	568,678	2,928,918	1,539,222	653,444	2,085,376
Canned fish and seafood	2,261,883	1,304,036	542,581	613,414	70,439	325,830	215,675	109,929	407,101
Fresh fish and shellfish	7,874,289	5,170,220	2,059,837	2,595,530	265,977	1,479,108	843,478	374,804	1,005,192
Frozen fish and shellfish	5,507,896	3,579,755	1,484,836	1,838,781	232,262	1,123,980	480,069	168,645	673,083
Eggs	6,604,001	3,990,061	1,439,707	2,111,117	297,195	1,120,281	689,863	330,375	1,082,770
Dairy products	**52,121,595**	**33,883,188**	**11,620,106**	**19,189,312**	**3,238,044**	**10,256,689**	**5,681,999**	**2,300,101**	**7,635,173**
Fresh milk and cream	18,893,814	11,987,707	3,776,022	7,033,058	1,274,376	3,676,907	2,079,596	949,177	2,781,733
Fresh milk, all types	15,960,084	10,084,225	3,127,622	5,941,374	1,122,372	3,145,546	1,673,526	813,673	2,409,727
Cream	2,933,729	1,904,086	648,400	1,091,685	152,003	531,360	406,070	135,503	372,006
Other dairy products	33,227,781	21,895,482	7,844,084	12,156,254	1,963,669	6,579,782	3,602,491	1,350,859	4,853,440
Butter	3,180,073	2,071,472	738,398	1,134,393	170,280	609,932	352,612	133,546	469,902
Cheese	16,356,972	10,930,217	4,006,075	6,004,558	976,840	3,179,431	1,842,766	617,366	2,401,230
Ice cream and related products	7,137,746	4,619,116	1,619,963	2,554,870	357,361	1,434,273	759,648	321,829	1,006,300
Miscellaneous dairy products	6,552,991	4,274,677	1,479,649	2,462,433	459,132	1,356,145	647,378	278,118	976,377
Fruits and vegetables	**90,945,608**	**57,613,264**	**21,393,050**	**30,998,344**	**4,870,122**	**16,275,368**	**9,816,437**	**4,411,203**	**14,170,951**
Fresh fruits	32,508,657	20,967,307	7,701,176	11,552,200	1,850,546	6,049,605	3,639,622	1,641,504	4,942,470
Apples	5,176,950	3,400,284	1,223,660	1,959,591	269,213	1,094,534	592,691	259,459	734,407
Bananas	5,450,665	3,304,203	1,181,644	1,769,161	280,678	921,705	564,777	337,813	843,016
Oranges	3,326,884	2,202,601	771,337	1,241,455	152,855	687,025	398,960	146,660	445,521
Citrus fruits, except oranges	4,970,419	3,154,946	1,107,467	1,781,447	286,184	869,768	623,062	272,964	747,706
Other fresh fruits	13,584,983	8,904,670	3,417,068	4,800,253	861,617	2,476,426	1,460,133	624,673	2,171,081
Fresh vegetables	28,135,434	18,029,298	7,056,667	9,282,245	1,477,236	4,877,683	2,917,281	1,152,726	4,368,392
Potatoes	4,782,551	2,951,908	1,087,756	1,567,615	229,935	834,255	500,873	245,041	681,210
Lettuce	4,022,369	2,537,372	978,565	1,314,585	213,815	663,645	435,389	158,207	647,963
Tomatoes	4,895,770	3,103,582	1,123,807	1,616,758	253,433	811,024	549,942	200,026	797,208
Other fresh vegetables	14,433,500	9,436,436	3,866,798	4,783,580	780,053	2,568,759	1,430,990	549,451	2,242,010
Processed fruits	14,153,564	8,866,600	3,170,157	4,878,941	803,892	2,601,757	1,469,437	723,381	2,369,090
Frozen fruits and fruit juices	1,581,327	1,114,292	478,260	581,530	41,151	342,255	195,925	63,479	217,219
Frozen fruits	890,819	675,585	297,745	349,854	11,693	197,392	139,044	26,814	125,972
Frozen fruit juices	690,509	438,103	180,255	231,383	29,458	144,863	56,881	36,665	91,247
Canned fruits	2,531,866	1,647,872	554,771	962,683	180,327	511,828	270,450	130,415	369,420
Dried fruits	1,083,663	736,013	305,526	354,534	97,627	173,569	84,444	41,036	168,086
Fresh fruit juice	2,122,537	1,287,721	432,094	738,320	127,710	395,376	214,798	96,099	381,611
Canned and bottled fruit juice	6,832,927	4,081,307	1,399,766	2,242,166	357,077	1,178,729	703,820	392,353	1,232,755
Processed vegetables	16,149,197	9,750,058	3,464,790	5,284,666	738,391	2,746,175	1,790,185	893,658	2,490,999
Frozen vegetables	4,665,600	2,897,523	1,037,181	1,601,254	197,695	828,484	571,097	274,073	721,847
Canned and dried vegetables and juices	11,483,597	6,851,931	2,427,610	3,683,412	540,696	1,917,839	1,219,089	619,584	1,769,152
Canned vegetables	6,791,869	4,115,751	1,568,350	2,137,736	315,869	1,119,689	698,904	344,859	1,059,497
Dried vegetables	2,266,860	1,319,748	425,350	709,946	88,148	359,715	260,531	123,043	324,720
Fresh and canned vegetable juices	2,361,416	1,380,176	417,310	818,178	135,259	428,965	253,158	150,117	371,637
Sugar and other sweets	**18,260,536**	**11,676,502**	**4,346,874**	**6,246,472**	**794,299**	**3,615,795**	**1,825,736**	**866,909**	**2,753,657**
Candy and chewing gum	10,931,190	7,064,033	2,617,202	3,786,379	431,319	2,317,210	1,030,713	515,461	1,708,198
Sugar	3,033,262	1,777,187	605,087	975,554	140,311	487,561	346,029	183,651	427,050
Artificial sweeteners	610,883	403,055	191,148	164,981	6,471	77,832	79,704	19,637	98,266
Jams, preserves, other sweets	3,683,958	2,431,623	933,437	1,319,558	216,199	733,339	369,290	148,160	520,513
Fats and oils	**14,194,621**	**8,772,937**	**3,137,478**	**4,756,668**	**695,026**	**2,474,206**	**1,579,777**	**707,984**	**2,161,107**
Margarine	1,087,396	615,761	261,176	294,568	33,999	190,585	69,434	73,330	162,914
Fats and oils	4,577,265	2,739,201	960,669	1,476,933	177,545	820,346	475,943	222,664	700,790
Salad dressings	3,892,977	2,528,912	994,386	1,256,081	208,877	622,066	423,626	157,489	591,441
Nondairy cream and imitation milk	2,312,893	1,391,657	494,600	773,130	130,151	347,877	293,887	112,539	347,255
Peanut butter	2,324,091	1,497,406	426,647	955,955	144,511	493,184	316,798	142,027	358,707

	total consumer units	total married couples	married couples, no children	married couples with children				single parent, at least one child under age 18	single person
				total	oldest child under age 6	oldest child aged 6 to 17	oldest child aged 18 or older		
Miscellaneous foods	**$87,000,376**	**$54,776,773**	**$19,057,513**	**$31,182,047**	**$5,270,450**	**$16,395,964**	**$9,492,793**	**$4,558,645**	**$13,088,920**
Frozen prepared foods	16,277,345	9,400,180	3,118,545	5,473,927	803,324	3,008,230	1,655,267	1,021,724	2,898,469
Frozen meals	7,540,854	4,239,024	1,594,805	2,212,914	361,107	1,088,615	760,438	485,320	1,633,945
Other frozen prepared foods	8,736,492	5,161,155	1,523,999	3,261,013	442,274	1,919,615	894,829	536,403	1,264,525
Canned and packaged soups	5,760,461	3,654,685	1,534,374	1,841,121	262,912	961,509	613,494	258,938	957,167
Potato chips, nuts, and other snacks	19,152,599	12,685,650	4,474,479	7,214,713	1,019,693	4,006,140	2,178,524	893,136	2,612,538
Potato chips and other snacks	13,883,581	9,107,104	2,765,296	5,612,874	776,136	3,179,727	1,648,860	742,888	1,761,395
Nuts	5,269,018	3,578,546	1,709,182	1,602,132	243,557	826,412	529,752	150,248	851,144
Condiments and seasonings	17,591,178	11,371,341	4,057,947	6,300,588	910,714	3,381,558	1,998,751	838,595	2,405,663
Salt, spices, and other seasonings	4,817,388	3,118,085	1,144,556	1,647,473	243,046	869,176	532,649	239,170	593,289
Olives, pickles, relishes	2,172,303	1,395,887	566,442	720,769	104,382	357,939	257,195	80,637	353,535
Sauces and gravies	7,498,552	4,837,866	1,672,094	2,731,259	394,936	1,508,850	823,728	368,997	1,019,599
Baking needs and miscellaneous products	3,104,179	2,019,504	675,114	1,200,795	168,350	645,445	385,091	149,791	439,240
Other canned/packaged prepared foods	28,218,793	17,664,917	5,872,170	10,351,990	2,273,749	5,038,674	3,046,756	1,546,253	4,214,713
Prepared salads	4,365,757	2,650,372	1,214,324	1,235,604	189,408	665,865	378,683	196,699	841,908
Prepared desserts	1,777,905	1,099,185	426,388	565,149	86,559	316,804	161,252	97,338	304,033
Baby food	3,116,621	2,013,461	180,774	1,629,336	1,114,880	474,096	65,747	390,592	136,316
Miscellaneous prepared foods	18,389,929	11,611,844	3,885,472	6,804,015	871,380	3,574,659	2,342,760	861,559	2,721,887
Nonalcoholic beverages	**46,050,094**	**27,931,634**	**10,292,183**	**14,695,620**	**1,898,281**	**7,761,322**	**5,004,426**	**2,355,034**	**7,389,139**
Carbonated drinks	17,385,892	10,468,547	3,744,899	5,472,172	793,732	2,801,516	1,867,607	911,468	2,675,709
Tea	3,777,270	2,342,189	883,640	1,211,618	140,708	668,085	399,750	224,621	535,290
Coffee	10,761,984	6,777,604	3,054,483	3,160,971	410,999	1,573,809	1,168,440	388,830	1,844,514
Noncarbonated fruit-flavored drinks	3,213,665	1,889,584	569,814	1,110,991	149,222	613,188	346,731	215,879	422,986
Other nonalcoholic beverages and ice	1,911,030	1,206,747	363,882	721,939	84,516	388,125	247,540	82,855	295,905
Bottled water	7,066,829	4,071,034	1,361,381	2,268,785	233,965	1,279,053	749,466	424,256	1,304,053
Sports drinks	1,881,170	1,155,383	301,895	741,831	85,083	437,547	217,607	107,189	276,696
Food prepared by consumer unit on trips	**6,249,416**	**4,477,715**	**2,313,751**	**1,931,510**	**256,896**	**1,152,686**	**521,852**	**169,950**	**878,111**

Note: Numbers do not add to total because not all types of consumer units are shown.
Source: Calculations by New Strategist based on the Bureau of Labor Statistics' 2012 Consumer Expenditure Survey

Table 19. Groceries: Market shares by household type, 2012

(percentage of total annual spending on groceries accounted for by types of consumer units, 2012)

	total consumer units	total married couples	married couples, no children	married couples with children				single parent, at least one child under age 18	single person
				total	oldest child under age 6	oldest child aged 6 to 17	oldest child aged 18 or older		
Share of total consumer units	100.0%	48.6%	20.8%	23.5%	4.6%	11.9%	7.1%	5.2%	29.7%
Share of total before-tax income	100.0	66.9	26.0	35.2	5.9	18.3	11.0	2.7	15.4
Share of total spending	100.0	63.6	24.8	33.3	5.7	17.3	10.3	3.9	17.7
GROCERIES	**100.0**	**63.0**	**22.7**	**34.4**	**5.2**	**18.5**	**10.7**	**4.9**	**14.9**
Cereals and bakery products	**100.0**	**63.0**	**21.6**	**35.1**	**5.3**	**19.4**	**10.4**	**5.0**	**14.9**
Cereals and cereal products	100.0	62.4	20.1	35.9	5.2	20.3	10.4	5.2	13.8
Flour	100.0	66.2	24.3	38.0	4.5	20.8	12.7	4.1	11.6
Prepared flour mixes	100.0	67.4	21.5	40.0	6.2	22.1	11.6	4.5	11.7
Ready-to-eat and cooked cereals	100.0	62.9	20.7	36.6	5.4	21.1	10.0	5.4	13.5
Rice	100.0	56.5	15.4	31.9	4.0	17.8	10.0	6.5	14.0
Pasta, cornmeal, and other cereal products	100.0	61.9	20.1	34.6	5.0	18.9	10.6	4.6	15.8
Bakery products	100.0	63.3	22.4	34.7	5.3	19.0	10.3	4.9	15.5
Bread	100.0	61.7	23.0	32.7	4.9	17.6	10.2	5.7	16.3
White bread	100.0	60.0	21.7	32.5	4.4	17.9	10.2	6.2	16.6
Bread other than white	100.0	62.9	24.0	32.9	5.2	17.4	10.3	5.3	16.1
Crackers and cookies	100.0	63.5	22.3	35.3	6.0	19.1	10.2	4.5	15.4
Cookies	100.0	62.4	22.5	33.5	5.1	18.0	10.3	4.6	15.4
Crackers	100.0	65.1	22.1	37.8	7.2	20.5	10.2	4.5	15.4
Frozen and refrigerated bakery products	100.0	67.7	22.4	40.1	6.6	22.7	10.7	5.3	12.9
Other bakery products	100.0	63.5	22.1	34.6	5.0	19.1	10.4	4.5	15.5
Biscuits and rolls	100.0	65.2	22.8	36.2	5.4	20.5	10.2	4.6	14.7
Cakes and cupcakes	100.0	62.9	22.0	33.8	4.7	18.6	10.4	3.8	16.4
Bread and cracker products	100.0	64.8	21.6	37.5	7.0	17.0	13.5	4.5	12.2
Sweetrolls, coffee cakes, doughnuts	100.0	61.8	22.5	31.6	4.2	17.4	10.0	5.0	15.7
Pies, tarts, turnovers	100.0	61.4	19.3	34.3	4.9	19.6	9.8	5.1	17.6
Meats, poultry, fish, and eggs	**100.0**	**62.4**	**22.6**	**33.5**	**4.4**	**18.2**	**10.8**	**4.9**	**13.7**
Beef	100.0	62.7	22.1	33.5	3.8	17.8	11.8	4.5	12.0
Ground beef	100.0	61.3	20.1	34.0	4.2	18.5	11.2	4.9	12.4
Roast	100.0	64.8	22.7	34.2	2.8	16.5	14.7	3.4	11.8
Chuck roast	100.0	65.0	23.4	34.7	2.9	15.6	16.1	2.8	10.4
Round roast	100.0	61.8	17.8	39.2	2.9	18.2	17.9	2.3	13.7
Other roast	100.0	65.9	24.2	32.0	2.7	16.4	12.9	4.2	11.7
Steak	100.0	64.0	23.5	33.8	4.0	18.3	11.4	4.3	12.2
Round steak	100.0	62.8	19.5	35.0	2.8	18.4	13.6	4.7	10.7
Sirloin steak	100.0	65.3	25.2	33.3	3.4	18.3	11.5	4.1	12.3
Other steak	100.0	63.7	24.2	33.5	4.8	18.2	10.5	4.2	12.7
Other beef	100.0	60.5	24.7	29.2	2.8	14.7	11.6	5.5	10.0
Pork	100.0	61.7	22.5	33.1	4.6	18.0	10.4	5.4	13.7
Bacon	100.0	59.1	21.3	31.9	5.5	16.6	9.7	4.9	14.9
Pork chops	100.0	58.1	21.0	31.3	4.2	17.5	9.6	6.7	14.7
Ham	100.0	63.2	21.5	34.9	3.6	20.6	10.7	4.5	14.8
Ham, not canned	100.0	63.1	22.0	34.4	3.7	21.0	9.7	4.4	15.1
Canned ham	100.0	64.4	9.3	48.2	1.0	9.6	37.2	6.2	8.4
Sausage	100.0	61.7	22.4	33.6	5.1	17.5	10.9	5.7	13.9
Other pork	100.0	65.1	25.5	33.5	4.7	17.8	11.0	5.4	11.1
Other meats	100.0	63.8	22.2	35.5	5.3	19.0	11.1	5.2	14.9
Frankfurters	100.0	61.2	18.6	34.6	5.5	18.4	10.7	6.1	13.3
Lunch meats (cold cuts)	100.0	64.3	22.2	36.6	5.2	20.6	10.8	5.2	15.1
Bologna, liverwurst, salami	100.0	62.0	21.5	35.8	4.8	19.9	11.1	6.6	15.6
Other lunch meats	100.0	65.2	22.4	37.0	5.4	20.8	10.7	4.7	14.9
Lamb, organ meats, and others	100.0	66.0	31.2	27.6	4.9	7.5	15.1	2.6	16.6

	total consumer units	total married couples	married couples, no children	married couples with children				single parent, at least one child under age 18	single person
				total	oldest child under age 6	oldest child aged 6 to 17	oldest child aged 18 or older		
Poultry	100.0%	60.9%	21.0%	33.7%	5.2%	18.1%	10.3%	5.5%	14.4%
Fresh and frozen chicken	100.0	60.6	20.0	33.8	5.1	18.5	10.2	5.5	14.3
Fresh and frozen whole chicken	100.0	61.2	21.2	33.0	4.1	18.0	10.8	5.6	13.6
Fresh and frozen chicken parts	100.0	60.4	19.4	34.1	5.5	18.7	9.9	5.5	14.6
Other poultry	100.0	62.1	24.9	33.1	5.4	16.7	11.0	5.3	14.6
Fish and seafood	100.0	64.3	26.1	32.3	3.6	18.7	9.8	4.2	13.3
Canned fish and seafood	100.0	57.7	24.0	27.1	3.1	14.4	9.5	4.9	18.0
Fresh fish and shellfish	100.0	65.7	26.2	33.0	3.4	18.8	10.7	4.8	12.8
Frozen fish and shellfish	100.0	65.0	27.0	33.4	4.2	20.4	8.7	3.1	12.2
Eggs	100.0	60.4	21.8	32.0	4.5	17.0	10.4	5.0	16.4
Dairy products	**100.0**	**65.0**	**22.3**	**36.8**	**6.2**	**19.7**	**10.9**	**4.4**	**14.6**
Fresh milk and cream	100.0	63.4	20.0	37.2	6.7	19.5	11.0	5.0	14.7
Fresh milk, all types	100.0	63.2	19.6	37.2	7.0	19.7	10.5	5.1	15.1
Cream	100.0	64.9	22.1	37.2	5.2	18.1	13.8	4.6	12.7
Other dairy products	100.0	65.9	23.6	36.6	5.9	19.8	10.8	4.1	14.6
Butter	100.0	65.1	23.2	35.7	5.4	19.2	11.1	4.2	14.8
Cheese	100.0	66.8	24.5	36.7	6.0	19.4	11.3	3.8	14.7
Ice cream and related products	100.0	64.7	22.7	35.8	5.0	20.1	10.6	4.5	14.1
Miscellaneous dairy products	100.0	65.2	22.6	37.6	7.0	20.7	9.9	4.2	14.9
Fruits and vegetables	**100.0**	**63.3**	**23.5**	**34.1**	**5.4**	**17.9**	**10.8**	**4.9**	**15.6**
Fresh fruits	100.0	64.5	23.7	35.5	5.7	18.6	11.2	5.0	15.2
Apples	100.0	65.7	23.6	37.9	5.2	21.1	11.4	5.0	14.2
Bananas	100.0	60.6	21.7	32.5	5.1	16.9	10.4	6.2	15.5
Oranges	100.0	66.2	23.2	37.3	4.6	20.7	12.0	4.4	13.4
Citrus fruits, except oranges	100.0	63.5	22.3	35.8	5.8	17.5	12.5	5.5	15.0
Other fresh fruits	100.0	65.5	25.2	35.3	6.3	18.2	10.7	4.6	16.0
Fresh vegetables	100.0	64.1	25.1	33.0	5.3	17.3	10.4	4.1	15.5
Potatoes	100.0	61.7	22.7	32.8	4.8	17.4	10.5	5.1	14.2
Lettuce	100.0	63.1	24.3	32.7	5.3	16.5	10.8	3.9	16.1
Tomatoes	100.0	63.4	23.0	33.0	5.2	16.6	11.2	4.1	16.3
Other fresh vegetables	100.0	65.4	26.8	33.1	5.4	17.8	9.9	3.8	15.5
Processed fruits	100.0	62.6	22.4	34.5	5.7	18.4	10.4	5.1	16.7
Frozen fruits and fruit juices	100.0	70.5	30.2	36.8	2.6	21.6	12.4	4.0	13.7
Frozen fruits	100.0	75.8	33.4	39.3	1.3	22.2	15.6	3.0	14.1
Frozen fruit juices	100.0	63.4	26.1	33.5	4.3	21.0	8.2	5.3	13.2
Canned fruits	100.0	65.1	21.9	38.0	7.1	20.2	10.7	5.2	14.6
Dried fruits	100.0	67.9	28.2	32.7	9.0	16.0	7.8	3.8	15.5
Fresh fruit juice	100.0	60.7	20.4	34.8	6.0	18.6	10.1	4.5	18.0
Canned and bottled fruit juice	100.0	59.7	20.5	32.8	5.2	17.3	10.3	5.7	18.0
Processed vegetables	100.0	60.4	21.5	32.7	4.6	17.0	11.1	5.5	15.4
Frozen vegetables	100.0	62.1	22.2	34.3	4.2	17.8	12.2	5.9	15.5
Canned and dried vegetables and juices	100.0	59.7	21.1	32.1	4.7	16.7	10.6	5.4	15.4
Canned vegetables	100.0	60.6	23.1	31.5	4.7	16.5	10.3	5.1	15.6
Dried vegetables	100.0	58.2	18.8	31.3	3.9	15.9	11.5	5.4	14.3
Fresh and canned vegetable juices	100.0	58.4	17.7	34.6	5.7	18.2	10.7	6.4	15.7
Sugar and other sweets	**100.0**	**63.9**	**23.8**	**34.2**	**4.3**	**19.8**	**10.0**	**4.7**	**15.1**
Candy and chewing gum	100.0	64.6	23.9	34.6	3.9	21.2	9.4	4.7	15.6
Sugar	100.0	58.6	19.9	32.2	4.6	16.1	11.4	6.1	14.1
Artificial sweeteners	100.0	66.0	31.3	27.0	1.1	12.7	13.0	3.2	16.1
Jams, preserves, other sweets	100.0	66.0	25.3	35.8	5.9	19.9	10.0	4.0	14.1
Fats and oils	**100.0**	**61.8**	**22.1**	**33.5**	**4.9**	**17.4**	**11.1**	**5.0**	**15.2**
Margarine	100.0	56.6	24.0	27.1	3.1	17.5	6.4	6.7	15.0
Fats and oils	100.0	59.8	21.0	32.3	3.9	17.9	10.4	4.9	15.3
Salad dressings	100.0	65.0	25.5	32.3	5.4	16.0	10.9	4.0	15.2
Nondairy cream and imitation milk	100.0	60.2	21.4	33.4	5.6	15.0	12.7	4.9	15.0
Peanut butter	100.0	64.4	18.4	41.1	6.2	21.2	13.6	6.1	15.4

	total consumer units	total married couples	married couples, no children	married couples with children				single parent, at least one child under age 18	single person
				total	oldest child under age 6	oldest child aged 6 to 17	oldest child aged 18 or older		
Miscellaneous foods	**100.0%**	**63.0%**	**21.9%**	**35.8%**	**6.1%**	**18.8%**	**10.9%**	**5.2%**	**15.0%**
Frozen prepared foods	100.0	57.8	19.2	33.6	4.9	18.5	10.2	6.3	17.8
Frozen meals	100.0	56.2	21.1	29.3	4.8	14.4	10.1	6.4	21.7
Other frozen prepared foods	100.0	59.1	17.4	37.3	5.1	22.0	10.2	6.1	14.5
Canned and packaged soups	100.0	63.4	26.6	32.0	4.6	16.7	10.7	4.5	16.6
Potato chips, nuts, and other snacks	100.0	66.2	23.4	37.7	5.3	20.9	11.4	4.7	13.6
Potato chips and other snacks	100.0	65.6	19.9	40.4	5.6	22.9	11.9	5.4	12.7
Nuts	100.0	67.9	32.4	30.4	4.6	15.7	10.1	2.9	16.2
Condiments and seasonings	100.0	64.6	23.1	35.8	5.2	19.2	11.4	4.8	13.7
Salt, spices, and other seasonings	100.0	64.7	23.8	34.2	5.0	18.0	11.1	5.0	12.3
Olives, pickles, relishes	100.0	64.3	26.1	33.2	4.8	16.5	11.8	3.7	16.3
Sauces and gravies	100.0	64.5	22.3	36.4	5.3	20.1	11.0	4.9	13.6
Baking needs and miscellaneous products	100.0	65.1	21.7	38.7	5.4	20.8	12.4	4.8	14.1
Other canned/packaged prepared foods	100.0	62.6	20.8	36.7	8.1	17.9	10.8	5.5	14.9
Prepared salads	100.0	60.7	27.8	28.3	4.3	15.3	8.7	4.5	19.3
Prepared desserts	100.0	61.8	24.0	31.8	4.9	17.8	9.1	5.5	17.1
Baby food	100.0	64.6	5.8	52.3	35.8	15.2	2.1	12.5	4.4
Miscellaneous prepared foods	100.0	63.1	21.1	37.0	4.7	19.4	12.7	4.7	14.8
Nonalcoholic beverages	**100.0**	**60.7**	**22.3**	**31.9**	**4.1**	**16.9**	**10.9**	**5.1**	**16.0**
Carbonated drinks	100.0	60.2	21.5	31.5	4.6	16.1	10.7	5.2	15.4
Tea	100.0	62.0	23.4	32.1	3.7	17.7	10.6	5.9	14.2
Coffee	100.0	63.0	28.4	29.4	3.8	14.6	10.9	3.6	17.1
Noncarbonated fruit-flavored drinks	100.0	58.8	17.7	34.6	4.6	19.1	10.8	6.7	13.2
Other nonalcoholic beverages and ice	100.0	63.1	19.0	37.8	4.4	20.3	13.0	4.3	15.5
Bottled water	100.0	57.6	19.3	32.1	3.3	18.1	10.6	6.0	18.5
Sports drinks	100.0	61.4	16.0	39.4	4.5	23.3	11.6	5.7	14.7
Food prepared by consumer unit on trips	**100.0**	**71.7**	**37.0**	**30.9**	**4.1**	**18.4**	**8.4**	**2.7**	**14.1**

Note: Market shares by type of consumer unit do not add to total because not all types of consumer units are shown.
Source: Calculations by New Strategist based on the Bureau of Labor Statistics' 2012 Consumer Expenditure Survey

Table 20. Groceries: Average spending by race and Hispanic origin, 2012

(average annual spending of consumer units on groceries, by race and Hispanic origin of consumer unit reference person, 2012)

	total consumer units	Asian	black	Hispanic	non-Hispanic white and other
Number of consumer units (in 000s)	124,416	5,393	15,637	15,597	93,385
Number of persons per consumer unit	2.5	2.8	2.5	3.3	2.3
Average before-tax income of consumer units	$65,596.00	$86,156.00	$47,119.00	$48,066.00	$71,552.00
Average spending of consumer units, total	51,441.87	61,399.02	38,626.84	42,267.55	55,096.53
GROCERIES	**3,920.65**	**4,366.72**	**2,972.73**	**4,115.78**	**4,049.81**
Cereals and bakery products	**537.85**	**584.39**	**404.22**	**533.76**	**561.27**
Cereals and cereal products	181.98	235.52	159.22	200.97	182.70
Flour	9.36	9.17	8.52	10.59	9.30
Prepared flour mixes	16.18	10.59	12.58	12.80	17.34
Ready-to-eat and cooked cereals	94.82	68.70	79.75	103.76	95.95
Rice	24.65	91.55	29.04	40.74	21.20
Pasta, cornmeal, and other cereal products	36.98	55.51	29.33	33.09	38.92
Bakery products	355.87	348.87	245.01	332.79	378.57
Bread	105.12	101.20	81.10	106.26	108.98
White bread	43.52	43.57	40.26	44.26	43.95
Bread other than white	61.60	57.63	40.84	62.00	65.03
Crackers and cookies	87.73	79.10	63.04	78.70	93.39
Cookies	50.56	51.90	39.63	49.55	52.57
Crackers	37.17	27.20	23.41	29.15	40.82
Frozen and refrigerated bakery products	28.77	32.68	18.95	20.48	31.83
Other bakery products	134.25	135.88	81.92	127.35	144.38
Biscuits and rolls	51.85	47.57	28.10	45.15	56.97
Cakes and cupcakes	37.94	40.21	23.59	39.05	40.31
Bread and cracker products	7.31	7.84	4.27	5.66	8.11
Sweetrolls, coffee cakes, doughnuts	23.73	26.52	16.04	28.07	24.35
Pies, tarts, turnovers	13.41	13.74	9.92	9.42	14.64
Meats, poultry, fish, and eggs	**852.41**	**1,033.82**	**835.89**	**1,036.54**	**824.72**
Beef	226.32	220.65	188.42	291.02	222.29
Ground beef	93.50	61.81	86.06	106.69	92.68
Roast	34.02	45.58	28.39	48.34	32.60
Chuck roast	9.42	6.82	6.18	22.40	7.80
Round roast	6.63	3.46	5.91	5.95	6.85
Other roast	17.97	35.30	16.29	19.99	17.95
Steak	79.44	71.52	51.37	104.92	80.00
Round steak	16.91	15.30	11.15	23.61	16.76
Sirloin steak	21.76	15.13	12.37	31.38	21.73
Other steak	40.77	41.09	27.85	49.93	41.50
Other beef	19.35	41.74	22.60	31.06	17.02
Pork	165.77	207.52	178.99	184.02	160.47
Bacon	32.18	31.38	34.71	33.09	31.62
Pork chops	28.04	26.53	39.00	29.51	25.95
Ham	33.42	30.13	22.98	45.28	33.20
Ham, not canned	32.19	26.69	21.50	44.13	31.99
Canned ham	1.23	3.44	1.48	1.15	1.20
Sausage	32.14	35.21	38.45	33.48	30.85
Other pork	39.99	84.27	43.85	42.67	38.85
Other meats	122.13	93.58	96.84	120.29	126.87
Frankfurters	24.71	18.32	25.19	29.03	23.99
Lunch meats (cold cuts)	87.23	61.82	56.99	83.96	92.95
Bologna, liverwurst, salami	25.65	20.76	19.22	24.42	26.93
Other lunch meats	61.58	41.05	37.77	59.54	66.02
Lamb, organ meats, and others	10.19	13.44	14.66	7.31	9.92

	total consumer units	Asian	black	Hispanic	non-Hispanic white and other
Poultry	$159.36	$159.58	$189.03	$210.62	$145.73
Fresh and frozen chicken	126.52	135.04	150.72	184.94	112.59
Fresh and frozen whole chicken	37.82	38.62	41.98	59.75	33.43
Fresh and frozen chicken parts	88.70	96.42	108.74	125.18	79.16
Other poultry	32.84	24.54	38.32	25.68	33.13
Fish and seafood	125.74	282.72	137.57	155.97	118.52
Canned fish and seafood	18.18	28.87	15.21	20.39	18.30
Fresh fish and shellfish	63.29	155.53	79.02	75.70	58.48
Frozen fish and shellfish	44.27	98.31	43.34	59.88	41.74
Eggs	53.08	69.78	45.03	74.62	50.85
Dairy products	**418.93**	**372.47**	**253.58**	**427.22**	**445.57**
Fresh milk and cream	151.86	181.22	96.39	184.82	155.71
Fresh milk, all types	128.28	160.78	85.31	162.35	129.85
Cream	23.58	20.44	11.08	22.47	25.86
Other dairy products	267.07	191.24	157.20	242.40	289.86
Butter	25.56	22.65	17.95	15.76	28.47
Cheese	131.47	63.20	68.30	119.66	144.20
Ice cream and related products	57.37	55.05	38.88	53.54	61.19
Miscellaneous dairy products	52.67	50.34	32.07	53.44	56.01
Fruits and vegetables	**730.98**	**1,037.20**	**530.27**	**820.47**	**750.10**
Fresh fruits	261.29	409.42	165.90	307.27	269.89
Apples	41.61	59.54	26.45	39.61	44.59
Bananas	43.81	62.66	32.20	60.74	42.93
Oranges	26.74	39.52	21.07	32.72	26.66
Citrus fruits, except oranges	39.95	79.81	21.62	60.13	39.76
Other fresh fruits	109.19	167.89	64.57	114.06	115.95
Fresh vegetables	226.14	385.62	148.65	259.06	233.73
Potatoes	38.44	52.68	30.29	39.60	39.55
Lettuce	32.33	41.93	20.89	34.02	34.05
Tomatoes	39.35	58.16	24.92	56.70	38.89
Other fresh vegetables	116.01	232.85	72.55	128.74	121.23
Processed fruits	113.76	116.71	97.16	122.42	115.16
Frozen fruits and fruit juices	12.71	17.21	6.92	12.34	13.84
Frozen fruits	7.16	10.78	2.53	5.20	8.33
Frozen fruit juices	5.55	6.43	4.39	7.14	5.52
Canned fruits	20.35	16.55	14.60	17.40	21.82
Dried fruits	8.71	6.78	4.06	5.64	9.99
Fresh fruit juice	17.06	18.52	15.05	17.00	17.39
Canned and bottled fruit juice	54.92	57.64	56.53	70.05	52.11
Processed vegetables	129.80	125.45	118.55	131.72	131.32
Frozen vegetables	37.50	26.13	39.32	24.87	39.25
Canned and dried vegetables and juices	92.30	99.31	79.23	106.84	92.06
Canned vegetables	54.59	42.40	45.91	55.14	56.00
Dried vegetables	18.22	33.52	16.92	31.00	16.30
Fresh and canned vegetable juices	18.98	23.29	16.29	20.00	19.24
Sugar and other sweets	**146.77**	**149.69**	**103.45**	**125.77**	**157.60**
Candy and chewing gum	87.86	99.63	50.62	66.61	97.69
Sugar	24.38	23.53	29.23	31.75	22.37
Artificial sweeteners	4.91	4.04	3.78	4.56	5.14
Jams, preserves, other sweets	29.61	22.48	19.83	22.85	32.40
Fats and oils	**114.09**	**107.79**	**92.16**	**128.80**	**115.49**
Margarine	8.74	4.93	8.61	7.17	9.01
Fats and oils	36.79	56.61	37.76	60.44	32.70
Salad dressings	31.29	15.93	22.27	29.27	33.22
Nondairy cream and imitation milk	18.59	15.23	11.98	16.42	20.09
Peanut butter	18.68	15.09	11.54	15.50	20.46

	total consumer units	Asian	black	Hispanic	non-Hispanic white and other
Miscellaneous foods	**$699.27**	**$709.39**	**$467.24**	**$625.60**	**$751.17**
Frozen prepared foods	130.83	103.07	106.31	101.18	139.92
Frozen meals	60.61	51.55	46.52	41.95	66.03
Other frozen prepared foods	70.22	51.52	59.79	59.23	73.90
Canned and packaged soups	46.30	46.13	27.29	34.12	51.52
Potato chips, nuts, and other snacks	153.94	140.82	88.56	130.80	168.91
Potato chips and other snacks	111.59	92.40	69.45	101.70	120.43
Nuts	42.35	48.42	19.11	29.10	48.49
Condiments and seasonings	141.39	149.89	108.68	122.60	150.13
Salt, spices, and other seasonings	38.72	61.41	34.18	42.01	38.97
Olives, pickles, relishes	17.46	8.48	10.94	11.77	19.49
Sauces and gravies	60.27	51.90	48.38	50.76	63.85
Baking needs and miscellaneous products	24.95	28.10	15.18	18.06	27.81
Other canned/packaged prepared foods	226.81	269.49	136.41	236.91	240.68
Prepared salads	35.09	32.48	21.63	22.64	39.50
Prepared desserts	14.29	12.48	9.02	12.57	15.48
Baby food	25.05	45.15	12.26	30.28	26.37
Miscellaneous prepared foods	147.81	175.55	93.07	170.85	153.41
Nonalcoholic beverages	**370.13**	**318.91**	**267.33**	**389.01**	**384.83**
Carbonated drinks	139.74	83.55	101.79	149.70	144.62
Tea	30.36	46.79	20.00	30.07	32.15
Coffee	86.50	75.06	40.47	61.78	98.41
Noncarbonated fruit-flavored drinks	25.83	23.52	26.75	34.69	24.18
Other nonalcoholic beverages and ice	15.36	13.31	12.18	16.22	15.77
Bottled water	56.80	69.52	53.84	75.45	54.39
Sports drinks	15.12	7.18	12.29	21.10	14.76
Food prepared by consumer unit on trips	**50.23**	**53.06**	**18.58**	**28.60**	**59.08**

Note: "Asian" and "black" include Hispanics and non-Hispanics who identify themselves as being of the respective race alone. "Hispanic" includes people of any race who identify themselves as Hispanic. "Other" includes people who identify themselves as non-Hispanic and as Alaska Native, American Indian, Asian (who are also included in the "Asian" column), Native Hawaiian or other Pacific Islander, as well as non-Hispanics reporting more than one race.
Source: Bureau of Labor Statistics, unpublished tables from the 2012 Consumer Expenditure Survey

Table 21. Groceries: Indexed spending by race and Hispanic origin, 2012

(indexed average annual spending of consumer units on groceries by race and Hispanic origin of consumer unit reference person, 2012; index definition: an index of 100 is the average for all consumer units; an index of 125 means that spending by consumer units in that group is 25 percent above the average for all consumer units; an index of 75 indicates spending that is 25 percent below the average for all consumer units)

	total consumer units	Asian	black	Hispanic	non-Hispanic white and other
Average spending of consumer units, total	$51,442	$61,399	$38,627	$42,268	$55,097
Average spending of consumer units, index	100	119	75	82	107
GROCERIES	**100**	**111**	**76**	**105**	**103**
Cereals and bakery products	**100**	**109**	**75**	**99**	**104**
Cereals and cereal products	100	129	87	110	100
Flour	100	98	91	113	99
Prepared flour mixes	100	65	78	79	107
Ready-to-eat and cooked cereals	100	72	84	109	101
Rice	100	371	118	165	86
Pasta, cornmeal, and other cereal products	100	150	79	89	105
Bakery products	100	98	69	94	106
Bread	100	96	77	101	104
White bread	100	100	93	102	101
Bread other than white	100	94	66	101	106
Crackers and cookies	100	90	72	90	106
Cookies	100	103	78	98	104
Crackers	100	73	63	78	110
Frozen and refrigerated bakery products	100	114	66	71	111
Other bakery products	100	101	61	95	108
Biscuits and rolls	100	92	54	87	110
Cakes and cupcakes	100	106	62	103	106
Bread and cracker products	100	107	58	77	111
Sweetrolls, coffee cakes, doughnuts	100	112	68	118	103
Pies, tarts, turnovers	100	102	74	70	109
Meats, poultry, fish, and eggs	**100**	**121**	**98**	**122**	**97**
Beef	100	97	83	129	98
Ground beef	100	66	92	114	99
Roast	100	134	83	142	96
Chuck roast	100	72	66	238	83
Round roast	100	52	89	90	103
Other roast	100	196	91	111	100
Steak	100	90	65	132	101
Round steak	100	90	66	140	99
Sirloin steak	100	70	57	144	100
Other steak	100	101	68	122	102
Other beef	100	216	117	161	88
Pork	100	125	108	111	97
Bacon	100	98	108	103	98
Pork chops	100	95	139	105	93
Ham	100	90	69	135	99
Ham, not canned	100	83	67	137	99
Canned ham	100	280	120	93	98
Sausage	100	110	120	104	96
Other pork	100	211	110	107	97
Other meats	100	77	79	98	104
Frankfurters	100	74	102	117	97
Lunch meats (cold cuts)	100	71	65	96	107
Bologna, liverwurst, salami	100	81	75	95	105
Other lunch meats	100	67	61	97	107
Lamb, organ meats, and others	100	132	144	72	97

	total consumer units	Asian	black	Hispanic	non-Hispanic white and other
Poultry	100	100	119	132	91
Fresh and frozen chicken	100	107	119	146	89
Fresh and frozen whole chicken	100	102	111	158	88
Fresh and frozen chicken parts	100	109	123	141	89
Other poultry	100	75	117	78	101
Fish and seafood	100	225	109	124	94
Canned fish and seafood	100	159	84	112	101
Fresh fish and shellfish	100	246	125	120	92
Frozen fish and shellfish	100	222	98	135	94
Eggs	100	131	85	141	96
Dairy products	**100**	**89**	**61**	**102**	**106**
Fresh milk and cream	100	119	63	122	103
Fresh milk, all types	100	125	67	127	101
Cream	100	87	47	95	110
Other dairy products	100	72	59	91	109
Butter	100	89	70	62	111
Cheese	100	48	52	91	110
Ice cream and related products	100	96	68	93	107
Miscellaneous dairy products	100	96	61	101	106
Fruits and vegetables	**100**	**142**	**73**	**112**	**103**
Fresh fruits	100	157	63	118	103
Apples	100	143	64	95	107
Bananas	100	143	73	139	98
Oranges	100	148	79	122	100
Citrus fruits, except oranges	100	200	54	151	100
Other fresh fruits	100	154	59	104	106
Fresh vegetables	100	171	66	115	103
Potatoes	100	137	79	103	103
Lettuce	100	130	65	105	105
Tomatoes	100	148	63	144	99
Other fresh vegetables	100	201	63	111	104
Processed fruits	100	103	85	108	101
Frozen fruits and fruit juices	100	135	54	97	109
Frozen fruits	100	151	35	73	116
Frozen fruit juices	100	116	79	129	99
Canned fruits	100	81	72	86	107
Dried fruits	100	78	47	65	115
Fresh fruit juice	100	109	88	100	102
Canned and bottled fruit juice	100	105	103	128	95
Processed vegetables	100	97	91	101	101
Frozen vegetables	100	70	105	66	105
Canned and dried vegetables and juices	100	108	86	116	100
Canned vegetables	100	78	84	101	103
Dried vegetables	100	184	93	170	89
Fresh and canned vegetable juices	100	123	86	105	101
Sugar and other sweets	**100**	**102**	**70**	**86**	**107**
Candy and chewing gum	100	113	58	76	111
Sugar	100	97	120	130	92
Artificial sweeteners	100	82	77	93	105
Jams, preserves, other sweets	100	76	67	77	109
Fats and oils	**100**	**94**	**81**	**113**	**101**
Margarine	100	56	99	82	103
Fats and oils	100	154	103	164	89
Salad dressings	100	51	71	94	106
Nondairy cream and imitation milk	100	82	64	88	108
Peanut butter	100	81	62	83	110

	total consumer units	Asian	black	Hispanic	non-Hispanic white and other
Miscellaneous foods	**100**	**101**	**67**	**89**	**107**
Frozen prepared foods	100	79	81	77	107
Frozen meals	100	85	77	69	109
Other frozen prepared foods	100	73	85	84	105
Canned and packaged soups	100	100	59	74	111
Potato chips, nuts, and other snacks	100	91	58	85	110
Potato chips and other snacks	100	83	62	91	108
Nuts	100	114	45	69	114
Condiments and seasonings	100	106	77	87	106
Salt, spices, and other seasonings	100	159	88	108	101
Olives, pickles, relishes	100	49	63	67	112
Sauces and gravies	100	86	80	84	106
Baking needs and miscellaneous products	100	113	61	72	111
Other canned/packaged prepared foods	100	119	60	104	106
Prepared salads	100	93	62	65	113
Prepared desserts	100	87	63	88	108
Baby food	100	180	49	121	105
Miscellaneous prepared foods	100	119	63	116	104
Nonalcoholic beverages	**100**	**86**	**72**	**105**	**104**
Carbonated drinks	100	60	73	107	103
Tea	100	154	66	99	106
Coffee	100	87	47	71	114
Noncarbonated fruit-flavored drinks	100	91	104	134	94
Other nonalcoholic beverages and ice	100	87	79	106	103
Bottled water	100	122	95	133	96
Sports drinks	100	47	81	140	98
Food prepared by consumer unit on trips	**100**	**106**	**37**	**57**	**118**

Note: "Asian" and "black" include Hispanics and non-Hispanics who identify themselves as being of the respective race alone. "Hispanic" includes people of any race who identify themselves as Hispanic. "Other" includes people who identify themselves as non-Hispanic and as Alaska Native, American Indian, Asian (who are also included in the "Asian" column), Native Hawaiian or other Pacific Islander, as well as non-Hispanics reporting more than one race.
Source: Calculations by New Strategist based on the Bureau of Labor Statistics' 2012 Consumer Expenditure Survey

Table 22. Groceries: Total spending by race and Hispanic origin, 2012

(total annual spending on groceries, by consumer unit race and Hispanic origin groups, 2012; consumer units and dollars in thousands)

	total consumer units	Asian	black	Hispanic	non-Hispanic white and other
Number of consumer units	124,416	5,393	15,637	15,597	93,385
Total spending of all consumer units	$6,400,191,698	$331,124,915	$604,007,897	$659,246,977	$5,145,189,454
GROCERIES	**487,791,590**	**23,549,721**	**46,484,579**	**64,193,821**	**378,191,507**
Cereals and bakery products	**66,917,146**	**3,151,615**	**6,320,788**	**8,325,055**	**52,414,199**
Cereals and cereal products	22,641,224	1,270,159	2,489,723	3,134,529	17,061,440
Flour	1,164,534	49,454	133,227	165,172	868,481
Prepared flour mixes	2,013,051	57,112	196,713	199,642	1,619,296
Ready-to-eat and cooked cereals	11,797,125	370,499	1,247,051	1,618,345	8,960,291
Rice	3,066,854	493,729	454,098	635,422	1,979,762
Pasta, cornmeal, and other cereal products	4,600,904	299,365	458,633	516,105	3,634,544
Bakery products	44,275,922	1,881,456	3,831,221	5,190,526	35,352,759
Bread	13,078,610	545,772	1,268,161	1,657,337	10,177,097
White bread	5,414,584	234,973	629,546	690,323	4,104,271
Bread other than white	7,664,026	310,799	638,615	967,014	6,072,827
Crackers and cookies	10,915,016	426,586	985,756	1,227,484	8,721,225
Cookies	6,290,473	279,897	619,694	772,831	4,909,249
Crackers	4,624,543	146,690	366,062	454,653	3,811,976
Frozen and refrigerated bakery products	3,579,448	176,243	296,321	319,427	2,972,445
Other bakery products	16,702,848	732,801	1,280,983	1,986,278	13,482,926
Biscuits and rolls	6,450,970	256,545	439,400	704,205	5,320,143
Cakes and cupcakes	4,720,343	216,853	368,877	609,063	3,764,349
Bread and cracker products	909,481	42,281	66,770	88,279	757,352
Sweetrolls, coffee cakes, doughnuts	2,952,392	143,022	250,817	437,808	2,273,925
Pies, tarts, turnovers	1,668,419	74,100	155,119	146,924	1,367,156
Meats, poultry, fish, and eggs	**106,053,443**	**5,575,391**	**13,070,812**	**16,166,914**	**77,016,477**
Beef	28,157,829	1,189,965	2,946,324	4,539,039	20,758,552
Ground beef	11,632,896	333,341	1,345,720	1,664,044	8,654,922
Roast	4,232,632	245,813	443,934	753,959	3,044,351
Chuck roast	1,171,999	36,780	96,637	349,373	728,403
Round roast	824,878	18,660	92,415	92,802	639,687
Other roast	2,235,756	190,373	254,727	311,784	1,676,261
Steak	9,883,607	385,707	803,273	1,636,437	7,470,800
Round steak	2,103,875	82,513	174,353	368,245	1,565,133
Sirloin steak	2,707,292	81,596	193,430	489,434	2,029,256
Other steak	5,072,440	221,598	435,490	778,758	3,875,478
Other beef	2,407,450	225,104	353,396	484,443	1,589,413
Pork	20,624,440	1,119,155	2,798,867	2,870,160	14,985,491
Bacon	4,003,707	169,232	542,760	516,105	2,952,834
Pork chops	3,488,625	143,076	609,843	460,267	2,423,341
Ham	4,157,983	162,491	359,338	706,232	3,100,382
Ham, not canned	4,004,951	143,939	336,196	688,296	2,987,386
Canned ham	153,032	18,552	23,143	17,937	112,062
Sausage	3,998,730	189,888	601,243	522,188	2,880,927
Other pork	4,975,396	454,468	685,682	665,524	3,628,007
Other meats	15,194,926	504,677	1,514,287	1,876,163	11,847,755
Frankfurters	3,074,319	98,800	393,896	452,781	2,240,306
Lunch meats (cold cuts)	10,852,808	333,395	891,153	1,309,524	8,680,136
Bologna, liverwurst, salami	3,191,270	111,959	300,543	380,879	2,514,858
Other lunch meats	7,661,537	221,383	590,609	928,645	6,165,278
Lamb, organ meats, and others	1,267,799	72,482	229,238	114,014	926,379

	total consumer units	Asian	black	Hispanic	non-Hispanic white and other
Poultry	$19,826,934	$860,615	$2,955,862	$3,285,040	$13,608,996
Fresh and frozen chicken	15,741,112	728,271	2,356,809	2,884,509	10,514,217
Fresh and frozen whole chicken	4,705,413	208,278	656,441	931,921	3,121,861
Fresh and frozen chicken parts	11,035,699	519,993	1,700,367	1,952,432	7,392,357
Other poultry	4,085,821	132,344	599,210	400,531	3,093,845
Fish and seafood	15,644,068	1,524,709	2,151,182	2,432,664	11,067,990
Canned fish and seafood	2,261,883	155,696	237,839	318,023	1,708,946
Fresh fish and shellfish	7,874,289	838,773	1,235,636	1,180,693	5,461,155
Frozen fish and shellfish	5,507,896	530,186	677,708	933,948	3,897,890
Eggs	6,604,001	376,324	704,134	1,163,848	4,748,627
Dairy products	**52,121,595**	**2,008,731**	**3,965,230**	**6,663,350**	**41,609,554**
Fresh milk and cream	18,893,814	977,319	1,507,250	2,882,638	14,540,978
Fresh milk, all types	15,960,084	867,087	1,333,992	2,532,173	12,126,042
Cream	2,933,729	110,233	173,258	350,465	2,414,936
Other dairy products	33,227,781	1,031,357	2,458,136	3,780,713	27,068,576
Butter	3,180,073	122,151	280,684	245,809	2,658,671
Cheese	16,356,972	340,838	1,068,007	1,866,337	13,466,117
Ice cream and related products	7,137,746	296,885	607,967	835,063	5,714,228
Miscellaneous dairy products	6,552,991	271,484	501,479	833,504	5,230,494
Fruits and vegetables	**90,945,608**	**5,593,620**	**8,291,832**	**12,796,871**	**70,048,089**
Fresh fruits	32,508,657	2,208,002	2,594,178	4,792,490	25,203,678
Apples	5,176,950	321,099	413,599	617,797	4,164,037
Bananas	5,450,665	337,925	503,511	947,362	4,009,018
Oranges	3,326,884	213,131	329,472	510,334	2,489,644
Citrus fruits, except oranges	4,970,419	430,415	338,072	937,848	3,712,988
Other fresh fruits	13,584,983	905,431	1,009,681	1,778,994	10,827,991
Fresh vegetables	28,135,434	2,079,649	2,324,440	4,040,559	21,826,876
Potatoes	4,782,551	284,103	473,645	617,641	3,693,377
Lettuce	4,022,369	226,128	326,657	530,610	3,179,759
Tomatoes	4,895,770	313,657	389,674	884,350	3,631,743
Other fresh vegetables	14,433,500	1,255,760	1,134,464	2,007,958	11,321,064
Processed fruits	14,153,564	629,417	1,519,291	1,909,385	10,754,217
Frozen fruits and fruit juices	1,581,327	92,814	108,208	192,467	1,292,448
Frozen fruits	890,819	58,137	39,562	81,104	777,897
Frozen fruit juices	690,509	34,677	68,646	111,363	515,485
Canned fruits	2,531,866	89,254	228,300	271,388	2,037,661
Dried fruits	1,083,663	36,565	63,486	87,967	932,916
Fresh fruit juice	2,122,537	99,878	235,337	265,149	1,623,965
Canned and bottled fruit juice	6,832,927	310,853	883,960	1,092,570	4,866,292
Processed vegetables	16,149,197	676,552	1,853,766	2,054,437	12,263,318
Frozen vegetables	4,665,600	140,919	614,847	387,897	3,665,361
Canned and dried vegetables and juices	11,483,597	535,579	1,238,920	1,666,383	8,597,023
Canned vegetables	6,791,869	228,663	717,895	860,019	5,229,560
Dried vegetables	2,266,860	180,773	264,578	483,507	1,522,176
Fresh and canned vegetable juices	2,361,416	125,603	254,727	311,940	1,796,727
Sugar and other sweets	**18,260,536**	**807,278**	**1,617,648**	**1,961,635**	**14,717,476**
Candy and chewing gum	10,931,190	537,305	791,545	1,038,916	9,122,781
Sugar	3,033,262	126,897	457,070	495,205	2,089,022
Artificial sweeteners	610,883	21,788	59,108	71,122	479,999
Jams, preserves, other sweets	3,683,958	121,235	310,082	356,391	3,025,674
Fats and oils	**14,194,621**	**581,311**	**1,441,106**	**2,008,894**	**10,785,034**
Margarine	1,087,396	26,587	134,635	111,830	841,399
Fats and oils	4,577,265	305,298	590,453	942,683	3,053,690
Salad dressings	3,892,977	85,910	348,236	456,524	3,102,250
Nondairy cream and imitation milk	2,312,893	82,135	187,331	256,103	1,876,105
Peanut butter	2,324,091	81,380	180,451	241,754	1,910,657

	total consumer units	Asian	black	Hispanic	non-Hispanic white and other
Miscellaneous foods	**$87,000,376**	**$3,825,740**	**$7,306,232**	**$9,757,483**	**$70,148,010**
Frozen prepared foods	16,277,345	555,857	1,662,369	1,578,104	13,066,429
Frozen meals	7,540,854	278,009	727,433	654,294	6,166,212
Other frozen prepared foods	8,736,492	277,847	934,936	923,810	6,901,152
Canned and packaged soups	5,760,461	248,779	426,734	532,170	4,811,195
Potato chips, nuts, and other snacks	19,152,599	759,442	1,384,813	2,040,088	15,773,660
Potato chips and other snacks	13,883,581	498,313	1,085,990	1,586,215	11,246,356
Nuts	5,269,018	261,129	298,823	453,873	4,528,239
Condiments and seasonings	17,591,178	808,357	1,699,429	1,912,192	14,019,890
Salt, spices, and other seasonings	4,817,388	331,184	534,473	655,230	3,639,213
Olives, pickles, relishes	2,172,303	45,733	171,069	183,577	1,820,074
Sauces and gravies	7,498,552	279,897	756,518	791,704	5,962,632
Baking needs and miscellaneous products	3,104,179	151,543	237,370	281,682	2,597,037
Other canned/packaged prepared foods	28,218,793	1,453,360	2,133,043	3,695,085	22,475,902
Prepared salads	4,365,757	175,165	338,228	353,116	3,688,708
Prepared desserts	1,777,905	67,305	141,046	196,054	1,445,600
Baby food	3,116,621	243,494	191,710	472,277	2,462,562
Miscellaneous prepared foods	18,389,929	946,741	1,455,336	2,664,747	14,326,193
Nonalcoholic beverages	**46,050,094**	**1,719,882**	**4,180,239**	**6,067,389**	**35,937,350**
Carbonated drinks	17,385,892	450,585	1,591,690	2,334,871	13,505,339
Tea	3,777,270	252,338	312,740	469,002	3,002,328
Coffee	10,761,984	404,799	632,829	963,583	9,190,018
Noncarbonated fruit-flavored drinks	3,213,665	126,843	418,290	541,060	2,258,049
Other nonalcoholic beverages and ice	1,911,030	71,781	190,459	252,983	1,472,681
Bottled water	7,066,829	374,921	841,896	1,176,794	5,079,210
Sports drinks	1,881,170	38,722	192,179	329,097	1,378,363
Food prepared by consumer unit on trips	**6,249,416**	**286,153**	**290,535**	**446,074**	**5,517,186**

Note: "Asian" and "black" include Hispanics and non-Hispanics who identify themselves as being of the respective race alone. "Hispanic" includes people of any race who identify themselves as Hispanic. "Other" includes people who identify themselves as non-Hispanic and as Alaska Native, American Indian, Asian (who are also included in the "Asian" column), Native Hawaiian or other Pacific Islander, as well as non-Hispanics reporting more than one race. Numbers may not add to total because of rounding.
Source: Calculations by New Strategist based on the Bureau of Labor Statistics' 2012 Consumer Expenditure Survey

Table 23. Groceries: Market shares by race and Hispanic origin, 2012

(percentage of total annual spending on groceries accounted for by consumer unit race and Hispanic origin groups, 2012)

	total consumer units	Asian	black	Hispanic	non-Hispanic white and other
Share of total consumer units	100.0%	4.3%	12.6%	12.5%	75.1%
Share of total before-tax income	100.0	5.7	9.0	9.2	81.9
Share of total spending	100.0	5.2	9.4	10.3	80.4
GROCERIES	100.0	4.8	9.5	13.2	77.5
Cereals and bakery products	100.0	4.7	9.4	12.4	78.3
Cereals and cereal products	100.0	5.6	11.0	13.8	75.4
Flour	100.0	4.2	11.4	14.2	74.6
Prepared flour mixes	100.0	2.8	9.8	9.9	80.4
Ready-to-eat and cooked cereals	100.0	3.1	10.6	13.7	76.0
Rice	100.0	16.1	14.8	20.7	64.6
Pasta, cornmeal, and other cereal products	100.0	6.5	10.0	11.2	79.0
Bakery products	100.0	4.2	8.7	11.7	79.8
Bread	100.0	4.2	9.7	12.7	77.8
White bread	100.0	4.3	11.6	12.7	75.8
Bread other than white	100.0	4.1	8.3	12.6	79.2
Crackers and cookies	100.0	3.9	9.0	11.2	79.9
Cookies	100.0	4.4	9.9	12.3	78.0
Crackers	100.0	3.2	7.9	9.8	82.4
Frozen and refrigerated bakery products	100.0	4.9	8.3	8.9	83.0
Other bakery products	100.0	4.4	7.7	11.9	80.7
Biscuits and rolls	100.0	4.0	6.8	10.9	82.5
Cakes and cupcakes	100.0	4.6	7.8	12.9	79.7
Bread and cracker products	100.0	4.6	7.3	9.7	83.3
Sweetrolls, coffee cakes, doughnuts	100.0	4.8	8.5	14.8	77.0
Pies, tarts, turnovers	100.0	4.4	9.3	8.8	81.9
Meats, poultry, fish, and eggs	100.0	5.3	12.3	15.2	72.6
Beef	100.0	4.2	10.5	16.1	73.7
Ground beef	100.0	2.9	11.6	14.3	74.4
Roast	100.0	5.8	10.5	17.8	71.9
Chuck roast	100.0	3.1	8.2	29.8	62.2
Round roast	100.0	2.3	11.2	11.3	77.5
Other roast	100.0	8.5	11.4	13.9	75.0
Steak	100.0	3.9	8.1	16.6	75.6
Round steak	100.0	3.9	8.3	17.5	74.4
Sirloin steak	100.0	3.0	7.1	18.1	75.0
Other steak	100.0	4.4	8.6	15.4	76.4
Other beef	100.0	9.4	14.7	20.1	66.0
Pork	100.0	5.4	13.6	13.9	72.7
Bacon	100.0	4.2	13.6	12.9	73.8
Pork chops	100.0	4.1	17.5	13.2	69.5
Ham	100.0	3.9	8.6	17.0	74.6
Ham, not canned	100.0	3.6	8.4	17.2	74.6
Canned ham	100.0	12.1	15.1	11.7	73.2
Sausage	100.0	4.7	15.0	13.1	72.0
Other pork	100.0	9.1	13.8	13.4	72.9
Other meats	100.0	3.3	10.0	12.3	78.0
Frankfurters	100.0	3.2	12.8	14.7	72.9
Lunch meats (cold cuts)	100.0	3.1	8.2	12.1	80.0
Bologna, liverwurst, salami	100.0	3.5	9.4	11.9	78.8
Other lunch meats	100.0	2.9	7.7	12.1	80.5
Lamb, organ meats, and others	100.0	5.7	18.1	9.0	73.1

	total consumer units	Asian	black	Hispanic	non-Hispanic white and other
Poultry	100.0%	4.3%	14.9%	16.6%	68.6%
Fresh and frozen chicken	100.0	4.6	15.0	18.3	66.8
Fresh and frozen whole chicken	100.0	4.4	14.0	19.8	66.3
Fresh and frozen chicken parts	100.0	4.7	15.4	17.7	67.0
Other poultry	100.0	3.2	14.7	9.8	75.7
Fish and seafood	100.0	9.7	13.8	15.6	70.7
Canned fish and seafood	100.0	6.9	10.5	14.1	75.6
Fresh fish and shellfish	100.0	10.7	15.7	15.0	69.4
Frozen fish and shellfish	100.0	9.6	12.3	17.0	70.8
Eggs	100.0	5.7	10.7	17.6	71.9
Dairy products	**100.0**	**3.9**	**7.6**	**12.8**	**79.8**
Fresh milk and cream	100.0	5.2	8.0	15.3	77.0
Fresh milk, all types	100.0	5.4	8.4	15.9	76.0
Cream	100.0	3.8	5.9	11.9	82.3
Other dairy products	100.0	3.1	7.4	11.4	81.5
Butter	100.0	3.8	8.8	7.7	83.6
Cheese	100.0	2.1	6.5	11.4	82.3
Ice cream and related products	100.0	4.2	8.5	11.7	80.1
Miscellaneous dairy products	100.0	4.1	7.7	12.7	79.8
Fruits and vegetables	**100.0**	**6.2**	**9.1**	**14.1**	**77.0**
Fresh fruits	100.0	6.8	8.0	14.7	77.5
Apples	100.0	6.2	8.0	11.9	80.4
Bananas	100.0	6.2	9.2	17.4	73.6
Oranges	100.0	6.4	9.9	15.3	74.8
Citrus fruits, except oranges	100.0	8.7	6.8	18.9	74.7
Other fresh fruits	100.0	6.7	7.4	13.1	79.7
Fresh vegetables	100.0	7.4	8.3	14.4	77.6
Potatoes	100.0	5.9	9.9	12.9	77.2
Lettuce	100.0	5.6	8.1	13.2	79.1
Tomatoes	100.0	6.4	8.0	18.1	74.2
Other fresh vegetables	100.0	8.7	7.9	13.9	78.4
Processed fruits	100.0	4.4	10.7	13.5	76.0
Frozen fruits and fruit juices	100.0	5.9	6.8	12.2	81.7
Frozen fruits	100.0	6.5	4.4	9.1	87.3
Frozen fruit juices	100.0	5.0	9.9	16.1	74.7
Canned fruits	100.0	3.5	9.0	10.7	80.5
Dried fruits	100.0	3.4	5.9	8.1	86.1
Fresh fruit juice	100.0	4.7	11.1	12.5	76.5
Canned and bottled fruit juice	100.0	4.5	12.9	16.0	71.2
Processed vegetables	100.0	4.2	11.5	12.7	75.9
Frozen vegetables	100.0	3.0	13.2	8.3	78.6
Canned and dried vegetables and juices	100.0	4.7	10.8	14.5	74.9
Canned vegetables	100.0	3.4	10.6	12.7	77.0
Dried vegetables	100.0	8.0	11.7	21.3	67.1
Fresh and canned vegetable juices	100.0	5.3	10.8	13.2	76.1
Sugar and other sweets	**100.0**	**4.4**	**8.9**	**10.7**	**80.6**
Candy and chewing gum	100.0	4.9	7.2	9.5	83.5
Sugar	100.0	4.2	15.1	16.3	68.9
Artificial sweeteners	100.0	3.6	9.7	11.6	78.6
Jams, preserves, other sweets	100.0	3.3	8.4	9.7	82.1
Fats and oils	**100.0**	**4.1**	**10.2**	**14.2**	**76.0**
Margarine	100.0	2.4	12.4	10.3	77.4
Fats and oils	100.0	6.7	12.9	20.6	66.7
Salad dressings	100.0	2.2	8.9	11.7	79.7
Nondairy cream and imitation milk	100.0	3.6	8.1	11.1	81.1
Peanut butter	100.0	3.5	7.8	10.4	82.2

	total consumer units	Asian	black	Hispanic	non-Hispanic white and other
Miscellaneous foods	**100.0%**	**4.4%**	**8.4%**	**11.2%**	**80.6%**
Frozen prepared foods	100.0	3.4	10.2	9.7	80.3
Frozen meals	100.0	3.7	9.6	8.7	81.8
Other frozen prepared foods	100.0	3.2	10.7	10.6	79.0
Canned and packaged soups	100.0	4.3	7.4	9.2	83.5
Potato chips, nuts, and other snacks	100.0	4.0	7.2	10.7	82.4
Potato chips and other snacks	100.0	3.6	7.8	11.4	81.0
Nuts	100.0	5.0	5.7	8.6	85.9
Condiments and seasonings	100.0	4.6	9.7	10.9	79.7
Salt, spices, and other seasonings	100.0	6.9	11.1	13.6	75.5
Olives, pickles, relishes	100.0	2.1	7.9	8.5	83.8
Sauces and gravies	100.0	3.7	10.1	10.6	79.5
Baking needs and miscellaneous products	100.0	4.9	7.6	9.1	83.7
Other canned/packaged prepared foods	100.0	5.2	7.6	13.1	79.6
Prepared salads	100.0	4.0	7.7	8.1	84.5
Prepared desserts	100.0	3.8	7.9	11.0	81.3
Baby food	100.0	7.8	6.2	15.2	79.0
Miscellaneous prepared foods	100.0	5.1	7.9	14.5	77.9
Nonalcoholic beverages	**100.0**	**3.7**	**9.1**	**13.2**	**78.0**
Carbonated drinks	100.0	2.6	9.2	13.4	77.7
Tea	100.0	6.7	8.3	12.4	79.5
Coffee	100.0	3.8	5.9	9.0	85.4
Noncarbonated fruit-flavored drinks	100.0	3.9	13.0	16.8	70.3
Other nonalcoholic beverages and ice	100.0	3.8	10.0	13.2	77.1
Bottled water	100.0	5.3	11.9	16.7	71.9
Sports drinks	100.0	2.1	10.2	17.5	73.3
Food prepared by consumer unit on trips	**100.0**	**4.6**	**4.6**	**7.1**	**88.3**

Note: "Asian" and "black" include Hispanics and non-Hispanics who identify themselves as being of the respective race alone. "Hispanic" includes people of any race who identify themselves as Hispanic. "Other" includes people who identify themselves as non-Hispanic and as Alaska Native, American Indian, Asian (who are also included in the "Asian" column), Native Hawaiian or other Pacific Islander, as well as non-Hispanics reporting more than one race.
Source: Calculations by New Strategist based on the 2012 Consumer Expenditure Survey

WHO'S BUYING GROCERIES 83

Table 24. Groceries: Average spending by region, 2012

(average annual spending of consumer units on groceries, by region in which consumer unit lives, 2012)

	total consumer units	Northeast	Midwest	South	West
Number of consumer units (in 000s)	124,416	22,459	27,584	46,338	28,035
Number of persons per consumer unit	2.5	2.4	2.4	2.5	2.6
Average before-tax income of consumer units	$65,596.00	$72,036.00	$65,217.00	$60,219.00	$69,700.00
Average spending of consumer units, total	51,441.87	55,883.88	48,602.08	47,756.69	56,782.20
GROCERIES	**3,920.65**	**4,056.05**	**3,906.42**	**3,651.74**	**4,271.67**
Cereals and bakery products	**537.85**	**585.53**	**555.67**	**488.17**	**563.81**
Cereals and cereal products	181.98	194.67	183.10	164.57	199.46
Flour	9.36	10.78	9.37	8.99	8.80
Prepared flour mixes	16.18	14.57	17.11	15.01	18.48
Ready-to-eat and cooked cereals	94.82	95.38	95.91	88.40	103.94
Rice	24.65	31.17	22.48	21.95	26.02
Pasta, cornmeal, and other cereal products	36.98	42.77	38.25	30.22	42.22
Bakery products	355.87	390.86	372.57	323.60	364.35
Bread	105.12	117.64	100.94	94.92	116.09
White bread	43.52	47.31	43.40	41.37	44.12
Bread other than white	61.60	70.33	57.54	53.55	71.97
Crackers and cookies	87.73	92.99	91.33	80.16	92.43
Cookies	50.56	54.73	51.20	46.89	52.65
Crackers	37.17	38.26	40.13	33.27	39.78
Frozen and refrigerated bakery products	28.77	27.91	31.97	30.20	23.91
Other bakery products	134.25	152.31	148.33	118.33	131.92
Biscuits and rolls	51.85	64.14	56.15	43.80	50.95
Cakes and cupcakes	37.94	38.37	46.49	35.79	32.60
Bread and cracker products	7.31	9.67	8.36	5.83	6.80
Sweetrolls, coffee cakes, doughnuts	23.73	24.51	24.50	20.21	28.18
Pies, tarts, turnovers	13.41	15.61	12.83	12.70	13.39
Meats, poultry, fish, and eggs	**852.41**	**897.95**	**797.39**	**838.76**	**893.22**
Beef	226.32	217.69	225.70	229.45	228.76
Ground beef	93.50	91.30	100.76	97.39	81.56
Roast	34.02	26.52	30.19	34.43	43.29
Chuck roast	9.42	5.60	7.52	9.56	14.21
Round roast	6.63	5.83	7.41	6.64	6.48
Other roast	17.97	15.09	15.26	18.23	22.61
Steak	79.44	78.40	78.43	76.89	85.51
Round steak	16.91	15.78	20.50	14.43	18.34
Sirloin steak	21.76	22.65	20.01	20.55	24.79
Other steak	40.77	39.97	37.92	41.92	42.38
Other beef	19.35	21.46	16.32	20.73	18.40
Pork	165.77	159.46	154.68	178.41	161.03
Bacon	32.18	29.39	32.84	33.77	31.16
Pork chops	28.04	28.75	22.39	34.57	22.27
Ham	33.42	33.23	30.41	35.57	33.03
Ham, not canned	32.19	32.27	29.72	34.91	30.07
Canned ham	1.23	0.95	0.70	0.66	2.96
Sausage	32.14	34.18	28.65	33.93	31.00
Other pork	39.99	33.91	40.39	40.57	43.57
Other meats	122.13	144.21	125.80	111.42	118.31
Frankfurters	24.71	29.60	25.28	23.34	22.46
Lunch meats (cold cuts)	87.23	98.89	94.43	78.70	84.71
Bologna, liverwurst, salami	25.65	28.95	28.41	24.47	22.16
Other lunch meats	61.58	69.94	66.02	54.24	62.54
Lamb, organ meats, and others	10.19	15.73	6.08	9.38	11.15

	total consumer units	Northeast	Midwest	South	West
Poultry	$159.36	$177.52	$137.82	$154.26	$174.68
Fresh and frozen chicken	126.52	145.41	109.04	120.41	138.84
Fresh and frozen whole chicken	37.82	43.52	32.20	35.04	43.44
Fresh and frozen chicken parts	88.70	101.89	76.84	85.38	95.40
Other poultry	32.84	32.11	28.77	33.84	35.84
Fish and seafood	125.74	143.77	103.70	115.63	149.98
Canned fish and seafood	18.18	23.50	15.68	15.23	21.26
Fresh fish and shellfish	63.29	81.36	38.41	59.11	80.48
Frozen fish and shellfish	44.27	38.91	49.61	41.28	48.24
Eggs	53.08	55.30	49.70	49.60	60.46
Dairy products	418.93	447.78	421.28	383.32	452.30
Fresh milk and cream	151.86	152.71	144.13	148.55	164.42
Fresh milk, all types	128.28	122.68	120.64	130.01	137.60
Cream	23.58	30.03	23.48	18.54	26.82
Other dairy products	267.07	295.07	277.15	234.77	287.88
Butter	25.56	32.31	27.23	20.69	26.49
Cheese	131.47	138.67	133.79	117.32	146.80
Ice cream and related products	57.37	60.88	60.91	54.59	55.59
Miscellaneous dairy products	52.67	63.21	55.22	42.18	59.00
Fruits and vegetables	730.98	798.28	727.52	637.07	835.85
Fresh fruits	261.29	285.29	261.53	217.99	313.53
Apples	41.61	48.33	44.46	33.44	46.87
Bananas	43.81	49.17	44.91	36.86	49.91
Oranges	26.74	30.55	28.12	22.27	29.70
Citrus fruits, except oranges	39.95	44.66	38.88	31.62	51.02
Other fresh fruits	109.19	112.58	105.16	93.80	136.04
Fresh vegetables	226.14	249.49	205.63	197.55	275.23
Potatoes	38.44	44.38	37.54	36.75	37.32
Lettuce	32.33	37.28	35.34	26.84	34.42
Tomatoes	39.35	43.37	38.39	32.57	48.34
Other fresh vegetables	116.01	124.47	94.37	101.39	155.14
Processed fruits	113.76	127.35	120.14	97.16	123.89
Frozen fruits and fruit juices	12.71	10.68	16.86	8.60	17.03
Frozen fruits	7.16	6.53	9.33	4.49	9.95
Frozen fruit juices	5.55	4.15	7.53	4.11	7.09
Canned fruits	20.35	22.91	26.22	17.73	16.75
Dried fruits	8.71	10.19	9.60	6.55	10.21
Fresh fruit juice	17.06	23.51	18.56	13.63	16.01
Canned and bottled fruit juice	54.92	60.05	48.91	50.64	63.89
Processed vegetables	129.80	136.15	140.22	124.38	123.20
Frozen vegetables	37.50	44.28	38.50	37.68	30.70
Canned and dried vegetables and juices	92.30	91.87	101.72	86.70	92.50
Canned vegetables	54.59	54.28	61.15	54.12	49.08
Dried vegetables	18.22	15.29	19.27	17.58	20.63
Fresh and canned vegetable juices	18.98	21.78	20.78	14.65	22.08
Sugar and other sweets	146.77	135.79	152.82	138.11	164.00
Candy and chewing gum	87.86	80.05	90.54	77.79	108.27
Sugar	24.38	24.04	25.33	26.11	20.84
Artificial sweeteners	4.91	4.35	3.48	6.48	4.18
Jams, preserves, other sweets	29.61	27.36	33.48	27.73	30.71
Fats and oils	114.09	114.32	117.29	106.32	123.61
Margarine	8.74	10.06	11.79	7.24	7.13
Fats and oils	36.79	37.15	31.57	35.61	43.67
Salad dressings	31.29	28.52	34.24	30.09	32.58
Nondairy cream and imitation milk	18.59	19.95	18.17	16.92	20.68
Peanut butter	18.68	18.65	21.53	16.46	19.55

	total consumer units	Northeast	Midwest	South	West
Miscellaneous foods	**$699.27**	**$656.28**	**$727.18**	**$645.57**	**$795.47**
Frozen prepared foods	130.83	123.10	149.59	126.54	125.44
Frozen meals	60.61	60.56	67.52	57.58	58.75
Other frozen prepared foods	70.22	62.54	82.07	68.96	66.69
Canned and packaged soups	46.30	44.82	47.31	40.72	55.75
Potato chips, nuts, and other snacks	153.94	148.53	163.26	143.57	166.22
Potato chips and other snacks	111.59	101.33	120.20	105.94	120.67
Nuts	42.35	47.19	43.05	37.62	45.55
Condiments and seasonings	141.39	143.64	150.70	125.17	157.19
Salt, spices, and other seasonings	38.72	38.78	38.40	36.21	43.17
Olives, pickles, relishes	17.46	15.57	20.21	15.44	19.57
Sauces and gravies	60.27	62.62	63.14	53.41	66.88
Baking needs and miscellaneous products	24.95	26.67	28.95	20.11	27.57
Other canned/packaged prepared foods	226.81	196.19	216.32	209.56	290.87
Prepared salads	35.09	38.37	38.48	28.72	39.60
Prepared desserts	14.29	17.15	16.41	12.49	12.85
Baby food	25.05	24.52	26.87	26.87	20.64
Miscellaneous prepared foods	147.81	114.39	130.55	138.57	207.62
Nonalcoholic beverages	**370.13**	**369.91**	**362.39**	**370.41**	**377.60**
Carbonated drinks	139.74	119.16	145.73	149.95	133.47
Tea	30.36	36.99	29.72	27.79	29.88
Coffee	86.50	99.85	80.23	80.46	91.97
Noncarbonated fruit-flavored drinks	25.83	25.07	24.62	25.90	27.54
Other nonalcoholic beverages and ice	15.36	15.00	14.77	13.30	19.67
Bottled water	56.80	60.98	49.99	58.06	58.14
Sports drinks	15.12	12.86	16.96	14.81	15.64
Food prepared by consumer unit on trips	**50.23**	**50.20**	**44.88**	**44.01**	**65.81**

Table 25. Groceries: Indexed spending by region, 2012

(indexed average annual spending of consumer units on groceries, by region in which consumer unit lives, 2012; index definition: an index of 100 is the average for all consumer units; an index of 125 means that spending by consumer units in that group is 25 percent above the average for all consumer units; an index of 75 indicates spending that is 25 percent below the average for all consumer units)

	total consumer units	Northeast	Midwest	South	West
Average spending of consumer units, total	$51,442	$55,884	$48,602	$47,757	$56,782
Average spending of consumer units, index	100	109	94	93	110
GROCERIES	**100**	**103**	**100**	**93**	**109**
Cereals and bakery products	**100**	**109**	**103**	**91**	**105**
Cereals and cereal products	100	107	101	90	110
Flour	100	115	100	96	94
Prepared flour mixes	100	90	106	93	114
Ready-to-eat and cooked cereals	100	101	101	93	110
Rice	100	126	91	89	106
Pasta, cornmeal, and other cereal products	100	116	103	82	114
Bakery products	100	110	105	91	102
Bread	100	112	96	90	110
White bread	100	109	100	95	101
Bread other than white	100	114	93	87	117
Crackers and cookies	100	106	104	91	105
Cookies	100	108	101	93	104
Crackers	100	103	108	90	107
Frozen and refrigerated bakery products	100	97	111	105	83
Other bakery products	100	113	110	88	98
Biscuits and rolls	100	124	108	84	98
Cakes and cupcakes	100	101	123	94	86
Bread and cracker products	100	132	114	80	93
Sweetrolls, coffee cakes, doughnuts	100	103	103	85	119
Pies, tarts, turnovers	100	116	96	95	100
Meats, poultry, fish, and eggs	**100**	**105**	**94**	**98**	**105**
Beef	100	96	100	101	101
Ground beef	100	98	108	104	87
Roast	100	78	89	101	127
Chuck roast	100	59	80	101	151
Round roast	100	88	112	100	98
Other roast	100	84	85	101	126
Steak	100	99	99	97	108
Round steak	100	93	121	85	108
Sirloin steak	100	104	92	94	114
Other steak	100	98	93	103	104
Other beef	100	111	84	107	95
Pork	100	96	93	108	97
Bacon	100	91	102	105	97
Pork chops	100	103	80	123	79
Ham	100	99	91	106	99
Ham, not canned	100	100	92	108	93
Canned ham	100	77	57	54	241
Sausage	100	106	89	106	96
Other pork	100	85	101	101	109
Other meats	100	118	103	91	97
Frankfurters	100	120	102	94	91
Lunch meats (cold cuts)	100	113	108	90	97
Bologna, liverwurst, salami	100	113	111	95	86
Other lunch meats	100	114	107	88	102
Lamb, organ meats, and others	100	154	60	92	109

	total consumer units	Northeast	Midwest	South	West
Poultry	100	111	86	97	110
Fresh and frozen chicken	100	115	86	95	110
Fresh and frozen whole chicken	100	115	85	93	115
Fresh and frozen chicken parts	100	115	87	96	108
Other poultry	100	98	88	103	109
Fish and seafood	100	114	82	92	119
Canned fish and seafood	100	129	86	84	117
Fresh fish and shellfish	100	129	61	93	127
Frozen fish and shellfish	100	88	112	93	109
Eggs	100	104	94	93	114
Dairy products	**100**	**107**	**101**	**91**	**108**
Fresh milk and cream	100	101	95	98	108
Fresh milk, all types	100	96	94	101	107
Cream	100	127	100	79	114
Other dairy products	100	110	104	88	108
Butter	100	126	107	81	104
Cheese	100	105	102	89	112
Ice cream and related products	100	106	106	95	97
Miscellaneous dairy products	100	120	105	80	112
Fruits and vegetables	**100**	**109**	**100**	**87**	**114**
Fresh fruits	100	109	100	83	120
Apples	100	116	107	80	113
Bananas	100	112	103	84	114
Oranges	100	114	105	83	111
Citrus fruits, except oranges	100	112	97	79	128
Other fresh fruits	100	103	96	86	125
Fresh vegetables	100	110	91	87	122
Potatoes	100	115	98	96	97
Lettuce	100	115	109	83	106
Tomatoes	100	110	98	83	123
Other fresh vegetables	100	107	81	87	134
Processed fruits	100	112	106	85	109
Frozen fruits and fruit juices	100	84	133	68	134
Frozen fruits	100	91	130	63	139
Frozen fruit juices	100	75	136	74	128
Canned fruits	100	113	129	87	82
Dried fruits	100	117	110	75	117
Fresh fruit juice	100	138	109	80	94
Canned and bottled fruit juice	100	109	89	92	116
Processed vegetables	100	105	108	96	95
Frozen vegetables	100	118	103	100	82
Canned and dried vegetables and juices	100	100	110	94	100
Canned vegetables	100	99	112	99	90
Dried vegetables	100	84	106	96	113
Fresh and canned vegetable juices	100	115	109	77	116
Sugar and other sweets	**100**	**93**	**104**	**94**	**112**
Candy and chewing gum	100	91	103	89	123
Sugar	100	99	104	107	85
Artificial sweeteners	100	89	71	132	85
Jams, preserves, other sweets	100	92	113	94	104
Fats and oils	**100**	**100**	**103**	**93**	**108**
Margarine	100	115	135	83	82
Fats and oils	100	101	86	97	119
Salad dressings	100	91	109	96	104
Nondairy cream and imitation milk	100	107	98	91	111
Peanut butter	100	100	115	88	105

	total consumer units	Northeast	Midwest	South	West
Miscellaneous foods	**100**	**94**	**104**	**92**	**114**
Frozen prepared foods	100	94	114	97	96
Frozen meals	100	100	111	95	97
Other frozen prepared foods	100	89	117	98	95
Canned and packaged soups	100	97	102	88	120
Potato chips, nuts, and other snacks	100	96	106	93	108
Potato chips and other snacks	100	91	108	95	108
Nuts	100	111	102	89	108
Condiments and seasonings	100	102	107	89	111
Salt, spices, and other seasonings	100	100	99	94	111
Olives, pickles, relishes	100	89	116	88	112
Sauces and gravies	100	104	105	89	111
Baking needs and miscellaneous products	100	107	116	81	111
Other canned/packaged prepared foods	100	86	95	92	128
Prepared salads	100	109	110	82	113
Prepared desserts	100	120	115	87	90
Baby food	100	98	107	107	82
Miscellaneous prepared foods	100	77	88	94	140
Nonalcoholic beverages	**100**	**100**	**98**	**100**	**102**
Carbonated drinks	100	85	104	107	96
Tea	100	122	98	92	98
Coffee	100	115	93	93	106
Noncarbonated fruit-flavored drinks	100	97	95	100	107
Other nonalcoholic beverages and ice	100	98	96	87	128
Bottled water	100	107	88	102	102
Sports drinks	100	85	112	98	103
Food prepared by consumer unit on trips	**100**	**100**	**89**	**88**	**131**

Source: Calculations by New Strategist based on the Bureau of Labor Statistics' 2012 Consumer Expenditure Survey

Table 26. Groceries: Total spending by region, 2012

(total annual spending on groceries, by region in which consumer unit lives, 2012; consumer units and dollars in thousands)

	total consumer units	Northeast	Midwest	South	West
Number of consumer units	124,416	22,459	27,584	46,338	28,035
Total spending of all consumer units	$6,400,191,698	$1,255,096,061	$1,340,639,775	$2,212,949,501	$1,591,888,977
GROCERIES	**487,791,590**	**91,094,827**	**107,754,689**	**169,214,328**	**119,756,268**
Cereals and bakery products	**66,917,146**	**13,150,418**	**15,327,601**	**22,620,821**	**15,806,413**
Cereals and cereal products	22,641,224	4,372,094	5,050,630	7,625,845	5,591,861
Flour	1,164,534	242,108	258,462	416,579	246,708
Prepared flour mixes	2,013,051	327,228	471,962	695,533	518,087
Ready-to-eat and cooked cereals	11,797,125	2,142,139	2,645,581	4,096,279	2,913,958
Rice	3,066,854	700,047	620,088	1,017,119	729,471
Pasta, cornmeal, and other cereal products	4,600,904	960,571	1,055,088	1,400,334	1,183,638
Bakery products	44,275,922	8,778,325	10,276,971	14,994,977	10,214,552
Bread	13,078,610	2,642,077	2,784,329	4,398,403	3,254,583
White bread	5,414,584	1,062,535	1,197,146	1,917,003	1,236,904
Bread other than white	7,664,026	1,579,541	1,587,183	2,481,400	2,017,679
Crackers and cookies	10,915,016	2,088,462	2,519,247	3,714,454	2,591,275
Cookies	6,290,473	1,229,181	1,412,301	2,172,789	1,476,043
Crackers	4,624,543	859,281	1,106,946	1,541,665	1,115,232
Frozen and refrigerated bakery products	3,579,448	626,831	881,860	1,399,408	670,317
Other bakery products	16,702,848	3,420,730	4,091,535	5,483,176	3,698,377
Biscuits and rolls	6,450,970	1,440,520	1,548,842	2,029,604	1,428,383
Cakes and cupcakes	4,720,343	861,752	1,282,380	1,658,437	913,941
Bread and cracker products	909,481	217,179	230,602	270,151	190,638
Sweetrolls, coffee cakes, doughnuts	2,952,392	550,470	675,808	936,491	790,026
Pies, tarts, turnovers	1,668,419	350,585	353,903	588,493	375,389
Meats, poultry, fish, and eggs	**106,053,443**	**20,167,059**	**21,995,206**	**38,866,461**	**25,041,423**
Beef	28,157,829	4,889,100	6,225,709	10,632,254	6,413,287
Ground beef	11,632,896	2,050,507	2,779,364	4,512,858	2,286,535
Roast	4,232,632	595,613	832,761	1,595,417	1,213,635
Chuck roast	1,171,999	125,770	207,432	442,991	398,377
Round roast	824,878	130,936	204,397	307,684	181,667
Other roast	2,235,756	338,906	420,932	844,742	633,871
Steak	9,883,607	1,760,786	2,163,413	3,562,929	2,397,273
Round steak	2,103,875	354,403	565,472	668,657	514,162
Sirloin steak	2,707,292	508,696	551,956	952,246	694,988
Other steak	5,072,440	897,686	1,045,985	1,942,489	1,188,123
Other beef	2,407,450	481,970	450,171	960,587	515,844
Pork	20,624,440	3,581,312	4,266,693	8,267,163	4,514,476
Bacon	4,003,707	660,070	905,859	1,564,834	873,571
Pork chops	3,488,625	645,696	617,606	1,601,905	624,339
Ham	4,157,983	746,313	838,829	1,648,243	925,996
Ham, not canned	4,004,951	724,752	819,796	1,617,660	843,012
Canned ham	153,032	21,336	19,309	30,583	82,984
Sausage	3,998,730	767,649	790,282	1,572,248	869,085
Other pork	4,975,396	761,585	1,114,118	1,879,933	1,221,485
Other meats	15,194,926	3,238,812	3,470,067	5,162,980	3,316,821
Frankfurters	3,074,319	664,786	697,324	1,081,529	629,666
Lunch meats (cold cuts)	10,852,808	2,220,971	2,604,757	3,646,801	2,374,845
Bologna, liverwurst, salami	3,191,270	650,188	783,661	1,133,891	621,256
Other lunch meats	7,661,537	1,570,782	1,821,096	2,513,373	1,753,309
Lamb, organ meats, and others	1,267,799	353,280	167,711	434,650	312,590

	total consumer units	Northeast	Midwest	South	West
Poultry	$19,826,934	$3,986,922	$3,801,627	$7,148,100	$4,897,154
Fresh and frozen chicken	15,741,112	3,265,763	3,007,759	5,579,559	3,892,379
Fresh and frozen whole chicken	4,705,413	977,416	888,205	1,623,684	1,217,840
Fresh and frozen chicken parts	11,035,699	2,288,348	2,119,555	3,956,338	2,674,539
Other poultry	4,085,821	721,158	793,592	1,568,078	1,004,774
Fish and seafood	15,644,068	3,228,930	2,860,461	5,358,063	4,204,689
Canned fish and seafood	2,261,883	527,787	432,517	705,728	596,024
Fresh fish and shellfish	7,874,289	1,827,264	1,059,501	2,739,039	2,256,257
Frozen fish and shellfish	5,507,896	873,880	1,368,442	1,912,833	1,352,408
Eggs	6,604,001	1,241,983	1,370,925	2,298,365	1,694,996
Dairy products	**52,121,595**	**10,056,691**	**11,620,588**	**17,762,282**	**12,680,231**
Fresh milk and cream	18,893,814	3,429,714	3,975,682	6,883,510	4,609,515
Fresh milk, all types	15,960,084	2,755,270	3,327,734	6,024,403	3,857,616
Cream	2,933,729	674,444	647,672	859,107	751,899
Other dairy products	33,227,781	6,626,977	7,644,906	10,878,772	8,070,716
Butter	3,180,073	725,650	751,112	958,733	742,647
Cheese	16,356,972	3,114,390	3,690,463	5,436,374	4,115,538
Ice cream and related products	7,137,746	1,367,304	1,680,141	2,529,591	1,558,466
Miscellaneous dairy products	6,552,991	1,419,633	1,523,188	1,954,537	1,654,065
Fruits and vegetables	**90,945,608**	**17,928,571**	**20,067,912**	**29,520,550**	**23,433,055**
Fresh fruits	32,508,657	6,407,328	7,214,044	10,101,221	8,789,814
Apples	5,176,950	1,085,443	1,226,385	1,549,543	1,314,000
Bananas	5,450,665	1,104,309	1,238,797	1,708,019	1,399,227
Oranges	3,326,884	686,122	775,662	1,031,947	832,640
Citrus fruits, except oranges	4,970,419	1,003,019	1,072,466	1,465,208	1,430,346
Other fresh fruits	13,584,983	2,528,434	2,900,733	4,346,504	3,813,881
Fresh vegetables	28,135,434	5,603,296	5,672,098	9,154,072	7,716,073
Potatoes	4,782,551	996,730	1,035,503	1,702,922	1,046,266
Lettuce	4,022,369	837,272	974,819	1,243,712	964,965
Tomatoes	4,895,770	974,047	1,058,950	1,509,229	1,355,212
Other fresh vegetables	14,433,500	2,795,472	2,603,102	4,698,210	4,349,350
Processed fruits	14,153,564	2,860,154	3,313,942	4,502,200	3,473,256
Frozen fruits and fruit juices	1,581,327	239,862	465,066	398,507	477,436
Frozen fruits	890,819	146,657	257,359	208,058	278,948
Frozen fruit juices	690,509	93,205	207,708	190,449	198,768
Canned fruits	2,531,866	514,536	723,252	821,573	469,586
Dried fruits	1,083,663	228,857	264,806	303,514	286,237
Fresh fruit juice	2,122,537	528,011	511,959	631,587	448,840
Canned and bottled fruit juice	6,832,927	1,348,663	1,349,133	2,346,556	1,791,156
Processed vegetables	16,149,197	3,057,793	3,867,828	5,763,520	3,453,912
Frozen vegetables	4,665,600	994,485	1,061,984	1,746,016	860,675
Canned and dried vegetables and juices	11,483,597	2,063,308	2,805,844	4,017,505	2,593,238
Canned vegetables	6,791,869	1,219,075	1,686,762	2,507,813	1,375,958
Dried vegetables	2,266,860	343,398	531,544	814,622	578,362
Fresh and canned vegetable juices	2,361,416	489,157	573,196	678,852	619,013
Sugar and other sweets	**18,260,536**	**3,049,708**	**4,215,387**	**6,399,741**	**4,597,740**
Candy and chewing gum	10,931,190	1,797,843	2,497,455	3,604,633	3,035,349
Sugar	3,033,262	539,914	698,703	1,209,885	584,249
Artificial sweeteners	610,883	97,697	95,992	300,270	117,186
Jams, preserves, other sweets	3,683,958	614,478	923,512	1,284,953	860,955
Fats and oils	**14,194,621**	**2,567,513**	**3,235,327**	**4,926,656**	**3,465,406**
Margarine	1,087,396	225,938	325,215	335,487	199,890
Fats and oils	4,577,265	834,352	870,827	1,650,096	1,224,288
Salad dressings	3,892,977	640,531	944,476	1,394,310	913,380
Nondairy cream and imitation milk	2,312,893	448,057	501,201	784,039	579,764
Peanut butter	2,324,091	418,860	593,884	762,723	548,084

	total consumer units	Northeast	Midwest	South	West
Miscellaneous foods	$87,000,376	$14,739,393	$20,058,533	$29,914,423	$22,301,001
Frozen prepared foods	16,277,345	2,764,703	4,126,291	5,863,611	3,516,710
Frozen meals	7,540,854	1,360,117	1,862,472	2,668,142	1,647,056
Other frozen prepared foods	8,736,492	1,404,586	2,263,819	3,195,468	1,869,654
Canned and packaged soups	5,760,461	1,006,612	1,304,999	1,886,883	1,562,951
Potato chips, nuts, and other snacks	19,152,599	3,335,835	4,503,364	6,652,747	4,659,978
Potato chips and other snacks	13,883,581	2,275,770	3,315,597	4,909,048	3,382,983
Nuts	5,269,018	1,059,840	1,187,491	1,743,236	1,276,994
Condiments and seasonings	17,591,178	3,226,011	4,156,909	5,800,127	4,406,822
Salt, spices, and other seasonings	4,817,388	870,960	1,059,226	1,677,899	1,210,271
Olives, pickles, relishes	2,172,303	349,687	557,473	715,459	548,645
Sauces and gravies	7,498,552	1,406,383	1,741,654	2,474,913	1,874,981
Baking needs and miscellaneous products	3,104,179	598,982	798,557	931,857	772,925
Other canned/packaged prepared foods	28,218,793	4,406,231	5,966,971	9,710,591	8,154,540
Prepared salads	4,365,757	861,752	1,061,432	1,330,827	1,110,186
Prepared desserts	1,777,905	385,172	452,653	578,762	360,250
Baby food	3,116,621	550,695	741,182	1,245,102	578,642
Miscellaneous prepared foods	18,389,929	2,569,085	3,601,091	6,421,057	5,820,627
Nonalcoholic beverages	46,050,094	8,307,809	9,996,166	17,164,059	10,586,016
Carbonated drinks	17,385,892	2,676,214	4,019,816	6,948,383	3,741,831
Tea	3,777,270	830,758	819,796	1,287,733	837,686
Coffee	10,761,984	2,242,531	2,213,064	3,728,355	2,578,379
Noncarbonated fruit-flavored drinks	3,213,665	563,047	679,118	1,200,154	772,084
Other nonalcoholic beverages and ice	1,911,030	336,885	407,416	616,295	551,448
Bottled water	7,066,829	1,369,550	1,378,924	2,690,384	1,629,955
Sports drinks	1,881,170	288,823	467,825	686,266	438,467
Food prepared by consumer unit on trips	6,249,416	1,127,442	1,237,970	2,039,335	1,844,983

Note: Numbers may not add to total because of rounding.
Source: Calculations by New Strategist based on the Bureau of Labor Statistics' 2012 Consumer Expenditure Survey

Table 27. Groceries: Market shares by region, 2012

(percentage of total annual spending on groceries accounted for by consumer units by region of residence, 2012)

	total consumer units	Northeast	Midwest	South	West
Share of total consumer units	100.0%	18.1%	22.2%	37.2%	22.5%
Share of total before-tax income	100.0	19.8	22.0	34.2	23.9
Share of total spending	100.0	19.6	20.9	34.6	24.9
GROCERIES	**100.0**	**18.7**	**22.1**	**34.7**	**24.6**
Cereals and bakery products	**100.0**	**19.7**	**22.9**	**33.8**	**23.6**
Cereals and cereal products	100.0	19.3	22.3	33.7	24.7
Flour	100.0	20.8	22.2	35.8	21.2
Prepared flour mixes	100.0	16.3	23.4	34.6	25.7
Ready-to-eat and cooked cereals	100.0	18.2	22.4	34.7	24.7
Rice	100.0	22.8	20.2	33.2	23.8
Pasta, cornmeal, and other cereal products	100.0	20.9	22.9	30.4	25.7
Bakery products	100.0	19.8	23.2	33.9	23.1
Bread	100.0	20.2	21.3	33.6	24.9
White bread	100.0	19.6	22.1	35.4	22.8
Bread other than white	100.0	20.6	20.7	32.4	26.3
Crackers and cookies	100.0	19.1	23.1	34.0	23.7
Cookies	100.0	19.5	22.5	34.5	23.5
Crackers	100.0	18.6	23.9	33.3	24.1
Frozen and refrigerated bakery products	100.0	17.5	24.6	39.1	18.7
Other bakery products	100.0	20.5	24.5	32.8	22.1
Biscuits and rolls	100.0	22.3	24.0	31.5	22.1
Cakes and cupcakes	100.0	18.3	27.2	35.1	19.4
Bread and cracker products	100.0	23.9	25.4	29.7	21.0
Sweetrolls, coffee cakes, doughnuts	100.0	18.6	22.9	31.7	26.8
Pies, tarts, turnovers	100.0	21.0	21.2	35.3	22.5
Meats, poultry, fish, and eggs	**100.0**	**19.0**	**20.7**	**36.6**	**23.6**
Beef	100.0	17.4	22.1	37.8	22.8
Ground beef	100.0	17.6	23.9	38.8	19.7
Roast	100.0	14.1	19.7	37.7	28.7
Chuck roast	100.0	10.7	17.7	37.8	34.0
Round roast	100.0	15.9	24.8	37.3	22.0
Other roast	100.0	15.2	18.8	37.8	28.4
Steak	100.0	17.8	21.9	36.0	24.3
Round steak	100.0	16.8	26.9	31.8	24.4
Sirloin steak	100.0	18.8	20.4	35.2	25.7
Other steak	100.0	17.7	20.6	38.3	23.4
Other beef	100.0	20.0	18.7	39.9	21.4
Pork	100.0	17.4	20.7	40.1	21.9
Bacon	100.0	16.5	22.6	39.1	21.8
Pork chops	100.0	18.5	17.7	45.9	17.9
Ham	100.0	17.9	20.2	39.6	22.3
Ham, not canned	100.0	18.1	20.5	40.4	21.0
Canned ham	100.0	13.9	12.6	20.0	54.2
Sausage	100.0	19.2	19.8	39.3	21.7
Other pork	100.0	15.3	22.4	37.8	24.6
Other meats	100.0	21.3	22.8	34.0	21.8
Frankfurters	100.0	21.6	22.7	35.2	20.5
Lunch meats (cold cuts)	100.0	20.5	24.0	33.6	21.9
Bologna, liverwurst, salami	100.0	20.4	24.6	35.5	19.5
Other lunch meats	100.0	20.5	23.8	32.8	22.9
Lamb, organ meats, and others	100.0	27.9	13.2	34.3	24.7

	total consumer units	Northeast	Midwest	South	West
Poultry	100.0%	20.1%	19.2%	36.1%	24.7%
Fresh and frozen chicken	100.0	20.7	19.1	35.4	24.7
Fresh and frozen whole chicken	100.0	20.8	18.9	34.5	25.9
Fresh and frozen chicken parts	100.0	20.7	19.2	35.9	24.2
Other poultry	100.0	17.7	19.4	38.4	24.6
Fish and seafood	100.0	20.6	18.3	34.2	26.9
Canned fish and seafood	100.0	23.3	19.1	31.2	26.4
Fresh fish and shellfish	100.0	23.2	13.5	34.8	28.7
Frozen fish and shellfish	100.0	15.9	24.8	34.7	24.6
Eggs	100.0	18.8	20.8	34.8	25.7
Dairy products	**100.0**	**19.3**	**22.3**	**34.1**	**24.3**
Fresh milk and cream	100.0	18.2	21.0	36.4	24.4
Fresh milk, all types	100.0	17.3	20.9	37.7	24.2
Cream	100.0	23.0	22.1	29.3	25.6
Other dairy products	100.0	19.9	23.0	32.7	24.3
Butter	100.0	22.8	23.6	30.1	23.4
Cheese	100.0	19.0	22.6	33.2	25.2
Ice cream and related products	100.0	19.2	23.5	35.4	21.8
Miscellaneous dairy products	100.0	21.7	23.2	29.8	25.2
Fruits and vegetables	**100.0**	**19.7**	**22.1**	**32.5**	**25.8**
Fresh fruits	100.0	19.7	22.2	31.1	27.0
Apples	100.0	21.0	23.7	29.9	25.4
Bananas	100.0	20.3	22.7	31.3	25.7
Oranges	100.0	20.6	23.3	31.0	25.0
Citrus fruits, except oranges	100.0	20.2	21.6	29.5	28.8
Other fresh fruits	100.0	18.6	21.4	32.0	28.1
Fresh vegetables	100.0	19.9	20.2	32.5	27.4
Potatoes	100.0	20.8	21.7	35.6	21.9
Lettuce	100.0	20.8	24.2	30.9	24.0
Tomatoes	100.0	19.9	21.6	30.8	27.7
Other fresh vegetables	100.0	19.4	18.0	32.6	30.1
Processed fruits	100.0	20.2	23.4	31.8	24.5
Frozen fruits and fruit juices	100.0	15.2	29.4	25.2	30.2
Frozen fruits	100.0	16.5	28.9	23.4	31.3
Frozen fruit juices	100.0	13.5	30.1	27.6	28.8
Canned fruits	100.0	20.3	28.6	32.4	18.5
Dried fruits	100.0	21.1	24.4	28.0	26.4
Fresh fruit juice	100.0	24.9	24.1	29.8	21.1
Canned and bottled fruit juice	100.0	19.7	19.7	34.3	26.2
Processed vegetables	100.0	18.9	24.0	35.7	21.4
Frozen vegetables	100.0	21.3	22.8	37.4	18.4
Canned and dried vegetables and juices	100.0	18.0	24.4	35.0	22.6
Canned vegetables	100.0	17.9	24.8	36.9	20.3
Dried vegetables	100.0	15.1	23.4	35.9	25.5
Fresh and canned vegetable juices	100.0	20.7	24.3	28.7	26.2
Sugar and other sweets	**100.0**	**16.7**	**23.1**	**35.0**	**25.2**
Candy and chewing gum	100.0	16.4	22.8	33.0	27.8
Sugar	100.0	17.8	23.0	39.9	19.3
Artificial sweeteners	100.0	16.0	15.7	49.2	19.2
Jams, preserves, other sweets	100.0	16.7	25.1	34.9	23.4
Fats and oils	**100.0**	**18.1**	**22.8**	**34.7**	**24.4**
Margarine	100.0	20.8	29.9	30.9	18.4
Fats and oils	100.0	18.2	19.0	36.0	26.7
Salad dressings	100.0	16.5	24.3	35.8	23.5
Nondairy cream and imitation milk	100.0	19.4	21.7	33.9	25.1
Peanut butter	100.0	18.0	25.6	32.8	23.6

	total consumer units	Northeast	Midwest	South	West
Miscellaneous foods	**100.0%**	**16.9%**	**23.1%**	**34.4%**	**25.6%**
Frozen prepared foods	100.0	17.0	25.3	36.0	21.6
Frozen meals	100.0	18.0	24.7	35.4	21.8
Other frozen prepared foods	100.0	16.1	25.9	36.6	21.4
Canned and packaged soups	100.0	17.5	22.7	32.8	27.1
Potato chips, nuts, and other snacks	100.0	17.4	23.5	34.7	24.3
Potato chips and other snacks	100.0	16.4	23.9	35.4	24.4
Nuts	100.0	20.1	22.5	33.1	24.2
Condiments and seasonings	100.0	18.3	23.6	33.0	25.1
Salt, spices, and other seasonings	100.0	18.1	22.0	34.8	25.1
Olives, pickles, relishes	100.0	16.1	25.7	32.9	25.3
Sauces and gravies	100.0	18.8	23.2	33.0	25.0
Baking needs and miscellaneous products	100.0	19.3	25.7	30.0	24.9
Other canned/packaged prepared foods	100.0	15.6	21.1	34.4	28.9
Prepared salads	100.0	19.7	24.3	30.5	25.4
Prepared desserts	100.0	21.7	25.5	32.6	20.3
Baby food	100.0	17.7	23.8	40.0	18.6
Miscellaneous prepared foods	100.0	14.0	19.6	34.9	31.7
Nonalcoholic beverages	**100.0**	**18.0**	**21.7**	**37.3**	**23.0**
Carbonated drinks	100.0	15.4	23.1	40.0	21.5
Tea	100.0	22.0	21.7	34.1	22.2
Coffee	100.0	20.8	20.6	34.6	24.0
Noncarbonated fruit-flavored drinks	100.0	17.5	21.1	37.3	24.0
Other nonalcoholic beverages and ice	100.0	17.6	21.3	32.2	28.9
Bottled water	100.0	19.4	19.5	38.1	23.1
Sports drinks	100.0	15.4	24.9	36.5	23.3
Food prepared by consumer unit on trips	**100.0**	**18.0**	**19.8**	**32.6**	**29.5**

Note: Numbers may not add to total because of rounding.
Source: Calculations by New Strategist based on the Bureau of Labor Statistics' 2012 Consumer Expenditure Survey

Table 28. Groceries: Average spending by education, 2012

(average annual spending of consumer units on groceries, by education of consumer unit reference person, 2012)

	total consumer units	less than high school graduate	high school graduate	some college	associate's degree	bachelor's degree or more total	bachelor's degree	master's, professional, doctorate
Number of consumer units (in 000s)	124,416	16,246	31,022	25,623	12,287	39,238	24,798	14,440
Number of persons per consumer unit	2.5	2.7	2.5	2.4	2.6	2.4	2.4	2.5
Average before-tax income of consumer units	$65,596.00	$33,154.00	$47,221.00	$55,987.00	$66,122.00	$99,667.00	$89,438.00	$117,233.00
Average spending of consumer units, total	51,441.87	31,193.61	39,989.36	46,118.38	52,414.41	71,926.33	66,420.24	81,363.01
GROCERIES	**3,920.65**	**3,492.14**	**3,584.63**	**3,555.34**	**4,150.44**	**4,517.47**	**4,351.33**	**4,798.66**
Cereals and bakery products	**537.85**	**458.70**	**503.31**	**482.10**	**573.24**	**620.79**	**590.37**	**672.22**
Cereals and cereal products	181.98	156.68	169.21	163.33	197.60	209.04	203.83	217.84
Flour	9.36	10.84	10.38	7.61	8.60	9.42	8.25	11.40
Prepared flour mixes	16.18	11.99	14.64	15.16	21.39	17.99	16.79	20.02
Ready-to-eat and cooked cereals	94.82	73.65	85.77	89.11	107.01	109.80	110.75	108.19
Rice	24.65	30.45	24.63	19.59	21.44	26.92	24.70	30.66
Pasta, cornmeal, and other cereal products	36.98	29.75	33.79	31.87	39.17	44.91	43.34	47.56
Bakery products	355.87	302.03	334.09	318.77	375.63	411.75	386.54	454.38
Bread	105.12	90.15	101.69	97.04	112.89	116.41	108.91	129.08
White bread	43.52	41.26	44.32	41.00	47.09	44.32	42.00	48.25
Bread other than white	61.60	48.90	57.37	56.04	65.79	72.09	66.92	80.83
Crackers and cookies	87.73	76.08	79.67	76.09	92.02	104.84	101.17	111.05
Cookies	50.56	47.83	48.20	45.46	52.73	56.17	53.39	60.88
Crackers	37.17	28.24	31.47	30.64	39.28	48.67	47.78	50.17
Frozen and refrigerated bakery products	28.77	22.87	28.58	25.35	32.63	32.24	29.92	36.16
Other bakery products	134.25	112.92	124.15	120.29	138.10	158.27	146.54	178.09
Biscuits and rolls	51.85	43.14	46.43	44.13	54.53	63.69	63.52	63.97
Cakes and cupcakes	37.94	31.74	31.36	34.34	35.37	48.59	39.32	64.27
Bread and cracker products	7.31	6.23	7.15	6.96	8.26	7.77	8.01	7.36
Sweetrolls, coffee cakes, doughnuts	23.73	24.74	23.91	23.75	24.50	22.96	21.67	25.15
Pies, tarts, turnovers	13.41	7.07	15.30	11.11	15.43	15.25	14.02	17.34
Meats, poultry, fish, and eggs	**852.41**	**827.30**	**887.65**	**751.17**	**913.81**	**883.64**	**867.68**	**910.61**
Beef	226.32	220.13	255.62	196.10	254.93	217.41	212.67	225.43
Ground beef	93.50	100.59	110.67	84.70	109.91	78.37	80.54	74.70
Roast	34.02	22.57	35.32	30.72	46.30	35.71	29.65	45.95
Chuck roast	9.42	3.52	7.96	11.17	17.33	9.11	8.00	10.99
Round roast	6.63	2.26	8.89	5.13	7.39	7.29	5.49	10.33
Other roast	17.97	16.79	18.47	14.42	21.58	19.31	16.15	24.64
Steak	79.44	73.37	83.56	65.36	79.66	87.95	85.50	92.09
Round steak	16.91	16.03	21.32	13.77	17.95	15.61	14.47	17.54
Sirloin steak	21.76	17.66	20.78	17.03	24.02	26.53	26.54	26.52
Other steak	40.77	39.67	41.46	34.56	37.69	45.81	44.50	48.03
Other beef	19.35	23.61	26.07	15.31	19.06	15.38	16.98	12.68
Pork	165.77	177.43	175.47	158.84	177.32	154.96	151.90	160.14
Bacon	32.18	31.20	33.98	31.68	37.28	29.91	29.83	30.04
Pork chops	28.04	32.96	34.03	24.56	27.08	24.21	22.67	26.82
Ham	33.42	38.24	33.41	32.22	37.19	31.25	28.49	35.93
Ham, not canned	32.19	36.42	32.55	31.49	37.01	29.28	25.75	35.25
Canned ham	1.23	1.82	0.86	0.73	0.18	1.97	2.74	0.68
Sausage	32.14	37.31	33.67	28.19	33.65	31.21	31.01	31.54
Other pork	39.99	37.72	40.38	42.20	42.12	38.38	39.90	35.81
Other meats	122.13	117.19	123.64	108.71	121.75	131.98	137.19	123.17
Frankfurters	24.71	29.29	29.27	22.76	23.19	21.25	21.71	20.48
Lunch meats (cold cuts)	87.23	76.99	81.97	76.29	93.54	100.54	106.93	89.72
Bologna, liverwurst, salami	25.65	25.64	26.17	20.12	28.49	28.09	30.76	23.58
Other lunch meats	61.58	51.35	55.81	56.17	65.05	72.45	76.18	66.14
Lamb, organ meats, and others	10.19	10.91	12.39	9.65	5.02	10.19	8.54	12.96

	total consumer units	less than high school graduate	high school graduate	some college	associate's degree	bachelor's degree or more		
						total	bachelor's degree	master's, professional, doctorate
Poultry	$159.36	$149.51	$158.46	$135.84	$178.70	$173.57	$171.50	$177.06
Fresh and frozen chicken	126.52	126.54	133.04	103.63	148.35	130.09	133.14	124.95
Fresh and frozen whole chicken	37.82	35.93	41.99	32.53	44.71	36.72	36.30	37.42
Fresh and frozen chicken parts	88.70	90.61	91.04	71.10	103.63	93.38	96.84	87.52
Other poultry	32.84	22.97	25.43	32.22	30.36	43.47	38.36	52.11
Fish and seafood	125.74	108.83	119.84	104.42	128.48	150.17	139.10	168.90
Canned fish and seafood	18.18	15.42	17.94	17.16	17.97	20.15	18.38	23.16
Fresh fish and shellfish	63.29	54.72	58.35	45.46	65.89	81.54	79.57	84.86
Frozen fish and shellfish	44.27	38.69	43.55	41.80	44.62	48.48	41.15	60.87
Eggs	53.08	54.21	54.60	47.26	52.63	55.55	55.32	55.92
Dairy products	**418.93**	**346.41**	**361.54**	**371.74**	**441.93**	**515.15**	**497.79**	**544.50**
Fresh milk and cream	151.86	142.53	147.83	133.91	161.06	167.71	165.85	170.84
Fresh milk, all types	128.28	120.85	125.99	114.52	133.75	140.40	138.95	142.86
Cream	23.58	21.68	21.84	19.39	27.30	27.31	26.91	27.98
Other dairy products	267.07	203.88	213.71	237.83	280.88	347.44	331.94	373.66
Butter	25.56	18.11	23.77	23.51	25.91	31.00	30.44	31.95
Cheese	131.47	92.60	105.75	117.47	134.97	174.29	168.30	184.40
Ice cream and related products	57.37	55.32	45.98	53.38	65.08	67.23	62.46	75.29
Miscellaneous dairy products	52.67	37.86	38.20	43.47	54.92	74.93	70.74	82.01
Fruits and vegetables	**730.98**	**658.26**	**625.70**	**630.40**	**735.28**	**906.20**	**861.84**	**981.18**
Fresh fruits	261.29	226.81	209.78	213.16	250.07	350.04	329.50	384.78
Apples	41.61	32.28	34.25	32.52	43.16	56.45	55.99	57.22
Bananas	43.81	44.42	39.39	39.64	44.67	49.55	48.26	51.74
Oranges	26.74	24.55	23.78	23.66	28.77	31.28	30.11	33.27
Citrus fruits, except oranges	39.95	43.13	31.32	30.44	36.78	52.82	48.84	59.55
Other fresh fruits	109.19	82.43	81.04	86.90	96.69	159.94	146.30	182.99
Fresh vegetables	226.14	212.98	191.57	185.27	227.44	284.97	271.17	308.31
Potatoes	38.44	39.84	37.28	32.93	43.57	40.92	40.15	42.22
Lettuce	32.33	27.94	30.36	28.25	32.36	38.25	37.07	40.24
Tomatoes	39.35	42.72	34.83	32.92	38.92	46.07	43.23	50.86
Other fresh vegetables	116.01	102.47	89.10	91.17	112.60	159.74	150.72	174.98
Processed fruits	113.76	94.72	96.41	105.03	113.13	140.39	131.48	155.46
Frozen fruits and fruit juices	12.71	8.15	9.84	11.31	16.56	16.39	14.33	19.86
Frozen fruits	7.16	3.30	4.40	5.36	10.36	10.97	9.72	13.08
Frozen fruit juices	5.55	4.85	5.44	5.95	6.20	5.41	4.62	6.77
Canned fruits	20.35	18.37	18.21	20.38	17.45	23.64	24.17	22.74
Dried fruits	8.71	6.04	7.45	7.25	9.62	11.40	10.61	12.73
Fresh fruit juice	17.06	15.81	14.48	14.21	18.09	21.12	18.79	25.07
Canned and bottled fruit juice	54.92	46.34	46.44	51.89	51.41	67.84	63.57	75.07
Processed vegetables	129.80	123.76	127.93	126.94	144.63	130.79	129.69	132.64
Frozen vegetables	37.50	31.78	35.28	39.61	38.19	39.73	39.86	39.51
Canned and dried vegetables and juices	92.30	91.98	92.65	87.34	106.45	91.06	89.83	93.13
Canned vegetables	54.59	50.56	54.77	52.49	61.57	55.20	56.40	53.18
Dried vegetables	18.22	24.89	19.48	17.64	18.21	15.16	13.43	18.07
Fresh and canned vegetable juices	18.98	16.02	17.93	16.87	25.61	20.24	19.63	21.26
Sugar and other sweets	**146.77**	**124.96**	**131.11**	**128.39**	**164.11**	**174.04**	**171.56**	**178.22**
Candy and chewing gum	87.86	66.27	71.02	75.47	105.08	111.97	110.60	114.30
Sugar	24.38	30.70	30.61	22.70	23.85	18.51	18.53	18.47
Artificial sweeteners	4.91	5.16	4.27	4.71	4.74	5.49	5.27	5.86
Jams, preserves, other sweets	29.61	22.83	25.21	25.52	30.44	38.07	37.17	39.60
Fats and oils	**114.09**	**114.83**	**106.77**	**106.12**	**126.94**	**120.83**	**118.76**	**124.32**
Margarine	8.74	9.18	8.87	8.37	12.07	7.69	7.10	8.70
Fats and oils	36.79	52.71	32.54	29.51	38.03	38.62	37.21	41.00
Salad dressings	31.29	23.23	31.42	31.65	33.50	33.28	32.63	34.37
Nondairy cream and imitation milk	18.59	16.53	19.23	20.38	19.57	17.35	17.75	16.68
Peanut butter	18.68	13.18	14.71	16.21	23.77	23.89	24.08	23.57

| | total consumer units | less than high school graduate | high school graduate | some college | associate's degree | bachelor's degree or more | | master's, professional, doctorate |
						total	bachelor's degree	
Miscellaneous foods	**$699.27**	**$592.71**	**$576.34**	**$685.29**	**$723.31**	**$836.27**	**$809.70**	**$881.18**
Frozen prepared foods	130.83	103.27	112.45	140.52	134.02	147.86	142.13	157.55
Frozen meals	60.61	43.38	49.20	64.92	58.12	73.77	64.89	88.78
Other frozen prepared foods	70.22	59.90	63.25	75.60	75.90	74.09	77.24	68.76
Canned and packaged soups	46.30	38.39	37.58	48.00	48.53	54.16	53.71	54.94
Potato chips, nuts, and other snacks	153.94	115.94	121.09	138.73	165.77	200.15	186.74	222.84
Potato chips and other snacks	111.59	90.22	92.90	105.10	126.05	133.92	129.20	141.88
Nuts	42.35	25.72	28.19	33.63	39.72	66.24	57.53	80.95
Condiments and seasonings	141.39	113.19	122.81	132.19	156.63	167.79	166.57	169.84
Salt, spices, and other seasonings	38.72	38.18	33.70	34.58	38.22	45.76	46.78	44.04
Olives, pickles, relishes	17.46	10.53	14.52	17.60	18.13	22.01	21.31	23.21
Sauces and gravies	60.27	45.47	53.39	56.75	73.03	69.53	69.04	70.35
Baking needs and miscellaneous products	24.95	19.01	21.21	23.27	27.24	30.49	29.44	32.25
Other canned/packaged prepared foods	226.81	221.92	182.40	225.85	218.36	266.30	260.55	276.02
Prepared salads	35.09	20.86	28.08	35.40	36.91	45.07	40.55	52.72
Prepared desserts	14.29	13.24	12.80	14.14	15.73	15.50	13.85	18.28
Baby food	25.05	23.05	18.24	26.71	22.60	30.73	29.36	33.04
Miscellaneous prepared foods	147.81	164.25	122.37	143.27	139.20	167.09	171.23	160.08
Nonalcoholic beverages	**370.13**	**351.20**	**365.51**	**354.62**	**420.05**	**375.67**	**360.81**	**400.78**
Carbonated drinks	139.74	144.88	149.58	136.68	159.16	126.18	121.35	134.35
Tea	30.36	26.90	28.36	27.98	38.43	32.29	31.24	34.07
Coffee	86.50	65.40	79.04	85.57	91.40	99.28	89.47	115.86
Noncarbonated fruit-flavored drinks	25.83	29.34	25.32	23.96	22.87	27.09	28.76	24.26
Other nonalcoholic beverages and ice	15.36	11.87	14.51	12.53	24.58	16.34	16.76	15.63
Bottled water	56.80	58.10	55.22	53.13	62.15	58.33	55.61	62.92
Sports drinks	15.12	14.71	13.16	13.71	21.46	15.77	17.01	13.67
Food prepared by consumer unit on trips	**50.23**	**17.76**	**26.69**	**45.50**	**51.76**	**84.90**	**72.82**	**105.63**

Source: Bureau of Labor Statistics, unpublished tables from the 2012 Consumer Expenditure Survey

Table 29. Groceries: Indexed spending by education, 2012

(indexed average annual spending of consumer units on groceries by education of consumer unit reference person, 2012; index definition: an index of 100 is the average for all consumer units; an index of 125 means that spending by consumer units in that group is 25 percent above the average for all consumer units; an index of 75 indicates spending that is 25 percent below the average for all consumer units)

	total consumer units	less than high school graduate	high school graduate	some college	associate's degree	bachelor's degree or more total	bachelor's degree	master's, professional, doctorate
Average spending of consumer units, total	$51,442	$31,194	$39,989	$46,118	$52,414	$71,926	$66,420	$81,363
Average spending of consumer units, index	100	61	78	90	102	140	129	158
GROCERIES	**100**	**89**	**91**	**91**	**106**	**115**	**111**	**122**
Cereals and bakery products	**100**	**85**	**94**	**90**	**107**	**115**	**110**	**125**
Cereals and cereal products	100	86	93	90	109	115	112	120
Flour	100	116	111	81	92	101	88	122
Prepared flour mixes	100	74	90	94	132	111	104	124
Ready-to-eat and cooked cereals	100	78	90	94	113	116	117	114
Rice	100	124	100	79	87	109	100	124
Pasta, cornmeal, and other cereal products	100	80	91	86	106	121	117	129
Bakery products	100	85	94	90	106	116	109	128
Bread	100	86	97	92	107	111	104	123
White bread	100	95	102	94	108	102	97	111
Bread other than white	100	79	93	91	107	117	109	131
Crackers and cookies	100	87	91	87	105	120	115	127
Cookies	100	95	95	90	104	111	106	120
Crackers	100	76	85	82	106	131	129	135
Frozen and refrigerated bakery products	100	79	99	88	113	112	104	126
Other bakery products	100	84	92	90	103	118	109	133
Biscuits and rolls	100	83	90	85	105	123	123	123
Cakes and cupcakes	100	84	83	91	93	128	104	169
Bread and cracker products	100	85	98	95	113	106	110	101
Sweetrolls, coffee cakes, doughnuts	100	104	101	100	103	97	91	106
Pies, tarts, turnovers	100	53	114	83	115	114	105	129
Meats, poultry, fish, and eggs	**100**	**97**	**104**	**88**	**107**	**104**	**102**	**107**
Beef	100	97	113	87	113	96	94	100
Ground beef	100	108	118	91	118	84	86	80
Roast	100	66	104	90	136	105	87	135
Chuck roast	100	37	85	119	184	97	85	117
Round roast	100	34	134	77	111	110	83	156
Other roast	100	93	103	80	120	107	90	137
Steak	100	92	105	82	100	111	108	116
Round steak	100	95	126	81	106	92	86	104
Sirloin steak	100	81	95	78	110	122	122	122
Other steak	100	97	102	85	92	112	109	118
Other beef	100	122	135	79	99	79	88	66
Pork	100	107	106	96	107	93	92	97
Bacon	100	97	106	98	116	93	93	93
Pork chops	100	118	121	88	97	86	81	96
Ham	100	114	100	96	111	94	85	108
Ham, not canned	100	113	101	98	115	91	80	110
Canned ham	100	148	70	59	15	160	223	55
Sausage	100	116	105	88	105	97	96	98
Other pork	100	94	101	106	105	96	100	90
Other meats	100	96	101	89	100	108	112	101
Frankfurters	100	119	118	92	94	86	88	83
Lunch meats (cold cuts)	100	88	94	87	107	115	123	103
Bologna, liverwurst, salami	100	100	102	78	111	110	120	92
Other lunch meats	100	83	91	91	106	118	124	107
Lamb, organ meats, and others	100	107	122	95	49	100	84	127

	total consumer units	less than high school graduate	high school graduate	some college	associate's degree	bachelor's degree or more total	bachelor's degree	master's, professional, doctorate
Poultry	100	94	99	85	112	109	108	111
Fresh and frozen chicken	100	100	105	82	117	103	105	99
Fresh and frozen whole chicken	100	95	111	86	118	97	96	99
Fresh and frozen chicken parts	100	102	103	80	117	105	109	99
Other poultry	100	70	77	98	92	132	117	159
Fish and seafood	100	87	95	83	102	119	111	134
Canned fish and seafood	100	85	99	94	99	111	101	127
Fresh fish and shellfish	100	86	92	72	104	129	126	134
Frozen fish and shellfish	100	87	98	94	101	110	93	137
Eggs	100	102	103	89	99	105	104	105
Dairy products	**100**	**83**	**86**	**89**	**105**	**123**	**119**	**130**
Fresh milk and cream	100	94	97	88	106	110	109	112
Fresh milk, all types	100	94	98	89	104	109	108	111
Cream	100	92	93	82	116	116	114	119
Other dairy products	100	76	80	89	105	130	124	140
Butter	100	71	93	92	101	121	119	125
Cheese	100	70	80	89	103	133	128	140
Ice cream and related products	100	96	80	93	113	117	109	131
Miscellaneous dairy products	100	72	73	83	104	142	134	156
Fruits and vegetables	**100**	**90**	**86**	**86**	**101**	**124**	**118**	**134**
Fresh fruits	100	87	80	82	96	134	126	147
Apples	100	78	82	78	104	136	135	138
Bananas	100	101	90	90	102	113	110	118
Oranges	100	92	89	88	108	117	113	124
Citrus fruits, except oranges	100	108	78	76	92	132	122	149
Other fresh fruits	100	75	74	80	89	146	134	168
Fresh vegetables	100	94	85	82	101	126	120	136
Potatoes	100	104	97	86	113	106	104	110
Lettuce	100	86	94	87	100	118	115	124
Tomatoes	100	109	89	84	99	117	110	129
Other fresh vegetables	100	88	77	79	97	138	130	151
Processed fruits	100	83	85	92	99	123	116	137
Frozen fruits and fruit juices	100	64	77	89	130	129	113	156
Frozen fruits	100	46	61	75	145	153	136	183
Frozen fruit juices	100	87	98	107	112	97	83	122
Canned fruits	100	90	89	100	86	116	119	112
Dried fruits	100	69	86	83	110	131	122	146
Fresh fruit juice	100	93	85	83	106	124	110	147
Canned and bottled fruit juice	100	84	85	94	94	124	116	137
Processed vegetables	100	95	99	98	111	101	100	102
Frozen vegetables	100	85	94	106	102	106	106	105
Canned and dried vegetables and juices	100	100	100	95	115	99	97	101
Canned vegetables	100	93	100	96	113	101	103	97
Dried vegetables	100	137	107	97	100	83	74	99
Fresh and canned vegetable juices	100	84	94	89	135	107	103	112
Sugar and other sweets	**100**	**85**	**89**	**87**	**112**	**119**	**117**	**121**
Candy and chewing gum	100	75	81	86	120	127	126	130
Sugar	100	126	126	93	98	76	76	76
Artificial sweeteners	100	105	87	96	97	112	107	119
Jams, preserves, other sweets	100	77	85	86	103	129	126	134
Fats and oils	**100**	**101**	**94**	**93**	**111**	**106**	**104**	**109**
Margarine	100	105	101	96	138	88	81	100
Fats and oils	100	143	88	80	103	105	101	111
Salad dressings	100	74	100	101	107	106	104	110
Nondairy cream and imitation milk	100	89	103	110	105	93	95	90
Peanut butter	100	71	79	87	127	128	129	126

	total consumer units	less than high school graduate	high school graduate	some college	associate's degree	bachelor's degree or more total	bachelor's degree	master's, professional, doctorate
Miscellaneous foods	**100**	**85**	**82**	**98**	**103**	**120**	**116**	**126**
Frozen prepared foods	100	79	86	107	102	113	109	120
Frozen meals	100	72	81	107	96	122	107	146
Other frozen prepared foods	100	85	90	108	108	106	110	98
Canned and packaged soups	100	83	81	104	105	117	116	119
Potato chips, nuts, and other snacks	100	75	79	90	108	130	121	145
Potato chips and other snacks	100	81	83	94	113	120	116	127
Nuts	100	61	67	79	94	156	136	191
Condiments and seasonings	100	80	87	93	111	119	118	120
Salt, spices, and other seasonings	100	99	87	89	99	118	121	114
Olives, pickles, relishes	100	60	83	101	104	126	122	133
Sauces and gravies	100	75	89	94	121	115	115	117
Baking needs and miscellaneous products	100	76	85	93	109	122	118	129
Other canned/packaged prepared foods	100	98	80	100	96	117	115	122
Prepared salads	100	59	80	101	105	128	116	150
Prepared desserts	100	93	90	99	110	108	97	128
Baby food	100	92	73	107	90	123	117	132
Miscellaneous prepared foods	100	111	83	97	94	113	116	108
Nonalcoholic beverages	**100**	**95**	**99**	**96**	**113**	**101**	**97**	**108**
Carbonated drinks	100	104	107	98	114	90	87	96
Tea	100	89	93	92	127	106	103	112
Coffee	100	76	91	99	106	115	103	134
Noncarbonated fruit-flavored drinks	100	114	98	93	89	105	111	94
Other nonalcoholic beverages and ice	100	77	94	82	160	106	109	102
Bottled water	100	102	97	94	109	103	98	111
Sports drinks	100	97	87	91	142	104	113	90
Food prepared by consumer unit on trips	**100**	**35**	**53**	**91**	**103**	**169**	**145**	**210**

Source: Calculations by New Strategist based on the Bureau of Labor Statistics' 2012 Consumer Expenditure Survey

Table 30. Groceries: Total spending by education, 2012

(total annual spending on groceries, by consumer unit educational attainment group, 2012; consumer units and dollars in thousands)

	total consumer units	less than high school graduate	high school graduate	some college	associate's degree	bachelor's degree or more total	bachelor's degree	master's, professional, doctorate
Number of consumer units	124,416	16,246	31,022	25,623	12,287	39,238	24,798	14,440
Total spending of all consumer units	$6,400,191,698	$506,771,388	$1,240,549,926	$1,181,691,251	$644,015,856	$2,822,245,337	$1,647,089,112	$1,174,881,864
GROCERIES	487,791,590	56,733,306	111,202,392	91,098,477	50,996,456	177,256,488	107,904,281	69,292,650
Cereals and bakery products	66,917,146	7,452,040	15,613,683	12,352,848	7,043,400	24,358,558	14,639,995	9,706,857
Cereals and cereal products	22,641,224	2,545,423	5,249,233	4,185,005	2,427,911	8,202,312	5,054,576	3,145,610
Flour	1,164,534	176,107	322,008	194,991	105,668	369,622	204,584	164,616
Prepared flour mixes	2,013,051	194,790	454,162	388,445	262,819	705,892	416,358	289,089
Ready-to-eat and cooked cereals	11,797,125	1,196,518	2,660,757	2,283,266	1,314,832	4,308,332	2,746,379	1,562,264
Rice	3,066,854	494,691	764,072	501,955	263,433	1,056,287	612,511	442,730
Pasta, cornmeal, and other cereal products	4,600,904	483,319	1,048,233	816,605	481,282	1,762,179	1,074,745	686,766
Bakery products	44,275,922	4,906,779	10,364,140	8,167,844	4,615,366	16,156,247	9,585,419	6,561,247
Bread	13,078,610	1,464,577	3,154,627	2,486,456	1,387,079	4,567,696	2,700,750	1,863,915
White bread	5,414,584	670,310	1,374,895	1,050,543	578,595	1,739,028	1,041,516	696,730
Bread other than white	7,664,026	794,429	1,779,732	1,435,913	808,362	2,828,667	1,659,482	1,167,185
Crackers and cookies	10,915,016	1,235,996	2,471,523	1,949,654	1,130,650	4,113,712	2,508,814	1,603,562
Cookies	6,290,473	777,046	1,495,260	1,164,822	647,894	2,203,998	1,323,965	879,107
Crackers	4,624,543	458,787	976,262	785,089	482,633	1,909,713	1,184,848	724,455
Frozen and refrigerated bakery products	3,579,448	371,546	886,609	649,543	400,925	1,265,033	741,956	522,150
Other bakery products	16,702,848	1,834,498	3,851,381	3,082,191	1,696,835	6,210,198	3,633,899	2,571,620
Biscuits and rolls	6,450,970	700,852	1,440,351	1,130,743	670,010	2,499,068	1,575,169	923,727
Cakes and cupcakes	4,720,343	515,648	972,850	879,894	434,591	1,906,574	975,057	928,059
Bread and cracker products	909,481	101,213	221,807	178,336	101,491	304,879	198,632	106,278
Sweetrolls, coffee cakes, doughnuts	2,952,392	401,926	741,736	608,546	301,032	900,904	537,373	363,166
Pies, tarts, turnovers	1,668,419	114,859	474,637	284,672	189,588	598,380	347,668	250,390
Meats, poultry, fish, and eggs	106,053,443	13,440,316	27,536,678	19,247,229	11,227,983	34,672,266	21,516,729	13,149,208
Beef	28,157,829	3,576,232	7,929,844	5,024,670	3,132,325	8,530,734	5,273,791	3,255,209
Ground beef	11,632,896	1,634,185	3,433,205	2,170,268	1,350,464	3,075,082	1,997,231	1,078,668
Roast	4,232,632	366,672	1,095,697	787,139	568,888	1,401,189	735,261	663,518
Chuck roast	1,171,999	57,186	246,935	286,209	212,934	357,458	198,384	158,696
Round roast	824,878	36,716	275,786	131,446	90,801	286,045	136,141	149,165
Other roast	2,235,756	272,770	572,976	369,484	265,153	757,686	400,488	355,802
Steak	9,883,607	1,191,969	2,592,198	1,674,719	978,782	3,450,982	2,120,229	1,329,780
Round steak	2,103,875	260,423	661,389	352,829	220,552	612,505	358,827	253,278
Sirloin steak	2,707,292	286,904	644,637	436,360	295,134	1,040,984	658,139	382,949
Other steak	5,072,440	644,479	1,286,172	885,531	463,097	1,797,493	1,103,511	693,553
Other beef	2,407,450	383,568	808,744	392,288	234,190	603,480	421,070	183,099
Pork	20,624,440	2,882,528	5,443,430	4,069,957	2,178,731	6,080,320	3,766,816	2,312,422
Bacon	4,003,707	506,875	1,054,128	811,737	458,059	1,173,609	739,724	433,778
Pork chops	3,488,625	535,468	1,055,679	629,301	332,732	949,952	562,171	387,281
Ham	4,157,983	621,247	1,036,445	825,573	456,954	1,226,188	706,495	518,829
Ham, not canned	4,004,951	591,679	1,009,766	806,868	454,742	1,148,889	638,549	509,010
Canned ham	153,032	29,568	26,679	18,705	2,212	77,299	67,947	9,819
Sausage	3,998,730	606,138	1,044,511	722,312	413,458	1,224,618	768,986	455,438
Other pork	4,975,396	612,799	1,252,668	1,081,291	517,528	1,505,954	989,440	517,096
Other meats	15,194,926	1,903,869	3,835,560	2,785,476	1,495,942	5,178,631	3,402,038	1,778,575
Frankfurters	3,074,319	475,845	908,014	583,179	284,936	833,808	538,365	295,731
Lunch meats (cold cuts)	10,852,808	1,250,780	2,542,873	1,954,779	1,149,326	3,944,989	2,651,650	1,295,557
Bologna, liverwurst, salami	3,191,270	416,547	811,846	515,535	350,057	1,102,195	762,786	340,495
Other lunch meats	7,661,537	834,232	1,731,338	1,439,244	799,269	2,842,793	1,889,112	955,062
Lamb, organ meats, and others	1,267,799	177,244	384,363	247,262	61,681	399,835	211,775	187,142

	total consumer units	less than high school graduate	high school graduate	some college	associate's degree	bachelor's degree or more		master's, professional, doctorate
						total	bachelor's degree	
Poultry	$19,826,934	$2,428,939	$4,915,746	$3,480,628	$2,195,687	$6,810,540	$4,252,857	$2,556,746
Fresh and frozen chicken	15,741,112	2,055,769	4,127,167	2,655,311	1,822,776	5,104,471	3,301,606	1,804,278
Fresh and frozen whole chicken	4,705,413	583,719	1,302,614	833,516	549,352	1,440,819	900,167	540,345
Fresh and frozen chicken parts	11,035,699	1,472,050	2,824,243	1,821,795	1,273,302	3,664,044	2,401,438	1,263,789
Other poultry	4,085,821	373,171	788,889	825,573	373,033	1,705,676	951,251	752,468
Fish and seafood	15,644,068	1,768,052	3,717,676	2,675,554	1,578,634	5,892,370	3,449,402	2,438,916
Canned fish and seafood	2,261,883	250,513	556,535	439,691	220,797	790,646	455,787	334,430
Fresh fish and shellfish	7,874,289	888,981	1,810,134	1,164,822	809,590	3,199,467	1,973,177	1,225,378
Frozen fish and shellfish	5,507,896	628,558	1,351,008	1,071,041	548,246	1,902,258	1,020,438	878,963
Eggs	6,604,001	880,696	1,693,801	1,210,943	646,665	2,179,671	1,371,825	807,485
Dairy products	**52,121,595**	**5,627,777**	**11,215,694**	**9,525,094**	**5,429,994**	**20,213,456**	**12,344,196**	**7,862,580**
Fresh milk and cream	18,893,814	2,315,542	4,585,982	3,431,176	1,978,944	6,580,605	4,112,748	2,466,930
Fresh milk, all types	15,960,084	1,963,329	3,908,462	2,934,346	1,643,386	5,509,015	3,445,682	2,062,898
Cream	2,933,729	352,213	677,520	496,830	335,435	1,071,590	667,314	404,031
Other dairy products	33,227,781	3,312,234	6,629,712	6,093,918	3,451,173	13,632,851	8,231,448	5,395,650
Butter	3,180,073	294,215	737,393	602,397	318,356	1,216,378	754,851	461,358
Cheese	16,356,972	1,504,380	3,280,577	3,009,934	1,658,376	6,838,791	4,173,503	2,662,736
Ice cream and related products	7,137,746	898,729	1,426,392	1,367,756	799,638	2,637,971	1,548,883	1,087,188
Miscellaneous dairy products	6,552,991	615,074	1,185,040	1,113,832	674,802	2,940,103	1,754,211	1,184,224
Fruits and vegetables	**90,945,608**	**10,694,092**	**19,410,465**	**16,152,739**	**9,034,385**	**35,557,476**	**21,371,908**	**14,168,239**
Fresh fruits	32,508,657	3,684,755	6,507,795	5,461,799	3,072,610	13,734,870	8,170,941	5,556,223
Apples	5,176,950	524,421	1,062,504	833,260	530,307	2,214,985	1,388,440	826,257
Bananas	5,450,665	721,647	1,221,957	1,015,696	548,860	1,944,243	1,196,751	747,126
Oranges	3,326,884	398,839	737,703	606,240	353,497	1,227,365	746,668	480,419
Citrus fruits, except oranges	4,970,419	700,690	971,609	779,964	451,916	2,072,551	1,211,134	859,902
Other fresh fruits	13,584,983	1,339,158	2,514,023	2,226,639	1,188,030	6,275,726	3,627,947	2,642,376
Fresh vegetables	28,135,434	3,460,073	5,942,885	4,747,173	2,794,555	11,181,653	6,724,474	4,451,996
Potatoes	4,782,551	647,241	1,156,500	843,765	535,345	1,605,619	995,640	609,657
Lettuce	4,022,369	453,913	941,828	723,850	397,607	1,500,854	919,262	581,066
Tomatoes	4,895,770	694,029	1,080,496	843,509	478,210	1,807,695	1,072,018	734,418
Other fresh vegetables	14,433,500	1,664,728	2,764,060	2,336,049	1,383,516	6,267,878	3,737,555	2,526,711
Processed fruits	14,153,564	1,538,821	2,990,831	2,691,184	1,390,028	5,508,623	3,260,441	2,244,842
Frozen fruits and fruit juices	1,581,327	132,405	305,256	289,796	203,473	643,111	355,355	286,778
Frozen fruits	890,819	53,612	136,497	137,339	127,293	430,441	241,037	188,875
Frozen fruit juices	690,509	78,793	168,760	152,457	76,179	212,278	114,567	97,759
Canned fruits	2,531,866	298,439	564,911	522,197	214,408	927,586	599,368	328,366
Dried fruits	1,083,663	98,126	231,114	185,767	118,201	447,313	263,107	183,821
Fresh fruit juice	2,122,537	256,849	449,199	364,103	222,272	828,707	465,954	362,011
Canned and bottled fruit juice	6,832,927	752,840	1,440,662	1,329,577	631,675	2,661,906	1,576,409	1,084,011
Processed vegetables	16,149,197	2,010,605	3,968,644	3,252,584	1,777,069	5,131,938	3,216,053	1,915,322
Frozen vegetables	4,665,600	516,298	1,094,456	1,014,927	469,241	1,558,926	988,448	570,524
Canned and dried vegetables and juices	11,483,597	1,494,307	2,874,188	2,237,913	1,307,951	3,573,012	2,227,604	1,344,797
Canned vegetables	6,791,869	821,398	1,699,075	1,344,951	756,511	2,165,938	1,398,607	767,919
Dried vegetables	2,266,860	404,363	604,309	451,990	223,746	594,848	333,037	260,931
Fresh and canned vegetable juices	2,361,416	260,261	556,224	432,260	314,670	794,177	486,785	306,994
Sugar and other sweets	**18,260,536**	**2,030,100**	**4,067,294**	**3,289,737**	**2,016,420**	**6,828,982**	**4,254,345**	**2,573,497**
Candy and chewing gum	10,931,190	1,076,622	2,203,182	1,933,768	1,291,118	4,393,479	2,742,659	1,650,492
Sugar	3,033,262	498,752	949,583	581,642	293,045	726,295	459,507	266,707
Artificial sweeteners	610,883	83,829	132,464	120,684	58,240	215,417	130,685	84,618
Jams, preserves, other sweets	3,683,958	370,896	782,065	653,899	374,016	1,493,791	921,742	571,824
Fats and oils	**14,194,621**	**1,865,528**	**3,312,219**	**2,719,113**	**1,559,712**	**4,741,128**	**2,945,010**	**1,795,181**
Margarine	1,087,396	149,138	275,165	214,465	148,304	301,740	176,066	125,628
Fats and oils	4,577,265	856,327	1,009,456	756,135	467,275	1,515,372	922,734	592,040
Salad dressings	3,892,977	377,395	974,711	810,968	411,615	1,305,841	809,159	496,303
Nondairy cream and imitation milk	2,312,893	268,546	596,553	522,197	240,457	680,779	440,165	240,859
Peanut butter	2,324,091	214,122	456,334	415,349	292,062	937,396	597,136	340,351

	total consumer units	less than high school graduate	high school graduate	some college	associate's degree	bachelor's degree or more		
						total	bachelor's degree	master's, professional, doctorate
Miscellaneous foods	**$87,000,376**	**$9,629,167**	**$17,879,219**	**$17,559,186**	**$8,887,310**	**$32,813,562**	**$20,078,941**	**$12,724,239**
Frozen prepared foods	16,277,345	1,677,724	3,488,424	3,600,544	1,646,704	5,801,731	3,524,540	2,275,022
Frozen meals	7,540,854	704,751	1,526,282	1,663,445	714,120	2,894,587	1,609,142	1,281,983
Other frozen prepared foods	8,736,492	973,135	1,962,142	1,937,099	932,583	2,907,143	1,915,398	992,894
Canned and packaged soups	5,760,461	623,684	1,165,807	1,229,904	596,288	2,125,130	1,331,901	793,334
Potato chips, nuts, and other snacks	19,152,599	1,883,561	3,756,454	3,554,679	2,036,816	7,853,486	4,630,779	3,217,810
Potato chips and other snacks	13,883,581	1,465,714	2,881,944	2,692,977	1,548,776	5,254,753	3,203,902	2,048,747
Nuts	5,269,018	417,847	874,510	861,701	488,040	2,599,125	1,426,629	1,168,918
Condiments and seasonings	17,591,178	1,838,885	3,809,812	3,387,104	1,924,513	6,583,744	4,130,603	2,452,490
Salt, spices, and other seasonings	4,817,388	620,272	1,045,441	886,043	469,609	1,795,531	1,160,050	635,938
Olives, pickles, relishes	2,172,303	171,070	450,439	450,965	222,763	863,628	528,445	335,152
Sauces and gravies	7,498,552	738,706	1,656,265	1,454,105	897,320	2,728,218	1,712,054	1,015,854
Baking needs and miscellaneous products	3,104,179	308,836	657,977	596,247	334,698	1,196,367	730,053	465,690
Other canned/packaged prepared foods	28,218,793	3,605,312	5,658,413	5,786,955	2,682,989	10,449,079	6,461,119	3,985,729
Prepared salads	4,365,757	338,892	871,098	907,054	453,513	1,768,457	1,005,559	761,277
Prepared desserts	1,777,905	215,097	397,082	362,309	193,275	608,189	343,452	263,963
Baby food	3,116,621	374,470	565,841	684,390	277,686	1,205,784	728,069	477,098
Miscellaneous prepared foods	18,389,929	2,668,406	3,796,162	3,671,007	1,710,350	6,556,277	4,246,162	2,311,555
Nonalcoholic beverages	**46,050,094**	**5,705,595**	**11,338,851**	**9,086,428**	**5,161,154**	**14,740,539**	**8,947,366**	**5,787,263**
Carbonated drinks	17,385,892	2,353,720	4,640,271	3,502,152	1,955,599	4,951,051	3,009,237	1,940,014
Tea	3,777,270	437,017	879,784	716,932	472,189	1,266,995	774,690	491,971
Coffee	10,761,984	1,062,488	2,451,979	2,192,560	1,123,032	3,895,549	2,218,677	1,673,018
Noncarbonated fruit-flavored drinks	3,213,665	476,658	785,477	613,927	281,004	1,062,957	713,190	350,314
Other nonalcoholic beverages and ice	1,911,030	192,840	450,129	321,056	302,014	641,149	415,614	225,697
Bottled water	7,066,829	943,893	1,713,035	1,361,350	763,637	2,288,753	1,379,017	908,565
Sports drinks	1,881,170	238,979	408,250	351,291	263,679	618,783	421,814	197,395
Food prepared by consumer unit on trips	**6,249,416**	**288,529**	**827,977**	**1,165,847**	**635,975**	**3,331,306**	**1,805,790**	**1,525,297**

Note: Numbers may not add to total because of rounding.
Source: Calculations by New Strategist based on the Bureau of Labor Statistics' 2012 Consumer Expenditure Survey

Table 31. Groceries: Market shares by education, 2012

(percentage of total annual spending on groceries accounted for by consumer unit educational attainment groups, 2012)

	total consumer units	less than high school graduate	high school graduate	some college	associate's degree	bachelor's degree or more total	bachelor's degree	master's, professional, doctorate
Share of total consumer units	100.0%	13.1%	24.9%	20.6%	9.9%	31.5%	19.9%	11.6%
Share of total before-tax income	100.0	6.6	17.9	17.6	10.0	47.9	27.2	20.7
Share of total spending	100.0	7.9	19.4	18.5	10.1	44.1	25.7	18.4
GROCERIES	100.0	11.6	22.8	18.7	10.5	36.3	22.1	14.2
Cereals and bakery products	100.0	11.1	23.3	18.5	10.5	36.4	21.9	14.5
Cereals and cereal products	100.0	11.2	23.2	18.5	10.7	36.2	22.3	13.9
Flour	100.0	15.1	27.7	16.7	9.1	31.7	17.6	14.1
Prepared flour mixes	100.0	9.7	22.6	19.3	13.1	35.1	20.7	14.4
Ready-to-eat and cooked cereals	100.0	10.1	22.6	19.4	11.1	36.5	23.3	13.2
Rice	100.0	16.1	24.9	16.4	8.6	34.4	20.0	14.4
Pasta, cornmeal, and other cereal products	100.0	10.5	22.8	17.7	10.5	38.3	23.4	14.9
Bakery products	100.0	11.1	23.4	18.4	10.4	36.5	21.6	14.8
Bread	100.0	11.2	24.1	19.0	10.6	34.9	20.7	14.3
White bread	100.0	12.4	25.4	19.4	10.7	32.1	19.2	12.9
Bread other than white	100.0	10.4	23.2	18.7	10.5	36.9	21.7	15.2
Crackers and cookies	100.0	11.3	22.6	17.9	10.4	37.7	23.0	14.7
Cookies	100.0	12.4	23.8	18.5	10.3	35.0	21.0	14.0
Crackers	100.0	9.9	21.1	17.0	10.4	41.3	25.6	15.7
Frozen and refrigerated bakery products	100.0	10.4	24.8	18.1	11.2	35.3	20.7	14.6
Other bakery products	100.0	11.0	23.1	18.5	10.2	37.2	21.8	15.4
Biscuits and rolls	100.0	10.9	22.3	17.5	10.4	38.7	24.4	14.3
Cakes and cupcakes	100.0	10.9	20.6	18.6	9.2	40.4	20.7	19.7
Bread and cracker products	100.0	11.1	24.4	19.6	11.2	33.5	21.8	11.7
Sweetrolls, coffee cakes, doughnuts	100.0	13.6	25.1	20.6	10.2	30.5	18.2	12.3
Pies, tarts, turnovers	100.0	6.9	28.4	17.1	11.4	35.9	20.8	15.0
Meats, poultry, fish, and eggs	100.0	12.7	26.0	18.1	10.6	32.7	20.3	12.4
Beef	100.0	12.7	28.2	17.8	11.1	30.3	18.7	11.6
Ground beef	100.0	14.0	29.5	18.7	11.6	26.4	17.2	9.3
Roast	100.0	8.7	25.9	18.6	13.4	33.1	17.4	15.7
Chuck roast	100.0	4.9	21.1	24.4	18.2	30.5	16.9	13.5
Round roast	100.0	4.5	33.4	15.9	11.0	34.7	16.5	18.1
Other roast	100.0	12.2	25.6	16.5	11.9	33.9	17.9	15.9
Steak	100.0	12.1	26.2	16.9	9.9	34.9	21.5	13.5
Round steak	100.0	12.4	31.4	16.8	10.5	29.1	17.1	12.0
Sirloin steak	100.0	10.6	23.8	16.1	10.9	38.5	24.3	14.1
Other steak	100.0	12.7	25.4	17.5	9.1	35.4	21.8	13.7
Other beef	100.0	15.9	33.6	16.3	9.7	25.1	17.5	7.6
Pork	100.0	14.0	26.4	19.7	10.6	29.5	18.3	11.2
Bacon	100.0	12.7	26.3	20.3	11.4	29.3	18.5	10.8
Pork chops	100.0	15.3	30.3	18.0	9.5	27.2	16.1	11.1
Ham	100.0	14.9	24.9	19.9	11.0	29.5	17.0	12.5
Ham, not canned	100.0	14.8	25.2	20.1	11.4	28.7	15.9	12.7
Canned ham	100.0	19.3	17.4	12.2	1.4	50.5	44.4	6.4
Sausage	100.0	15.2	26.1	18.1	10.3	30.6	19.2	11.4
Other pork	100.0	12.3	25.2	21.7	10.4	30.3	19.9	10.4
Other meats	100.0	12.5	25.2	18.3	9.8	34.1	22.4	11.7
Frankfurters	100.0	15.5	29.5	19.0	9.3	27.1	17.5	9.6
Lunch meats (cold cuts)	100.0	11.5	23.4	18.0	10.6	36.3	24.4	11.9
Bologna, liverwurst, salami	100.0	13.1	25.4	16.2	11.0	34.5	23.9	10.7
Other lunch meats	100.0	10.9	22.6	18.8	10.4	37.1	24.7	12.5
Lamb, organ meats, and others	100.0	14.0	30.3	19.5	4.9	31.5	16.7	14.8

	total consumer units	less than high school graduate	high school graduate	some college	associate's degree	bachelor's degree or more		master's, professional, doctorate
						total	bachelor's degree	
Poultry	100.0%	12.3%	24.8%	17.6%	11.1%	34.3%	21.4%	12.9%
Fresh and frozen chicken	100.0	13.1	26.2	16.9	11.6	32.4	21.0	11.5
Fresh and frozen whole chicken	100.0	12.4	27.7	17.7	11.7	30.6	19.1	11.5
Fresh and frozen chicken parts	100.0	13.3	25.6	16.5	11.5	33.2	21.8	11.5
Other poultry	100.0	9.1	19.3	20.2	9.1	41.7	23.3	18.4
Fish and seafood	100.0	11.3	23.8	17.1	10.1	37.7	22.0	15.6
Canned fish and seafood	100.0	11.1	24.6	19.4	9.8	35.0	20.2	14.8
Fresh fish and shellfish	100.0	11.3	23.0	14.8	10.3	40.6	25.1	15.6
Frozen fish and shellfish	100.0	11.4	24.5	19.4	10.0	34.5	18.5	16.0
Eggs	100.0	13.3	25.6	18.3	9.8	33.0	20.8	12.2
Dairy products	**100.0**	**10.8**	**21.5**	**18.3**	**10.4**	**38.8**	**23.7**	**15.1**
Fresh milk and cream	100.0	12.3	24.3	18.2	10.5	34.8	21.8	13.1
Fresh milk, all types	100.0	12.3	24.5	18.4	10.3	34.5	21.6	12.9
Cream	100.0	12.0	23.1	16.9	11.4	36.5	22.7	13.8
Other dairy products	100.0	10.0	20.0	18.3	10.4	41.0	24.8	16.2
Butter	100.0	9.3	23.2	18.9	10.0	38.3	23.7	14.5
Cheese	100.0	9.2	20.1	18.4	10.1	41.8	25.5	16.3
Ice cream and related products	100.0	12.6	20.0	19.2	11.2	37.0	21.7	15.2
Miscellaneous dairy products	100.0	9.4	18.1	17.0	10.3	44.9	26.8	18.1
Fruits and vegetables	**100.0**	**11.8**	**21.3**	**17.8**	**9.9**	**39.1**	**23.5**	**15.6**
Fresh fruits	100.0	11.3	20.0	16.8	9.5	42.2	25.1	17.1
Apples	100.0	10.1	20.5	16.1	10.2	42.8	26.8	16.0
Bananas	100.0	13.2	22.4	18.6	10.1	35.7	22.0	13.7
Oranges	100.0	12.0	22.2	18.2	10.6	36.9	22.4	14.4
Citrus fruits, except oranges	100.0	14.1	19.5	15.7	9.1	41.7	24.4	17.3
Other fresh fruits	100.0	9.9	18.5	16.4	8.7	46.2	26.7	19.5
Fresh vegetables	100.0	12.3	21.1	16.9	9.9	39.7	23.9	15.8
Potatoes	100.0	13.5	24.2	17.6	11.2	33.6	20.8	12.7
Lettuce	100.0	11.3	23.4	18.0	9.9	37.3	22.9	14.4
Tomatoes	100.0	14.2	22.1	17.2	9.8	36.9	21.9	15.0
Other fresh vegetables	100.0	11.5	19.2	16.2	9.6	43.4	25.9	17.5
Processed fruits	100.0	10.9	21.1	19.0	9.8	38.9	23.0	15.9
Frozen fruits and fruit juices	100.0	8.4	19.3	18.3	12.9	40.7	22.5	18.1
Frozen fruits	100.0	6.0	15.3	15.4	14.3	48.3	27.1	21.2
Frozen fruit juices	100.0	11.4	24.4	22.1	11.0	30.7	16.6	14.2
Canned fruits	100.0	11.8	22.3	20.6	8.5	36.6	23.7	13.0
Dried fruits	100.0	9.1	21.3	17.1	10.9	41.3	24.3	17.0
Fresh fruit juice	100.0	12.1	21.2	17.2	10.5	39.0	22.0	17.1
Canned and bottled fruit juice	100.0	11.0	21.1	19.5	9.2	39.0	23.1	15.9
Processed vegetables	100.0	12.5	24.6	20.1	11.0	31.8	19.9	11.9
Frozen vegetables	100.0	11.1	23.5	21.8	10.1	33.4	21.2	12.2
Canned and dried vegetables and juices	100.0	13.0	25.0	19.5	11.4	31.1	19.4	11.7
Canned vegetables	100.0	12.1	25.0	19.8	11.1	31.9	20.6	11.3
Dried vegetables	100.0	17.8	26.7	19.9	9.9	26.2	14.7	11.5
Fresh and canned vegetable juices	100.0	11.0	23.6	18.3	13.3	33.6	20.6	13.0
Sugar and other sweets	**100.0**	**11.1**	**22.3**	**18.0**	**11.0**	**37.4**	**23.3**	**14.1**
Candy and chewing gum	100.0	9.8	20.2	17.7	11.8	40.2	25.1	15.1
Sugar	100.0	16.4	31.3	19.2	9.7	23.9	15.1	8.8
Artificial sweeteners	100.0	13.7	21.7	19.8	9.5	35.3	21.4	13.9
Jams, preserves, other sweets	100.0	10.1	21.2	17.7	10.2	40.5	25.0	15.5
Fats and oils	**100.0**	**13.1**	**23.3**	**19.2**	**11.0**	**33.4**	**20.7**	**12.6**
Margarine	100.0	13.7	25.3	19.7	13.6	27.7	16.2	11.6
Fats and oils	100.0	18.7	22.1	16.5	10.2	33.1	20.2	12.9
Salad dressings	100.0	9.7	25.0	20.8	10.6	33.5	20.8	12.7
Nondairy cream and imitation milk	100.0	11.6	25.8	22.6	10.4	29.4	19.0	10.4
Peanut butter	100.0	9.2	19.6	17.9	12.6	40.3	25.7	14.6

	total consumer units	less than high school graduate	high school graduate	some college	associate's degree	bachelor's degree or more		
						total	bachelor's degree	master's, professional, doctorate
Miscellaneous foods	**100.0%**	**11.1%**	**20.6%**	**20.2%**	**10.2%**	**37.7%**	**23.1%**	**14.6%**
Frozen prepared foods	100.0	10.3	21.4	22.1	10.1	35.6	21.7	14.0
Frozen meals	100.0	9.3	20.2	22.1	9.5	38.4	21.3	17.0
Other frozen prepared foods	100.0	11.1	22.5	22.2	10.7	33.3	21.9	11.4
Canned and packaged soups	100.0	10.8	20.2	21.4	10.4	36.9	23.1	13.8
Potato chips, nuts, and other snacks	100.0	9.8	19.6	18.6	10.6	41.0	24.2	16.8
Potato chips and other snacks	100.0	10.6	20.8	19.4	11.2	37.8	23.1	14.8
Nuts	100.0	7.9	16.6	16.4	9.3	49.3	27.1	22.2
Condiments and seasonings	100.0	10.5	21.7	19.3	10.9	37.4	23.5	13.9
Salt, spices, and other seasonings	100.0	12.9	21.7	18.4	9.7	37.3	24.1	13.2
Olives, pickles, relishes	100.0	7.9	20.7	20.8	10.3	39.8	24.3	15.4
Sauces and gravies	100.0	9.9	22.1	19.4	12.0	36.4	22.8	13.5
Baking needs and miscellaneous products	100.0	9.9	21.2	19.2	10.8	38.5	23.5	15.0
Other canned/packaged prepared foods	100.0	12.8	20.1	20.5	9.5	37.0	22.9	14.1
Prepared salads	100.0	7.8	20.0	20.8	10.4	40.5	23.0	17.4
Prepared desserts	100.0	12.1	22.3	20.4	10.9	34.2	19.3	14.8
Baby food	100.0	12.0	18.2	22.0	8.9	38.7	23.4	15.3
Miscellaneous prepared foods	100.0	14.5	20.6	20.0	9.3	35.7	23.1	12.6
Nonalcoholic beverages	**100.0**	**12.4**	**24.6**	**19.7**	**11.2**	**32.0**	**19.4**	**12.6**
Carbonated drinks	100.0	13.5	26.7	20.1	11.2	28.5	17.3	11.2
Tea	100.0	11.6	23.3	19.0	12.5	33.5	20.5	13.0
Coffee	100.0	9.9	22.8	20.4	10.4	36.2	20.6	15.5
Noncarbonated fruit-flavored drinks	100.0	14.8	24.4	19.1	8.7	33.1	22.2	10.9
Other nonalcoholic beverages and ice	100.0	10.1	23.6	16.8	15.8	33.5	21.7	11.8
Bottled water	100.0	13.4	24.2	19.3	10.8	32.4	19.5	12.9
Sports drinks	100.0	12.7	21.7	18.7	14.0	32.9	22.4	10.5
Food prepared by consumer unit on trips	**100.0**	**4.6**	**13.2**	**18.7**	**10.2**	**53.3**	**28.9**	**24.4**

Note: Numbers may not add to total because of rounding.
Source: Calculations by New Strategist based on the Bureau of Labor Statistics' 2012 Consumer Expenditure Survey

Apples

Best customers:	**Householders aged 35 to 54**
	Married couples with children at home
	Asians
Customer trends:	**Average household spending on apples may fall as the population ages and household size shrinks.**

The largest households spend the most on apples. Married couples with children at home spend 61 percent more than the average household on apples. Householders aged 35 to 54, most with children at home, spend 16 to 25 percent more than average on apples and control 45 percent of the market. The spending on apples by Asian householders is 43 percent above average.

Average household spending on apples remained steady from 2000 to 2010, after adjusting for inflation, and then increased by 6 percent between 2010 and 2012. Behind these trends is the greater availability of conveniently packaged sliced apples, boosting household purchasing despite the baby-boom generation's exit from the best-customer lifestage. Average household spending on apples may fall as the population ages and household size shrinks.

Table 32. Apples

Total household spending	$5,176,949,760.00
Average household spends	41.61

	AVERAGE HOUSEHOLD SPENDING	BEST CUSTOMERS (index)	BIGGEST CUSTOMERS (market share)
AGE OF HOUSEHOLDER			
Average household	**$41.61**	**100**	**100.0%**
Under age 25	32.09	77	5.1
Aged 25 to 34	40.38	97	15.7
Aged 35 to 44	52.08	125	21.7
Aged 45 to 54	48.45	116	23.0
Aged 55 to 64	38.33	92	16.9
Aged 65 to 74	35.26	85	10.2
Aged 75 or older	30.93	74	7.3

	AVERAGE HOUSEHOLD SPENDING	BEST CUSTOMERS (index)	BIGGEST CUSTOMERS (market share)
HOUSEHOLD INCOME			
Average household	**$41.61**	**100**	**100.0%**
Under $20,000	21.70	52	11.0
$20,000 to $39,999	27.89	67	15.1
$40,000 to $49,999	36.47	88	7.8
$50,000 to $69,999	41.39	99	14.4
$70,000 to $79,999	47.82	115	6.4
$80,000 to $99,999	52.27	126	11.1
$100,000 or more	76.07	183	34.2
HOUSEHOLD TYPE			
Average household	**41.61**	**100**	**100.0**
Married couples	56.27	135	65.7
Married couples, no children	47.18	113	23.6
Married couples with children	66.99	161	37.9
Oldest child under age 6	47.43	114	5.2
Oldest child aged 6 to 17	73.97	178	21.1
Oldest child aged 18 or older	67.52	162	11.4
Single parent with child under age 18	39.77	96	5.0
Single person	19.88	48	14.2
RACE AND HISPANIC ORIGIN			
Average household	**41.61**	**100**	**100.0**
Asian	59.54	143	6.2
Black	26.45	64	8.0
Hispanic	39.61	95	11.9
Non-Hispanic white and other	44.59	107	80.4
REGION			
Average household	**41.61**	**100**	**100.0**
Northeast	48.33	116	21.0
Midwest	44.46	107	23.7
South	33.44	80	29.9
West	46.87	113	25.4
EDUCATION			
Average household	**41.61**	**100**	**100.0**
Less than high school graduate	32.28	78	10.1
High school graduate	34.25	82	20.5
Some college	32.52	78	16.1
Associate's degree	43.16	104	10.2
Bachelor's degree or more	56.45	136	42.8
Bachelor's degree	55.99	135	26.8
Master's, professional, doctoral degree	57.22	138	16.0

Note: Market shares may not sum to 100.0 because of rounding and missing categories by household type. "Asian" and "black" include Hispanics and non-Hispanics who identify themselves as being of the respective race alone. "Hispanic" includes people of any race who identify themselves as Hispanic. "Other" includes people who identify themselves as non-Hispanic and as Alaska Native, American Indian, Asian (who are also included in the "Asian" row), or Native Hawaiian or other Pacific Islander, as well as non-Hispanics reporting more than one race.
Source: Calculations by New Strategist based on the Bureau of Labor Statistics' 2012 Consumer Expenditure Survey

Artificial Sweeteners

Best customers:
Householders aged 55 or older
Married couples without children at home
Married couples with adult children at home
Households in the South

Customer trends:
Average household spending on artificial sweeteners should stabilize now that the large baby-boom generation is in the best-customer age groups.

Older householders spend the most on artificial sweeteners. Householders aged 55 to 64 spend 70 percent more than the average household on artificial sweeteners. Those aged 65 or older spend 8 to 14 percent more than average on this item. Married couples without children at home (most of them older) spend one-half more than the average household on artificial sweeteners, while married couples with adult children at home outspend the average by 85 percent. Households in the South spend 32 percent more than average on this item.

Average household spending on artificial sweeteners grew 18 percent between 2000 and 2006, after adjusting for inflation, but fell 26 percent between 2006 and 2012. Spending on artificial sweeteners should stabilize now that the large baby-boom generation is in the best-customer age groups.

Table 33. Artificial sweeteners

Total household spending $610,882,560.00
Average household spends 4.91

	AVERAGE HOUSEHOLD SPENDING	BEST CUSTOMERS (index)	BIGGEST CUSTOMERS (market share)
AGE OF HOUSEHOLDER			
Average household	**$4.91**	**100**	**100.0%**
Under age 25	2.30	47	3.1
Aged 25 to 34	2.84	58	9.4
Aged 35 to 44	4.35	89	15.4
Aged 45 to 54	4.32	88	17.4
Aged 55 to 64	8.34	170	31.1
Aged 65 to 74	5.62	114	13.8
Aged 75 or older	5.31	108	10.6

	AVERAGE HOUSEHOLD SPENDING	BEST CUSTOMERS (index)	BIGGEST CUSTOMERS (market share)
HOUSEHOLD INCOME			
Average household	**$4.91**	**100**	**100.0%**
Under $20,000	4.28	87	18.4
$20,000 to $39,999	3.54	72	16.2
$40,000 to $49,999	5.06	103	9.1
$50,000 to $69,999	3.89	79	11.4
$70,000 to $79,999	7.87	160	8.9
$80,000 to $99,999	5.36	109	9.6
$100,000 or more	6.66	136	25.4
HOUSEHOLD TYPE			
Average household	**4.91**	**100**	**100.0**
Married couples	6.67	136	66.0
Married couples, no children	7.37	150	31.3
Married couples with children	5.64	115	27.0
Oldest child under age 6	1.14	23	1.1
Oldest child aged 6 to 17	5.26	107	12.7
Oldest child aged 18 or older	9.08	185	13.0
Single parent with child under age 18	3.01	61	3.2
Single person	2.66	54	16.1
RACE AND HISPANIC ORIGIN			
Average household	**4.91**	**100**	**100.0**
Asian	4.04	82	3.6
Black	3.78	77	9.7
Hispanic	4.56	93	11.6
Non-Hispanic white and other	5.14	105	78.6
REGION			
Average household	**4.91**	**100**	**100.0**
Northeast	4.35	89	16.0
Midwest	3.48	71	15.7
South	6.48	132	49.2
West	4.18	85	19.2
EDUCATION			
Average household	**4.91**	**100**	**100.0**
Less than high school graduate	5.16	105	13.7
High school graduate	4.27	87	21.7
Some college	4.71	96	19.8
Associate's degree	4.74	97	9.5
Bachelor's degree or more	5.49	112	35.3
Bachelor's degree	5.27	107	21.4
Master's, professional, doctoral degree	5.86	119	13.9

Note: Market shares may not sum to 100.0 because of rounding and missing categories by household type. "Asian" and "black" include Hispanics and non-Hispanics who identify themselves as being of the respective race alone. "Hispanic" includes people of any race who identify themselves as Hispanic. "Other" includes people who identify themselves as non-Hispanic and as Alaska Native, American Indian, Asian (who are also included in the "Asian" row), or Native Hawaiian or other Pacific Islander, as well as non-Hispanics reporting more than one race.
Source: Calculations by New Strategist based on the Bureau of Labor Statistics' 2012 Consumer Expenditure Survey

Baby Food

Best customers: Householders aged 25 to 34
Married couples with preschoolers
Single parents
Asians and Hispanics

Customer trends: Average household spending on baby food should stabilize when
the baby bust comes to an end.

Not surprisingly, married couples with preschoolers spend much more on baby food than any other household type, almost eight times the average. Householders aged 25 to 34, many with infants, spend more than twice the average on baby food. Single parents, whose spending on most items is below average, spend well over twice the average on this item. Hispanics spend 21 percent more than average, and Asians spend 80 percent more.

Average household spending on baby food is in long-term decline. It fell 42 percent between 2000 and 2012, after adjusting for inflation. Behind the decline are price discounting, belt tightening during the economic downturn, and the ongoing baby bust. Average household spending on baby food should stabilize when the large millennial generation begins to have more children, although the low incomes of young adults may limit the increase.

Table 34. Baby food

Total household spending $3,116,620,800.00
Average household spends   25.05

	AVERAGE HOUSEHOLD SPENDING	BEST CUSTOMERS (index)	BIGGEST CUSTOMERS (market share)
AGE OF HOUSEHOLDER			
Average household	**$25.05**	**100**	**100.0%**
Under age 25	21.05	84	5.5
Aged 25 to 34	65.77	263	42.4
Aged 35 to 44	36.66	146	25.4
Aged 45 to 54	18.70	75	14.8
Aged 55 to 64	8.37	33	6.1
Aged 65 to 74	5.29	21	2.5
Aged 75 or older	4.78	19	1.9

	AVERAGE HOUSEHOLD SPENDING	BEST CUSTOMERS (index)	BIGGEST CUSTOMERS (market share)
HOUSEHOLD INCOME			
Average household	**$25.05**	**100**	**100.0%**
Under $20,000	14.72	59	12.4
$20,000 to $39,999	18.76	75	16.9
$40,000 to $49,999	38.02	152	13.4
$50,000 to $69,999	25.55	102	14.7
$70,000 to $79,999	28.68	114	6.4
$80,000 to $99,999	26.85	107	9.5
$100,000 or more	35.73	143	26.7
HOUSEHOLD TYPE			
Average household	**25.05**	**100**	**100.0**
Married couples	33.32	133	64.6
Married couples, no children	6.97	28	5.8
Married couples with children	55.70	222	52.3
Oldest child under age 6	196.42	784	35.8
Oldest child aged 6 to 17	32.04	128	15.2
Oldest child aged 18 or older	7.49	30	2.1
Single parent with child under age 18	59.87	239	12.5
Single person	3.69	15	4.4
RACE AND HISPANIC ORIGIN			
Average household	**25.05**	**100**	**100.0**
Asian	45.15	180	7.8
Black	12.26	49	6.2
Hispanic	30.28	121	15.2
Non-Hispanic white and other	26.37	105	79.0
REGION			
Average household	**25.05**	**100**	**100.0**
Northeast	24.52	98	17.7
Midwest	26.87	107	23.8
South	26.87	107	40.0
West	20.64	82	18.6
EDUCATION			
Average household	**25.05**	**100**	**100.0**
Less than high school graduate	23.05	92	12.0
High school graduate	18.24	73	18.2
Some college	26.71	107	22.0
Associate's degree	22.60	90	8.9
Bachelor's degree or more	30.73	123	38.7
Bachelor's degree	29.36	117	23.4
Master's, professional, doctoral degree	33.04	132	15.3

Note: Market shares may not sum to 100.0 because of rounding and missing categories by household type. "Asian" and "black" include Hispanics and non-Hispanics who identify themselves as being of the respective race alone. "Hispanic" includes people of any race who identify themselves as Hispanic. "Other" includes people who identify themselves as non-Hispanic and as Alaska Native, American Indian, Asian (who are also included in the "Asian" row), or Native Hawaiian or other Pacific Islander, as well as non-Hispanics reporting more than one race.
Source: Calculations by New Strategist based on the Bureau of Labor Statistics' 2012 Consumer Expenditure Survey

Bacon

Best customers:	**Householders aged 35 to 64**
	Married couples with children at home
	Blacks and Hispanics
Customer trends:	**Average household spending on bacon may continue to decline as**
	the large baby-boom generation ages and household size shrinks.

Married couples with children at home spend the most on bacon—36 percent more than the average household. Householders ranging in age from 35 to 64, many with children in the household, outspend the average by 7 to 20 percent. Black and Hispanic households spend slightly more than average on bacon.

Average household spending on bacon has been on a rollercoaster ride over the past 12 years. It declined 10 percent between 2000 and 2006, after adjusting for inflation, then rebounded between 2006 and 2010, only to decline again—by 3 percent—between 2010 and 2012. One factor behind the earlier spending decline was the growing propensity for households to eat fast-food breakfasts or no breakfast at all. More home-cooked meals in the aftermath of the Great Recession may be responsible for the 2006-to-2010 rise in spending on bacon. Average household spending on bacon may continue to decline in the years ahead as the large baby-boom generation ages and household size shrinks.

Table 35. Bacon

Total household spending	$4,003,706,880.00
Average household spends	32.18

	AVERAGE HOUSEHOLD SPENDING	BEST CUSTOMERS (index)	BIGGEST CUSTOMERS (market share)
AGE OF HOUSEHOLDER			
Average household	**$32.18**	**100**	**100.0%**
Under age 25	21.70	67	4.4
Aged 25 to 34	29.13	91	14.6
Aged 35 to 44	34.40	107	18.6
Aged 45 to 54	38.76	120	23.8
Aged 55 to 64	36.79	114	20.9
Aged 65 to 74	29.31	91	11.0
Aged 75 or older	22.12	69	6.7

	AVERAGE HOUSEHOLD SPENDING	BEST CUSTOMERS (index)	BIGGEST CUSTOMERS (market share)
HOUSEHOLD INCOME			
Average household	**$32.18**	**100**	**100.0%**
Under $20,000	23.55	73	15.4
$20,000 to $39,999	24.29	75	17.0
$40,000 to $49,999	31.85	99	8.8
$50,000 to $69,999	31.40	98	14.1
$70,000 to $79,999	37.95	118	6.6
$80,000 to $99,999	45.65	142	12.5
$100,000 or more	44.17	137	25.7
HOUSEHOLD TYPE			
Average household	**32.18**	**100**	**100.0**
Married couples	39.17	122	59.1
Married couples, no children	32.90	102	21.3
Married couples with children	43.64	136	31.9
Oldest child under age 6	38.92	121	5.5
Oldest child aged 6 to 17	45.01	140	16.6
Oldest child aged 18 or older	44.29	138	9.7
Single parent with child under age 18	29.85	93	4.9
Single person	16.10	50	14.9
RACE AND HISPANIC ORIGIN			
Average household	**32.18**	**100**	**100.0**
Asian	31.38	98	4.2
Black	34.71	108	13.6
Hispanic	33.09	103	12.9
Non-Hispanic white and other	31.62	98	73.8
REGION			
Average household	**32.18**	**100**	**100.0**
Northeast	29.39	91	16.5
Midwest	32.84	102	22.6
South	33.77	105	39.1
West	31.16	97	21.8
EDUCATION			
Average household	**32.18**	**100**	**100.0**
Less than high school graduate	31.20	97	12.7
High school graduate	33.98	106	26.3
Some college	31.68	98	20.3
Associate's degree	37.28	116	11.4
Bachelor's degree or more	29.91	93	29.3
Bachelor's degree	29.83	93	18.5
Master's, professional, doctoral degree	30.04	93	10.8

Note: Market shares may not sum to 100.0 because of rounding and missing categories by household type. "Asian" and "black" include Hispanics and non-Hispanics who identify themselves as being of the respective race alone. "Hispanic" includes people of any race who identify themselves as Hispanic. "Other" includes people who identify themselves as non-Hispanic and as Alaska Native, American Indian, Asian (who are also included in the "Asian" row), or Native Hawaiian or other Pacific Islander, as well as non-Hispanics reporting more than one race.
Source: Calculations by New Strategist based on the Bureau of Labor Statistics' 2012 Consumer Expenditure Survey

Bakery Products, Frozen and Refrigerated

Best customers:	**Householders aged 35 to 44**
	Married couples with children at home
	Single parents
Customer trends:	**Average household spending on frozen and refrigerated bakery products may rise as the large millennial generation begins to fill the best-customer age group.**

Households with children spend the most on frozen and refrigerated bakery products. Married couples with children spend 71 percent more than the average household on this item. Many are busy two-earner couples trying to save time by buying heat-and-serve foods. Householders aged 35 to 44, most with children, spend 35 percent more than average on frozen and refrigerated bakery products. Single parents, whose spending on most items is below average, spend an average amount on frozen and refrigerated bakery products.

Average household spending on frozen and refrigerated bakery products fell 12 percent between 2000 and 2012, after adjusting for inflation. But the category made some gains at the end of the time period, rising 8 percent between 2010 and 2012. Behind the decline was the entry of the small generation X into the best-customer lifestage. Average household spending on frozen and refrigerated bakery products may rise in the years ahead as the large millennial generation fills the best-customer age group.

Table 36. Bakery products, frozen and refrigerated

Total household spending	$3,579,448,320.00
Average household spends	28.77

	AVERAGE HOUSEHOLD SPENDING	BEST CUSTOMERS (index)	BIGGEST CUSTOMERS (market share)
AGE OF HOUSEHOLDER			
Average household	**$28.77**	**100**	**100.0%**
Under age 25	19.96	69	4.5
Aged 25 to 34	30.63	106	17.2
Aged 35 to 44	38.74	135	23.4
Aged 45 to 54	30.74	107	21.1
Aged 55 to 64	26.60	92	16.9
Aged 65 to 74	22.91	80	9.6
Aged 75 or older	20.66	72	7.0

	AVERAGE HOUSEHOLD SPENDING	BEST CUSTOMERS (index)	BIGGEST CUSTOMERS (market share)
HOUSEHOLD INCOME			
Average household	**$28.77**	**100**	**100.0%**
Under $20,000	17.02	59	12.4
$20,000 to $39,999	22.13	77	17.3
$40,000 to $49,999	24.90	87	7.7
$50,000 to $69,999	29.77	103	14.9
$70,000 to $79,999	42.11	146	8.2
$80,000 to $99,999	35.05	122	10.7
$100,000 or more	43.87	152	28.5
HOUSEHOLD TYPE			
Average household	**28.77**	**100**	**100.0**
Married couples	40.09	139	67.7
Married couples, no children	30.85	107	22.4
Married couples with children	49.10	171	40.1
Oldest child under age 6	41.84	145	6.6
Oldest child aged 6 to 17	55.02	191	22.7
Oldest child aged 18 or older	43.75	152	10.7
Single parent with child under age 18	29.02	101	5.3
Single person	12.50	43	12.9
RACE AND HISPANIC ORIGIN			
Average household	**28.77**	**100**	**100.0**
Asian	32.68	114	4.9
Black	18.95	66	8.3
Hispanic	20.48	71	8.9
Non-Hispanic white and other	31.83	111	83.0
REGION			
Average household	**28.77**	**100**	**100.0**
Northeast	27.91	97	17.5
Midwest	31.97	111	24.6
South	30.20	105	39.1
West	23.91	83	18.7
EDUCATION			
Average household	**28.77**	**100**	**100.0**
Less than high school graduate	22.87	79	10.4
High school graduate	28.58	99	24.8
Some college	25.35	88	18.1
Associate's degree	32.63	113	11.2
Bachelor's degree or more	32.24	112	35.3
Bachelor's degree	29.92	104	20.7
Master's, professional, doctoral degree	36.16	126	14.6

Note: Market shares may not sum to 100.0 because of rounding and missing categories by household type. "Asian" and "black" include Hispanics and non-Hispanics who identify themselves as being of the respective race alone. "Hispanic" includes people of any race who identify themselves as Hispanic. "Other" includes people who identify themselves as non-Hispanic and as Alaska Native, American Indian, Asian (who are also included in the "Asian" row), or Native Hawaiian or other Pacific Islander, as well as non-Hispanics reporting more than one race.
Source: Calculations by New Strategist based on the Bureau of Labor Statistics' 2012 Consumer Expenditure Survey

Baking Needs and Miscellaneous Products

Best customers: **Married couples with children at home**

Customer trends: **Average household spending on baking needs and miscellaneous products is**
                              likely to fall as cooking-challenged younger generations marry and have children.

Although cooking from scratch has become a lot less common than it once was, many people enjoy whipping up a home-cooked meal or dessert every now and then. Most are married couples, often with children at home. Married couples with children at home spend 65 percent more than the average household on products for baking, the figure peaking at 76 percent above average among couples with the largest households—those with adult children at home.

Average household spending on products for baking rose steadily over the entire decade of the 2000s, for a cumulative gain of 22 percent between 2000 and 2010, after adjusting for inflation. The trend then reversed and average household spending on baking products fell 9 percent between 2010 and 2012. The popularity of televised cooking programs may account for some of the increase. In the long term, however, average household spending on products for baking is likely to decline as cooking-challenged younger generations have children.

Table 37. Baking needs and miscellaneous products

Total household spending	$3,104,179,200.00		
Average household spends	24.95		

	AVERAGE HOUSEHOLD SPENDING	BEST CUSTOMERS (index)	BIGGEST CUSTOMERS (market share)
AGE OF HOUSEHOLDER			
Average household	**$24.95**	**100**	**100.0%**
Under age 25	12.80	51	3.4
Aged 25 to 34	26.34	106	17.1
Aged 35 to 44	26.79	107	18.6
Aged 45 to 54	31.29	125	24.8
Aged 55 to 64	23.97	96	17.6
Aged 65 to 74	26.01	104	12.6
Aged 75 or older	15.07	60	5.9

	AVERAGE HOUSEHOLD SPENDING	BEST CUSTOMERS (index)	BIGGEST CUSTOMERS (market share)
HOUSEHOLD INCOME			
Average household	**$24.95**	**100**	**100.0%**
Under $20,000	13.52	54	11.4
$20,000 to $39,999	19.51	78	17.6
$40,000 to $49,999	24.92	100	8.8
$50,000 to $69,999	25.22	101	14.6
$70,000 to $79,999	27.54	110	6.2
$80,000 to $99,999	28.13	113	9.9
$100,000 or more	41.51	166	31.1
HOUSEHOLD TYPE			
Average household	**24.95**	**100**	**100.0**
Married couples	33.42	134	65.1
Married couples, no children	26.03	104	21.7
Married couples with children	41.05	165	38.7
Oldest child under age 6	29.66	119	5.4
Oldest child aged 6 to 17	43.62	175	20.8
Oldest child aged 18 or older	43.87	176	12.4
Single parent with child under age 18	22.96	92	4.8
Single person	11.89	48	14.1
RACE AND HISPANIC ORIGIN			
Average household	**24.95**	**100**	**100.0**
Asian	28.10	113	4.9
Black	15.18	61	7.6
Hispanic	18.06	72	9.1
Non-Hispanic white and other	27.81	111	83.7
REGION			
Average household	**24.95**	**100**	**100.0**
Northeast	26.67	107	19.3
Midwest	28.95	116	25.7
South	20.11	81	30.0
West	27.57	111	24.9
EDUCATION			
Average household	**24.95**	**100**	**100.0**
Less than high school graduate	19.01	76	9.9
High school graduate	21.21	85	21.2
Some college	23.27	93	19.2
Associate's degree	27.24	109	10.8
Bachelor's degree or more	30.49	122	38.5
Bachelor's degree	29.44	118	23.5
Master's, professional, doctoral degree	32.25	129	15.0

Note: Market shares may not sum to 100.0 because of rounding and missing categories by household type. "Asian" and "black" include Hispanics and non-Hispanics who identify themselves as being of the respective race alone. "Hispanic" includes people of any race who identify themselves as Hispanic. "Other" includes people who identify themselves as non-Hispanic and as Alaska Native, American Indian, Asian (who are also included in the "Asian" row), or Native Hawaiian or other Pacific Islander, as well as non-Hispanics reporting more than one race.
Source: Calculations by New Strategist based on the Bureau of Labor Statistics' 2012 Consumer Expenditure Survey

Bananas

Best customers: Householders aged 35 to 54
Married couples with children at home
Single parents
Asians and Hispanics

Customer trends: Average household spending on bananas may decline as the large
baby-boom generation ages and household size shrinks.

Households with children spend the most on bananas. Married couples with children at home spend 38 percent more than the average household on bananas. Householders aged 35 to 54, most with children at home, spend 11 to 22 percent more on bananas than the average household. Single parents, whose spending approaches average on only a few items, spend 18 percent more than average on bananas. Hispanics, who tend to have large families, spend 39 percent more than average and Asians spend 43 percent more.

Average household spending on bananas fell 22 percent between 2000 and 2006, after adjusting for inflation, but rebounded with a 34 percent gain between 2006 and 2012. The greater propensity to eat out and the exit of the baby-boom generation from the best-customer lifestage were factors in the earlier spending decline. The increased spending since 2006 is due to less eating out as households tightened their belts following the Great Recession. Average household spending on bananas may decline again in the years ahead as the large baby-boom generation ages and household size shrinks.

Table 38. Bananas

Total household spending $5,450,664,960.00
Average household spends   43.81

	AVERAGE HOUSEHOLD SPENDING	BEST CUSTOMERS (index)	BIGGEST CUSTOMERS (market share)
AGE OF HOUSEHOLDER			
Average household	**$43.81**	**100**	**100.0%**
Under age 25	27.94	64	4.2
Aged 25 to 34	39.98	91	14.8
Aged 35 to 44	48.55	111	19.2
Aged 45 to 54	53.35	122	24.1
Aged 55 to 64	43.12	98	18.0
Aged 65 to 74	39.00	89	10.7
Aged 75 or older	40.44	92	9.0

	AVERAGE HOUSEHOLD SPENDING	BEST CUSTOMERS (index)	BIGGEST CUSTOMERS (market share)
HOUSEHOLD INCOME			
Average household	**$43.81**	**100**	**100.0%**
Under $20,000	26.51	61	12.7
$20,000 to $39,999	34.35	78	17.7
$40,000 to $49,999	45.47	104	9.2
$50,000 to $69,999	47.47	108	15.7
$70,000 to $79,999	49.25	112	6.3
$80,000 to $99,999	56.11	128	11.3
$100,000 or more	63.14	144	27.0
HOUSEHOLD TYPE			
Average household	**43.81**	**100**	**100.0**
Married couples	54.68	125	60.6
Married couples, no children	45.56	104	21.7
Married couples with children	60.48	138	32.5
Oldest child under age 6	49.45	113	5.1
Oldest child aged 6 to 17	62.29	142	16.9
Oldest child aged 18 or older	64.34	147	10.4
Single parent with child under age 18	51.78	118	6.2
Single person	22.82	52	15.5
RACE AND HISPANIC ORIGIN			
Average household	**43.81**	**100**	**100.0**
Asian	62.66	143	6.2
Black	32.20	73	9.2
Hispanic	60.74	139	17.4
Non-Hispanic white and other	42.93	98	73.6
REGION			
Average household	**43.81**	**100**	**100.0**
Northeast	49.17	112	20.3
Midwest	44.91	103	22.7
South	36.86	84	31.3
West	49.91	114	25.7
EDUCATION			
Average household	**43.81**	**100**	**100.0**
Less than high school graduate	44.42	101	13.2
High school graduate	39.39	90	22.4
Some college	39.64	90	18.6
Associate's degree	44.67	102	10.1
Bachelor's degree or more	49.55	113	35.7
Bachelor's degree	48.26	110	22.0
Master's, professional, doctoral degree	51.74	118	13.7

Note: Market shares may not sum to 100.0 because of rounding and missing categories by household type. "Asian" and "black" include Hispanics and non-Hispanics who identify themselves as being of the respective race alone. "Hispanic" includes people of any race who identify themselves as Hispanic. "Other" includes people who identify themselves as non-Hispanic and as Alaska Native, American Indian, Asian (who are also included in the "Asian" row), or Native Hawaiian or other Pacific Islander, as well as non-Hispanics reporting more than one race.
Source: Calculations by New Strategist based on the Bureau of Labor Statistics' 2012 Consumer Expenditure Survey

Beef, Ground

Best customers:	Householders aged 35 to 54
	Married couples with school-aged or older children at home
	Hispanics
	Householders without a high school diploma
Customer trends:	Average household spending on ground beef may decline as the small generation X passes through the best-customer age groups and eating out claims more of the food dollar.

Households with children are the biggest spenders on ground beef. Married couples with school-aged or older children at home spend 56 to 58 percent more than average on this item. Householders aged 35 to 54, most with children at home, spend 16 to 21 percent more than average on ground beef and control 44 percent of the market. Hispanics, with their relatively large families, outspend the average by 14 percent. Householders with no more than a high school education, many of them Hispanic, spend 8 to 18 percent more on ground beef than the average household.

Average household spending on ground beef declined 24 percent between 2000 and 2010, after adjusting for inflation, but then grew 5 percent during the 2010-to-2012 time period. Behind the decline was the growing popularity of fast food as a substitute for home-cooked meals. The recent increase in spending on ground beef could be short-lived, a sign of economic recovery. Average household spending on ground beef is likely to resume its decline as the small generation X passes through the best-customer age groups and eating out claims more of the food dollar.

Table 39. Beef, ground

Total household spending	$11,632,896,000.00
Average household spends	93.50

	AVERAGE HOUSEHOLD SPENDING	BEST CUSTOMERS (index)	BIGGEST CUSTOMERS (market share)
AGE OF HOUSEHOLDER			
Average household	**$93.50**	**100**	**100.0%**
Under age 25	64.24	69	4.5
Aged 25 to 34	90.01	96	15.6
Aged 35 to 44	108.48	116	20.1
Aged 45 to 54	112.67	121	23.8
Aged 55 to 64	101.04	108	19.8
Aged 65 to 74	80.44	86	10.4
Aged 75 or older	54.95	59	5.7

	AVERAGE HOUSEHOLD SPENDING	BEST CUSTOMERS (index)	BIGGEST CUSTOMERS (market share)
HOUSEHOLD INCOME			
Average household	**$93.50**	**100**	**100.0%**
Under $20,000	66.31	71	14.9
$20,000 to $39,999	83.23	89	20.1
$40,000 to $49,999	92.15	99	8.7
$50,000 to $69,999	97.80	105	15.1
$70,000 to $79,999	117.76	126	7.0
$80,000 to $99,999	119.62	128	11.3
$100,000 or more	114.03	122	22.8
HOUSEHOLD TYPE			
Average household	**93.50**	**100**	**100.0**
Married couples	118.02	126	61.3
Married couples, no children	90.36	97	20.1
Married couples with children	135.03	144	34.0
Oldest child under age 6	86.42	92	4.2
Oldest child aged 6 to 17	145.44	156	18.5
Oldest child aged 18 or older	147.95	158	11.2
Single parent with child under age 18	86.75	93	4.9
Single person	39.20	42	12.4
RACE AND HISPANIC ORIGIN			
Average household	**93.50**	**100**	**100.0**
Asian	61.81	66	2.9
Black	86.06	92	11.6
Hispanic	106.69	114	14.3
Non-Hispanic white and other	92.68	99	74.4
REGION			
Average household	**93.50**	**100**	**100.0**
Northeast	91.30	98	17.6
Midwest	100.76	108	23.9
South	97.39	104	38.8
West	81.56	87	19.7
EDUCATION			
Average household	**93.50**	**100**	**100.0**
Less than high school graduate	100.59	108	14.0
High school graduate	110.67	118	29.5
Some college	84.70	91	18.7
Associate's degree	109.91	118	11.6
Bachelor's degree or more	78.37	84	26.4
Bachelor's degree	80.54	86	17.2
Master's, professional, doctoral degree	74.70	80	9.3

Note: Market shares may not sum to 100.0 because of rounding and missing categories by household type. "Asian" and "black" include Hispanics and non-Hispanics who identify themselves as being of the respective race alone. "Hispanic" includes people of any race who identify themselves as Hispanic. "Other" includes people who identify themselves as non-Hispanic and as Alaska Native, American Indian, Asian (who are also included in the "Asian" row), or Native Hawaiian or other Pacific Islander, as well as non-Hispanics reporting more than one race.
Source: Calculations by New Strategist based on the Bureau of Labor Statistics' 2012 Consumer Expenditure Survey

Beef, Roast

Best customers: Householders aged 45 to 54
                        Married couples with school-aged or older children at home
                        Hispanics and Asians
                        Households in the West

Customer trends: Average household spending on roast beef may decline as the small
                        generation X enters the best-customer age group and eating out claims
                        more of the food dollar.

The largest households are the biggest spenders on roast beef. Married couples with adult children at home spend over twice the average on this item, and those with school-aged children spend 39 percent more. Householders aged 45 to 54, many with children at home, spend 34 percent more than average on roast beef. Hispanics, who have the largest families, spend 42 percent more than average on this item. Asians spend 34 percent more. Households in the West, where many Hispanics and Asians reside, outspend the average household by 27 percent.

Average household spending on roast beef fell a steep 42 percent between 2000 and 2010, after adjusting for inflation, but then increased 10 percent in the 2010-to-2012 time period. Behind the decline was the growing consumer preference for prepared foods and eating out as well as belt tightening in the aftermath of the Great Recession. The recent increase in spending on roast beef could be short-lived, a sign of economic recovery. Average household spending on roast beef is likely to resume its decline as the small generation X enters the best-customer age group and eating out claims more of the food dollar.

Table 40. Beef, roast

| Total household spending | $4,232,632,320.00 |
| Average household spends | 34.02 |

	AVERAGE HOUSEHOLD SPENDING	BEST CUSTOMERS (index)	BIGGEST CUSTOMERS (market share)
AGE OF HOUSEHOLDER			
Average household	**$34.02**	**100**	**100.0%**
Under age 25	25.04	74	4.8
Aged 25 to 34	23.42	69	11.1
Aged 35 to 44	35.62	105	18.2
Aged 45 to 54	45.64	134	26.6
Aged 55 to 64	37.18	109	20.0
Aged 65 to 74	33.02	97	11.7
Aged 75 or older	27.01	79	7.8

	AVERAGE HOUSEHOLD SPENDING	BEST CUSTOMERS (index)	BIGGEST CUSTOMERS (market share)
HOUSEHOLD INCOME			
Average household	**$34.02**	**100**	**100.0%**
Under $20,000	14.38	42	8.9
$20,000 to $39,999	25.32	74	16.8
$40,000 to $49,999	35.36	104	9.2
$50,000 to $69,999	29.95	88	12.7
$70,000 to $79,999	41.72	123	6.8
$80,000 to $99,999	41.24	121	10.7
$100,000 or more	62.99	185	34.7
HOUSEHOLD TYPE			
Average household	**34.02**	**100**	**100.0**
Married couples	45.41	133	64.8
Married couples, no children	37.09	109	22.7
Married couples with children	49.43	145	34.2
Oldest child under age 6	20.74	61	2.8
Oldest child aged 6 to 17	47.20	139	16.5
Oldest child aged 18 or older	71.01	209	14.7
Single parent with child under age 18	22.11	65	3.4
Single person	13.47	40	11.8
RACE AND HISPANIC ORIGIN			
Average household	**34.02**	**100**	**100.0**
Asian	45.58	134	5.8
Black	28.39	83	10.5
Hispanic	48.34	142	17.8
Non-Hispanic white and other	32.60	96	71.9
REGION			
Average household	**34.02**	**100**	**100.0**
Northeast	26.52	78	14.1
Midwest	30.19	89	19.7
South	34.43	101	37.7
West	43.29	127	28.7
EDUCATION			
Average household	**34.02**	**100**	**100.0**
Less than high school graduate	22.57	66	8.7
High school graduate	35.32	104	25.9
Some college	30.72	90	18.6
Associate's degree	46.30	136	13.4
Bachelor's degree or more	35.71	105	33.1
Bachelor's degree	29.65	87	17.4
Master's, professional, doctoral degree	45.95	135	15.7

Note: Market shares may not sum to 100.0 because of rounding and missing categories by household type. "Asian" and "black" include Hispanics and non-Hispanics who identify themselves as being of the respective race alone. "Hispanic" includes people of any race who identify themselves as Hispanic. "Other" includes people who identify themselves as non-Hispanic and as Alaska Native, American Indian, Asian (who are also included in the "Asian" row), or Native Hawaiian or other Pacific Islander, as well as non-Hispanics reporting more than one race.
Source: Calculations by New Strategist based on the Bureau of Labor Statistics' 2012 Consumer Expenditure Survey

Beef, Steak

Best customers: Householders aged 35 to 54
Married couples with school-aged or older children at home
Hispanics

Customer trends: Average household spending on steak should continue to decline
as the small generation X passes through the best-customer age
groups and prepared meals claim more of the food dollar.

The best customers of steak are the largest households. Married couples with school-aged or older children at home spend 54 to 62 percent more than average on steak. Householders aged 35 to 54, most with children at home, spend 22 to 25 percent more than average on steak. Hispanics, who tend to have large families, spend 32 percent more than average on steak.

Average household spending on steak is in long-term decline. Spending on steak fell 23 percent between 2000 and 2006 and another 18 percent between 2006 and 2012, after adjusting for inflation. Average household spending on steak should continue to decline as the small generation X passes through the best-customer age groups and prepared meals claim more of the food dollar.

Table 41. Beef, steak

| Total household spending | $9,883,607,040.00 |
| Average household spends | 79.44 |

	AVERAGE HOUSEHOLD SPENDING	BEST CUSTOMERS (index)	BIGGEST CUSTOMERS (market share)
AGE OF HOUSEHOLDER			
Average household	**$79.44**	**100**	**100.0%**
Under age 25	59.84	75	4.9
Aged 25 to 34	64.13	81	13.0
Aged 35 to 44	97.02	122	21.2
Aged 45 to 54	99.24	125	24.7
Aged 55 to 64	85.36	107	19.7
Aged 65 to 74	71.22	90	10.8
Aged 75 or older	45.30	57	5.6

	AVERAGE HOUSEHOLD SPENDING	BEST CUSTOMERS (index)	BIGGEST CUSTOMERS (market share)
HOUSEHOLD INCOME			
Average household	**$79.44**	**100**	**100.0%**
Under $20,000	41.25	52	10.9
$20,000 to $39,999	55.01	69	15.6
$40,000 to $49,999	87.59	110	9.8
$50,000 to $69,999	75.30	95	13.7
$70,000 to $79,999	95.43	120	6.7
$80,000 to $99,999	87.30	110	9.7
$100,000 or more	141.19	178	33.3
HOUSEHOLD TYPE			
Average household	**79.44**	**100**	**100.0**
Married couples	104.63	132	64.0
Married couples, no children	89.47	113	23.5
Married couples with children	114.10	144	33.8
Oldest child under age 6	69.49	87	4.0
Oldest child aged 6 to 17	122.08	154	18.3
Oldest child aged 18 or older	128.59	162	11.4
Single parent with child under age 18	65.24	82	4.3
Single person	32.58	41	12.2
RACE AND HISPANIC ORIGIN			
Average household	**79.44**	**100**	**100.0**
Asian	71.52	90	3.9
Black	51.37	65	8.1
Hispanic	104.92	132	16.6
Non-Hispanic white and other	80.00	101	75.6
REGION			
Average household	**79.44**	**100**	**100.0**
Northeast	78.40	99	17.8
Midwest	78.43	99	21.9
South	76.89	97	36.0
West	85.51	108	24.3
EDUCATION			
Average household	**79.44**	**100**	**100.0**
Less than high school graduate	73.37	92	12.1
High school graduate	83.56	105	26.2
Some college	65.36	82	16.9
Associate's degree	79.66	100	9.9
Bachelor's degree or more	87.95	111	34.9
Bachelor's degree	85.50	108	21.5
Master's, professional, doctoral degree	92.09	116	13.5

Note: Market shares may not sum to 100.0 because of rounding and missing categories by household type. "Asian" and "black" include Hispanics and non-Hispanics who identify themselves as being of the respective race alone. "Hispanic" includes people of any race who identify themselves as Hispanic. "Other" includes people who identify themselves as non-Hispanic and as Alaska Native, American Indian, Asian (who are also included in the "Asian" row), or Native Hawaiian or other Pacific Islander, as well as non-Hispanics reporting more than one race.
Source: Calculations by New Strategist based on the Bureau of Labor Statistics' 2012 Consumer Expenditure Survey

Biscuits and Rolls

Best customers: Householders aged 35 to 64

Married couples with children at home

Households in the Northeast

Customer trends: Average household spending on biscuits and rolls may resume its decline as

the large baby-boom generation ages and household size shrinks.

The largest households spend the most on biscuits and rolls. Married couples with school-aged children spend 73 percent more than the average household on this item, and those with adult children at home spend 45 percent more. Householders ranging in age from 35 to 64, many with children at home, spend 10 to 22 percent more than average on biscuits and rolls and control 63 percent of the market. Households in the Northeast spend 24 percent more than average on this item.

Average household spending on biscuits and rolls fell 7 percent between 2000 and 2006, then climbed 9 percent between 2006 and 2012, after adjusting for inflation. Behind the increase was the shift to homemade meals by financially strapped consumers. Average household spending on biscuits and rolls may resume its decline as the large baby-boom generation ages and household size shrinks.

Table 42. Biscuits and rolls

Total household spending	$6,450,969,600.00
Average household spends	51.85

	AVERAGE HOUSEHOLD SPENDING	BEST CUSTOMERS (index)	BIGGEST CUSTOMERS (market share)
AGE OF HOUSEHOLDER			
Average household	**$51.85**	**100**	**100.0%**
Under age 25	27.14	52	3.4
Aged 25 to 34	44.52	86	13.9
Aged 35 to 44	63.28	122	21.2
Aged 45 to 54	57.59	111	22.0
Aged 55 to 64	57.18	110	20.2
Aged 65 to 74	50.52	97	11.7
Aged 75 or older	40.81	79	7.7

	AVERAGE HOUSEHOLD SPENDING	BEST CUSTOMERS (index)	BIGGEST CUSTOMERS (market share)
HOUSEHOLD INCOME			
Average household	**$51.85**	**100**	**100.0%**
Under $20,000	29.73	57	12.1
$20,000 to $39,999	38.23	74	16.6
$40,000 to $49,999	46.16	89	7.9
$50,000 to $69,999	51.65	100	14.4
$70,000 to $79,999	64.20	124	6.9
$80,000 to $99,999	62.26	120	10.6
$100,000 or more	86.94	168	31.4
HOUSEHOLD TYPE			
Average household	**51.85**	**100**	**100.0**
Married couples	69.57	134	65.2
Married couples, no children	56.64	109	22.8
Married couples with children	79.85	154	36.2
Oldest child under age 6	61.71	119	5.4
Oldest child aged 6 to 17	89.56	173	20.5
Oldest child aged 18 or older	74.97	145	10.2
Single parent with child under age 18	45.05	87	4.6
Single person	25.61	49	14.7
RACE AND HISPANIC ORIGIN			
Average household	**51.85**	**100**	**100.0**
Asian	47.57	92	4.0
Black	28.10	54	6.8
Hispanic	45.15	87	10.9
Non-Hispanic white and other	56.97	110	82.5
REGION			
Average household	**51.85**	**100**	**100.0**
Northeast	64.14	124	22.3
Midwest	56.15	108	24.0
South	43.80	84	31.5
West	50.95	98	22.1
EDUCATION			
Average household	**51.85**	**100**	**100.0**
Less than high school graduate	43.14	83	10.9
High school graduate	46.43	90	22.3
Some college	44.13	85	17.5
Associate's degree	54.53	105	10.4
Bachelor's degree or more	63.69	123	38.7
Bachelor's degree	63.52	123	24.4
Master's, professional, doctoral degree	63.97	123	14.3

Note: Market shares may not sum to 100.0 because of rounding and missing categories by household type. "Asian" and "black" include Hispanics and non-Hispanics who identify themselves as being of the respective race alone. "Hispanic" includes people of any race who identify themselves as Hispanic. "Other" includes people who identify themselves as non-Hispanic and as Alaska Native, American Indian, Asian (who are also included in the "Asian" row), or Native Hawaiian or other Pacific Islander, as well as non-Hispanics reporting more than one race.
Source: Calculations by New Strategist based on the Bureau of Labor Statistics' 2012 Consumer Expenditure Survey

Bread and Cracker Products

Best customers: Householders aged 35 to 54
                   Married couples with children at home
                   Households in the Northeast

Customer trends: Average household spending on bread and cracker products is likely
                   to continue to decline as restaurant meals replace home cooking
                   among younger generations.

The biggest spenders on bread and cracker products are the largest households. Married couples with children at home spend 59 percent more than average on this item. Householders aged 35 to 54, most with children at home, spend 11 to 20 percent more than average on bread and cracker products. Households in the Northeast spend 32 percent more.

Average household spending on bread and cracker products fell 16 percent between 2000 and 2006, after adjusting for inflation, then climbed 48 percent between 2006 and 2010 before falling again in the ensuing two years. Behind the 2006-to-2010 increase in spending was belt tightening in the face of the Great Recession as households opted for more meals at home rather than in restaurants. Average household spending on bread and cracker products is likely to continue to decline as restaurant meals replace home cooking among younger generations.

Table 43. Bread and cracker products

Total household spending $909,480,960.00
Average household spends   7.31

	AVERAGE HOUSEHOLD SPENDING	BEST CUSTOMERS (index)	BIGGEST CUSTOMERS (market share)
AGE OF HOUSEHOLDER			
Average household	**$7.31**	**100**	**100.0%**
Under age 25	6.03	82	5.4
Aged 25 to 34	7.31	100	16.2
Aged 35 to 44	8.09	111	19.2
Aged 45 to 54	8.78	120	23.8
Aged 55 to 64	6.55	90	16.4
Aged 65 to 74	7.03	96	11.6
Aged 75 or older	5.48	75	7.3

	AVERAGE HOUSEHOLD SPENDING	BEST CUSTOMERS (index)	BIGGEST CUSTOMERS (market share)
HOUSEHOLD INCOME			
Average household	**$7.31**	**100**	**100.0%**
Under $20,000	3.97	54	11.4
$20,000 to $39,999	5.75	79	17.7
$40,000 to $49,999	9.16	125	11.1
$50,000 to $69,999	7.74	106	15.3
$70,000 to $79,999	8.78	120	6.7
$80,000 to $99,999	8.77	120	10.6
$100,000 or more	10.51	144	26.9
HOUSEHOLD TYPE			
Average household	**7.31**	**100**	**100.0**
Married couples	9.75	133	64.8
Married couples, no children	7.58	104	21.6
Married couples with children	11.65	159	37.5
Oldest child under age 6	11.16	153	7.0
Oldest child aged 6 to 17	10.42	143	17.0
Oldest child aged 18 or older	14.00	192	13.5
Single parent with child under age 18	6.33	87	4.5
Single person	3.00	41	12.2
RACE AND HISPANIC ORIGIN			
Average household	**7.31**	**100**	**100.0**
Asian	7.84	107	4.6
Black	4.27	58	7.3
Hispanic	5.66	77	9.7
Non-Hispanic white and other	8.11	111	83.3
REGION			
Average household	**7.31**	**100**	**100.0**
Northeast	9.67	132	23.9
Midwest	8.36	114	25.4
South	5.83	80	29.7
West	6.80	93	21.0
EDUCATION			
Average household	**7.31**	**100**	**100.0**
Less than high school graduate	6.23	85	11.1
High school graduate	7.15	98	24.4
Some college	6.96	95	19.6
Associate's degree	8.26	113	11.2
Bachelor's degree or more	7.77	106	33.5
Bachelor's degree	8.01	110	21.8
Master's, professional, doctoral degree	7.36	101	11.7

Note: Market shares may not sum to 100.0 because of rounding and missing categories by household type. "Asian" and "black" include Hispanics and non-Hispanics who identify themselves as being of the respective race alone. "Hispanic" includes people of any race who identify themselves as Hispanic. "Other" includes people who identify themselves as non-Hispanic and as Alaska Native, American Indian, Asian (who are also included in the "Asian" row), or Native Hawaiian or other Pacific Islander, as well as non-Hispanics reporting more than one race.
Source: Calculations by New Strategist based on the Bureau of Labor Statistics' 2012 Consumer Expenditure Survey

Bread Other than White

Best customers: Householders aged 35 to 64
                         Married couples with school-aged or older children at home
                         Single parents

Customer trends: Average household spending on nonwhite bread should remain stable
                         as households switch from white to other bread types, but shrinking
                         household size may limit gains.

Bread took a beating a few years back as low-carb diets became popular. Nonwhite bread held its own, however. In 2000, nonwhite bread accounted for 56 percent of total household spending on bread. By 2012, the figure had grown to 59 percent of the total. The best customers of nonwhite bread are the largest households. Married couples with school-aged or older children at home spend 46 percent more than the average household on nonwhite bread. Householders aged 35 to 64, many with children at home, spend 8 to 18 percent more than average on this item. Nonwhite bread is one of the relatively few items on which single parents, with their lower incomes, spend an average amount.

Spending on nonwhite bread, in slow decline before the Great Recession, held steady between 2006 and 2012, after adjusting for inflation. Average household spending on nonwhite bread should remain stable in the years ahead because of the shift away from white bread, but shrinking household size may take a toll on all bread buying.

Table 44. Bread other than white

Total household spending	$7,664,025,600.00
Average household spends	61.60

	AVERAGE HOUSEHOLD SPENDING	BEST CUSTOMERS (index)	BIGGEST CUSTOMERS (market share)
AGE OF HOUSEHOLDER			
Average household	**$61.60**	**100**	**100.0%**
Under age 25	32.37	53	3.4
Aged 25 to 34	54.36	88	14.3
Aged 35 to 44	66.54	108	18.8
Aged 45 to 54	72.53	118	23.3
Aged 55 to 64	68.43	111	20.3
Aged 65 to 74	61.73	100	12.1
Aged 75 or older	50.20	81	8.0

	AVERAGE HOUSEHOLD SPENDING	BEST CUSTOMERS (index)	BIGGEST CUSTOMERS (market share)
HOUSEHOLD INCOME			
Average household	**$61.60**	**100**	**100.0%**
Under $20,000	38.61	63	13.2
$20,000 to $39,999	50.45	82	18.5
$40,000 to $49,999	52.54	85	7.5
$50,000 to $69,999	63.26	103	14.8
$70,000 to $79,999	78.15	127	7.1
$80,000 to $99,999	76.49	124	11.0
$100,000 or more	91.67	149	27.9
HOUSEHOLD TYPE			
Average household	**61.60**	**100**	**100.0**
Married couples	79.77	129	62.9
Married couples, no children	70.92	115	24.0
Married couples with children	86.17	140	32.9
Oldest child under age 6	69.55	113	5.2
Oldest child aged 6 to 17	90.17	146	17.4
Oldest child aged 18 or older	89.86	146	10.3
Single parent with child under age 18	62.26	101	5.3
Single person	33.42	54	16.1
RACE AND HISPANIC ORIGIN			
Average household	**61.60**	**100**	**100.0**
Asian	57.63	94	4.1
Black	40.84	66	8.3
Hispanic	62.00	101	12.6
Non-Hispanic white and other	65.03	106	79.2
REGION			
Average household	**61.60**	**100**	**100.0**
Northeast	70.33	114	20.6
Midwest	57.54	93	20.7
South	53.55	87	32.4
West	71.97	117	26.3
EDUCATION			
Average household	**61.60**	**100**	**100.0**
Less than high school graduate	48.90	79	10.4
High school graduate	57.37	93	23.2
Some college	56.04	91	18.7
Associate's degree	65.79	107	10.5
Bachelor's degree or more	72.09	117	36.9
Bachelor's degree	66.92	109	21.7
Master's, professional, doctoral degree	80.83	131	15.2

Note: Market shares may not sum to 100.0 because of rounding and missing categories by household type. "Asian" and "black" include Hispanics and non-Hispanics who identify themselves as being of the respective race alone. "Hispanic" includes people of any race who identify themselves as Hispanic. "Other" includes people who identify themselves as non-Hispanic and as Alaska Native, American Indian, Asian (who are also included in the "Asian" row), or Native Hawaiian or other Pacific Islander, as well as non-Hispanics reporting more than one race.
Source: Calculations by New Strategist based on the Bureau of Labor Statistics' 2012 Consumer Expenditure Survey

Bread, White

Best customers:	**Householders aged 35 to 54**
	Married couples with school-aged or older children at home
	Single parents
Customer trends:	**Average household spending on white bread is likely to resume its decline**
	in the years ahead as consumers switch to nonwhite bread.

White bread accounts for 41 percent of the average household's bread spending, down from 44 percent in 2000. The best customers of white bread are the largest households. Married couples with school-aged or older children at home spend 44 to 50 percent more than the average household on this item. Householders aged 35 to 54, many with children at home, spend 14 to 19 percent more than average on white bread. Single parents, whose spending approaches average on only a few items, spend 18 percent more than average on white bread.

Average household spending on white bread declined by a substantial 26 percent between 2000 and 2006, after adjusting for inflation, but rebounded by 20 percent between 2006 and 2012. Behind the decline was the switch to nonwhite bread, and behind the more recent increase is the renewed popularity of brown-bag lunches as the Great Recession cut incomes and spending. Average household spending on white bread is likely to resume its decline in the years ahead as consumers continue to switch to more nutritious whole-grain bread.

Table 45. Bread, white

Total household spending	$5,414,584,320.00
Average household spends	43.52

	AVERAGE HOUSEHOLD SPENDING	BEST CUSTOMERS (index)	BIGGEST CUSTOMERS (market share)
AGE OF HOUSEHOLDER			
Average household	**$43.52**	**100**	**100.0%**
Under age 25	26.38	61	4.0
Aged 25 to 34	42.02	97	15.6
Aged 35 to 44	51.89	119	20.7
Aged 45 to 54	49.56	114	22.5
Aged 55 to 64	45.14	104	19.0
Aged 65 to 74	38.46	88	10.6
Aged 75 or older	33.51	77	7.5

	AVERAGE HOUSEHOLD SPENDING	BEST CUSTOMERS (index)	BIGGEST CUSTOMERS (market share)
HOUSEHOLD INCOME			
Average household	**$43.52**	**100**	**100.0%**
Under $20,000	30.36	70	14.7
$20,000 to $39,999	37.75	87	19.5
$40,000 to $49,999	44.42	102	9.0
$50,000 to $69,999	43.81	101	14.5
$70,000 to $79,999	52.64	121	6.8
$80,000 to $99,999	52.62	121	10.7
$100,000 or more	57.07	131	24.6
HOUSEHOLD TYPE			
Average household	**43.52**	**100**	**100.0**
Married couples	53.77	124	60.0
Married couples, no children	45.20	104	21.7
Married couples with children	60.20	138	32.5
Oldest child under age 6	42.24	97	4.4
Oldest child aged 6 to 17	65.36	150	17.9
Oldest child aged 18 or older	62.79	144	10.2
Single parent with child under age 18	51.24	118	6.2
Single person	24.28	56	16.6
RACE AND HISPANIC ORIGIN			
Average household	**43.52**	**100**	**100.0**
Asian	43.57	100	4.3
Black	40.26	93	11.6
Hispanic	44.26	102	12.7
Non-Hispanic white and other	43.95	101	75.8
REGION			
Average household	**43.52**	**100**	**100.0**
Northeast	47.31	109	19.6
Midwest	43.40	100	22.1
South	41.37	95	35.4
West	44.12	101	22.8
EDUCATION			
Average household	**43.52**	**100**	**100.0**
Less than high school graduate	41.26	95	12.4
High school graduate	44.32	102	25.4
Some college	41.00	94	19.4
Associate's degree	47.09	108	10.7
Bachelor's degree or more	44.32	102	32.1
Bachelor's degree	42.00	97	19.2
Master's, professional, doctoral degree	48.25	111	12.9

Note: Market shares may not sum to 100.0 because of rounding and missing categories by household type. "Asian" and "black" include Hispanics and non-Hispanics who identify themselves as being of the respective race alone. "Hispanic" includes people of any race who identify themselves as Hispanic. "Other" includes people who identify themselves as non-Hispanic and as Alaska Native, American Indian, Asian (who are also included in the "Asian" row), or Native Hawaiian or other Pacific Islander, as well as non-Hispanics reporting more than one race.
Source: Calculations by New Strategist based on the Bureau of Labor Statistics' 2012 Consumer Expenditure Survey

Butter

Best customers: Householders aged 45 to 64

Married couples with school-aged or older children at home

Households in the Northeast

Customer trends: Average household spending on butter may continue to climb as butter's reputation improves, but shrinking household size due to the aging of the baby-boom generation may limit the increase.

The best customers of butter are households headed by baby boomers and the largest households—married couples with children at home. Householders aged 45 to 64, members of the baby-boom generation, spend 18 to 19 percent more than average on butter. Not only do these households have the income to afford butter, but unlike older adults they never made the switch to margarine. The largest households—married couples with school-aged or older children at home—spend 57 to 61 percent more than the average household on butter. Households in the Northeast spend 26 percent more.

After dropping by 8 percent between 2000 and 2006, average household spending on butter rebounded with a 23 percent rise between 2006 and 2012, after adjusting for inflation. Spending on butter may continue to climb in the years ahead as butter's reputation improves, but shrinking household size due to the aging of the baby-boom generation may limit the increase.

Table 46. Butter

Total household spending	$3,180,072,960.00
Average household spends	25.56

	AVERAGE HOUSEHOLD SPENDING	BEST CUSTOMERS (index)	BIGGEST CUSTOMERS (market share)
AGE OF HOUSEHOLDER			
Average household	**$25.56**	**100**	**100.0%**
Under age 25	10.47	41	2.7
Aged 25 to 34	22.68	89	14.3
Aged 35 to 44	26.08	102	17.7
Aged 45 to 54	30.25	118	23.4
Aged 55 to 64	30.30	119	21.7
Aged 65 to 74	25.04	98	11.8
Aged 75 or older	22.35	87	8.5

	AVERAGE HOUSEHOLD SPENDING	BEST CUSTOMERS (index)	BIGGEST CUSTOMERS (market share)
HOUSEHOLD INCOME			
Average household	**$25.56**	**100**	**100.0%**
Under $20,000	13.58	53	11.2
$20,000 to $39,999	18.24	71	16.1
$40,000 to $49,999	24.65	96	8.5
$50,000 to $69,999	27.65	108	15.6
$70,000 to $79,999	33.06	129	7.2
$80,000 to $99,999	31.12	122	10.7
$100,000 or more	41.21	161	30.2
HOUSEHOLD TYPE			
Average household	**25.56**	**100**	**100.0**
Married couples	34.28	134	65.1
Married couples, no children	28.47	111	23.2
Married couples with children	38.78	152	35.7
Oldest child under age 6	30.00	117	5.4
Oldest child aged 6 to 17	41.22	161	19.2
Oldest child aged 18 or older	40.17	157	11.1
Single parent with child under age 18	20.47	80	4.2
Single person	12.72	50	14.8
RACE AND HISPANIC ORIGIN			
Average household	**25.56**	**100**	**100.0**
Asian	22.65	89	3.8
Black	17.95	70	8.8
Hispanic	15.76	62	7.7
Non-Hispanic white and other	28.47	111	83.6
REGION			
Average household	**$25.56**	**100**	**100.0**
Northeast	32.31	126	22.8
Midwest	27.23	107	23.6
South	20.69	81	30.1
West	26.49	104	23.4
EDUCATION			
Average household	**25.56**	**100**	**100.0**
Less than high school graduate	18.11	71	9.3
High school graduate	23.77	93	23.2
Some college	23.51	92	18.9
Associate's degree	25.91	101	10.0
Bachelor's degree or more	31.00	121	38.3
Bachelor's degree	30.44	119	23.7
Master's, professional, doctoral degree	31.95	125	14.5

Note: Market shares may not sum to 100.0 because of rounding and missing categories by household type. "Asian" and "black" include Hispanics and non-Hispanics who identify themselves as being of the respective race alone. "Hispanic" includes people of any race who identify themselves as Hispanic. "Other" includes people who identify themselves as non-Hispanic and as Alaska Native, American Indian, Asian (who are also included in the "Asian" row), or Native Hawaiian or other Pacific Islander, as well as non-Hispanics reporting more than one race.
Source: Calculations by New Strategist based on the Bureau of Labor Statistics' 2012 Consumer Expenditure Survey

Cakes and Cupcakes

Best customers:	**Householders aged 35 to 54**
	Married couples with school-aged or older children at home
	Households in the Midwest
Customer trends:	**Average household spending on cakes and cupcakes should continue to decline as the small generation X passes through the best-customer age groups and household size shrinks.**

The largest households—those with children—spend the most on cakes and cupcakes. Married couples with school-aged children spend 56 percent more than the average household on this item, and those with adult children at home spend 47 percent more. Householders aged 35 to 54, most with children, spend 8 to 11 percent more than average on cakes and cupcakes. Households in the Midwest spend 23 percent more than average on this item.

Average household spending on cakes and cupcakes fell 26 percent between 2000 and 2012, after adjusting for inflation. The baby-boom generation's exit from the best-customer lifestage is one factor behind the decline. Average household spending on cakes and cupcakes should continue to decline as the small generation X passes through the best-customer age groups and household size shrinks.

Table 47. Cakes and cupcakes

Total household spending	$4,720,343,040.00
Average household spends	37.94

	AVERAGE HOUSEHOLD SPENDING	BEST CUSTOMERS (index)	BIGGEST CUSTOMERS (market share)
AGE OF HOUSEHOLDER			
Average household	**$37.94**	**100**	**100.0%**
Under age 25	21.02	55	3.6
Aged 25 to 34	38.61	102	16.5
Aged 35 to 44	41.93	111	19.2
Aged 45 to 54	40.92	108	21.3
Aged 55 to 64	37.60	99	18.1
Aged 65 to 74	35.39	93	11.2
Aged 75 or older	39.11	103	10.1

	AVERAGE HOUSEHOLD SPENDING	BEST CUSTOMERS (index)	BIGGEST CUSTOMERS (market share)
HOUSEHOLD INCOME			
Average household	**$37.94**	**100**	**100.0%**
Under $20,000	24.41	64	13.5
$20,000 to $39,999	22.68	60	13.5
$40,000 to $49,999	52.60	139	12.3
$50,000 to $69,999	36.58	96	13.9
$70,000 to $79,999	50.24	132	7.4
$80,000 to $99,999	49.28	130	11.5
$100,000 or more	55.98	148	27.6
HOUSEHOLD TYPE			
Average household	**37.94**	**100**	**100.0**
Married couples	49.11	129	62.9
Married couples, no children	40.09	106	22.0
Married couples with children	54.49	144	33.8
Oldest child under age 6	39.38	104	4.7
Oldest child aged 6 to 17	59.30	156	18.6
Oldest child aged 18 or older	55.89	147	10.4
Single parent with child under age 18	27.78	73	3.8
Single person	20.94	55	16.4
RACE AND HISPANIC ORIGIN			
Average household	**37.94**	**100**	**100.0**
Asian	40.21	106	4.6
Black	23.59	62	7.8
Hispanic	39.05	103	12.9
Non-Hispanic white and other	40.31	106	79.7
REGION			
Average household	**37.94**	**100**	**100.0**
Northeast	38.37	101	18.3
Midwest	46.49	123	27.2
South	35.79	94	35.1
West	32.60	86	19.4
EDUCATION			
Average household	**37.94**	**100**	**100.0**
Less than high school graduate	31.74	84	10.9
High school graduate	31.36	83	20.6
Some college	34.34	91	18.6
Associate's degree	35.37	93	9.2
Bachelor's degree or more	48.59	128	40.4
Bachelor's degree	39.32	104	20.7
Master's, professional, doctoral degree	64.27	169	19.7

Note: Market shares may not sum to 100.0 because of rounding and missing categories by household type. "Asian" and "black" include Hispanics and non-Hispanics who identify themselves as being of the respective race alone. "Hispanic" includes people of any race who identify themselves as Hispanic. "Other" includes people who identify themselves as non-Hispanic and as Alaska Native, American Indian, Asian (who are also included in the "Asian" row), or Native Hawaiian or other Pacific Islander, as well as non-Hispanics reporting more than one race.
Source: Calculations by New Strategist based on the Bureau of Labor Statistics' 2012 Consumer Expenditure Survey

Candy and Chewing Gum

Best customers: Householders aged 35 to 64
Married couples with school-aged or older children at home
Households in the West

Customer trends: Average household spending on candy and chewing gum should fall as the large baby-boom generation ages and household size shrinks.

Households with children spend the most on candy and chewing gum. Married couples with school-aged children spend 78 percent more than the average household on this item, and those with adult children at home spend 34 percent more. Householders aged 35 to 64, many with children and grandchildren, spend 10 to 15 percent more than average on candy and chewing gum. Households in the West spend 23 percent more than average on this item.

Average household spending on candy and chewing gum fell 14 percent between 2000 and 2012, after adjusting for inflation, although spending climbed in the 2010-to-2012 time period. Average household spending on candy and chewing gum is likely to resume its decline as the large baby-boom generation ages and household size shrinks.

Table 48. Candy and chewing gum

Total household spending	$10,931,189,760.00
Average household spends	87.86

	AVERAGE HOUSEHOLD SPENDING	BEST CUSTOMERS (index)	BIGGEST CUSTOMERS (market share)
AGE OF HOUSEHOLDER			
Average household	**$87.86**	**100**	**100.0%**
Under age 25	49.30	56	3.7
Aged 25 to 34	82.87	94	15.2
Aged 35 to 44	101.13	115	20.0
Aged 45 to 54	98.40	112	22.2
Aged 55 to 64	96.90	110	20.2
Aged 65 to 74	87.26	99	12.0
Aged 75 or older	61.37	70	6.8

	AVERAGE HOUSEHOLD SPENDING	BEST CUSTOMERS (index)	BIGGEST CUSTOMERS (market share)
HOUSEHOLD INCOME			
Average household	**$87.86**	**100**	**100.0%**
Under $20,000	46.60	53	11.2
$20,000 to $39,999	66.73	76	17.1
$40,000 to $49,999	74.22	84	7.5
$50,000 to $69,999	88.48	101	14.5
$70,000 to $79,999	128.02	146	8.1
$80,000 to $99,999	98.54	112	9.9
$100,000 or more	147.18	168	31.4
HOUSEHOLD TYPE			
Average household	**87.86**	**100**	**100.0**
Married couples	116.90	133	64.6
Married couples, no children	100.91	115	23.9
Married couples with children	129.44	147	34.6
Oldest child under age 6	75.99	86	3.9
Oldest child aged 6 to 17	156.60	178	21.2
Oldest child aged 18 or older	117.42	134	9.4
Single parent with child under age 18	79.01	90	4.7
Single person	46.24	53	15.6
RACE AND HISPANIC ORIGIN			
Average household	**87.86**	**100**	**100.0**
Asian	99.63	113	4.9
Black	50.62	58	7.2
Hispanic	66.61	76	9.5
Non-Hispanic white and other	97.69	111	83.5
REGION			
Average household	**87.86**	**100**	**100.0**
Northeast	80.05	91	16.4
Midwest	90.54	103	22.8
South	77.79	89	33.0
West	108.27	123	27.8
EDUCATION			
Average household	**87.86**	**100**	**100.0**
Less than high school graduate	66.27	75	9.8
High school graduate	71.02	81	20.2
Some college	75.47	86	17.7
Associate's degree	105.08	120	11.8
Bachelor's degree or more	111.97	127	40.2
Bachelor's degree	110.60	126	25.1
Master's, professional, doctoral degree	114.30	130	15.1

Note: Market shares may not sum to 100.0 because of rounding and missing categories by household type. "Asian" and "black" include Hispanics and non-Hispanics who identify themselves as being of the respective race alone. "Hispanic" includes people of any race who identify themselves as Hispanic. "Other" includes people who identify themselves as non-Hispanic and as Alaska Native, American Indian, Asian (who are also included in the "Asian" row), or Native Hawaiian or other Pacific Islander, as well as non-Hispanics reporting more than one race.
Source: Calculations by New Strategist based on the Bureau of Labor Statistics' 2012 Consumer Expenditure Survey

Carbonated Drinks

Best customers:	**Householders aged 35 to 54**
	Married couples with school-aged or older children at home
	Hispanics
Customer trends:	**Average household spending on carbonated beverages may continue to fall**
	as boomers age and household size shrinks, but the substitution of colas
	for coffee among younger generations may limit the decline.

The best customers of carbonated drinks are the largest households. Married couples with school-aged or older children at home spend 35 to 52 percent more than average on this item. Householders ranging in age from 35 to 54, many with children at home, spend 16 to 22 percent more than average on sodas and control 44 percent of the market. Hispanics, who have the largest households, outspend the average by 7 percent.

Average household spending on carbonated beverages purchased at grocery or convenience stores fell 22 percent between 2000 and 2012, after adjusting for inflation. Lower-priced private brands and discounters are one factor behind the decline. Average household spending on sodas may continue to fall as boomers age and household size shrinks. But younger generations, drinking cola rather than coffee, may limit the decline.

Table 49. Carbonated drinks

Total household spending	$17,385,891,840.00
Average household spends	139.74

	AVERAGE HOUSEHOLD SPENDING	BEST CUSTOMERS (index)	BIGGEST CUSTOMERS (market share)
AGE OF HOUSEHOLDER			
Average household	**$139.74**	**100**	**100.0%**
Under age 25	112.25	80	5.3
Aged 25 to 34	130.56	93	15.1
Aged 35 to 44	161.92	116	20.1
Aged 45 to 54	171.16	122	24.2
Aged 55 to 64	148.37	106	19.4
Aged 65 to 74	122.32	88	10.5
Aged 75 or older	74.19	53	5.2

	AVERAGE HOUSEHOLD SPENDING	BEST CUSTOMERS (index)	BIGGEST CUSTOMERS (market share)
HOUSEHOLD INCOME			
Average household	**$139.74**	**100**	**100.0%**
Under $20,000	94.08	67	14.2
$20,000 to $39,999	123.52	88	19.9
$40,000 to $49,999	138.48	99	8.8
$50,000 to $69,999	145.14	104	15.0
$70,000 to $79,999	190.44	136	7.6
$80,000 to $99,999	151.96	109	9.6
$100,000 or more	184.03	132	24.7
HOUSEHOLD TYPE			
Average household	**139.74**	**100**	**100.0**
Married couples	173.24	124	60.2
Married couples, no children	144.39	103	21.5
Married couples with children	187.07	134	31.5
Oldest child under age 6	139.84	100	4.6
Oldest child aged 6 to 17	189.33	135	16.1
Oldest child aged 18 or older	212.76	152	10.7
Single parent with child under age 18	139.71	100	5.2
Single person	72.43	52	15.4
RACE AND HISPANIC ORIGIN			
Average household	**139.74**	**100**	**100.0**
Asian	83.55	60	2.6
Black	101.79	73	9.2
Hispanic	149.70	107	13.4
Non-Hispanic white and other	144.62	103	77.7
REGION			
Average household	**139.74**	**100**	**100.0**
Northeast	119.16	85	15.4
Midwest	145.73	104	23.1
South	149.95	107	40.0
West	133.47	96	21.5
EDUCATION			
Average household	**139.74**	**100**	**100.0**
Less than high school graduate	144.88	104	13.5
High school graduate	149.58	107	26.7
Some college	136.68	98	20.1
Associate's degree	159.16	114	11.2
Bachelor's degree or more	126.18	90	28.5
Bachelor's degree	121.35	87	17.3
Master's, professional, doctoral degree	134.35	96	11.2

Note: Market shares may not sum to 100.0 because of rounding and missing categories by household type. "Asian" and "black" include Hispanics and non-Hispanics who identify themselves as being of the respective race alone. "Hispanic" includes people of any race who identify themselves as Hispanic. "Other" includes people who identify themselves as non-Hispanic and as Alaska Native, American Indian, Asian (who are also included in the "Asian" row), or Native Hawaiian or other Pacific Islander, as well as non-Hispanics reporting more than one race.
Source: Calculations by New Strategist based on the Bureau of Labor Statistics' 2012 Consumer Expenditure Survey

Cereal, Ready-to-Eat and Cooked

Best customers:	**Householders aged 35 to 54**
	Married couples with children at home
	Single parents
Customer trends:	**Average household spending on cereal should grow as the large millennial**
	generation enters the best-customer age groups, but the ongoing
	baby bust may limit the gains.

The biggest spenders on cereal are households with children. Married couples with children at home spend 56 percent more than the average household on cereal, the figure peaking at 77 percent among those with school-aged children. Householders aged 35 to 54, most of them parents, spend 22 to 23 percent more than average on cereal. Single parents, whose spending approaches the average on only a few items, spend just over an average amount on cereal.

Average household spending on cereal fell 25 percent between 2000 and 2010, after adjusting for inflation, then grew 9 percent in the ensuing two years. Behind the decline was the entry of the small generation X into the best-customer lifestage. Average household spending on cereal may grow as the large millennial generation enters the best-customer age groups, but the ongoing baby bust may limit the gains.

Table 50. Cereal, ready-to-eat and cooked

Total household spending	$11,797,125,120.00
Average household spends	94.82

	AVERAGE HOUSEHOLD SPENDING	BEST CUSTOMERS (index)	BIGGEST CUSTOMERS (market share)
AGE OF HOUSEHOLDER			
Average household	**$94.82**	**100**	**100.0%**
Under age 25	75.05	79	5.2
Aged 25 to 34	99.18	105	16.9
Aged 35 to 44	116.50	123	21.3
Aged 45 to 54	115.79	122	24.2
Aged 55 to 64	82.67	87	16.0
Aged 65 to 74	76.06	80	9.7
Aged 75 or older	63.54	67	6.5

	AVERAGE HOUSEHOLD SPENDING	BEST CUSTOMERS (index)	BIGGEST CUSTOMERS (market share)
HOUSEHOLD INCOME			
Average household	**$94.82**	**100**	**100.0%**
Under $20,000	57.41	61	12.7
$20,000 to $39,999	70.70	75	16.8
$40,000 to $49,999	92.91	98	8.7
$50,000 to $69,999	97.37	103	14.8
$70,000 to $79,999	123.96	131	7.3
$80,000 to $99,999	120.22	127	11.2
$100,000 or more	143.75	152	28.4
HOUSEHOLD TYPE			
Average household	**94.82**	**100**	**100.0**
Married couples	122.89	130	62.9
Married couples, no children	93.96	99	20.7
Married couples with children	147.53	156	36.6
Oldest child under age 6	112.48	119	5.4
Oldest child aged 6 to 17	168.24	177	21.1
Oldest child aged 18 or older	134.83	142	10.0
Single parent with child under age 18	97.55	103	5.4
Single person	43.12	45	13.5
RACE AND HISPANIC ORIGIN			
Average household	**94.82**	**100**	**100.0**
Asian	68.70	72	3.1
Black	79.75	84	10.6
Hispanic	103.76	109	13.7
Non-Hispanic white and other	95.95	101	76.0
REGION			
Average household	**94.82**	**100**	**100.0**
Northeast	95.38	101	18.2
Midwest	95.91	101	22.4
South	88.40	93	34.7
West	103.94	110	24.7
EDUCATION			
Average household	**94.82**	**100**	**100.0**
Less than high school graduate	73.65	78	10.1
High school graduate	85.77	90	22.6
Some college	89.11	94	19.4
Associate's degree	107.01	113	11.1
Bachelor's degree or more	109.80	116	36.5
Bachelor's degree	110.75	117	23.3
Master's, professional, doctoral degree	108.19	114	13.2

Note: Market shares may not sum to 100.0 because of rounding and missing categories by household type. "Asian" and "black" include Hispanics and non-Hispanics who identify themselves as being of the respective race alone. "Hispanic" includes people of any race who identify themselves as Hispanic. "Other" includes people who identify themselves as non-Hispanic and as Alaska Native, American Indian, Asian (who are also included in the "Asian" row), or Native Hawaiian or other Pacific Islander, as well as non-Hispanics reporting more than one race.
Source: Calculations by New Strategist based on the Bureau of Labor Statistics' 2012 Consumer Expenditure Survey

Cheese

Best customers: **Householders aged 35 to 64**
              Married couples with children at home

Customer trends: **Average household spending on cheese may decline in the years ahead as the**
              large baby-boom generation ages and household size shrinks.

The largest households spend the most on cheese. Married couples with children at home spend 56 percent more than the average household on this item, the figure peaking at 63 percent among couples with school-aged children. Householders aged 35 to 64, many with children at home, spend 12 to 18 percent more than average on cheese.

Average household spending on cheese, the fifth-largest grocery item in dollar amount spent, declined 5 percent between 2000 and 2010, after adjusting for inflation. In the two years that followed, average spending on cheese rebounded by 8 percent. Spending on cheese may resume its decline in the years ahead as the large baby-boom generation ages and household size shrinks.

Table 51. Cheese

Total household spending	$16,356,971,520.00
Average household spends	131.47

	AVERAGE HOUSEHOLD SPENDING	BEST CUSTOMERS (index)	BIGGEST CUSTOMERS (market share)
AGE OF HOUSEHOLDER			
Average household	**$131.47**	**100**	**100.0%**
Under age 25	67.10	51	3.3
Aged 25 to 34	123.26	94	15.2
Aged 35 to 44	154.60	118	20.4
Aged 45 to 54	152.14	116	22.9
Aged 55 to 64	146.85	112	20.4
Aged 65 to 74	128.43	98	11.8
Aged 75 or older	80.72	61	6.0

	AVERAGE HOUSEHOLD SPENDING	BEST CUSTOMERS (index)	BIGGEST CUSTOMERS (market share)
HOUSEHOLD INCOME			
Average household	**$131.47**	**100**	**100.0%**
Under $20,000	68.50	52	11.0
$20,000 to $39,999	93.61	71	16.0
$40,000 to $49,999	117.19	89	7.9
$50,000 to $69,999	125.86	96	13.8
$70,000 to $79,999	169.54	129	7.2
$80,000 to $99,999	167.23	127	11.2
$100,000 or more	230.47	175	32.8
HOUSEHOLD TYPE			
Average household	**131.47**	**100**	**100.0**
Married couples	180.88	138	66.8
Married couples, no children	154.46	117	24.5
Married couples with children	205.27	156	36.7
Oldest child under age 6	172.10	131	6.0
Oldest child aged 6 to 17	214.87	163	19.4
Oldest child aged 18 or older	209.93	160	11.3
Single parent with child under age 18	94.63	72	3.8
Single person	65.00	49	14.7
RACE AND HISPANIC ORIGIN			
Average household	**131.47**	**100**	**100.0**
Asian	63.20	48	2.1
Black	68.30	52	6.5
Hispanic	119.66	91	11.4
Non-Hispanic white and other	144.20	110	82.3
REGION			
Average household	**131.47**	**100**	**100.0**
Northeast	138.67	105	19.0
Midwest	133.79	102	22.6
South	117.32	89	33.2
West	146.80	112	25.2
EDUCATION			
Average household	**131.47**	**100**	**100.0**
Less than high school graduate	92.60	70	9.2
High school graduate	105.75	80	20.1
Some college	117.47	89	18.4
Associate's degree	134.97	103	10.1
Bachelor's degree or more	174.29	133	41.8
Bachelor's degree	168.30	128	25.5
Master's, professional, doctoral degree	184.40	140	16.3

Note: Market shares may not sum to 100.0 because of rounding and missing categories by household type. "Asian" and "black" include Hispanics and non-Hispanics who identify themselves as being of the respective race alone. "Hispanic" includes people of any race who identify themselves as Hispanic. "Other" includes people who identify themselves as non-Hispanic and as Alaska Native, American Indian, Asian (who are also included in the "Asian" row), or Native Hawaiian or other Pacific Islander, as well as non-Hispanics reporting more than one race.
Source: Calculations by New Strategist based on the Bureau of Labor Statistics' 2012 Consumer Expenditure Survey

Chicken, Fresh and Frozen

Best customers: Householders aged 35 to 54

Married couples with children at home

Single parents

Hispanics, blacks, and Asians

Customer trends: Average household spending on chicken may rise as minority populations grow and the large millennial generation begins to fill the best-customer age groups.

Families with children are the best customers of chicken. Married couples with children at home spend 44 percent more than the average household on this item. Single parents, whose spending approaches average on only a few items, spend 5 percent more than average on chicken. Householders aged 35 to 54, most with children at home, spend 15 to 29 percent more than average on chicken. Asians spend 7 percent more, blacks spend 19 percent more, and Hispanics spend 46 percent more than average on chicken. Together, the minority groups, which represent 29 percent of the population, account for 38 percent of household spending on chicken.

Average household spending on chicken fell 24 percent between 2000 and 2010, after adjusting for inflation, then grew 9 percent in the ensuing two years. One factor behind the decline was the baby-boom generation's exit from the best-customer lifestage, as well as competition from fast-food restaurants. Spending on chicken may continue to rise in the years ahead as minority populations grow and the large millennial generation fills the best-customer age groups.

Table 52. Chicken, fresh and frozen

| Total household spending | $15,741,112,320.00 |
| Average household spends | 126.52 |

	AVERAGE HOUSEHOLD SPENDING	BEST CUSTOMERS (index)	BIGGEST CUSTOMERS (market share)
AGE OF HOUSEHOLDER			
Average household	**$126.52**	**100**	**100.0%**
Under age 25	95.41	75	4.9
Aged 25 to 34	133.05	105	17.0
Aged 35 to 44	145.33	115	19.9
Aged 45 to 54	163.66	129	25.6
Aged 55 to 64	122.15	97	17.7
Aged 65 to 74	97.45	77	9.3
Aged 75 or older	69.52	55	5.4

	AVERAGE HOUSEHOLD SPENDING	BEST CUSTOMERS (index)	BIGGEST CUSTOMERS (market share)
HOUSEHOLD INCOME			
Average household	**$126.52**	**100**	**100.0%**
Under $20,000	87.31	69	14.5
$20,000 to $39,999	108.10	85	19.3
$40,000 to $49,999	123.10	97	8.6
$50,000 to $69,999	119.74	95	13.7
$70,000 to $79,999	169.16	134	7.5
$80,000 to $99,999	154.48	122	10.8
$100,000 or more	173.54	137	25.7
HOUSEHOLD TYPE			
Average household	**126.52**	**100**	**100.0**
Married couples	157.92	125	60.6
Married couples, no children	121.14	96	20.0
Married couples with children	181.91	144	33.8
Oldest child under age 6	141.64	112	5.1
Oldest child aged 6 to 17	196.84	156	18.5
Oldest child aged 18 or older	182.10	144	10.2
Single parent with child under age 18	132.71	105	5.5
Single person	60.86	48	14.3
RACE AND HISPANIC ORIGIN			
Average household	**126.52**	**100**	**100.0**
Asian	135.04	107	4.6
Black	150.72	119	15.0
Hispanic	184.94	146	18.3
Non-Hispanic white and other	112.59	89	66.8
REGION			
Average household	**126.52**	**100**	**100.0**
Northeast	145.41	115	20.7
Midwest	109.04	86	19.1
South	120.41	95	35.4
West	138.84	110	24.7
EDUCATION			
Average household	**126.52**	**100**	**100.0**
Less than high school graduate	126.54	100	13.1
High school graduate	133.04	105	26.2
Some college	103.63	82	16.9
Associate's degree	148.35	117	11.6
Bachelor's degree or more	130.09	103	32.4
Bachelor's degree	133.14	105	21.0
Master's, professional, doctoral degree	124.95	99	11.5

Note: Market shares may not sum to 100.0 because of rounding and missing categories by household type. "Asian" and "black" include Hispanics and non-Hispanics who identify themselves as being of the respective race alone. "Hispanic" includes people of any race who identify themselves as Hispanic. "Other" includes people who identify themselves as non-Hispanic and as Alaska Native, American Indian, Asian (who are also included in the "Asian" row), or Native Hawaiian or other Pacific Islander, as well as non-Hispanics reporting more than one race.
Source: Calculations by New Strategist based on the Bureau of Labor Statistics' 2012 Consumer Expenditure Survey

Citrus Fruit Other than Oranges

Best customers:	Householders aged 35 to 54
	Married couples with children at home
	Single parents
	Asians and Hispanics
	Households in the West
Customer trends:	Average household spending on fresh citrus fruit other than oranges should rise as the Asian and Hispanic populations grow.

The largest households are the best customers of fresh citrus fruit other than oranges. Married couples with children at home spend 52 percent more than average on fresh citrus. Single parents, whose spending approaches average on only a few items, spend 5 percent more. Householders aged 35 to 54, most with children, spend 12 to 24 percent more than average on this item. Hispanics, whose families tend to be relatively large, spend 51 percent more than average and Asians spend twice the average. Together the two minority groups account for a sizeable 28 percent of the market. Households in the West, where many Asians and Hispanics reside and where fresh citrus fruit is widely available, spend 28 percent more than average on this item.

Average household spending on fresh citrus fruit other than oranges, which had stagnated between 2000 and 2006, more than doubled between 2006 and 2012, after adjusting for inflation. One factor behind the increase is the greater availability of a variety of citrus fruit in grocery stores. Average household spending on fresh citrus may continue to rise as the Asian and Hispanic populations grow.

Table 53. Citrus fruit other than oranges

Total household spending $4,970,419,200.00
Average household spends   39.95

	AVERAGE HOUSEHOLD SPENDING	BEST CUSTOMERS (index)	BIGGEST CUSTOMERS (market share)
AGE OF HOUSEHOLDER			
Average household	**$39.95**	**100**	**100.0%**
Under age 25	24.06	60	3.9
Aged 25 to 34	37.88	95	15.3
Aged 35 to 44	44.65	112	19.4
Aged 45 to 54	49.50	124	24.5
Aged 55 to 64	39.51	99	18.1
Aged 65 to 74	36.82	92	11.1
Aged 75 or older	30.97	78	7.6

	AVERAGE HOUSEHOLD SPENDING	BEST CUSTOMERS (index)	BIGGEST CUSTOMERS (market share)
HOUSEHOLD INCOME			
Average household	**$39.95**	**100**	**100.0%**
Under $20,000	22.06	55	11.6
$20,000 to $39,999	30.61	77	17.3
$40,000 to $49,999	34.30	86	7.6
$50,000 to $69,999	42.04	105	15.2
$70,000 to $79,999	44.43	111	6.2
$80,000 to $99,999	48.36	121	10.7
$100,000 or more	66.95	168	31.4
HOUSEHOLD TYPE			
Average household	**39.95**	**100**	**100.0**
Married couples	52.21	131	63.5
Married couples, no children	42.70	107	22.3
Married couples with children	60.90	152	35.8
Oldest child under age 6	50.42	126	5.8
Oldest child aged 6 to 17	58.78	147	17.5
Oldest child aged 18 or older	70.98	178	12.5
Single parent with child under age 18	41.84	105	5.5
Single person	20.24	51	15.0
RACE AND HISPANIC ORIGIN			
Average household	**39.95**	**100**	**100.0**
Asian	79.81	200	8.7
Black	21.62	54	6.8
Hispanic	60.13	151	18.9
Non-Hispanic white and other	39.76	100	74.7
REGION			
Average household	**39.95**	**100**	**100.0**
Northeast	44.66	112	20.2
Midwest	38.88	97	21.6
South	31.62	79	29.5
West	51.02	128	28.8
EDUCATION			
Average household	**39.95**	**100**	**100.0**
Less than high school graduate	43.13	108	14.1
High school graduate	31.32	78	19.5
Some college	30.44	76	15.7
Associate's degree	36.78	92	9.1
Bachelor's degree or more	52.82	132	41.7
Bachelor's degree	48.84	122	24.4
Master's, professional, doctoral degree	59.55	149	17.3

Note: Market shares may not sum to 100.0 because of rounding and missing categories by household type. "Asian" and "black" include Hispanics and non-Hispanics who identify themselves as being of the respective race alone. "Hispanic" includes people of any race who identify themselves as Hispanic. "Other" includes people who identify themselves as non-Hispanic and as Alaska Native, American Indian, Asian (who are also included in the "Asian" row), or Native Hawaiian or other Pacific Islander, as well as non-Hispanics reporting more than one race.
Source: Calculations by New Strategist based on the Bureau of Labor Statistics' 2012 Consumer Expenditure Survey

Coffee

Best customers: Householders aged 45 to 74

Married couples without children at home

Married couples with school-aged or older children at home

Customer trends: Average household spending on coffee may decline in the years ahead as the millennial generation—which prefers cola to coffee—enters middle age.

Starbucks has been successful in promoting coffee to the masses, and Keurig has made it easy to brew a cup of coffee at home. These factors may account for the much greater spending in the past few years on coffee purchased at grocery and convenience stores. The best customers of coffee are householders ranging in age from 45 to 74, who spend 15 to 25 percent more than average on coffee. Married couples without children at home (most of them middle aged or older) spend 36 percent more than average on this item, while those with adult children at home spend 54 percent more.

Average household spending on coffee purchased at grocery or convenience stores climbed slightly between 2000 and 2006 (up 2 percent after adjusting for inflation), then rose much more strongly between 2006 and 2012 (up 52 percent). Much of that growth occurred between 2010 and 2012. The surprising growth in spending on coffee purchased at groceries and convenience stores may be due to fewer trips to Starbucks and other coffee shops as the Great Recession reduced restaurant spending. Some of it is also due to the newfound convenience of single-cup coffee brewing. Average household spending on coffee could decline in the years ahead, however, as the millennial generation—which prefers cola to coffee—enters middle age.

Table 54. Coffee

Total household spending $10,761,984,000.00
Average household spends   86.50

	AVERAGE HOUSEHOLD SPENDING	BEST CUSTOMERS (index)	BIGGEST CUSTOMERS (market share)
AGE OF HOUSEHOLDER			
Average household	**$86.50**	**100**	**100.0%**
Under age 25	45.53	53	3.5
Aged 25 to 34	63.79	74	11.9
Aged 35 to 44	78.12	90	15.7
Aged 45 to 54	106.55	123	24.4
Aged 55 to 64	99.16	115	21.0
Aged 65 to 74	108.29	125	15.1
Aged 75 or older	78.06	90	8.8

	AVERAGE HOUSEHOLD SPENDING	BEST CUSTOMERS (index)	BIGGEST CUSTOMERS (market share)
HOUSEHOLD INCOME			
Average household	**$86.50**	**100**	**100.0%**
Under $20,000	50.50	58	12.3
$20,000 to $39,999	59.27	69	15.4
$40,000 to $49,999	73.50	85	7.5
$50,000 to $69,999	85.90	99	14.3
$70,000 to $79,999	118.64	137	7.7
$80,000 to $99,999	106.42	123	10.9
$100,000 or more	146.71	170	31.8
HOUSEHOLD TYPE			
Average household	**86.50**	**100**	**100.0**
Married couples	112.16	130	63.0
Married couples, no children	117.77	136	28.4
Married couples with children	108.06	125	29.4
Oldest child under age 6	72.41	84	3.8
Oldest child aged 6 to 17	106.36	123	14.6
Oldest child aged 18 or older	133.11	154	10.9
Single parent with child under age 18	59.60	69	3.6
Single person	49.93	58	17.1
RACE AND HISPANIC ORIGIN			
Average household	**86.50**	**100**	**100.0**
Asian	75.06	87	3.8
Black	40.47	47	5.9
Hispanic	61.78	71	9.0
Non-Hispanic white and other	98.41	114	85.4
REGION			
Average household	**86.50**	**100**	**100.0**
Northeast	99.85	115	20.8
Midwest	80.23	93	20.6
South	80.46	93	34.6
West	91.97	106	24.0
EDUCATION			
Average household	**86.50**	**100**	**100.0**
Less than high school graduate	65.40	76	9.9
High school graduate	79.04	91	22.8
Some college	85.57	99	20.4
Associate's degree	91.40	106	10.4
Bachelor's degree or more	99.28	115	36.2
Bachelor's degree	89.47	103	20.6
Master's, professional, doctoral degree	115.86	134	15.5

Note: Market shares may not sum to 100.0 because of rounding and missing categories by household type. "Asian" and "black" include Hispanics and non-Hispanics who identify themselves as being of the respective race alone. "Hispanic" includes people of any race who identify themselves as Hispanic. "Other" includes people who identify themselves as non-Hispanic and as Alaska Native, American Indian, Asian (who are also included in the "Asian" row), or Native Hawaiian or other Pacific Islander, as well as non-Hispanics reporting more than one race.
Source: Calculations by New Strategist based on the Bureau of Labor Statistics' 2012 Consumer Expenditure Survey

Cookies

Best customers: Householders aged 35 to 54

Married couples with school-aged or older children at home

Customer trends: Average household spending on cookies may resume its decline because

of the ongoing baby bust.

The biggest spenders on cookies are households with children. Married couples with school-aged or older children at home spend 46 to 52 percent more than the average household on this item. Householders aged 35 to 54, many with children at home, spend 9 to 12 percent more than average on cookies.

Average household spending on cookies fell 24 percent between 2000 and 2010, after adjusting for inflation, then increased by 5 percent in the ensuing two years. Behind the decline was increased competition with other snack foods for the dollars of shoppers as well as the baby-boom generation's exit from the best-customer lifestage. The recent increase is a sign of economic recovery and may be short-lived. Average household spending on cookies may resume its decline because of the ongoing baby bust.

Table 55. Cookies

| Total household spending | $6,290,472,960.00 |
| Average household spends | 50.56 |

	AVERAGE HOUSEHOLD SPENDING	BEST CUSTOMERS (index)	BIGGEST CUSTOMERS (market share)
AGE OF HOUSEHOLDER			
Average household	**$50.56**	**100**	**100.0%**
Under age 25	34.75	69	4.5
Aged 25 to 34	45.30	90	14.5
Aged 35 to 44	54.98	109	18.9
Aged 45 to 54	56.65	112	22.2
Aged 55 to 64	52.60	104	19.0
Aged 65 to 74	52.56	104	12.5
Aged 75 or older	43.81	87	8.5

	AVERAGE HOUSEHOLD SPENDING	BEST CUSTOMERS (index)	BIGGEST CUSTOMERS (market share)
HOUSEHOLD INCOME			
Average household	**$50.56**	**100**	**100.0%**
Under $20,000	31.18	62	13.0
$20,000 to $39,999	37.88	75	16.9
$40,000 to $49,999	44.58	88	7.8
$50,000 to $69,999	56.01	111	16.0
$70,000 to $79,999	55.56	110	6.1
$80,000 to $99,999	60.72	120	10.6
$100,000 or more	79.30	157	29.4
HOUSEHOLD TYPE			
Average household	**50.56**	**100**	**100.0**
Married couples	64.94	128	62.4
Married couples, no children	54.51	108	22.5
Married couples with children	71.94	142	33.5
Oldest child under age 6	56.47	112	5.1
Oldest child aged 6 to 17	76.66	152	18.0
Oldest child aged 18 or older	73.72	146	10.3
Single parent with child under age 18	44.04	87	4.6
Single person	26.20	52	15.4
RACE AND HISPANIC ORIGIN			
Average household	**50.56**	**100**	**100.0**
Asian	51.90	103	4.4
Black	39.63	78	9.9
Hispanic	49.55	98	12.3
Non-Hispanic white and other	52.57	104	78.0
REGION			
Average household	**50.56**	**100**	**100.0**
Northeast	54.73	108	19.5
Midwest	51.20	101	22.5
South	46.89	93	34.5
West	52.65	104	23.5
EDUCATION			
Average household	**50.56**	**100**	**100.0**
Less than high school graduate	47.83	95	12.4
High school graduate	48.20	95	23.8
Some college	45.46	90	18.5
Associate's degree	52.73	104	10.3
Bachelor's degree or more	56.17	111	35.0
Bachelor's degree	53.39	106	21.0
Master's, professional, doctoral degree	60.88	120	14.0

Note: Market shares may not sum to 100.0 because of rounding and missing categories by household type. "Asian" and "black" include Hispanics and non-Hispanics who identify themselves as being of the respective race alone. "Hispanic" includes people of any race who identify themselves as Hispanic. "Other" includes people who identify themselves as non-Hispanic and as Alaska Native, American Indian, Asian (who are also included in the "Asian" row), or Native Hawaiian or other Pacific Islander, as well as non-Hispanics reporting more than one race.
Source: Calculations by New Strategist based on the Bureau of Labor Statistics' 2012 Consumer Expenditure Survey

Crackers

Best customers: Householders aged 35 to 54
Married couples with children at home

Customer trends: Average household spending on crackers is likely to stabilize as the small generation X passes through the best-customer age groups.

Married couples with children at home are the biggest spenders on crackers. This household type spends 61 percent more than the average household on crackers. The figure peaks at 72 percent more than average among households with school-aged children. Householders aged 35 to 54, most with children, spend 12 to 22 percent more than average on this item and account for 43 percent of the market.

Average household spending on crackers grew 20 percent between 2000 and 2012, after adjusting for inflation. Several factors account for this increase, including the greater variety of crackers available and consumers' substitution of crackers for cookies in an attempt to cut calories. Average household spending on crackers is likely to stabilize as the small generation X passes through the best-customer age groups.

Table 56. Crackers

Total household spending $4,624,542,720.00
Average household spends   37.17

	AVERAGE HOUSEHOLD SPENDING	BEST CUSTOMERS (index)	BIGGEST CUSTOMERS (market share)
AGE OF HOUSEHOLDER			
Average household	**$37.17**	**100**	**100.0%**
Under age 25	23.14	62	4.1
Aged 25 to 34	35.33	95	15.4
Aged 35 to 44	41.52	112	19.4
Aged 45 to 54	45.17	122	24.1
Aged 55 to 64	36.42	98	17.9
Aged 65 to 74	36.62	99	11.9
Aged 75 or older	27.71	75	7.3

	AVERAGE HOUSEHOLD SPENDING	BEST CUSTOMERS (index)	BIGGEST CUSTOMERS (market share)
HOUSEHOLD INCOME			
Average household	**$37.17**	**100**	**100.0%**
Under $20,000	21.84	59	12.4
$20,000 to $39,999	26.46	71	16.0
$40,000 to $49,999	36.28	98	8.6
$50,000 to $69,999	34.82	94	13.5
$70,000 to $79,999	44.84	121	6.7
$80,000 to $99,999	47.21	127	11.2
$100,000 or more	62.51	168	31.5
HOUSEHOLD TYPE			
Average household	**37.17**	**100**	**100.0**
Married couples	49.80	134	65.1
Married couples, no children	39.36	106	22.1
Married couples with children	59.79	161	37.8
Oldest child under age 6	58.59	158	7.2
Oldest child aged 6 to 17	64.01	172	20.5
Oldest child aged 18 or older	53.51	144	10.2
Single parent with child under age 18	31.82	86	4.5
Single person	19.33	52	15.4
RACE AND HISPANIC ORIGIN			
Average household	**37.17**	**100**	**100.0**
Asian	27.20	73	3.2
Black	23.41	63	7.9
Hispanic	29.15	78	9.8
Non-Hispanic white and other	40.82	110	82.4
REGION			
Average household	**37.17**	**100**	**100.0**
Northeast	38.26	103	18.6
Midwest	40.13	108	23.9
South	33.27	90	33.3
West	39.78	107	24.1
EDUCATION			
Average household	**37.17**	**100**	**100.0**
Less than high school graduate	28.24	76	9.9
High school graduate	31.47	85	21.1
Some college	30.64	82	17.0
Associate's degree	39.28	106	10.4
Bachelor's degree or more	48.67	131	41.3
Bachelor's degree	47.78	129	25.6
Master's, professional, doctoral degree	50.17	135	15.7

Note: Market shares may not sum to 100.0 because of rounding and missing categories by household type. "Asian" and "black" include Hispanics and non-Hispanics who identify themselves as being of the respective race alone. "Hispanic" includes people of any race who identify themselves as Hispanic. "Other" includes people who identify themselves as non-Hispanic and as Alaska Native, American Indian, Asian (who are also included in the "Asian" row), or Native Hawaiian or other Pacific Islander, as well as non-Hispanics reporting more than one race.
Source: Calculations by New Strategist based on the Bureau of Labor Statistics' 2012 Consumer Expenditure Survey

Cream

Best customers: Householders aged 35 to 54
                        Married couples with school-aged or older children at home
                        Households in the Northeast and West

Customer trends: Average household spending on cream should stabilize as the large baby-boom
                        generation ages and household size shrinks.

Like butter, cream made a comeback when lower-carb diets became popular, especially among baby boomers. The biggest spenders on cream are the largest households—middle-aged married couples with children. Householders aged 35 to 54 spend 15 to 24 percent more than the average household on cream, and those aged 55 to 74 are also above-average spenders on this item. Married couples with school-aged or older children at home spend 52 to 96 percent more than average on this item. Households in the Northeast spend 27 percent more than average on cream, and those in the West spend 14 percent more.

Average household spending on cream rose 52 percent between 2000 and 2012, after adjusting for inflation. Behind the increase is the improved reputation of cream because of the popularity of low-carb diets. Spending on cream should stabilize as the large baby-boom generation ages and household size shrinks.

Table 57. Cream

Total household spending $2,933,729,280.00
Average household spends   23.58

	AVERAGE HOUSEHOLD SPENDING	BEST CUSTOMERS (index)	BIGGEST CUSTOMERS (market share)
AGE OF HOUSEHOLDER			
Average household	**$23.58**	**100**	**100.0%**
Under age 25	11.01	47	3.1
Aged 25 to 34	20.58	87	14.1
Aged 35 to 44	27.20	115	20.0
Aged 45 to 54	29.14	124	24.5
Aged 55 to 64	24.77	105	19.2
Aged 65 to 74	23.98	102	12.3
Aged 75 or older	16.76	71	6.9

	AVERAGE HOUSEHOLD SPENDING	BEST CUSTOMERS (index)	BIGGEST CUSTOMERS (market share)
HOUSEHOLD INCOME			
Average household	**$23.58**	**100**	**100.0%**
Under $20,000	13.19	56	11.8
$20,000 to $39,999	17.76	75	17.0
$40,000 to $49,999	23.45	99	8.8
$50,000 to $69,999	23.14	98	14.2
$70,000 to $79,999	28.33	120	6.7
$80,000 to $99,999	27.62	117	10.3
$100,000 or more	38.84	165	30.8
HOUSEHOLD TYPE			
Average household	**23.58**	**100**	**100.0**
Married couples	31.51	134	64.9
Married couples, no children	25.00	106	22.1
Married couples with children	37.32	158	37.2
Oldest child under age 6	26.78	114	5.2
Oldest child aged 6 to 17	35.91	152	18.1
Oldest child aged 18 or older	46.26	196	13.8
Single parent with child under age 18	20.77	88	4.6
Single person	10.07	43	12.7
RACE AND HISPANIC ORIGIN			
Average household	**23.58**	**100**	**100.0**
Asian	20.44	87	3.8
Black	11.08	47	5.9
Hispanic	22.47	95	11.9
Non-Hispanic white and other	25.86	110	82.3
REGION			
Average household	**23.58**	**100**	**100.0**
Northeast	30.03	127	23.0
Midwest	23.48	100	22.1
South	18.54	79	29.3
West	26.82	114	25.6
EDUCATION			
Average household	**23.58**	**100**	**100.0**
Less than high school graduate	21.68	92	12.0
High school graduate	21.84	93	23.1
Some college	19.39	82	16.9
Associate's degree	27.30	116	11.4
Bachelor's degree or more	27.31	116	36.5
Bachelor's degree	26.91	114	22.7
Master's, professional, doctoral degree	27.98	119	13.8

Note: Market shares may not sum to 100.0 because of rounding and missing categories by household type. "Asian" and "black" include Hispanics and non-Hispanics who identify themselves as being of the respective race alone. "Hispanic" includes people of any race who identify themselves as Hispanic. "Other" includes people who identify themselves as non-Hispanic and as Alaska Native, American Indian, Asian (who are also included in the "Asian" row), or Native Hawaiian or other Pacific Islander, as well as non-Hispanics reporting more than one race.
Source: Calculations by New Strategist based on the Bureau of Labor Statistics' 2012 Consumer Expenditure Survey

Dairy Products Other than Butter, Cheese, Cream, Ice Cream, and Milk

Best customers:	Householders aged 35 to 54
	Married couples with children at home
	Households in the Northeast and West
Customer trends:	Average household spending on dairy products other than butter, cheese, cream, ice cream, and milk should continue to grow as more consumers seek the health benefits of yogurt.

Some dairy products, such as yogurt, are growing in popularity. The biggest spenders on dairy products other than butter, cheese, cream, ice cream, and milk—a category that includes yogurt—are the largest households. Married couples with children at home spend 60 percent more than the average household on such dairy products. Householders aged 35 to 54, many with children, spend 21 to 23 percent more than average and account for 45 percent of the market. Households in the Northeast spend 20 percent more than average on other dairy, and households in the West spend 12 percent more.

Average household spending on other dairy products rose by a substantial 65 percent between 2000 and 2012, after adjusting for inflation. Behind the increase is the growing popularity of yogurt and yogurt-based drinks. Average household spending on such dairy products may continue to rise as more consumers seek the health benefits of yogurt.

Table 58. Dairy products other than butter, cheese, cream, ice cream, and milk

Total household spending	$6,552,990,720.00
Average household spends	52.67

	AVERAGE HOUSEHOLD SPENDING	BEST CUSTOMERS (index)	BIGGEST CUSTOMERS (market share)
AGE OF HOUSEHOLDER			
Average household	**$52.67**	**100**	**100.0%**
Under age 25	37.11	70	4.6
Aged 25 to 34	52.14	99	16.0
Aged 35 to 44	63.50	121	20.9
Aged 45 to 54	64.65	123	24.3
Aged 55 to 64	51.41	98	17.9
Aged 65 to 74	43.60	83	10.0
Aged 75 or older	33.35	63	6.2

	AVERAGE HOUSEHOLD SPENDING	BEST CUSTOMERS (index)	BIGGEST CUSTOMERS (market share)
HOUSEHOLD INCOME			
Average household	**$52.67**	**100**	**100.0%**
Under $20,000	24.17	46	9.7
$20,000 to $39,999	36.54	69	15.6
$40,000 to $49,999	43.53	83	7.3
$50,000 to $69,999	51.97	99	14.3
$70,000 to $79,999	70.86	135	7.5
$80,000 to $99,999	72.08	137	12.1
$100,000 or more	94.45	179	33.6
HOUSEHOLD TYPE			
Average household	**52.67**	**100**	**100.0**
Married couples	70.74	134	65.2
Married couples, no children	57.05	108	22.6
Married couples with children	84.18	160	37.6
Oldest child under age 6	80.89	154	7.0
Oldest child aged 6 to 17	91.65	174	20.7
Oldest child aged 18 or older	73.75	140	9.9
Single parent with child under age 18	42.63	81	4.2
Single person	26.43	50	14.9
RACE AND HISPANIC ORIGIN			
Average household	**52.67**	**100**	**100.0**
Asian	50.34	96	4.1
Black	32.07	61	7.7
Hispanic	53.44	101	12.7
Non-Hispanic white and other	56.01	106	79.8
REGION			
Average household	**52.67**	**100**	**100.0**
Northeast	63.21	120	21.7
Midwest	55.22	105	23.2
South	42.18	80	29.8
West	59.00	112	25.2
EDUCATION			
Average household	**52.67**	**100**	**100.0**
Less than high school graduate	37.86	72	9.4
High school graduate	38.20	73	18.1
Some college	43.47	83	17.0
Associate's degree	54.92	104	10.3
Bachelor's degree or more	74.93	142	44.9
Bachelor's degree	70.74	134	26.8
Master's, professional, doctoral degree	82.01	156	18.1

Note: Market shares may not sum to 100.0 because of rounding and missing categories by household type. "Asian" and "black" include Hispanics and non-Hispanics who identify themselves as being of the respective race alone. "Hispanic" includes people of any race who identify themselves as Hispanic. "Other" includes people who identify themselves as non-Hispanic and as Alaska Native, American Indian, Asian (who are also included in the "Asian" row), or Native Hawaiian or other Pacific Islander, as well as non-Hispanics reporting more than one race.
Source: Calculations by New Strategist based on the Bureau of Labor Statistics' 2012 Consumer Expenditure Survey

Desserts, Prepared

Best customers: Married couples with school-aged or older children at home

                            Single parents

                            Households in the Northeast and Midwest

Customer trends: Average household spending on prepared desserts may decline in the years

                            ahead as the large baby-boom generation ages and household size shrinks.

The best customers of prepared desserts are the largest households. For convenience, they are buying prepared desserts rather than cooking from scratch. Couples with school-aged children spend 50 percent more than the average household on this item, and those with adult children at home spend 29 percent more. Prepared desserts are one of the relatively few items on which single parents, with their lower incomes, spend an average amount. Households in the Northeast spend 20 percent more than average on prepared desserts, and households in the Midwest spend 15 percent more.

Average household spending on prepared desserts climbed 40 percent between 2000 and 2010, after adjusting for inflation, then dropped by 18 percent in the ensuing two years. Behind the increase was the consumer preference for the convenience of prepared food. Average household spending on prepared desserts may continue to decline in the years ahead as the large baby-boom generation ages and household size shrinks.

Table 59. Desserts, prepared

Total household spending $1,777,904,640.00
Average household spends   14.29

	AVERAGE HOUSEHOLD SPENDING	BEST CUSTOMERS (index)	BIGGEST CUSTOMERS (market share)
AGE OF HOUSEHOLDER			
Average household	**$14.29**	**100**	**100.0%**
Under age 25	11.74	82	5.4
Aged 25 to 34	12.17	85	13.8
Aged 35 to 44	14.90	104	18.1
Aged 45 to 54	14.98	105	20.7
Aged 55 to 64	14.14	99	18.1
Aged 65 to 74	15.82	111	13.3
Aged 75 or older	15.64	109	10.7

	AVERAGE HOUSEHOLD SPENDING	BEST CUSTOMERS (index)	BIGGEST CUSTOMERS (market share)
HOUSEHOLD INCOME			
Average household	**$14.29**	**100**	**100.0%**
Under $20,000	8.49	59	12.5
$20,000 to $39,999	12.08	85	19.1
$40,000 to $49,999	12.01	84	7.4
$50,000 to $69,999	16.74	117	16.9
$70,000 to $79,999	14.92	104	5.8
$80,000 to $99,999	17.74	124	11.0
$100,000 or more	20.82	146	27.3
HOUSEHOLD TYPE			
Average household	**14.29**	**100**	**100.0**
Married couples	18.19	127	61.8
Married couples, no children	16.44	115	24.0
Married couples with children	19.32	135	31.8
Oldest child under age 6	15.25	107	4.9
Oldest child aged 6 to 17	21.41	150	17.8
Oldest child aged 18 or older	18.37	129	9.1
Single parent with child under age 18	14.92	104	5.5
Single person	8.23	58	17.1
RACE AND HISPANIC ORIGIN			
Average household	**14.29**	**100**	**100.0**
Asian	12.48	87	3.8
Black	9.02	63	7.9
Hispanic	12.57	88	11.0
Non-Hispanic white and other	15.48	108	81.3
REGION			
Average household	**14.29**	**100**	**100.0**
Northeast	17.15	120	21.7
Midwest	16.41	115	25.5
South	12.49	87	32.6
West	12.85	90	20.3
EDUCATION			
Average household	**14.29**	**100**	**100.0**
Less than high school graduate	13.24	93	12.1
High school graduate	12.80	90	22.3
Some college	14.14	99	20.4
Associate's degree	15.73	110	10.9
Bachelor's degree or more	15.50	108	34.2
Bachelor's degree	13.85	97	19.3
Master's, professional, doctoral degree	18.28	128	14.8

Note: Market shares may not sum to 100.0 because of rounding and missing categories by household type. "Asian" and "black" include Hispanics and non-Hispanics who identify themselves as being of the respective race alone. "Hispanic" includes people of any race who identify themselves as Hispanic. "Other" includes people who identify themselves as non-Hispanic and as Alaska Native, American Indian, Asian (who are also included in the "Asian" row), or Native Hawaiian or other Pacific Islander, as well as non-Hispanics reporting more than one race.
Source: Calculations by New Strategist based on the Bureau of Labor Statistics' 2012 Consumer Expenditure Survey

Eggs

Best customers: Householders aged 35 to 54

Married couples with school-aged or older children at home

Hispanics and Asians

Households in the West

Customer trends: Average household spending on eggs may stabilize or even decline as the small

generation X passes through the best-customer lifestage.

Household size is the most important factor in determining spending on eggs, the largest households spending the most. Married couples with school-aged children spend 43 percent more than the average household on eggs, and those with adult children at home spend 48 percent more. Householders aged 35 to 54, most with children, outspend the average by 13 to 14 percent. Hispanics, whose families are larger than average, spend 41 percent more than average on eggs, and Asians spend 31 percent more. Households in the West, where many Asians and Hispanics reside, spend 14 percent more than average on this item.

Average household spending on eggs declined 9 percent between 2000 and 2006, after adjusting for inflation, but rebounded by 27 percent between 2006 and 2012. Behind the rise was the improving reputation of eggs thanks to the popularity of low-carb diets, as well as consumers' increased propensity to eat at home as the Great Recession reduced incomes. Spending on eggs may stabilize or even decline as the small generation X passes through the best-customer lifestage.

Table 60. Eggs

Total household spending $6,604,001,280.00
Average household spends   53.08

	AVERAGE HOUSEHOLD SPENDING	BEST CUSTOMERS (index)	BIGGEST CUSTOMERS (market share)
AGE OF HOUSEHOLDER			
Average household	**$53.08**	**100**	**100.0%**
Under age 25	38.69	73	4.8
Aged 25 to 34	50.47	95	15.4
Aged 35 to 44	60.46	114	19.8
Aged 45 to 54	59.86	113	22.3
Aged 55 to 64	53.10	100	18.3
Aged 65 to 74	52.32	99	11.9
Aged 75 or older	41.01	77	7.6

	AVERAGE HOUSEHOLD SPENDING	BEST CUSTOMERS (index)	BIGGEST CUSTOMERS (market share)
HOUSEHOLD INCOME			
Average household	**$53.08**	**100**	**100.0%**
Under $20,000	39.83	75	15.8
$20,000 to $39,999	46.30	87	19.7
$40,000 to $49,999	49.58	93	8.3
$50,000 to $69,999	50.68	95	13.8
$70,000 to $79,999	63.96	120	6.7
$80,000 to $99,999	61.27	115	10.2
$100,000 or more	72.35	136	25.5
HOUSEHOLD TYPE			
Average household	**53.08**	**100**	**100.0**
Married couples	66.03	124	60.4
Married couples, no children	55.51	105	21.8
Married couples with children	72.17	136	32.0
Oldest child under age 6	52.36	99	4.5
Oldest child aged 6 to 17	75.71	143	17.0
Oldest child aged 18 or older	78.59	148	10.4
Single parent with child under age 18	50.64	95	5.0
Single person	29.31	55	16.4
RACE AND HISPANIC ORIGIN			
Average household	**53.08**	**100**	**100.0**
Asian	69.78	131	5.7
Black	45.03	85	10.7
Hispanic	74.62	141	17.6
Non-Hispanic white and other	50.85	96	71.9
REGION			
Average household	**53.08**	**100**	**100.0**
Northeast	55.30	104	18.8
Midwest	49.70	94	20.8
South	49.60	93	34.8
West	60.46	114	25.7
EDUCATION			
Average household	**53.08**	**100**	**100.0**
Less than high school graduate	54.21	102	13.3
High school graduate	54.60	103	25.6
Some college	47.26	89	18.3
Associate's degree	52.63	99	9.8
Bachelor's degree or more	55.55	105	33.0
Bachelor's degree	55.32	104	20.8
Master's, professional, doctoral degree	55.92	105	12.2

Note: Market shares may not sum to 100.0 because of rounding and missing categories by household type. "Asian" and "black" include Hispanics and non-Hispanics who identify themselves as being of the respective race alone. "Hispanic" includes people of any race who identify themselves as Hispanic. "Other" includes people who identify themselves as non-Hispanic and as Alaska Native, American Indian, Asian (who are also included in the "Asian" row), or Native Hawaiian or other Pacific Islander, as well as non-Hispanics reporting more than one race.
Source: Calculations by New Strategist based on the Bureau of Labor Statistics' 2012 Consumer Expenditure Survey

Fats and Oils

Best customers: Householders aged 35 to 54
Married couples with school-aged or older children at home
Hispanics, Asians, and blacks
Householders without a high school diploma

Customer trends: Average household spending on fats and oils may level out in the years ahead
if eating out regains its pre–Great Recession popularity.

The biggest spenders on fats and oils are Hispanics, Asians, and blacks. Hispanics spend 64 percent more than average on this item, Asians spend 54 percent more, and blacks spend 3 percent more. Together the three minorities, which represent 29 percent of the population, account for 40 percent of the market for fats and oils. Married couples with school-aged or older children at home spend 47 to 51 percent more than average on fats and oils. Householders aged 35 to 54, many with children, spend 20 to 23 percent more than average on this item. Householders who did not complete high school, many of them Hispanic, spend 43 percent above average on fats and oils.

Average household spending on fats and oils rose 18 percent between 2000 and 2012, after adjusting for inflation. Behind the increase was the popularity of high-priced specialty oils, as well as the growth of the Asian, black, and Hispanic populations. Average household spending on fats and oils may level out in the years ahead if eating out regains its pre–Great Recession popularity.

Table 61. Fats and oils

Total household spending $4,577,264,640.00
Average household spends   36.79

AGE OF HOUSEHOLDER	AVERAGE HOUSEHOLD SPENDING	BEST CUSTOMERS (index)	BIGGEST CUSTOMERS (market share)
Average household	**$36.79**	**100**	**100.0%**
Under age 25	31.44	85	5.6
Aged 25 to 34	32.70	89	14.4
Aged 35 to 44	45.27	123	21.4
Aged 45 to 54	44.33	120	23.8
Aged 55 to 64	33.40	91	16.6
Aged 65 to 74	31.56	86	10.3
Aged 75 or older	29.09	79	7.7

	AVERAGE HOUSEHOLD SPENDING	BEST CUSTOMERS (index)	BIGGEST CUSTOMERS (market share)
HOUSEHOLD INCOME			
Average household	**$36.79**	**100**	**100.0%**
Under $20,000	27.13	74	15.5
$20,000 to $39,999	32.88	89	20.1
$40,000 to $49,999	34.91	95	8.4
$50,000 to $69,999	31.23	85	12.3
$70,000 to $79,999	43.50	118	6.6
$80,000 to $99,999	44.50	121	10.7
$100,000 or more	51.86	141	26.4
HOUSEHOLD TYPE			
Average household	**36.79**	**100**	**100.0**
Married couples	45.33	123	59.8
Married couples, no children	37.04	101	21.0
Married couples with children	50.49	137	32.3
Oldest child under age 6	31.28	85	3.9
Oldest child aged 6 to 17	55.44	151	17.9
Oldest child aged 18 or older	54.22	147	10.4
Single parent with child under age 18	34.13	93	4.9
Single person	18.97	52	15.3
RACE AND HISPANIC ORIGIN			
Average household	**36.79**	**100**	**100.0**
Asian	56.61	154	6.7
Black	37.76	103	12.9
Hispanic	60.44	164	20.6
Non-Hispanic white and other	32.70	89	66.7
REGION			
Average household	**36.79**	**100**	**100.0**
Northeast	37.15	101	18.2
Midwest	31.57	86	19.0
South	35.61	97	36.0
West	43.67	119	26.7
EDUCATION			
Average household	**36.79**	**100**	**100.0**
Less than high school graduate	52.71	143	18.7
High school graduate	32.54	88	22.1
Some college	29.51	80	16.5
Associate's degree	38.03	103	10.2
Bachelor's degree or more	38.62	105	33.1
Bachelor's degree	37.21	101	20.2
Master's, professional, doctoral degree	41.00	111	12.9

Note: Market shares may not sum to 100.0 because of rounding and missing categories by household type. "Asian" and "black" include Hispanics and non-Hispanics who identify themselves as being of the respective race alone. "Hispanic" includes people of any race who identify themselves as Hispanic. "Other" includes people who identify themselves as non-Hispanic and as Alaska Native, American Indian, Asian (who are also included in the "Asian" row), or Native Hawaiian or other Pacific Islander, as well as non-Hispanics reporting more than one race.
Source: Calculations by New Strategist based on the Bureau of Labor Statistics' 2012 Consumer Expenditure Survey

Fish and Seafood, Canned

Best customers: Householders aged 35 to 74
                      Married couples with school-aged or older children at home
                      Asians
                      Households in the Northeast and West

Customer trends: Average household spending on canned fish and seafood may resume its slow
                      decline as consumer preferences shift from canned to frozen fish.

The biggest spenders on canned fish and seafood are middle-aged and older householders. Householders ranging in age from 35 to 74 spend more than average on this item, the figure peaking at 24 percent more than average among householders aged 65 to 74. Couples with adult children at home spend 35 percent more than average on canned fish and seafood, and those with school-aged children spend 21 percent more. Asians outspend the average by 59 percent. Households in the Northeast spend 29 percent more than average on canned fish, and those in the West spend 17 percent more.

Average household spending on canned fish and seafood fell 10 percent between 2000 and 2006, grew 13 percent between 2006 and 2010, then fell 14 percent between 2010 and 2012, after adjusting for inflation. Behind the earlier decline was the shift from canned to frozen fish and the then-growing preference for eating out rather than preparing meals from scratch. The 2006-to-2010 growth was the result of more home cooking because of the Great Recession. The current decline is likely due to changing consumer preferences. Average household spending on canned fish and seafood may continue its decline as consumer preferences shift.

Table 62. Fish and seafood, canned

Total household spending $2,261,882,880.00
Average household spends   18.18

	AVERAGE HOUSEHOLD SPENDING	BEST CUSTOMERS (index)	BIGGEST CUSTOMERS (market share)
AGE OF HOUSEHOLDER			
Average household	**$18.18**	**100**	**100.0%**
Under age 25	7.79	43	2.8
Aged 25 to 34	13.49	74	12.0
Aged 35 to 44	20.22	111	19.3
Aged 45 to 54	18.55	102	20.2
Aged 55 to 64	21.34	117	21.5
Aged 65 to 74	22.46	124	14.9
Aged 75 or older	17.97	99	9.7

	AVERAGE HOUSEHOLD SPENDING	BEST CUSTOMERS (index)	BIGGEST CUSTOMERS (market share)
HOUSEHOLD INCOME			
Average household	**$18.18**	**100**	**100.0%**
Under $20,000	13.07	72	15.1
$20,000 to $39,999	15.03	83	18.6
$40,000 to $49,999	15.96	88	7.8
$50,000 to $69,999	18.65	103	14.8
$70,000 to $79,999	23.81	131	7.3
$80,000 to $99,999	25.14	138	12.2
$100,000 or more	23.50	129	24.2
HOUSEHOLD TYPE			
Average household	**18.18**	**100**	**100.0**
Married couples	21.58	119	57.7
Married couples, no children	20.92	115	24.0
Married couples with children	20.97	115	27.1
Oldest child under age 6	12.41	68	3.1
Oldest child aged 6 to 17	22.02	121	14.4
Oldest child aged 18 or older	24.57	135	9.5
Single parent with child under age 18	16.85	93	4.9
Single person	11.02	61	18.0
RACE AND HISPANIC ORIGIN			
Average household	**18.18**	**100**	**100.0**
Asian	28.87	159	6.9
Black	15.21	84	10.5
Hispanic	20.39	112	14.1
Non-Hispanic white and other	18.30	101	75.6
REGION			
Average household	**18.18**	**100**	**100.0**
Northeast	23.50	129	23.3
Midwest	15.68	86	19.1
South	15.23	84	31.2
West	21.26	117	26.4
EDUCATION			
Average household	**18.18**	**100**	**100.0**
Less than high school graduate	15.42	85	11.1
High school graduate	17.94	99	24.6
Some college	17.16	94	19.4
Associate's degree	17.97	99	9.8
Bachelor's degree or more	20.15	111	35.0
Bachelor's degree	18.38	101	20.2
Master's, professional, doctoral degree	23.16	127	14.8

Note: Market shares may not sum to 100.0 because of rounding and missing categories by household type. "Asian" and "black" include Hispanics and non-Hispanics who identify themselves as being of the respective race alone. "Hispanic" includes people of any race who identify themselves as Hispanic. "Other" includes people who identify themselves as non-Hispanic and as Alaska Native, American Indian, Asian (who are also included in the "Asian" row), or Native Hawaiian or other Pacific Islander, as well as non-Hispanics reporting more than one race.
Source: Calculations by New Strategist based on the Bureau of Labor Statistics' 2012 Consumer Expenditure Survey

Fish and Shellfish, Fresh

Best customers: Householders aged 35 to 64
Married couples without children at home
Married couples with school-aged or older children at home
Asians, blacks, and Hispanics
Households in the Northeast and West

Customer trends: Average household spending on fresh fish may resume its decline in the years
ahead if consumers opt for prepared meals rather than home cooking.

The best customers of fresh fish and shellfish are minorities and the largest households. Asians spend two-and-one-half times the average on fresh fish, while blacks and Hispanics spend, respectively, 25 and 20 percent more than average on this item. Together the three minority groups, which represent 29 percent of the population, account for 41 percent of the market for fresh fish. Householders ranging in age from 35 to 64 spend 15 to 26 percent more than average on fresh fish. Married couples with school-aged or older children at home spend 52 to 58 percent more than average on this item. Married couples without children at home, most of them older empty-nesters, spend 25 percent more than average on fresh fish. Households in the Northeast and West spend, respectively, 29 and 27 percent more than average on this item.

Average household spending on fresh fish fell 20 percent between 2000 and 2006, after adjusting for inflation, and fell another 18 percent between 2006 and 2010—the year in which overall household spending bottomed out. In the ensuing two years, however, spending on fresh fish grew by 9 percent. Behind the earlier decline was the shift from fresh to frozen fish, as well as the then-growing propensity of Americans to eat out rather than prepare a meal from scratch. The recent increase in spending on fresh fish may be a sign of economic recovery. Average household spending on fresh fish may resume its decline in the years ahead if consumers opt for prepared meals rather than home cooking.

Table 63. Fish and shellfish, fresh

Total household spending $7,874,288,640.00
Average household spends   63.29

AGE OF HOUSEHOLDER	AVERAGE HOUSEHOLD SPENDING	BEST CUSTOMERS (index)	BIGGEST CUSTOMERS (market share)
Average household	**$63.29**	**100**	**100.0%**
Under age 25	23.78	38	2.5
Aged 25 to 34	49.93	79	12.8
Aged 35 to 44	72.84	115	20.0
Aged 45 to 54	79.94	126	25.0
Aged 55 to 64	77.24	122	22.3
Aged 65 to 74	64.79	102	12.3
Aged 75 or older	34.34	54	5.3

	AVERAGE HOUSEHOLD SPENDING	BEST CUSTOMERS (index)	BIGGEST CUSTOMERS (market share)
HOUSEHOLD INCOME			
Average household	**$63.29**	**100**	**100.0%**
Under $20,000	41.39	65	13.8
$20,000 to $39,999	41.79	66	14.9
$40,000 to $49,999	48.04	76	6.7
$50,000 to $69,999	54.48	86	12.4
$70,000 to $79,999	78.67	124	6.9
$80,000 to $99,999	90.83	144	12.7
$100,000 or more	111.68	176	33.0
HOUSEHOLD TYPE			
Average household	**63.29**	**100**	**100.0**
Married couples	85.56	135	65.7
Married couples, no children	79.42	125	26.2
Married couples with children	88.73	140	33.0
Oldest child under age 6	46.86	74	3.4
Oldest child aged 6 to 17	99.96	158	18.8
Oldest child aged 18 or older	96.09	152	10.7
Single parent with child under age 18	57.45	91	4.8
Single person	27.21	43	12.8
RACE AND HISPANIC ORIGIN			
Average household	**63.29**	**100**	**100.0**
Asian	155.53	246	10.7
Black	79.02	125	15.7
Hispanic	75.70	120	15.0
Non-Hispanic white and other	58.48	92	69.4
REGION			
Average household	**63.29**	**100**	**100.0**
Northeast	81.36	129	23.2
Midwest	38.41	61	13.5
South	59.11	93	34.8
West	80.48	127	28.7
EDUCATION			
Average household	**63.29**	**100**	**100.0**
Less than high school graduate	54.72	86	11.3
High school graduate	58.35	92	23.0
Some college	45.46	72	14.8
Associate's degree	65.89	104	10.3
Bachelor's degree or more	81.54	129	40.6
Bachelor's degree	79.57	126	25.1
Master's, professional, doctoral degree	84.86	134	15.6

Note: Market shares may not sum to 100.0 because of rounding and missing categories by household type. "Asian" and "black" include Hispanics and non-Hispanics who identify themselves as being of the respective race alone. "Hispanic" includes people of any race who identify themselves as Hispanic. "Other" includes people who identify themselves as non-Hispanic and as Alaska Native, American Indian, Asian (who are also included in the "Asian" row), or Native Hawaiian or other Pacific Islander, as well as non-Hispanics reporting more than one race.
Source: Calculations by New Strategist based on the Bureau of Labor Statistics' 2012 Consumer Expenditure Survey

Fish and Shellfish, Frozen

Best customers: Householders aged 35 to 54 and 65 to 74
Married couples without children at home
Married couples with school-aged or older children at home
Asians and Hispanics

Customer trends: Average household spending on frozen fish may continue to decline because
the small generation X is in the best-customer lifestage, but the spending
of aging boomers may limit the loss.

The largest households and older householders are the best customers of frozen fish. Married couples with school-aged or older children at home spend 24 to 72 percent more than average on frozen fish. Householders aged 35 to 54, most with children at home, spend 25 to 28 percent more. Couples without children at home, most of them older empty-nesters, spend 29 percent more than average on frozen fish, and householders aged 65 to 74 spend 13 percent more. Asian households spend more than twice the average on this item. Hispanics, who have the largest families, spend 35 percent above average on frozen fish. Frozen fish is one of the relatively few items on which blacks spend an average amount. Together the three minority groups, which represent 29 percent of the population, account for 39 percent of the market for frozen fish.

Average household spending on frozen fish rose by a healthy 32 percent between 2000 and 2006, after adjusting for inflation, but spending declined 9 percent between 2006 and 2012. Behind the earlier increase were nutritional claims regarding the benefits of fish consumption and the shift away from canned and fresh fish to the greater convenience of frozen fish. Average household spending on frozen fish may continue to decline because the small generation X is in the best-customer lifestage, but the spending of aging boomers may limit the loss.

Table 64. Fish and shellfish, frozen

Total household spending $5,507,896,320.00
Average household spends   44.27

AGE OF HOUSEHOLDER	AVERAGE HOUSEHOLD SPENDING	BEST CUSTOMERS (index)	BIGGEST CUSTOMERS (market share)
Average household	**$44.27**	**100**	**100.0%**
Under age 25	41.42	94	6.1
Aged 25 to 34	29.77	67	10.9
Aged 35 to 44	56.55	128	22.2
Aged 45 to 54	55.23	125	24.7
Aged 55 to 64	39.18	89	16.2
Aged 65 to 74	49.98	113	13.6
Aged 75 or older	28.24	64	6.2

	AVERAGE HOUSEHOLD SPENDING	BEST CUSTOMERS (index)	BIGGEST CUSTOMERS (market share)
HOUSEHOLD INCOME			
Average household	**$44.27**	**100**	**100.0%**
Under $20,000	28.03	63	13.3
$20,000 to $39,999	32.39	73	16.5
$40,000 to $49,999	35.26	80	7.0
$50,000 to $69,999	42.20	95	13.8
$70,000 to $79,999	54.23	122	6.8
$80,000 to $99,999	67.02	151	13.4
$100,000 or more	69.47	157	29.4
HOUSEHOLD TYPE			
Average household	**44.27**	**100**	**100.0**
Married couples	59.24	134	65.0
Married couples, no children	57.25	129	27.0
Married couples with children	62.86	142	33.4
Oldest child under age 6	40.92	92	4.2
Oldest child aged 6 to 17	75.96	172	20.4
Oldest child aged 18 or older	54.69	124	8.7
Single parent with child under age 18	25.85	58	3.1
Single person	18.22	41	12.2
RACE AND HISPANIC ORIGIN			
Average household	**44.27**	**100**	**100.0**
Asian	98.31	222	9.6
Black	43.34	98	12.3
Hispanic	59.88	135	17.0
Non-Hispanic white and other	41.74	94	70.8
REGION			
Average household	**44.27**	**100**	**100.0**
Northeast	38.91	88	15.9
Midwest	49.61	112	24.8
South	41.28	93	34.7
West	48.24	109	24.6
EDUCATION			
Average household	**44.27**	**100**	**100.0**
Less than high school graduate	38.69	87	11.4
High school graduate	43.55	98	24.5
Some college	41.80	94	19.4
Associate's degree	44.62	101	10.0
Bachelor's degree or more	48.48	110	34.5
Bachelor's degree	41.15	93	18.5
Master's, professional, doctoral degree	60.87	137	16.0

Note: Market shares may not sum to 100.0 because of rounding and missing categories by household type. "Asian" and "black" include Hispanics and non-Hispanics who identify themselves as being of the respective race alone. "Hispanic" includes people of any race who identify themselves as Hispanic. "Other" includes people who identify themselves as non-Hispanic and as Alaska Native, American Indian, Asian (who are also included in the "Asian" row), or Native Hawaiian or other Pacific Islander, as well as non-Hispanics reporting more than one race.
Source: Calculations by New Strategist based on the Bureau of Labor Statistics' 2012 Consumer Expenditure Survey

Flour

Best customers:
Householders aged 25 to 64
Married couples with school-aged or older children at home
Hispanics
Householders without a high school diploma

Customer trends:
Average household spending on flour should resume its decline
as eating out regains its popularity.

The biggest spenders on flour are households most likely to cook from scratch—typically married couples with children at home. This household type spends 62 percent more than average on flour, the figure peaking at 80 percent above average among couples with adult children at home. Householders aged 25 to 64, many with children, spend more than average on this item. Hispanics, who have the largest households, spend 13 percent more. Households headed by people without a high school diploma, many of them Hispanic, spend 16 percent more than average on flour.

Average household spending on flour fell by a precipitous 47 percent between 2000 and 2006, after adjusting for inflation, then rebounded with a strong 66 percent increase between 2006 and 2012. Behind the earlier decline was the rise of eating out as busy families found less time to cook from scratch. The Great Recession then shifted restaurant dollars back to the grocery store as families endeavored to cut spending. Average household spending on flour should resume its decline as eating out regains its popularity.

Table 65. Flour

Total household spending $1,164,533,760.00
Average household spends   9.36

	AVERAGE HOUSEHOLD SPENDING	BEST CUSTOMERS (index)	BIGGEST CUSTOMERS (market share)
AGE OF HOUSEHOLDER			
Average household	**$9.36**	**100**	**100.0%**
Under age 25	6.15	66	4.3
Aged 25 to 34	9.95	106	17.2
Aged 35 to 44	9.82	105	18.2
Aged 45 to 54	11.47	123	24.3
Aged 55 to 64	10.01	107	19.6
Aged 65 to 74	7.24	77	9.3
Aged 75 or older	6.77	72	7.1

	AVERAGE HOUSEHOLD SPENDING	BEST CUSTOMERS (index)	BIGGEST CUSTOMERS (market share)
HOUSEHOLD INCOME			
Average household	**$9.36**	**100**	**100.0%**
Under $20,000	6.58	70	14.8
$20,000 to $39,999	7.04	75	16.9
$40,000 to $49,999	12.19	130	11.5
$50,000 to $69,999	8.96	96	13.8
$70,000 to $79,999	8.95	96	5.3
$80,000 to $99,999	10.01	107	9.4
$100,000 or more	13.77	147	27.5
HOUSEHOLD TYPE			
Average household	**9.36**	**100**	**100.0**
Married couples	12.76	136	66.2
Married couples, no children	10.90	116	24.3
Married couples with children	15.13	162	38.0
Oldest child under age 6	9.16	98	4.5
Oldest child aged 6 to 17	16.36	175	20.8
Oldest child aged 18 or older	16.81	180	12.7
Single parent with child under age 18	7.40	79	4.1
Single person	3.65	39	11.6
RACE AND HISPANIC ORIGIN			
Average household	**9.36**	**100**	**100.0**
Asian	9.17	98	4.2
Black	8.52	91	11.4
Hispanic	10.59	113	14.2
Non-Hispanic white and other	9.30	99	74.6
REGION			
Average household	**9.36**	**100**	**100.0**
Northeast	10.78	115	20.8
Midwest	9.37	100	22.2
South	8.99	96	35.8
West	8.80	94	21.2
EDUCATION			
Average household	**9.36**	**100**	**100.0**
Less than high school graduate	10.84	116	15.1
High school graduate	10.38	111	27.7
Some college	7.61	81	16.7
Associate's degree	8.60	92	9.1
Bachelor's degree or more	9.42	101	31.7
Bachelor's degree	8.25	88	17.6
Master's, professional, doctoral degree	11.40	122	14.1

Note: Market shares may not sum to 100.0 because of rounding and missing categories by household type. "Asian" and "black" include Hispanics and non-Hispanics who identify themselves as being of the respective race alone. "Hispanic" includes people of any race who identify themselves as Hispanic. "Other" includes people who identify themselves as non-Hispanic and as Alaska Native, American Indian, Asian (who are also included in the "Asian" row), or Native Hawaiian or other Pacific Islander, as well as non-Hispanics reporting more than one race.
Source: Calculations by New Strategist based on the Bureau of Labor Statistics' 2012 Consumer Expenditure Survey

Flour, Prepared Mixes

Best customers: Householders aged 35 to 54
                           Married couples with children at home

Customer trends: Average household spending on flour mixes should resume its decline
                           as eating out regains its popularity.

The biggest spenders on prepared flour mixes—such as cake and biscuit mixes—are married couples with children at home. These households spend 70 percent more than average on flour mixes. Householders aged 35 to 54, most with children at home, spend 15 to 30 percent more than average on prepared flour mixes.

Average household spending on prepared flour mixes fell 28 percent between 2000 and 2006, after adjusting for inflation, then rebounded with a 26 percent increase between 2006 and 2012. Behind the earlier spending cut was the decline in home cooking. Behind the rebound is the Great Recession, leading more consumers to bake at home to save money. Average household spending on flour mixes should resume its decline as eating out regains its popularity.

Table 66. Flour, prepared mixes

Total household spending $2,013,050,880.00
Average household spends   16.18

	AVERAGE HOUSEHOLD SPENDING	BEST CUSTOMERS (index)	BIGGEST CUSTOMERS (market share)
AGE OF HOUSEHOLDER			
Average household	**$16.18**	**100**	**100.0%**
Under age 25	9.40	58	3.8
Aged 25 to 34	13.60	84	13.6
Aged 35 to 44	18.61	115	20.0
Aged 45 to 54	21.09	130	25.8
Aged 55 to 64	16.27	101	18.4
Aged 65 to 74	15.09	93	11.2
Aged 75 or older	11.93	74	7.2

	AVERAGE HOUSEHOLD SPENDING	BEST CUSTOMERS (index)	BIGGEST CUSTOMERS (market share)
HOUSEHOLD INCOME			
Average household	**$16.18**	**100**	**100.0%**
Under $20,000	9.55	59	12.4
$20,000 to $39,999	12.54	77	17.5
$40,000 to $49,999	18.11	112	9.9
$50,000 to $69,999	12.41	77	11.1
$70,000 to $79,999	20.54	127	7.1
$80,000 to $99,999	23.19	143	12.6
$100,000 or more	25.11	155	29.1
HOUSEHOLD TYPE			
Average household	**16.18**	**100**	**100.0**
Married couples	22.44	139	67.4
Married couples, no children	16.72	103	21.5
Married couples with children	27.50	170	40.0
Oldest child under age 6	22.04	136	6.2
Oldest child aged 6 to 17	30.09	186	22.1
Oldest child aged 18 or older	26.59	164	11.6
Single parent with child under age 18	13.92	86	4.5
Single person	6.35	39	11.7
RACE AND HISPANIC ORIGIN			
Average household	**16.18**	**100**	**100.0**
Asian	10.59	65	2.8
Black	12.58	78	9.8
Hispanic	12.80	79	9.9
Non-Hispanic white and other	17.34	107	80.4
REGION			
Average household	**16.18**	**100**	**100.0**
Northeast	14.57	90	16.3
Midwest	17.11	106	23.4
South	15.01	93	34.6
West	18.48	114	25.7
EDUCATION			
Average household	**16.18**	**100**	**100.0**
Less than high school graduate	11.99	74	9.7
High school graduate	14.64	90	22.6
Some college	15.16	94	19.3
Associate's degree	21.39	132	13.1
Bachelor's degree or more	17.99	111	35.1
Bachelor's degree	16.79	104	20.7
Master's, professional, doctoral degree	20.02	124	14.4

Note: Market shares may not sum to 100.0 because of rounding and missing categories by household type. "Asian" and "black" include Hispanics and non-Hispanics who identify themselves as being of the respective race alone. "Hispanic" includes people of any race who identify themselves as Hispanic. "Other" includes people who identify themselves as non-Hispanic and as Alaska Native, American Indian, Asian (who are also included in the "Asian" row), or Native Hawaiian or other Pacific Islander, as well as non-Hispanics reporting more than one race.
Source: Calculations by New Strategist based on the Bureau of Labor Statistics' 2012 Consumer Expenditure Survey

Frankfurters

Best customers:	Householders aged 35 to 54
	Married couples with children at home
	Single parents
	Hispanics
	Households in the Northeast
	Householders with a high school diploma or less education
Customer trends:	Average household spending on frankfurters may resume its decline because the small generation X is in the best-customer lifestage.

Households with children are the biggest spenders on frankfurters. Married couples with children at home spend 47 percent more than average on this item. Householders aged 35 to 54, most with children, spend 11 to 31 percent more than average on hot dogs. Single parents, whose spending approaches the average on only a few items, spend 16 percent more than average on frankfurters. Hispanics, who have the largest families, spend 17 percent more. Households in the Northeast outspend the average on this item by 20 percent. Householders with no more than a high school education, many of them Hispanic, spend 18 to 19 percent more than average on frankfurters.

Average household spending on frankfurters fell 17 percent between 2000 and 2006, after adjusting for inflation, and then rebounded by 7 percent between 2006 and 2012. Average household spending on hot dogs may resume its decline because the small generation X is in the best-customer lifestage.

Table 67. Frankfurters

Total household spending $3,074,319,360.00
Average household spends   24.71

	AVERAGE HOUSEHOLD SPENDING	BEST CUSTOMERS (index)	BIGGEST CUSTOMERS (market share)
AGE OF HOUSEHOLDER			
Average household	**$24.71**	**100**	**100.0%**
Under age 25	19.14	77	5.1
Aged 25 to 34	23.50	95	15.4
Aged 35 to 44	32.33	131	22.7
Aged 45 to 54	27.55	111	22.1
Aged 55 to 64	26.11	106	19.3
Aged 65 to 74	19.86	80	9.7
Aged 75 or older	14.19	57	5.6

	AVERAGE HOUSEHOLD SPENDING	BEST CUSTOMERS (index)	BIGGEST CUSTOMERS (market share)
HOUSEHOLD INCOME			
Average household	**$24.71**	**100**	**100.0%**
Under $20,000	17.49	71	14.9
$20,000 to $39,999	23.46	95	21.4
$40,000 to $49,999	23.15	94	8.3
$50,000 to $69,999	22.16	90	13.0
$70,000 to $79,999	31.45	127	7.1
$80,000 to $99,999	29.14	118	10.4
$100,000 or more	32.52	132	24.6
HOUSEHOLD TYPE			
Average household	**24.71**	**100**	**100.0**
Married couples	31.16	126	61.2
Married couples, no children	21.99	89	18.6
Married couples with children	36.33	147	34.6
Oldest child under age 6	29.79	121	5.5
Oldest child aged 6 to 17	38.16	154	18.4
Oldest child aged 18 or older	37.34	151	10.7
Single parent with child under age 18	28.57	116	6.1
Single person	11.09	45	13.3
RACE AND HISPANIC ORIGIN			
Average household	**24.71**	**100**	**100.0**
Asian	18.32	74	3.2
Black	25.19	102	12.8
Hispanic	29.03	117	14.7
Non-Hispanic white and other	23.99	97	72.9
REGION			
Average household	**24.71**	**100**	**100.0**
Northeast	29.60	120	21.6
Midwest	25.28	102	22.7
South	23.34	94	35.2
West	22.46	91	20.5
EDUCATION			
Average household	**24.71**	**100**	**100.0**
Less than high school graduate	29.29	119	15.5
High school graduate	29.27	118	29.5
Some college	22.76	92	19.0
Associate's degree	23.19	94	9.3
Bachelor's degree or more	21.25	86	27.1
Bachelor's degree	21.71	88	17.5
Master's, professional, doctoral degree	20.48	83	9.6

Note: Market shares may not sum to 100.0 because of rounding and missing categories by household type. "Asian" and "black" include Hispanics and non-Hispanics who identify themselves as being of the respective race alone. "Hispanic" includes people of any race who identify themselves as Hispanic. "Other" includes people who identify themselves as non-Hispanic and as Alaska Native, American Indian, Asian (who are also included in the "Asian" row), or Native Hawaiian or other Pacific Islander, as well as non-Hispanics reporting more than one race.
Source: Calculations by New Strategist based on the Bureau of Labor Statistics' 2012 Consumer Expenditure Survey

Fruit-Flavored Drinks, Noncarbonated

Best customers: Householders aged 35 to 54
Married couples with school-aged or older children at home
Single parents
Hispanics and blacks

Customer trends: Average household spending on noncarbonated fruit-flavored drinks
should continue to grow in the years ahead as the millennial generation
enters the best-customer lifestage.

The best customers of noncarbonated fruit-flavored drinks are parents with children. Married couples with school-aged or older children at home spend 53 to 60 percent more than the average household on this item. Single parents, whose spending approaches average on only a few items, spend 28 percent more than average on fruit-flavored drinks. Householders aged 35 to 54, most with children at home, spend 20 to 30 percent more than average on this item and account for 46 percent of the market. Hispanics spend 34 percent more than average on fruit-flavored drinks, and blacks spend 4 percent more.

Average household spending on noncarbonated fruit-flavored drinks purchased at grocery or convenience stores declined rapidly before the Great Recession, then rebounded strongly along with overall grocery spending. Behind the spending increase is the switch from fruit juice to less-expensive fruit-flavored drinks by some households. Average household spending on noncarbonated fruit-flavored drinks should continue to grow in the years ahead as the millennial generation enters the best-customer lifestage.

Table 68. Fruit-flavored drinks, noncarbonated

Total household spending $3,213,665,280.00
Average household spends 25.83

	AVERAGE HOUSEHOLD SPENDING	BEST CUSTOMERS (index)	BIGGEST CUSTOMERS (market share)
AGE OF HOUSEHOLDER			
Average household	**$25.83**	**100**	**100.0%**
Under age 25	29.14	113	7.4
Aged 25 to 34	23.60	91	14.8
Aged 35 to 44	33.70	130	22.6
Aged 45 to 54	31.11	120	23.8
Aged 55 to 64	19.62	76	13.9
Aged 65 to 74	20.92	81	9.8
Aged 75 or older	19.47	75	7.4

	AVERAGE HOUSEHOLD SPENDING	BEST CUSTOMERS (index)	BIGGEST CUSTOMERS (market share)
HOUSEHOLD INCOME			
Average household	**$25.83**	**100**	**100.0%**
Under $20,000	16.61	64	13.5
$20,000 to $39,999	23.66	92	20.6
$40,000 to $49,999	23.85	92	8.2
$50,000 to $69,999	32.09	124	17.9
$70,000 to $79,999	31.65	123	6.8
$80,000 to $99,999	31.01	120	10.6
$100,000 or more	30.63	119	22.2
HOUSEHOLD TYPE			
Average household	**25.83**	**100**	**100.0**
Married couples	31.27	121	58.8
Married couples, no children	21.97	85	17.7
Married couples with children	37.98	147	34.6
Oldest child under age 6	26.29	102	4.6
Oldest child aged 6 to 17	41.44	160	19.1
Oldest child aged 18 or older	39.50	153	10.8
Single parent with child under age 18	33.09	128	6.7
Single person	11.45	44	13.2
RACE AND HISPANIC ORIGIN			
Average household	**25.83**	**100**	**100.0**
Asian	23.52	91	3.9
Black	26.75	104	13.0
Hispanic	34.69	134	16.8
Non-Hispanic white and other	24.18	94	70.3
REGION			
Average household	**25.83**	**100**	**100.0**
Northeast	25.07	97	17.5
Midwest	24.62	95	21.1
South	25.90	100	37.3
West	27.54	107	24.0
EDUCATION			
Average household	**25.83**	**100**	**100.0**
Less than high school graduate	29.34	114	14.8
High school graduate	25.32	98	24.4
Some college	23.96	93	19.1
Associate's degree	22.87	89	8.7
Bachelor's degree or more	27.09	105	33.1
Bachelor's degree	28.76	111	22.2
Master's, professional, doctoral degree	24.26	94	10.9

Note: Market shares may not sum to 100.0 because of rounding and missing categories by household type. "Asian" and "black" include Hispanics and non-Hispanics who identify themselves as being of the respective race alone. "Hispanic" includes people of any race who identify themselves as Hispanic. "Other" includes people who identify themselves as non-Hispanic and as Alaska Native, American Indian, Asian (who are also included in the "Asian" row), or Native Hawaiian or other Pacific Islander, as well as non-Hispanics reporting more than one race.
Source: Calculations by New Strategist based on the Bureau of Labor Statistics' 2012 Consumer Expenditure Survey

Fruit, Canned

Best customers:	Householders aged 35 to 54
	Married couples with children at home
	Households in the Northeast and Midwest
Customer trends:	Average household spending on canned fruit is likely to continue to decline
	because the small generation X is in the best customer lifestage and
	packaged fresh fruit is becoming more widely available.

The biggest spenders on canned fruit are the largest households. Married couples with children at home spend 62 percent more than average on this item, the figure peaking at 70 percent among those with school-aged children. Householders aged 35 to 54, many with children, spend 11 to 19 percent more than average on canned fruit. Households in the Midwest spend 29 percent more than average on this item, and those in the Northeast spend 13 percent more.

Average household spending on canned fruit fell by 1 percent between 2000 and 2012, after adjusting for inflation. Behind the relative stability were two competing trends: the attempt by consumers to add more fruit to their diet, which boosted spending on canned fruit, and competition from sliced and conveniently packaged fresh fruit, which reduced spending on canned fruit. Average household spending on canned fruit is likely to continue to decline because the small generation X is in the best-customer lifestage and packaged fresh fruit is becoming more widely available.

Table 69. Fruit, canned

Total household spending	$2,531,865,600.00
Average household spends	20.35

	AVERAGE HOUSEHOLD SPENDING	BEST CUSTOMERS (index)	BIGGEST CUSTOMERS (market share)
AGE OF HOUSEHOLDER			
Average household	**$20.35**	**100**	**100.0%**
Under age 25	10.34	51	3.3
Aged 25 to 34	19.21	94	15.3
Aged 35 to 44	22.41	110	19.1
Aged 45 to 54	24.12	119	23.5
Aged 55 to 64	18.78	92	16.9
Aged 65 to 74	19.96	98	11.8
Aged 75 or older	21.27	105	10.2

	AVERAGE HOUSEHOLD SPENDING	BEST CUSTOMERS (index)	BIGGEST CUSTOMERS (market share)
HOUSEHOLD INCOME			
Average household	**$20.35**	**100**	**100.0%**
Under $20,000	12.44	61	12.9
$20,000 to $39,999	19.16	94	21.2
$40,000 to $49,999	13.60	67	5.9
$50,000 to $69,999	21.43	105	15.2
$70,000 to $79,999	23.79	117	6.5
$80,000 to $99,999	27.38	135	11.9
$100,000 or more	29.10	143	26.8
HOUSEHOLD TYPE			
Average household	**20.35**	**100**	**100.0**
Married couples	27.27	134	65.1
Married couples, no children	21.39	105	21.9
Married couples with children	32.91	162	38.0
Oldest child under age 6	31.77	156	7.1
Oldest child aged 6 to 17	34.59	170	20.2
Oldest child aged 18 or older	30.81	151	10.7
Single parent with child under age 18	19.99	98	5.2
Single person	10.00	49	14.6
RACE AND HISPANIC ORIGIN			
Average household	**20.35**	**100**	**100.0**
Asian	16.55	81	3.5
Black	14.60	72	9.0
Hispanic	17.40	86	10.7
Non-Hispanic white and other	21.82	107	80.5
REGION			
Average household	**20.35**	**100**	**100.0**
Northeast	22.91	113	20.3
Midwest	26.22	129	28.6
South	17.73	87	32.4
West	16.75	82	18.5
EDUCATION			
Average household	**20.35**	**100**	**100.0**
Less than high school graduate	18.37	90	11.8
High school graduate	18.21	89	22.3
Some college	20.38	100	20.6
Associate's degree	17.45	86	8.5
Bachelor's degree or more	23.64	116	36.6
Bachelor's degree	24.17	119	23.7
Master's, professional, doctoral degree	22.74	112	13.0

Note: Market shares may not sum to 100.0 because of rounding and missing categories by household type. "Asian" and "black" include Hispanics and non-Hispanics who identify themselves as being of the respective race alone. "Hispanic" includes people of any race who identify themselves as Hispanic. "Other" includes people who identify themselves as non-Hispanic and as Alaska Native, American Indian, Asian (who are also included in the "Asian" row), or Native Hawaiian or other Pacific Islander, as well as non-Hispanics reporting more than one race.
Source: Calculations by New Strategist based on the Bureau of Labor Statistics' 2012 Consumer Expenditure Survey

Fruit, Dried

Best customers: Householders aged 25 to 34 and 65 or older
Married couples without children at home
Married couples with children under age 18

Customer trends: Average household spending on dried fruit should increase again
as the population ages.

The biggest spenders on dried fruit are older householders and the largest households. Married couples with preschoolers spend twice the average on dried fruit, and those with school-aged children spend one-third more than average. Householders aged 25 to 34, many with children, spend 21 percent more than average on dried fruit, and those aged 65 or older spend 11 to 19 percent more. Married couples without children at home (most of them older empty-nesters) spend 35 percent more than average on this item.

Average household spending on dried fruit, which had grown strongly between 2000 and 2006, declined 15 percent between 2006 and 2012, after adjusting for inflation. Behind the earlier increase was the greater availability of dried fruit and its growing popularity as a snack food. Spending on dried fruit should increase again as the population ages.

Table 70. Fruit, dried

Total household spending	$1,083,663,360.00
Average household spends	8.71

	AVERAGE HOUSEHOLD SPENDING	BEST CUSTOMERS (index)	BIGGEST CUSTOMERS (market share)
AGE OF HOUSEHOLDER			
Average household	**$8.71**	**100**	**100.0%**
Under age 25	3.29	38	2.5
Aged 25 to 34	10.52	121	19.5
Aged 35 to 44	7.53	86	15.0
Aged 45 to 54	8.52	98	19.4
Aged 55 to 64	8.86	102	18.6
Aged 65 to 74	10.39	119	14.4
Aged 75 or older	9.69	111	10.9

	AVERAGE HOUSEHOLD SPENDING	BEST CUSTOMERS (index)	BIGGEST CUSTOMERS (market share)
HOUSEHOLD INCOME			
Average household	**$8.71**	**100**	**100.0%**
Under $20,000	3.38	39	8.2
$20,000 to $39,999	7.32	84	18.9
$40,000 to $49,999	7.11	82	7.2
$50,000 to $69,999	9.83	113	16.3
$70,000 to $79,999	9.02	104	5.8
$80,000 to $99,999	10.12	116	10.3
$100,000 or more	15.37	176	33.0
HOUSEHOLD TYPE			
Average household	**8.71**	**100**	**100.0**
Married couples	12.18	140	67.9
Married couples, no children	11.78	135	28.2
Married couples with children	12.12	139	32.7
Oldest child under age 6	17.20	197	9.0
Oldest child aged 6 to 17	11.73	135	16.0
Oldest child aged 18 or older	9.62	110	7.8
Single parent with child under age 18	6.29	72	3.8
Single person	4.55	52	15.5
RACE AND HISPANIC ORIGIN			
Average household	**8.71**	**100**	**100.0**
Asian	6.78	78	3.4
Black	4.06	47	5.9
Hispanic	5.64	65	8.1
Non-Hispanic white and other	9.99	115	86.1
REGION			
Average household	**8.71**	**100**	**100.0**
Northeast	10.19	117	21.1
Midwest	9.60	110	24.4
South	6.55	75	28.0
West	10.21	117	26.4
EDUCATION			
Average household	**8.71**	**100**	**100.0**
Less than high school graduate	6.04	69	9.1
High school graduate	7.45	86	21.3
Some college	7.25	83	17.1
Associate's degree	9.62	110	10.9
Bachelor's degree or more	11.40	131	41.3
Bachelor's degree	10.61	122	24.3
Master's, professional, doctoral degree	12.73	146	17.0

Note: Market shares may not sum to 100.0 because of rounding and missing categories by household type. "Asian" and "black" include Hispanics and non-Hispanics who identify themselves as being of the respective race alone. "Hispanic" includes people of any race who identify themselves as Hispanic. "Other" includes people who identify themselves as non-Hispanic and as Alaska Native, American Indian, Asian (who are also included in the "Asian" row), or Native Hawaiian or other Pacific Islander, as well as non-Hispanics reporting more than one race.
Source: Calculations by New Strategist based on the Bureau of Labor Statistics' 2012 Consumer Expenditure Survey

Fruit, Fresh, Total

Best customers:
Householders aged 35 to 54
Married couples with children at home
Asians and Hispanics
Households in the West

Customer trends:
Average household spending on fresh fruit should continue to rise because of growing minority populations and the interest in healthy eating.

The biggest spenders on fresh fruit are the largest households. Married couples with children at home spend 51 percent more than average on fresh fruit. Householders aged 35 to 54, most with children, spend 14 to 18 percent more than average on fresh fruit. Asians spend 57 percent more than average on this item. Hispanics, who have the largest households, spend 18 percent more. Households in the West, where many Asians and Hispanics live, spend 20 percent more than average on fresh fruit.

Fresh fruit is the grocery category on which the average household spends the most. Average household spending on fresh fruit climbed 20 percent between 2000 and 2012, after adjusting for inflation. Behind the increase was the growing variety of sliced and packaged fresh fruit available in grocery stores, boosting sales. Average household spending on fresh fruit should continue to rise because of growing minority populations and the interest in healthy eating.

Table 71. Fruit, fresh, total

Total household spending $32,508,656,640.00
Average household spends 261.29

	AVERAGE HOUSEHOLD SPENDING	BEST CUSTOMERS (index)	BIGGEST CUSTOMERS (market share)
AGE OF HOUSEHOLDER			
Average household	**$261.29**	**100**	**100.0%**
Under age 25	162.19	62	4.1
Aged 25 to 34	236.97	91	14.7
Aged 35 to 44	296.71	114	19.7
Aged 45 to 54	308.31	118	23.4
Aged 55 to 64	257.81	99	18.1
Aged 65 to 74	259.75	99	12.0
Aged 75 or older	219.11	84	8.2

	AVERAGE HOUSEHOLD SPENDING	BEST CUSTOMERS (index)	BIGGEST CUSTOMERS (market share)
HOUSEHOLD INCOME			
Average household	**$261.29**	**100**	**100.0%**
Under $20,000	141.93	54	11.4
$20,000 to $39,999	186.03	71	16.0
$40,000 to $49,999	232.87	89	7.9
$50,000 to $69,999	261.43	100	14.5
$70,000 to $79,999	306.16	117	6.5
$80,000 to $99,999	332.65	127	11.2
$100,000 or more	451.13	173	32.3
HOUSEHOLD TYPE			
Average household	**261.29**	**100**	**100.0**
Married couples	346.98	133	64.5
Married couples, no children	296.93	114	23.7
Married couples with children	394.92	151	35.5
Oldest child under age 6	326.03	125	5.7
Oldest child aged 6 to 17	408.84	156	18.6
Oldest child aged 18 or older	414.63	159	11.2
Single parent with child under age 18	251.61	96	5.0
Single person	133.79	51	15.2
RACE AND HISPANIC ORIGIN			
Average household	**261.29**	**100**	**100.0**
Asian	409.42	157	6.8
Black	165.90	63	8.0
Hispanic	307.27	118	14.7
Non-Hispanic white and other	269.89	103	77.5
REGION			
Average household	**261.29**	**100**	**100.0**
Northeast	285.29	109	19.7
Midwest	261.53	100	22.2
South	217.99	83	31.1
West	313.53	120	27.0
EDUCATION			
Average household	**261.29**	**100**	**100.0**
Less than high school graduate	226.81	87	11.3
High school graduate	209.78	80	20.0
Some college	213.16	82	16.8
Associate's degree	250.07	96	9.5
Bachelor's degree or more	350.04	134	42.2
Bachelor's degree	329.50	126	25.1
Master's, professional, doctoral degree	384.78	147	17.1

Note: Market shares may not sum to 100.0 because of rounding and missing categories by household type. "Asian" and "black" include Hispanics and non-Hispanics who identify themselves as being of the respective race alone. "Hispanic" includes people of any race who identify themselves as Hispanic. "Other" includes people who identify themselves as non-Hispanic and as Alaska Native, American Indian, Asian (who are also included in the "Asian" row), or Native Hawaiian or other Pacific Islander, as well as non-Hispanics reporting more than one race.
Source: Calculations by New Strategist based on the Bureau of Labor Statistics' 2012 Consumer Expenditure Survey

Fruit, Frozen

Best customers: Married couples without children at home
Married couples with school-aged or older children at home
Asians
Households in the Midwest and West

Customer trends: Average household spending on frozen fruit may continue to rise as consumers attempt to improve their diet.

The largest households are the best customers of frozen fruit. Married couples with school-aged children spend 86 percent more than average on frozen fruit, and those with adult children at home spend more than twice the average. Couples without children at home, most of them older empty-nesters, outspend the average by 60 percent. Asian households spend 51 percent more than average on frozen fruit. Households in the Midwest and West spend, respectively, 30 and 39 percent more than average on frozen fruit.

Average household spending on frozen fruit grew by a substantial 48 percent between 2000 and 2012, after adjusting for inflation. One factor behind the rise was growing health consciousness among consumers, who were adding more fruit to their diet. Average household spending on frozen fruit may continue to rise as consumers attempt to improve their diet.

Table 72. Fruit, frozen

Total household spending $890,818,560.00
Average household spends 7.16

AGE OF HOUSEHOLDER	AVERAGE HOUSEHOLD SPENDING	BEST CUSTOMERS (index)	BIGGEST CUSTOMERS (market share)
Average household	$7.16	100	100.0%
Under age 25	2.65	37	2.4
Aged 25 to 34	4.70	66	10.6
Aged 35 to 44	7.47	104	18.1
Aged 45 to 54	11.86	166	32.8
Aged 55 to 64	7.24	101	18.5
Aged 65 to 74	6.92	97	11.6
Aged 75 or older	4.44	62	6.1

	AVERAGE HOUSEHOLD SPENDING	BEST CUSTOMERS (index)	BIGGEST CUSTOMERS (market share)
HOUSEHOLD INCOME			
Average household	**$7.16**	**100**	**100.0%**
Under $20,000	2.87	40	8.4
$20,000 to $39,999	4.87	68	15.3
$40,000 to $49,999	4.40	61	5.4
$50,000 to $69,999	7.29	102	14.7
$70,000 to $79,999	11.97	167	9.3
$80,000 to $99,999	11.40	159	14.0
$100,000 or more	12.73	178	33.3
HOUSEHOLD TYPE			
Average household	**7.16**	**100**	**100.0**
Married couples	11.18	156	75.8
Married couples, no children	11.48	160	33.4
Married couples with children	11.96	167	39.3
Oldest child under age 6	2.06	29	1.3
Oldest child aged 6 to 17	13.34	186	22.2
Oldest child aged 18 or older	15.84	221	15.6
Single parent with child under age 18	4.11	57	3.0
Single person	3.41	48	14.1
RACE AND HISPANIC ORIGIN			
Average household	**7.16**	**100**	**100.0**
Asian	10.78	151	6.5
Black	2.53	35	4.4
Hispanic	5.20	73	9.1
Non-Hispanic white and other	8.33	116	87.3
REGION			
Average household	**7.16**	**100**	**100.0**
Northeast	6.53	91	16.5
Midwest	9.33	130	28.9
South	4.49	63	23.4
West	9.95	139	31.3
EDUCATION			
Average household	**7.16**	**100**	**100.0**
Less than high school graduate	3.30	46	6.0
High school graduate	4.40	61	15.3
Some college	5.36	75	15.4
Associate's degree	10.36	145	14.3
Bachelor's degree or more	10.97	153	48.3
Bachelor's degree	9.72	136	27.1
Master's, professional, doctoral degree	13.08	183	21.2

Note: Market shares may not sum to 100.0 because of rounding and missing categories by household type. "Asian" and "black" include Hispanics and non-Hispanics who identify themselves as being of the respective race alone. "Hispanic" includes people of any race who identify themselves as Hispanic. "Other" includes people who identify themselves as non-Hispanic and as Alaska Native, American Indian, Asian (who are also included in the "Asian" row), or Native Hawaiian or other Pacific Islander, as well as non-Hispanics reporting more than one race.
Source: Calculations by New Strategist based on the Bureau of Labor Statistics' 2012 Consumer Expenditure Survey

Fruit Juice, Canned and Bottled

Best customers:	Householders aged 35 to 54
	Married couples with children at home
	Single parents
	Hispanics, Asians, and blacks
	Households in the West
Customer trends:	Average household spending on canned and bottled fruit juice may begin to grow again as the large millennial generation fills the best-customer lifestage.

Households with children are the biggest spenders on canned and bottled fruit juice, which dominates fruit juice sales. Married couples with children at home spend 40 percent more than average on canned and bottled fruit juice. Despite their low incomes single parents spend 10 percent more than the average household on this item. Householders aged 35 to 54, most with children at home, spend 8 to 14 percent more than average on canned and bottled fruit juice. Blacks, Asians, and Hispanics outspend the average by 3 to 28 percent and account for one-third of the market. Households in the West outspend the average household on this item by 16 percent.

Average household spending on canned and bottled fruit juice purchased at grocery or convenience stores fell 27 percent between 2000 and 2010, but has held steady since then. Behind the decline was the growing propensity of consumers to eat fast-food breakfasts or no breakfast at all, and the rise of fruit-flavored drinks as a substitute for juice. Spending on canned and bottled fruit juice may begin to grow again as the large millennial generation fills the best-customer lifestage.

Table 73. Fruit juice, canned and bottled

Total household spending $6,832,926,720.00
Average household spends   54.92

	AVERAGE HOUSEHOLD SPENDING	BEST CUSTOMERS (index)	BIGGEST CUSTOMERS (market share)
AGE OF HOUSEHOLDER			
Average household	$54.92	100	100.0%
Under age 25	45.51	83	5.4
Aged 25 to 34	56.60	103	16.7
Aged 35 to 44	59.27	108	18.7
Aged 45 to 54	62.55	114	22.5
Aged 55 to 64	54.46	99	18.1
Aged 65 to 74	44.56	81	9.8
Aged 75 or older	48.54	88	8.6

	AVERAGE HOUSEHOLD SPENDING	BEST CUSTOMERS (index)	BIGGEST CUSTOMERS (market share)
HOUSEHOLD INCOME			
Average household	**$54.92**	**100**	**100.0%**
Under $20,000	35.94	65	13.8
$20,000 to $39,999	45.64	83	18.7
$40,000 to $49,999	51.34	93	8.3
$50,000 to $69,999	51.34	93	13.5
$70,000 to $79,999	78.87	144	8.0
$80,000 to $99,999	63.16	115	10.1
$100,000 or more	80.91	147	27.6
HOUSEHOLD TYPE			
Average household	**54.92**	**100**	**100.0**
Married couples	67.54	123	59.7
Married couples, no children	53.97	98	20.5
Married couples with children	76.65	140	32.8
Oldest child under age 6	62.91	115	5.2
Oldest child aged 6 to 17	79.66	145	17.3
Oldest child aged 18 or older	80.18	146	10.3
Single parent with child under age 18	60.14	110	5.7
Single person	33.37	61	18.0
RACE AND HISPANIC ORIGIN			
Average household	**54.92**	**100**	**100.0**
Asian	57.64	105	4.5
Black	56.53	103	12.9
Hispanic	70.05	128	16.0
Non-Hispanic white and other	52.11	95	71.2
REGION			
Average household	**54.92**	**100**	**100.0**
Northeast	60.05	109	19.7
Midwest	48.91	89	19.7
South	50.64	92	34.3
West	63.89	116	26.2
EDUCATION			
Average household	**54.92**	**100**	**100.0**
Less than high school graduate	46.34	84	11.0
High school graduate	46.44	85	21.1
Some college	51.89	94	19.5
Associate's degree	51.41	94	9.2
Bachelor's degree or more	67.84	124	39.0
Bachelor's degree	63.57	116	23.1
Master's, professional, doctoral degree	75.07	137	15.9

Note: Market shares may not sum to 100.0 because of rounding and missing categories by household type. "Asian" and "black" include Hispanics and non-Hispanics who identify themselves as being of the respective race alone. "Hispanic" includes people of any race who identify themselves as Hispanic. "Other" includes people who identify themselves as non-Hispanic and as Alaska Native, American Indian, Asian (who are also included in the "Asian" row), or Native Hawaiian or other Pacific Islander, as well as non-Hispanics reporting more than one race.
Source: Calculations by New Strategist based on the Bureau of Labor Statistics' 2012 Consumer Expenditure Survey

Fruit Juice, Fresh

Best customers: Householders aged 35 to 54
                         Married couples with children at home
                         Households in the Northeast

Customer trends: Average household spending on fresh fruit juice may stabilize as the large
                         millennial generation enters the best-customer lifestage.

Middle-aged married couples are the biggest spenders on fresh fruit juice. Householders aged 35 to 54 spend 25 to 27 percent more than average on this item. Married couples with children at home spend 48 percent more than average on fresh fruit juice, the figure peaking among those with school-aged children at 57 percent above average. Households in the Northeast outspend the average by 38 percent.

Average household spending on fresh fruit juice purchased at grocery or convenience stores fell by a substantial 36 percent between 2000 and 2006, after adjusting for inflation. Spending on this item fell another 14 percent between 2006 and 2012. Behind the long decline in spending on fresh fruit juice is the baby-boom generation's exit from the best-customer lifestage and the growing propensity of consumers to eat fast-food breakfasts or no breakfast at all. Average household spending on fresh fruit juice may stabilize as the large millennial generation enters the best-customer lifestage.

Table 74. Fruit juice, fresh

Total household spending	$2,122,536,960.00
Average household spends	17.06

	AVERAGE HOUSEHOLD SPENDING	BEST CUSTOMERS (index)	BIGGEST CUSTOMERS (market share)
AGE OF HOUSEHOLDER			
Average household	**$17.06**	**100**	**100.0%**
Under age 25	10.35	61	4.0
Aged 25 to 34	14.40	84	13.6
Aged 35 to 44	21.68	127	22.1
Aged 45 to 54	21.28	125	24.7
Aged 55 to 64	17.69	104	19.0
Aged 65 to 74	13.28	78	9.4
Aged 75 or older	12.66	74	7.3

	AVERAGE HOUSEHOLD SPENDING	BEST CUSTOMERS (index)	BIGGEST CUSTOMERS (market share)
HOUSEHOLD INCOME			
Average household	**$17.06**	**100**	**100.0%**
Under $20,000	10.03	59	12.4
$20,000 to $39,999	13.67	80	18.1
$40,000 to $49,999	14.42	85	7.5
$50,000 to $69,999	16.19	95	13.7
$70,000 to $79,999	18.13	106	5.9
$80,000 to $99,999	22.68	133	11.7
$100,000 or more	28.12	165	30.9
HOUSEHOLD TYPE			
Average household	**17.06**	**100**	**100.0**
Married couples	21.31	125	60.7
Married couples, no children	16.66	98	20.4
Married couples with children	25.24	148	34.8
Oldest child under age 6	22.50	132	6.0
Oldest child aged 6 to 17	26.72	157	18.6
Oldest child aged 18 or older	24.47	143	10.1
Single parent with child under age 18	14.73	86	4.5
Single person	10.33	61	18.0
RACE AND HISPANIC ORIGIN			
Average household	**17.06**	**100**	**100.0**
Asian	18.52	109	4.7
Black	15.05	88	11.1
Hispanic	17.00	100	12.5
Non-Hispanic white and other	17.39	102	76.5
REGION			
Average household	**17.06**	**100**	**100.0**
Northeast	23.51	138	24.9
Midwest	18.56	109	24.1
South	13.63	80	29.8
West	16.01	94	21.1
EDUCATION			
Average household	**17.06**	**100**	**100.0**
Less than high school graduate	15.81	93	12.1
High school graduate	14.48	85	21.2
Some college	14.21	83	17.2
Associate's degree	18.09	106	10.5
Bachelor's degree or more	21.12	124	39.0
Bachelor's degree	18.79	110	22.0
Master's, professional, doctoral degree	25.07	147	17.1

Note: Market shares may not sum to 100.0 because of rounding and missing categories by household type. "Asian" and "black" include Hispanics and non-Hispanics who identify themselves as being of the respective race alone. "Hispanic" includes people of any race who identify themselves as Hispanic. "Other" includes people who identify themselves as non-Hispanic and as Alaska Native, American Indian, Asian (who are also included in the "Asian" row), or Native Hawaiian or other Pacific Islander, as well as non-Hispanics reporting more than one race.
Source: Calculations by New Strategist based on the Bureau of Labor Statistics' 2012 Consumer Expenditure Survey

Fruit Juice, Frozen

Best customers: Married couples without children at home
Married couples with school-aged children
Hispanics and Asians
Households in the Midwest and West

Customer trends: Average household spending on frozen fruit juice may continue its decline
as consumer preferences shift.

Households with school-aged children are the best customers of frozen fruit juice. Married couples with school-aged children spend 76 percent more than average on frozen fruit juice. Hispanic householders, who have the largest families, outspend the average by 29 percent. Asians spend 16 percent more. Married couples without children at home (most of them older empty-nesters) spend one-quarter more than average on frozen fruit juice. Households in the Midwest and West spend, respectively, 36 and 28 percent more than average on frozen fruit juice.

Average household spending on frozen fruit juice fell steeply between 2000 and 2006 (down 60 percent, after adjusting for inflation) and continued to decline—although more slowly—between 2006 and 2012. The declines occurred because consumers were looking for more convenience from fruit juice, and they were increasingly eating breakfast away from home—a trend slowed by household belt tightening in face of the Great Recession. Average household spending on frozen fruit juice is likely to continue its decline as consumer preferences shift.

Table 75. Fruit juice, frozen

| Total household spending | $690,508,800.00 |
| Average household spends | 5.55 |

	AVERAGE HOUSEHOLD SPENDING	BEST CUSTOMERS (index)	BIGGEST CUSTOMERS (market share)
AGE OF HOUSEHOLDER			
Average household	**$5.55**	**100**	**100.0%**
Under age 25	4.65	84	5.5
Aged 25 to 34	6.49	117	18.9
Aged 35 to 44	5.70	103	17.8
Aged 45 to 54	6.58	119	23.5
Aged 55 to 64	3.88	70	12.8
Aged 65 to 74	4.45	80	9.7
Aged 75 or older	6.60	119	11.6

	AVERAGE HOUSEHOLD SPENDING	BEST CUSTOMERS (index)	BIGGEST CUSTOMERS (market share)
HOUSEHOLD INCOME			
Average household	**$5.55**	**100**	**100.0%**
Under $20,000	4.27	77	16.2
$20,000 to $39,999	4.69	85	19.0
$40,000 to $49,999	4.17	75	6.6
$50,000 to $69,999	7.21	130	18.8
$70,000 to $79,999	7.87	142	7.9
$80,000 to $99,999	5.88	106	9.3
$100,000 or more	6.52	117	22.0
HOUSEHOLD TYPE			
Average household	**5.55**	**100**	**100.0**
Married couples	7.25	131	63.4
Married couples, no children	6.95	125	26.1
Married couples with children	7.91	143	33.5
Oldest child under age 6	5.19	94	4.3
Oldest child aged 6 to 17	9.79	176	21.0
Oldest child aged 18 or older	6.48	117	8.2
Single parent with child under age 18	5.62	101	5.3
Single person	2.47	45	13.2
RACE AND HISPANIC ORIGIN			
Average household	**5.55**	**100**	**100.0**
Asian	6.43	116	5.0
Black	4.39	79	9.9
Hispanic	7.14	129	16.1
Non-Hispanic white and other	5.52	99	74.7
REGION			
Average household	**5.55**	**100**	**100.0**
Northeast	4.15	75	13.5
Midwest	7.53	136	30.1
South	4.11	74	27.6
West	7.09	128	28.8
EDUCATION			
Average household	**5.55**	**100**	**100.0**
Less than high school graduate	4.85	87	11.4
High school graduate	5.44	98	24.4
Some college	5.95	107	22.1
Associate's degree	6.20	112	11.0
Bachelor's degree or more	5.41	97	30.7
Bachelor's degree	4.62	83	16.6
Master's, professional, doctoral degree	6.77	122	14.2

Note: Market shares may not sum to 100.0 because of rounding and missing categories by household type. "Asian" and "black" include Hispanics and non-Hispanics who identify themselves as being of the respective race alone. "Hispanic" includes people of any race who identify themselves as Hispanic. "Other" includes people who identify themselves as non-Hispanic and as Alaska Native, American Indian, Asian (who are also included in the "Asian" row), or Native Hawaiian or other Pacific Islander, as well as non-Hispanics reporting more than one race.
Source: Calculations by New Strategist based on the Bureau of Labor Statistics' 2012 Consumer Expenditure Survey

Ham

Best customers: Householders aged 35 to 54
Married couples with school-aged or older children at home
Hispanics
Householders without a high school diploma

Customer trends: Average household spending on ham may continue its decline as the small
generation X passes through the best-customer lifestage.

Households with children are the biggest spenders on ham. Married couples with school-aged or older children at home spend 52 to 73 percent more than average on this item. Householders aged 35 to 54, most with children at home, spend one-fifth more than average on ham. Hispanics, who tend to have larger families, outspend the average by 35 percent. Householders without a high school diploma, many of them Hispanic, spend 14 percent more than average on ham.

Average household spending on ham declined 31 percent between 2000 and 2012, after adjusting for inflation. Average household spending on ham may continue its decline as the small generation X passes through the best-customer lifestage.

Table 76. Ham

Total household spending $4,157,982,720.00
Average household spends   33.42

	AVERAGE HOUSEHOLD SPENDING	BEST CUSTOMERS (index)	BIGGEST CUSTOMERS (market share)
AGE OF HOUSEHOLDER			
Average household	**$33.42**	**100**	**100.0%**
Under age 25	20.85	62	4.1
Aged 25 to 34	28.37	85	13.7
Aged 35 to 44	39.99	120	20.8
Aged 45 to 54	39.72	119	23.5
Aged 55 to 64	33.92	101	18.6
Aged 65 to 74	35.39	106	12.8
Aged 75 or older	22.45	67	6.6

	AVERAGE HOUSEHOLD SPENDING	BEST CUSTOMERS (index)	BIGGEST CUSTOMERS (market share)
HOUSEHOLD INCOME			
Average household	**$33.42**	**100**	**100.0%**
Under $20,000	24.94	75	15.7
$20,000 to $39,999	27.78	83	18.7
$40,000 to $49,999	27.06	81	7.2
$50,000 to $69,999	34.55	103	14.9
$70,000 to $79,999	50.17	150	8.4
$80,000 to $99,999	42.01	126	11.1
$100,000 or more	43.34	130	24.3
HOUSEHOLD TYPE			
Average household	**33.42**	**100**	**100.0**
Married couples	43.48	130	63.2
Married couples, no children	34.48	103	21.5
Married couples with children	49.67	149	34.9
Oldest child under age 6	26.10	78	3.6
Oldest child aged 6 to 17	57.78	173	20.6
Oldest child aged 18 or older	50.82	152	10.7
Single parent with child under age 18	28.70	86	4.5
Single person	16.67	50	14.8
RACE AND HISPANIC ORIGIN			
Average household	**33.42**	**100**	**100.0**
Asian	30.13	90	3.9
Black	22.98	69	8.6
Hispanic	45.28	135	17.0
Non-Hispanic white and other	33.20	99	74.6
REGION			
Average household	**33.42**	**100**	**100.0**
Northeast	33.23	99	17.9
Midwest	30.41	91	20.2
South	35.57	106	39.6
West	33.03	99	22.3
EDUCATION			
Average household	**33.42**	**100**	**100.0**
Less than high school graduate	38.24	114	14.9
High school graduate	33.41	100	24.9
Some college	32.22	96	19.9
Associate's degree	37.19	111	11.0
Bachelor's degree or more	31.25	94	29.5
Bachelor's degree	28.49	85	17.0
Master's, professional, doctoral degree	35.93	108	12.5

Note: Market shares may not sum to 100.0 because of rounding and missing categories by household type. "Asian" and "black" include Hispanics and non-Hispanics who identify themselves as being of the respective race alone. "Hispanic" includes people of any race who identify themselves as Hispanic. "Other" includes people who identify themselves as non-Hispanic and as Alaska Native, American Indian, Asian (who are also included in the "Asian" row), or Native Hawaiian or other Pacific Islander, as well as non-Hispanics reporting more than one race.
Source: Calculations by New Strategist based on the Bureau of Labor Statistics' 2012 Consumer Expenditure Survey

Ice Cream and Related Products

Best customers: Householders aged 35 to 74

Married couples with school-aged or older children at home

Customer trends: Average household spending on ice cream may continue to fall as the large baby-boom generation ages and household size shrinks.

Households with children spend the most on ice cream and related products. Married couples with school-aged or older children at home spend 51 to 69 percent more than the average household on this item. Because ice cream is such a commonly purchased item, householders ranging in age from 35 to 75 spend more than average on ice cream.

Average household spending on ice cream and related products fell 24 percent between 2000 and 2012, after adjusting for inflation. Behind the decline was price discounting as private-label brands competed with premium brands in the grocery store. Average household spending on ice cream may continue to fall as the large baby-boom generation ages and household size shrinks.

Table 77. Ice cream and related products

Total household spending	$7,137,745,920.00
Average household spends	57.37

	AVERAGE HOUSEHOLD SPENDING	BEST CUSTOMERS (index)	BIGGEST CUSTOMERS (market share)
AGE OF HOUSEHOLDER			
Average household	**$57.37**	**100**	**100.0%**
Under age 25	36.91	64	4.2
Aged 25 to 34	46.19	81	13.0
Aged 35 to 44	62.96	110	19.1
Aged 45 to 54	69.27	121	23.9
Aged 55 to 64	62.34	109	19.9
Aged 65 to 74	61.75	108	13.0
Aged 75 or older	41.48	72	7.1

	AVERAGE HOUSEHOLD SPENDING	BEST CUSTOMERS (index)	BIGGEST CUSTOMERS (market share)
HOUSEHOLD INCOME			
Average household	**$57.37**	**100**	**100.0%**
Under $20,000	34.85	61	12.8
$20,000 to $39,999	42.28	74	16.6
$40,000 to $49,999	46.75	81	7.2
$50,000 to $69,999	57.06	99	14.4
$70,000 to $79,999	75.09	131	7.3
$80,000 to $99,999	77.64	135	11.9
$100,000 or more	91.07	159	29.7
HOUSEHOLD TYPE			
Average household	**57.37**	**100**	**100.0**
Married couples	76.44	133	64.7
Married couples, no children	62.46	109	22.7
Married couples with children	87.34	152	35.8
Oldest child under age 6	62.96	110	5.0
Oldest child aged 6 to 17	96.93	169	20.1
Oldest child aged 18 or older	86.54	151	10.6
Single parent with child under age 18	49.33	86	4.5
Single person	27.24	47	14.1
RACE AND HISPANIC ORIGIN			
Average household	**57.37**	**100**	**100.0**
Asian	55.05	96	4.2
Black	38.88	68	8.5
Hispanic	53.54	93	11.7
Non-Hispanic white and other	61.19	107	80.1
REGION			
Average household	**57.37**	**100**	**100.0**
Northeast	60.88	106	19.2
Midwest	60.91	106	23.5
South	54.59	95	35.4
West	55.59	97	21.8
EDUCATION			
Average household	**57.37**	**100**	**100.0**
Less than high school graduate	55.32	96	12.6
High school graduate	45.98	80	20.0
Some college	53.38	93	19.2
Associate's degree	65.08	113	11.2
Bachelor's degree or more	67.23	117	37.0
Bachelor's degree	62.46	109	21.7
Master's, professional, doctoral degree	75.29	131	15.2

Note: Market shares may not sum to 100.0 because of rounding and missing categories by household type. "Asian" and "black" include Hispanics and non-Hispanics who identify themselves as being of the respective race alone. "Hispanic" includes people of any race who identify themselves as Hispanic. "Other" includes people who identify themselves as non-Hispanic and as Alaska Native, American Indian, Asian (who are also included in the "Asian" row), or Native Hawaiian or other Pacific Islander, as well as non-Hispanics reporting more than one race.
Source: Calculations by New Strategist based on the Bureau of Labor Statistics' 2012 Consumer Expenditure Survey

Jams, Preserves, and Other Sweets

Best customers: Householders aged 35 to 54
Married couples

Customer trends: Average household spending on jams, preserves, and other sweets is likely to decline as the large baby-boom generation ages and household size shrinks.

Married couples with children at home spend the most on jams, preserves, and other sweets—52 percent more than the average household. Couples without children at home spend 22 percent more than average on this item. Householders aged 35 to 54, most with children at home, spend 13 to 17 percent more than average on jams.

Average household spending on jams, preserves, and other sweets held steady between 2000 and 2006, but increased 13 percent between 2006 and 2012, after adjusting for inflation. One factor behind the increase was more brown-bag lunches as the Great Recession reduced eating out. Average household spending on jams is likely to fall in the years ahead as the large baby-boom generation ages and household size shrinks.

Table 78. Jams, preserves, and other sweets

Total household spending $3,683,957,760.00
Average household spends   29.61

	AVERAGE HOUSEHOLD SPENDING	BEST CUSTOMERS (index)	BIGGEST CUSTOMERS (market share)
AGE OF HOUSEHOLDER			
Average household	**$29.61**	**100**	**100.0%**
Under age 25	17.82	60	3.9
Aged 25 to 34	25.39	86	13.9
Aged 35 to 44	34.55	117	20.3
Aged 45 to 54	33.52	113	22.4
Aged 55 to 64	30.72	104	19.0
Aged 65 to 74	26.29	89	10.7
Aged 75 or older	30.17	102	10.0

	AVERAGE HOUSEHOLD SPENDING	BEST CUSTOMERS (index)	BIGGEST CUSTOMERS (market share)
HOUSEHOLD INCOME			
Average household	**$29.61**	**100**	**100.0%**
Under $20,000	18.06	61	12.8
$20,000 to $39,999	21.73	73	16.5
$40,000 to $49,999	25.57	86	7.6
$50,000 to $69,999	29.05	98	14.2
$70,000 to $79,999	32.50	110	6.1
$80,000 to $99,999	39.96	135	11.9
$100,000 or more	48.70	164	30.8
HOUSEHOLD TYPE			
Average household	**29.61**	**100**	**100.0**
Married couples	40.24	136	66.0
Married couples, no children	35.99	122	25.3
Married couples with children	45.11	152	35.8
Oldest child under age 6	38.09	129	5.9
Oldest child aged 6 to 17	49.56	167	19.9
Oldest child aged 18 or older	42.07	142	10.0
Single parent with child under age 18	22.71	77	4.0
Single person	14.09	48	14.1
RACE AND HISPANIC ORIGIN			
Average household	**29.61**	**100**	**100.0**
Asian	22.48	76	3.3
Black	19.83	67	8.4
Hispanic	22.85	77	9.7
Non-Hispanic white and other	32.40	109	82.1
REGION			
Average household	**29.61**	**100**	**100.0**
Northeast	27.36	92	16.7
Midwest	33.48	113	25.1
South	27.73	94	34.9
West	30.71	104	23.4
EDUCATION			
Average household	**29.61**	**100**	**100.0**
Less than high school graduate	22.83	77	10.1
High school graduate	25.21	85	21.2
Some college	25.52	86	17.7
Associate's degree	30.44	103	10.2
Bachelor's degree or more	38.07	129	40.5
Bachelor's degree	37.17	126	25.0
Master's, professional, doctoral degree	39.60	134	15.5

Note: Market shares may not sum to 100.0 because of rounding and missing categories by household type. "Asian" and "black" include Hispanics and non-Hispanics who identify themselves as being of the respective race alone. "Hispanic" includes people of any race who identify themselves as Hispanic. "Other" includes people who identify themselves as non-Hispanic and as Alaska Native, American Indian, Asian (who are also included in the "Asian" row), or Native Hawaiian or other Pacific Islander, as well as non-Hispanics reporting more than one race.
Source: Calculations by New Strategist based on the Bureau of Labor Statistics' 2012 Consumer Expenditure Survey

Lettuce

Best customers:	**Householders aged 35 to 74**
	Married couples
	Asians
Customer trends:	**Average household spending on lettuce may continue to rise as Americans strive to improve their diet.**

Because lettuce is a common purchase, there is little variation in spending on lettuce by household segment. The best customers of lettuce tend to be the largest households. Married couples with school-aged or older children at home spend 39 to 53 percent more than average on this item. Married couples without children at home spend 17 percent more. Householders aged 35 to 54, most with children, spend 12 to 16 percent more than average on lettuce. Spending is average or above average in the 55-to-74 age groups as well. Asians spend 30 percent more than average on lettuce.

Average household spending on lettuce climbed 17 percent between 2000 and 2012, after adjusting for inflation. Among the factors behind the growth were the attempt by many Americans to eat a healthier diet and the convenience of bagged lettuce available in the grocery store. Average household spending on lettuce may continue to rise as Americans strive to improve their diet.

Table 79. Lettuce

Total household spending	$4,022,369,280.00
Average household spends	32.33

	AVERAGE HOUSEHOLD SPENDING	BEST CUSTOMERS (index)	BIGGEST CUSTOMERS (market share)
AGE OF HOUSEHOLDER			
Average household	**$32.33**	**100**	**100.0%**
Under age 25	18.93	59	3.8
Aged 25 to 34	29.73	92	14.9
Aged 35 to 44	36.22	112	19.4
Aged 45 to 54	37.38	116	22.9
Aged 55 to 64	32.37	100	18.3
Aged 65 to 74	34.24	106	12.8
Aged 75 or older	26.24	81	7.9

	AVERAGE HOUSEHOLD SPENDING	BEST CUSTOMERS (index)	BIGGEST CUSTOMERS (market share)
HOUSEHOLD INCOME			
Average household	**$32.33**	**100**	**100.0%**
Under $20,000	19.16	59	12.5
$20,000 to $39,999	23.71	73	16.5
$40,000 to $49,999	28.46	88	7.8
$50,000 to $69,999	33.91	105	15.2
$70,000 to $79,999	45.37	140	7.8
$80,000 to $99,999	37.49	116	10.2
$100,000 or more	51.53	159	29.8
HOUSEHOLD TYPE			
Average household	**32.33**	**100**	**100.0**
Married couples	41.99	130	63.1
Married couples, no children	37.73	117	24.3
Married couples with children	44.94	139	32.7
Oldest child under age 6	37.67	117	5.3
Oldest child aged 6 to 17	44.85	139	16.5
Oldest child aged 18 or older	49.60	153	10.8
Single parent with child under age 18	24.25	75	3.9
Single person	17.54	54	16.1
RACE AND HISPANIC ORIGIN			
Average household	**32.33**	**100**	**100.0**
Asian	41.93	130	5.6
Black	20.89	65	8.1
Hispanic	34.02	105	13.2
Non-Hispanic white and other	34.05	105	79.1
REGION			
Average household	**32.33**	**100**	**100.0**
Northeast	37.28	115	20.8
Midwest	35.34	109	24.2
South	26.84	83	30.9
West	34.42	106	24.0
EDUCATION			
Average household	**32.33**	**100**	**100.0**
Less than high school graduate	27.94	86	11.3
High school graduate	30.36	94	23.4
Some college	28.25	87	18.0
Associate's degree	32.36	100	9.9
Bachelor's degree or more	38.25	118	37.3
Bachelor's degree	37.07	115	22.9
Master's, professional, doctoral degree	40.24	124	14.4

Note: Market shares may not sum to 100.0 because of rounding and missing categories by household type. "Asian" and "black" include Hispanics and non-Hispanics who identify themselves as being of the respective race alone. "Hispanic" includes people of any race who identify themselves as Hispanic. "Other" includes people who identify themselves as non-Hispanic and as Alaska Native, American Indian, Asian (who are also included in the "Asian" row), or Native Hawaiian or other Pacific Islander, as well as non-Hispanics reporting more than one race.
Source: Calculations by New Strategist based on the Bureau of Labor Statistics' 2012 Consumer Expenditure Survey

Lunch Meats (Cold Cuts)

Best customers: Householders aged 35 to 54

Married couples with school-aged or older children at home

Single parents

Customer trends: Average household spending on lunch meats will continue to decline as the small generation X passes through the best-customer lifestage.

The best customers of lunch meats are the largest households. Married couples with school-aged or older children at home spend 53 to 73 percent more than the average household on this item. Householders aged 35 to 54, most with children, spend 20 to 27 percent more than average on lunch meats. Cold cuts are one of the relatively few items on which single parents, with their lower incomes, spend an average amount.

Average household spending on lunch meats fell 5 percent between 2000 and 2006, after adjusting for inflation, then increased by 1 percent from 2006 to 2012. Behind the earlier decline was the substitution of fast food for brown-bag lunches, a pattern that reversed following the Great Recession. Average household spending on lunch meats will continue to decline as the small generation X passes through the best-customer lifestage.

Table 80. Lunch meats (cold cuts)

Total household spending	$10,852,807,680.00
Average household spends	87.23

	AVERAGE HOUSEHOLD SPENDING	BEST CUSTOMERS (index)	BIGGEST CUSTOMERS (market share)
AGE OF HOUSEHOLDER			
Average household	**$87.23**	**100**	**100.0%**
Under age 25	49.46	57	3.7
Aged 25 to 34	79.71	91	14.8
Aged 35 to 44	110.73	127	22.0
Aged 45 to 54	104.25	120	23.7
Aged 55 to 64	86.42	99	18.1
Aged 65 to 74	80.49	92	11.1
Aged 75 or older	58.13	67	6.5

	AVERAGE HOUSEHOLD SPENDING	BEST CUSTOMERS (index)	BIGGEST CUSTOMERS (market share)
HOUSEHOLD INCOME			
Average household	**$87.23**	**100**	**100.0%**
Under $20,000	50.30	58	12.1
$20,000 to $39,999	68.36	78	17.7
$40,000 to $49,999	82.60	95	8.4
$50,000 to $69,999	86.92	100	14.4
$70,000 to $79,999	117.67	135	7.5
$80,000 to $99,999	107.16	123	10.8
$100,000 or more	134.29	154	28.8
HOUSEHOLD TYPE			
Average household	**87.23**	**100**	**100.0**
Married couples	115.42	132	64.3
Married couples, no children	92.69	106	22.2
Married couples with children	135.87	156	36.6
Oldest child under age 6	100.25	115	5.2
Oldest child aged 6 to 17	150.75	173	20.6
Oldest child aged 18 or older	133.22	153	10.8
Single parent with child under age 18	87.03	100	5.2
Single person	44.41	51	15.1
RACE AND HISPANIC ORIGIN			
Average household	**87.23**	**100**	**100.0**
Asian	61.82	71	3.1
Black	56.99	65	8.2
Hispanic	83.96	96	12.1
Non-Hispanic white and other	92.95	107	80.0
REGION			
Average household	**87.23**	**100**	**100.0**
Northeast	98.89	113	20.5
Midwest	94.43	108	24.0
South	78.70	90	33.6
West	84.71	97	21.9
EDUCATION			
Average household	**87.23**	**100**	**100.0**
Less than high school graduate	76.99	88	11.5
High school graduate	81.97	94	23.4
Some college	76.29	87	18.0
Associate's degree	93.54	107	10.6
Bachelor's degree or more	100.54	115	36.3
Bachelor's degree	106.93	123	24.4
Master's, professional, doctoral degree	89.72	103	11.9

Note: Market shares may not sum to 100.0 because of rounding and missing categories by household type. "Asian" and "black" include Hispanics and non-Hispanics who identify themselves as being of the respective race alone. "Hispanic" includes people of any race who identify themselves as Hispanic. "Other" includes people who identify themselves as non-Hispanic and as Alaska Native, American Indian, Asian (who are also included in the "Asian" row), or Native Hawaiian or other Pacific Islander, as well as non-Hispanics reporting more than one race.
Source: Calculations by New Strategist based on the Bureau of Labor Statistics' 2012 Consumer Expenditure Survey

Margarine

Best customers:	**Householders aged 65 or older**
	Married couples without children at home
	Married couples with school-aged children
	Single parents
	Households in the Midwest
Customer trends:	**Average household spending on margarine may depend more on marketing than demographics in the years ahead.**

Margarine's fortunes have been waning as the reputation of butter improved. In 2000, the average household spent 68 percent as much on margarine as on butter. By 2012, the figure had fallen to 34 percent. Some of the best customers of margarine are the oldest consumers. Householders aged 65 or older spend 15 to 25 percent more than average on margarine. Married couples without children at home (most of them older empty-nesters) spend 15 percent more than the average household on this item. Couples with school-aged children spend 47 percent more than average on margarine. Single parents, whose spending approaches average on only a few items, spend 29 percent more. Households in the Midwest spend 35 percent more than average on margarine.

Average household spending on margarine fell 44 percent between 2000 and 2012, after adjusting for inflation. Behind the downward slide were health warnings about transfats in margarine and the improving reputation of butter. Average household spending on margarine may depend more on marketing than demographics in the years ahead.

Table 81. Margarine

Total household spending	$1,087,395,840.00
Average household spends	8.74

	AVERAGE HOUSEHOLD SPENDING	BEST CUSTOMERS (index)	BIGGEST CUSTOMERS (market share)
AGE OF HOUSEHOLDER			
Average household	**$8.74**	**100**	**100.0%**
Under age 25	7.40	85	5.6
Aged 25 to 34	6.40	73	11.8
Aged 35 to 44	9.96	114	19.8
Aged 45 to 54	8.38	96	19.0
Aged 55 to 64	8.60	98	18.0
Aged 65 to 74	10.01	115	13.8
Aged 75 or older	10.95	125	12.2

	AVERAGE HOUSEHOLD SPENDING	BEST CUSTOMERS (index)	BIGGEST CUSTOMERS (market share)
HOUSEHOLD INCOME			
Average household	**$8.74**	**100**	**100.0%**
Under $20,000	7.35	84	17.7
$20,000 to $39,999	7.73	88	19.9
$40,000 to $49,999	6.28	72	6.4
$50,000 to $69,999	10.45	120	17.3
$70,000 to $79,999	11.54	132	7.4
$80,000 to $99,999	9.23	106	9.3
$100,000 or more	10.42	119	22.3
HOUSEHOLD TYPE			
Average household	**8.74**	**100**	**100.0**
Married couples	10.19	117	56.6
Married couples, no children	10.07	115	24.0
Married couples with children	10.07	115	27.1
Oldest child under age 6	5.99	69	3.1
Oldest child aged 6 to 17	12.88	147	17.5
Oldest child aged 18 or older	7.91	91	6.4
Single parent with child under age 18	11.24	129	6.7
Single person	4.41	50	15.0
RACE AND HISPANIC ORIGIN			
Average household	**8.74**	**100**	**100.0**
Asian	4.93	56	2.4
Black	8.61	99	12.4
Hispanic	7.17	82	10.3
Non-Hispanic white and other	9.01	103	77.4
REGION			
Average household	**8.74**	**100**	**100.0**
Northeast	10.06	115	20.8
Midwest	11.79	135	29.9
South	7.24	83	30.9
West	7.13	82	18.4
EDUCATION			
Average household	**8.74**	**100**	**100.0**
Less than high school graduate	9.18	105	13.7
High school graduate	8.87	101	25.3
Some college	8.37	96	19.7
Associate's degree	12.07	138	13.6
Bachelor's degree or more	7.69	88	27.7
Bachelor's degree	7.10	81	16.2
Master's, professional, doctoral degree	8.70	100	11.6

Note: Market shares may not sum to 100.0 because of rounding and missing categories by household type. "Asian" and "black" include Hispanics and non-Hispanics who identify themselves as being of the respective race alone. "Hispanic" includes people of any race who identify themselves as Hispanic. "Other" includes people who identify themselves as non-Hispanic and as Alaska Native, American Indian, Asian (who are also included in the "Asian" row), or Native Hawaiian or other Pacific Islander, as well as non-Hispanics reporting more than one race.
Source: Calculations by New Strategist based on the Bureau of Labor Statistics' 2012 Consumer Expenditure Survey

Milk, Fresh

Best customers: Householders aged 35 to 54
Married couples with children at home
Asians and Hispanics

Customer trends: Average household spending on milk is unlikely to grow much in the years
ahead because the small generation X is in the best customer lifestage.

The best customers of milk are the largest households. Married couples with children at home spend 58 percent more than the average household on milk. Householders aged 35 to 54, most with children, spend 19 to 27 percent more than average on milk. Hispanics, who have the largest households, spend 27 percent more than average, while Asians spend 25 percent more.

Average household spending on milk purchased at grocery or convenience stores declined 20 percent between 2000 and 2010, after adjusting for inflation, as the large baby-boom generation exited the best-customer lifestage and was replaced by the small generation X. From 2010 to 2012, however, average household spending on fresh milk stabilized, rising 1 percent. Average household spending on milk is unlikely to grow much in the years ahead because the small generation X is in the best customer lifestage.

Table 82. Milk, fresh

Total household spending $15,960,084,480.00
Average household spends   128.28

	AVERAGE HOUSEHOLD SPENDING	BEST CUSTOMERS (index)	BIGGEST CUSTOMERS (market share)
AGE OF HOUSEHOLDER			
Average household	**$128.28**	**100**	**100.0%**
Under age 25	88.89	69	4.5
Aged 25 to 34	129.01	101	16.3
Aged 35 to 44	162.73	127	22.0
Aged 45 to 54	152.50	119	23.5
Aged 55 to 64	117.35	91	16.7
Aged 65 to 74	101.83	79	9.6
Aged 75 or older	94.21	73	7.2

	AVERAGE HOUSEHOLD SPENDING	BEST CUSTOMERS (index)	BIGGEST CUSTOMERS (market share)
HOUSEHOLD INCOME			
Average household	**$128.28**	**100**	**100.0%**
Under $20,000	87.93	69	14.4
$20,000 to $39,999	108.80	85	19.1
$40,000 to $49,999	118.36	92	8.2
$50,000 to $69,999	128.43	100	14.5
$70,000 to $79,999	164.55	128	7.2
$80,000 to $99,999	157.02	122	10.8
$100,000 or more	176.59	138	25.8
HOUSEHOLD TYPE			
Average household	**128.28**	**100**	**100.0**
Married couples	166.88	130	63.2
Married couples, no children	120.59	94	19.6
Married couples with children	203.11	158	37.2
Oldest child under age 6	197.74	154	7.0
Oldest child aged 6 to 17	212.58	166	19.7
Oldest child aged 18 or older	190.65	149	10.5
Single parent with child under age 18	124.72	97	5.1
Single person	65.23	51	15.1
RACE AND HISPANIC ORIGIN			
Average household	**128.28**	**100**	**100.0**
Asian	160.78	125	5.4
Black	85.31	67	8.4
Hispanic	162.35	127	15.9
Non-Hispanic white and other	129.85	101	76.0
REGION			
Average household	**128.28**	**100**	**100.0**
Northeast	122.68	96	17.3
Midwest	120.64	94	20.9
South	130.01	101	37.7
West	137.60	107	24.2
EDUCATION			
Average household	**128.28**	**100**	**100.0**
Less than high school graduate	120.85	94	12.3
High school graduate	125.99	98	24.5
Some college	114.52	89	18.4
Associate's degree	133.75	104	10.3
Bachelor's degree or more	140.40	109	34.5
Bachelor's degree	138.95	108	21.6
Master's, professional, doctoral degree	142.86	111	12.9

Note: Market shares may not sum to 100.0 because of rounding and missing categories by household type. "Asian" and "black" include Hispanics and non-Hispanics who identify themselves as being of the respective race alone. "Hispanic" includes people of any race who identify themselves as Hispanic. "Other" includes people who identify themselves as non-Hispanic and as Alaska Native, American Indian, Asian (who are also included in the "Asian" row), or Native Hawaiian or other Pacific Islander, as well as non-Hispanics reporting more than one race.
Source: Calculations by New Strategist based on the Bureau of Labor Statistics' 2012 Consumer Expenditure Survey

Nondairy Cream and Imitation Milk

| Best customers: | Householders aged 45 to 54 |
| | Married couples with children at home |

| Customer trends: | Average household spending on nondairy cream and imitation milk may continue |
| | to rise in the years ahead as soy products become more commonly consumed. |

Older householders and the largest households are the biggest spenders on nondairy cream and imitation milk. Married couples with children at home spend 42 percent more than average on this item, the figure peaking at 80 percent above average among couples with adult children at home. Householders aged 45 to 54, many with (adult) children at home, spend 33 percent more than average on nondairy cream and imitation milk.

Average household spending on nondairy cream and imitation milk grew by an enormous 52 percent between 2000 and 2012, after adjusting for inflation. Behind the increase was the growing popularity of soy products. Average household spending on nondairy cream and imitation milk may continue to rise in the years ahead as soy products become more commonly consumed.

Table 83. Nondairy cream and imitation milk

Total household spending $2,312,893,440.00
Average household spends   18.59

	AVERAGE HOUSEHOLD SPENDING	BEST CUSTOMERS (index)	BIGGEST CUSTOMERS (market share)
AGE OF HOUSEHOLDER			
Average household	**$18.59**	**100**	**100.0%**
Under age 25	12.06	65	4.3
Aged 25 to 34	15.84	85	13.8
Aged 35 to 44	19.98	107	18.7
Aged 45 to 54	24.73	133	26.3
Aged 55 to 64	19.43	105	19.1
Aged 65 to 74	16.82	90	10.9
Aged 75 or older	13.29	71	7.0

	AVERAGE HOUSEHOLD SPENDING	BEST CUSTOMERS (index)	BIGGEST CUSTOMERS (market share)
HOUSEHOLD INCOME			
Average household	**$18.59**	**100**	**100.0%**
Under $20,000	12.05	65	13.6
$20,000 to $39,999	14.57	78	17.7
$40,000 to $49,999	21.85	118	10.4
$50,000 to $69,999	20.34	109	15.8
$70,000 to $79,999	23.83	128	7.2
$80,000 to $99,999	18.27	98	8.7
$100,000 or more	26.10	140	26.3
HOUSEHOLD TYPE			
Average household	**18.59**	**100**	**100.0**
Married couples	23.03	124	60.2
Married couples, no children	19.07	103	21.4
Married couples with children	26.43	142	33.4
Oldest child under age 6	22.93	123	5.6
Oldest child aged 6 to 17	23.51	126	15.0
Oldest child aged 18 or older	33.48	180	12.7
Single parent with child under age 18	17.25	93	4.9
Single person	9.40	51	15.0
RACE AND HISPANIC ORIGIN			
Average household	**18.59**	**100**	**100.0**
Asian	15.23	82	3.6
Black	11.98	64	8.1
Hispanic	16.42	88	11.1
Non-Hispanic white and other	20.09	108	81.1
REGION			
Average household	**18.59**	**100**	**100.0**
Northeast	19.95	107	19.4
Midwest	18.17	98	21.7
South	16.92	91	33.9
West	20.68	111	25.1
EDUCATION			
Average household	**18.59**	**100**	**100.0**
Less than high school graduate	16.53	89	11.6
High school graduate	19.23	103	25.8
Some college	20.38	110	22.6
Associate's degree	19.57	105	10.4
Bachelor's degree or more	17.35	93	29.4
Bachelor's degree	17.75	95	19.0
Master's, professional, doctoral degree	16.68	90	10.4

Note: Market shares may not sum to 100.0 because of rounding and missing categories by household type. "Asian" and "black" include Hispanics and non-Hispanics who identify themselves as being of the respective race alone. "Hispanic" includes people of any race who identify themselves as Hispanic. "Other" includes people who identify themselves as non-Hispanic and as Alaska Native, American Indian, Asian (who are also included in the "Asian" row), or Native Hawaiian or other Pacific Islander, as well as non-Hispanics reporting more than one race.
Source: Calculations by New Strategist based on the Bureau of Labor Statistics' 2012 Consumer Expenditure Survey

Nuts

Best customers:	Householders aged 45 to 74
	Married couples without children at home
	Married couples with school-aged or older children at home
Customer trends:	Average household spending on nuts will continue to climb as boomers age.

Older Americans are the biggest spenders on nuts. Householders ranging in age from 45 to 74 spend 16 to 43 percent more than the average household on nuts and control 62 percent of the market. Married couples without children at home (most of them older) spend 56 percent more than average on nuts, while those with school-aged or older children at home (the largest households) spend 32 to 43 percent more.

Average household spending on nuts increased 52 percent between 2000 and 2012, after adjusting for inflation. Behind the increase was the aging of the baby-boom generation into the best-customer age groups, as well as the increased attention to the health benefits of nut consumption. Average household spending on nuts should continue to climb as boomers age.

Table 84. Nuts

Total household spending	$5,269,017,600.00
Average household spends	42.35

	AVERAGE HOUSEHOLD SPENDING	BEST CUSTOMERS (index)	BIGGEST CUSTOMERS (market share)
AGE OF HOUSEHOLDER			
Average household	$42.35	100	100.0%
Under age 25	23.37	55	3.6
Aged 25 to 34	30.24	71	11.5
Aged 35 to 44	39.57	93	16.2
Aged 45 to 54	51.08	121	23.9
Aged 55 to 64	49.13	116	21.2
Aged 65 to 74	60.36	143	17.2
Aged 75 or older	28.69	68	6.6

	AVERAGE HOUSEHOLD SPENDING	BEST CUSTOMERS (index)	BIGGEST CUSTOMERS (market share)
HOUSEHOLD INCOME			
Average household	**$42.35**	**100**	**100.0%**
Under $20,000	19.28	46	9.6
$20,000 to $39,999	27.13	64	14.4
$40,000 to $49,999	39.90	94	8.3
$50,000 to $69,999	38.89	92	13.3
$70,000 to $79,999	58.24	138	7.7
$80,000 to $99,999	60.32	142	12.6
$100,000 or more	76.78	181	33.9
HOUSEHOLD TYPE			
Average household	**42.35**	**100**	**100.0**
Married couples	59.22	140	67.9
Married couples, no children	65.90	156	32.4
Married couples with children	54.77	129	30.4
Oldest child under age 6	42.91	101	4.6
Oldest child aged 6 to 17	55.85	132	15.7
Oldest child aged 18 or older	60.35	143	10.1
Single parent with child under age 18	23.03	54	2.9
Single person	23.04	54	16.2
RACE AND HISPANIC ORIGIN			
Average household	**42.35**	**100**	**100.0**
Asian	48.42	114	5.0
Black	19.11	45	5.7
Hispanic	29.10	69	8.6
Non-Hispanic white and other	48.49	114	85.9
REGION			
Average household	**42.35**	**100**	**100.0**
Northeast	47.19	111	20.1
Midwest	43.05	102	22.5
South	37.62	89	33.1
West	45.55	108	24.2
EDUCATION			
Average household	**42.35**	**100**	**100.0**
Less than high school graduate	25.72	61	7.9
High school graduate	28.19	67	16.6
Some college	33.63	79	16.4
Associate's degree	39.72	94	9.3
Bachelor's degree or more	66.24	156	49.3
Bachelor's degree	57.53	136	27.1
Master's, professional, doctoral degree	80.95	191	22.2

Note: Market shares may not sum to 100.0 because of rounding and missing categories by household type. "Asian" and "black" include Hispanics and non-Hispanics who identify themselves as being of the respective race alone. "Hispanic" includes people of any race who identify themselves as Hispanic. "Other" includes people who identify themselves as non-Hispanic and as Alaska Native, American Indian, Asian (who are also included in the "Asian" row), or Native Hawaiian or other Pacific Islander, as well as non-Hispanics reporting more than one race.
Source: Calculations by New Strategist based on the Bureau of Labor Statistics' 2012 Consumer Expenditure Survey

Olives, Pickles, and Relishes

Best customers: Householders aged 45 to 64
                        Married couples without children at home
                        Married couples with school-aged or older children at home
                        Households in the Midwest and West

Customer trends: Average household spending on olives, pickles, and relishes should stabilize
                        now that boomers have filled the best-customer age groups.

The best customers of olives, pickles, and relishes are the largest households and older householders. Married couples with school-aged children spend 39 percent more than the average household on this item, and those with adult children at home spend 68 percent more. Married couples without children at home, most of them older empty-nesters, outspend the average by one-quarter. Householders aged 45 to 64 spend 19 to 21 percent more than average on olives, pickles, and relishes. Households in the Midwest spend 16 percent more than average, and those in the West spend 12 percent more.

Average household spending on olives, pickles, and relishes increased 34 percent between 2000 and 2012, after adjusting for inflation. Behind the increase is the greater availability of fresh olives and relishes in grocery stores. Average household spending on olives, pickles, and relishes should stabilize now that boomers have filled the best-customer age groups.

Table 85. Olives, pickles, and relishes

Total household spending $2,172,303,360.00
Average household spends   17.46

	AVERAGE HOUSEHOLD SPENDING	BEST CUSTOMERS (index)	BIGGEST CUSTOMERS (market share)
AGE OF HOUSEHOLDER			
Average household	**$17.46**	**100**	**100.0%**
Under age 25	9.32	53	3.5
Aged 25 to 34	13.70	78	12.7
Aged 35 to 44	17.73	102	17.6
Aged 45 to 54	20.84	119	23.6
Aged 55 to 64	21.12	121	22.1
Aged 65 to 74	19.26	110	13.3
Aged 75 or older	13.11	75	7.3

	AVERAGE HOUSEHOLD SPENDING	BEST CUSTOMERS (index)	BIGGEST CUSTOMERS (market share)
HOUSEHOLD INCOME			
Average household	**$17.46**	**100**	**100.0%**
Under $20,000	9.55	55	11.5
$20,000 to $39,999	13.07	75	16.9
$40,000 to $49,999	13.67	78	6.9
$50,000 to $69,999	19.63	112	16.2
$70,000 to $79,999	24.52	140	7.8
$80,000 to $99,999	24.37	140	12.3
$100,000 or more	26.43	151	28.3
HOUSEHOLD TYPE			
Average household	**17.46**	**100**	**100.0**
Married couples	23.10	132	64.3
Married couples, no children	21.84	125	26.1
Married couples with children	24.64	141	33.2
Oldest child under age 6	18.39	105	4.8
Oldest child aged 6 to 17	24.19	139	16.5
Oldest child aged 18 or older	29.30	168	11.8
Single parent with child under age 18	12.36	71	3.7
Single person	9.57	55	16.3
RACE AND HISPANIC ORIGIN			
Average household	**17.46**	**100**	**100.0**
Asian	8.48	49	2.1
Black	10.94	63	7.9
Hispanic	11.77	67	8.5
Non-Hispanic white and other	19.49	112	83.8
REGION			
Average household	**17.46**	**100**	**100.0**
Northeast	15.57	89	16.1
Midwest	20.21	116	25.7
South	15.44	88	32.9
West	19.57	112	25.3
EDUCATION			
Average household	**17.46**	**100**	**100.0**
Less than high school graduate	10.53	60	7.9
High school graduate	14.52	83	20.7
Some college	17.60	101	20.8
Associate's degree	18.13	104	10.3
Bachelor's degree or more	22.01	126	39.8
Bachelor's degree	21.31	122	24.3
Master's, professional, doctoral degree	23.21	133	15.4

Note: Market shares may not sum to 100.0 because of rounding and missing categories by household type. "Asian" and "black" include Hispanics and non-Hispanics who identify themselves as being of the respective race alone. "Hispanic" includes people of any race who identify themselves as Hispanic. "Other" includes people who identify themselves as non-Hispanic and as Alaska Native, American Indian, Asian (who are also included in the "Asian" row), or Native Hawaiian or other Pacific Islander, as well as non-Hispanics reporting more than one race.
Source: Calculations by New Strategist based on the Bureau of Labor Statistics' 2012 Consumer Expenditure Survey

Oranges

Best customers: Householders aged 35 to 54
Married couples with school-aged or older children at home
Asians and Hispanics
Households in the Northeast and West

Customer trends: Average household spending on oranges may continue to rise due to the growth of the Asian and Hispanic populations, but the presence of the small generation X in the best-customer lifestage may limit gains.

The biggest spenders on oranges are the largest households. Married couples with school-aged or older children at home spend 70 to 74 percent more than average on oranges. Householders aged 35 to 54, many with children at home, spend 23 to 29 percent more than average on oranges. Asians spend 48 percent more than average. Hispanics, who have the largest families, spend 22 percent more. Households in the Northeast spend 14 percent more than average on oranges, and those in the West spend 11 percent more.

Average household spending on oranges grew 6 percent between 2000 and 2012, after adjusting for inflation. Behind the increase was the rapid growth in the Asian and Hispanic populations. Spending on oranges may continue to rise due to the ongoing increase in those populations, but the presence of the small generation X in the best-customer lifestage may limit gains.

Table 86. Oranges

Total household spending $3,326,883,840.00
Average household spends   26.74

	AVERAGE HOUSEHOLD SPENDING	BEST CUSTOMERS (index)	BIGGEST CUSTOMERS (market share)
AGE OF HOUSEHOLDER			
Average household	**$26.74**	**100**	**100.0%**
Under age 25	19.10	71	4.7
Aged 25 to 34	21.41	80	12.9
Aged 35 to 44	34.47	129	22.4
Aged 45 to 54	32.91	123	24.4
Aged 55 to 64	25.19	94	17.2
Aged 65 to 74	26.34	99	11.9
Aged 75 or older	17.61	66	6.4

	AVERAGE HOUSEHOLD SPENDING	BEST CUSTOMERS (index)	BIGGEST CUSTOMERS (market share)
HOUSEHOLD INCOME			
Average household	**$26.74**	**100**	**100.0%**
Under $20,000	12.93	48	10.2
$20,000 to $39,999	20.45	76	17.2
$40,000 to $49,999	21.82	82	7.2
$50,000 to $69,999	27.92	104	15.1
$70,000 to $79,999	30.32	113	6.3
$80,000 to $99,999	38.57	144	12.7
$100,000 or more	44.47	166	31.1
HOUSEHOLD TYPE			
Average household	**26.74**	**100**	**100.0**
Married couples	36.45	136	66.2
Married couples, no children	29.74	111	23.2
Married couples with children	42.44	159	37.3
Oldest child under age 6	26.93	101	4.6
Oldest child aged 6 to 17	46.43	174	20.7
Oldest child aged 18 or older	45.45	170	12.0
Single parent with child under age 18	22.48	84	4.4
Single person	12.06	45	13.4
RACE AND HISPANIC ORIGIN			
Average household	**26.74**	**100**	**100.0**
Asian	39.52	148	6.4
Black	21.07	79	9.9
Hispanic	32.72	122	15.3
Non-Hispanic white and other	26.66	100	74.8
REGION			
Average household	**26.74**	**100**	**100.0**
Northeast	30.55	114	20.6
Midwest	28.12	105	23.3
South	22.27	83	31.0
West	29.70	111	25.0
EDUCATION			
Average household	**26.74**	**100**	**100.0**
Less than high school graduate	24.55	92	12.0
High school graduate	23.78	89	22.2
Some college	23.66	88	18.2
Associate's degree	28.77	108	10.6
Bachelor's degree or more	31.28	117	36.9
Bachelor's degree	30.11	113	22.4
Master's, professional, doctoral degree	33.27	124	14.4

Note: Market shares may not sum to 100.0 because of rounding and missing categories by household type. "Asian" and "black" include Hispanics and non-Hispanics who identify themselves as being of the respective race alone. "Hispanic" includes people of any race who identify themselves as Hispanic. "Other" includes people who identify themselves as non-Hispanic and as Alaska Native, American Indian, Asian (who are also included in the "Asian" row), or Native Hawaiian or other Pacific Islander, as well as non-Hispanics reporting more than one race.
Source: Calculations by New Strategist based on the Bureau of Labor Statistics' 2012 Consumer Expenditure Survey

Pasta, Cornmeal, and Other Cereal Products

Best customers: Householders aged 35 to 54
                       Married couples with school-aged or older children at home
                       Asians
                       Households in the Northeast and West

Customer trends: Average household spending on pasta should resume its decline as the
                       baby-boom generation ages and household size shrinks.

The biggest spenders on pasta, cornmeal, and other cereal products are households with children. Married couples with children at home spend 47 percent more than the average household on this item. Householders aged 35 to 54, most with children at home, spend one-quarter more than average on pasta. Asians spend 50 percent more. Households in the Northeast spend 16 percent more than average on pasta, and those in the West spend 14 percent more.

Average household spending on pasta, cornmeal, and other cereal products fell 28 percent between 2000 and 2006, after adjusting for inflation, then grew 34 percent between 2006 and 2012. Behind the decline was the growing propensity of consumers to eat out rather than cook a meal at home. Efforts at belt tightening and a renewed surge of home cooking may have been responsible for the ensuing rise in average household spending on pasta. Average household spending on pasta should resume its decline as the baby-boom generation ages and household size shrinks.

Table 87. Pasta, cornmeal, and other cereal products

| Total household spending | $4,600,903,680.00 |
| Average household spends | 36.98 |

	AVERAGE HOUSEHOLD SPENDING	BEST CUSTOMERS (index)	BIGGEST CUSTOMERS (market share)
AGE OF HOUSEHOLDER			
Average household	**$36.98**	**100**	**100.0%**
Under age 25	27.23	74	4.8
Aged 25 to 34	37.07	100	16.2
Aged 35 to 44	46.21	125	21.7
Aged 45 to 54	46.48	126	24.9
Aged 55 to 64	32.02	87	15.8
Aged 65 to 74	29.04	79	9.5
Aged 75 or older	25.98	70	6.9

	AVERAGE HOUSEHOLD SPENDING	BEST CUSTOMERS (index)	BIGGEST CUSTOMERS (market share)
HOUSEHOLD INCOME			
Average household	**$36.98**	**100**	**100.0%**
Under $20,000	24.19	65	13.8
$20,000 to $39,999	28.20	76	17.2
$40,000 to $49,999	29.59	80	7.1
$50,000 to $69,999	33.85	92	13.2
$70,000 to $79,999	51.79	140	7.8
$80,000 to $99,999	48.17	130	11.5
$100,000 or more	58.45	158	29.6
HOUSEHOLD TYPE			
Average household	**36.98**	**100**	**100.0**
Married couples	47.11	127	61.9
Married couples, no children	35.63	96	20.1
Married couples with children	54.39	147	34.6
Oldest child under age 6	40.51	110	5.0
Oldest child aged 6 to 17	58.81	159	18.9
Oldest child aged 18 or older	55.69	151	10.6
Single parent with child under age 18	32.45	88	4.6
Single person	19.70	53	15.8
RACE AND HISPANIC ORIGIN			
Average household	**36.98**	**100**	**100.0**
Asian	55.51	150	6.5
Black	29.33	79	10.0
Hispanic	33.09	89	11.2
Non-Hispanic white and other	38.92	105	79.0
REGION			
Average household	**36.98**	**100**	**100.0**
Northeast	42.77	116	20.9
Midwest	38.25	103	22.9
South	30.22	82	30.4
West	42.22	114	25.7
EDUCATION			
Average household	**36.98**	**100**	**100.0**
Less than high school graduate	29.75	80	10.5
High school graduate	33.79	91	22.8
Some college	31.87	86	17.7
Associate's degree	39.17	106	10.5
Bachelor's degree or more	44.91	121	38.3
Bachelor's degree	43.34	117	23.4
Master's, professional, doctoral degree	47.56	129	14.9

Note: Market shares may not sum to 100.0 because of rounding and missing categories by household type. "Asian" and "black" include Hispanics and non-Hispanics who identify themselves as being of the respective race alone. "Hispanic" includes people of any race who identify themselves as Hispanic. "Other" includes people who identify themselves as non-Hispanic and as Alaska Native, American Indian, Asian (who are also included in the "Asian" row), or Native Hawaiian or other Pacific Islander, as well as non-Hispanics reporting more than one race.
Source: Calculations by New Strategist based on the Bureau of Labor Statistics' 2012 Consumer Expenditure Survey

Peanut Butter

Best customers: Householders aged 35 to 54
Married couples with children at home
Single parents
Households in the Midwest

Customer trends: Average household spending on peanut butter may decline because the small generation X is in the best-customer lifestage.

Married couples with children at home spend the most on peanut butter, 75 percent more than average. The figure peaks among those with adult children at home at 93 percent above average. Householders aged 35 to 54, most with children, spend 26 to 34 percent more than the average household on peanut butter. Single parents, whose spending approaches average on only a few items, surpass the average on peanut butter by 17 percent. Households in the Midwest spend 15 percent more than average on this item.

Average household spending on peanut butter fell 19 percent between 2000 and 2006, after adjusting for inflation, then rebounded 46 percent between 2006 and 2012. Behind the rebound was belt tightening by parents who substituted homemade sandwiches for school-bought meals in an effort to cut costs. Average household spending on peanut butter may decline because the small generation X is in the best-customer lifestage.

Table 88. Peanut butter

Total household spending $2,324,090,880.00
Average household spends 18.68

	AVERAGE HOUSEHOLD SPENDING	BEST CUSTOMERS (index)	BIGGEST CUSTOMERS (market share)
AGE OF HOUSEHOLDER			
Average household	**$18.68**	**100**	**100.0%**
Under age 25	11.37	61	4.0
Aged 25 to 34	16.10	86	13.9
Aged 35 to 44	24.97	134	23.2
Aged 45 to 54	23.62	126	25.0
Aged 55 to 64	16.98	91	16.6
Aged 65 to 74	16.74	90	10.8
Aged 75 or older	12.04	64	6.3

	AVERAGE HOUSEHOLD SPENDING	BEST CUSTOMERS (index)	BIGGEST CUSTOMERS (market share)
HOUSEHOLD INCOME			
Average household	**$18.68**	**100**	**100.0%**
Under $20,000	9.87	53	11.1
$20,000 to $39,999	15.59	83	18.8
$40,000 to $49,999	18.32	98	8.7
$50,000 to $69,999	18.45	99	14.3
$70,000 to $79,999	24.56	131	7.3
$80,000 to $99,999	18.27	98	8.6
$100,000 or more	30.54	163	30.6
HOUSEHOLD TYPE			
Average household	**18.68**	**100**	**100.0**
Married couples	24.78	133	64.4
Married couples, no children	16.45	88	18.4
Married couples with children	32.68	175	41.1
Oldest child under age 6	25.46	136	6.2
Oldest child aged 6 to 17	33.33	178	21.2
Oldest child aged 18 or older	36.09	193	13.6
Single parent with child under age 18	21.77	117	6.1
Single person	9.71	52	15.4
RACE AND HISPANIC ORIGIN			
Average household	**18.68**	**100**	**100.0**
Asian	15.09	81	3.5
Black	11.54	62	7.8
Hispanic	15.50	83	10.4
Non-Hispanic white and other	20.46	110	82.2
REGION			
Average household	**18.68**	**100**	**100.0**
Northeast	18.65	100	18.0
Midwest	21.53	115	25.6
South	16.46	88	32.8
West	19.55	105	23.6
EDUCATION			
Average household	**18.68**	**100**	**100.0**
Less than high school graduate	13.18	71	9.2
High school graduate	14.71	79	19.6
Some college	16.21	87	17.9
Associate's degree	23.77	127	12.6
Bachelor's degree or more	23.89	128	40.3
Bachelor's degree	24.08	129	25.7
Master's, professional, doctoral degree	23.57	126	14.6

Note: Market shares may not sum to 100.0 because of rounding and missing categories by household type. "Asian" and "black" include Hispanics and non-Hispanics who identify themselves as being of the respective race alone. "Hispanic" includes people of any race who identify themselves as Hispanic. "Other" includes people who identify themselves as non-Hispanic and as Alaska Native, American Indian, Asian (who are also included in the "Asian" row), or Native Hawaiian or other Pacific Islander, as well as non-Hispanics reporting more than one race.
Source: Calculations by New Strategist based on the Bureau of Labor Statistics' 2012 Consumer Expenditure Survey

Pies, Tarts, and Turnovers

Best customers: Householders aged 35 to 54 and 65 to 74

Married couples with school-aged or older children at home

Households in the Northeast

Customer trends: Average household spending on pies, tarts, and turnovers is likely to continue to decline because the small generation X is in the best-customer lifestage.

The best customers of pies, tarts, and turnovers are households with children. Married couples with school-aged or older children at home spend 39 to 65 percent more than average on pies. Householders aged 35 to 54, many with children, spend 21 to 23 percent more than average on this item and control 45 percent of the market. Householders aged 65 to 74 spend 25 percent more than average on pies, tarts, and turnovers. Households in the Northeast spend 16 percent more.

Average household spending on pies, tarts, and turnovers fell 25 percent between 2000 and 2012, after adjusting for inflation. Behind the decline is the substitution of other snack categories for this one and the propensity to buy snacks from restaurants rather than grocery stores. Spending on pies, tarts, and turnovers is likely to continue to decline because the small generation X is in the best-customer lifestage.

Table 89. Pies, tarts, and turnovers

Total household spending	$1,668,418,560.00
Average household spends	13.41

	AVERAGE HOUSEHOLD SPENDING	BEST CUSTOMERS (index)	BIGGEST CUSTOMERS (market share)
AGE OF HOUSEHOLDER			
Average household	**$13.41**	**100**	**100.0%**
Under age 25	6.78	51	3.3
Aged 25 to 34	9.43	70	11.4
Aged 35 to 44	16.23	121	21.0
Aged 45 to 54	16.50	123	24.4
Aged 55 to 64	12.49	93	17.0
Aged 65 to 74	16.81	125	15.1
Aged 75 or older	10.87	81	7.9

	AVERAGE HOUSEHOLD SPENDING	BEST CUSTOMERS (index)	BIGGEST CUSTOMERS (market share)
HOUSEHOLD INCOME			
Average household	**$13.41**	**100**	**100.0%**
Under $20,000	8.38	62	13.1
$20,000 to $39,999	11.44	85	19.2
$40,000 to $49,999	9.95	74	6.6
$50,000 to $69,999	16.86	126	18.2
$70,000 to $79,999	17.52	131	7.3
$80,000 to $99,999	19.11	143	12.6
$100,000 or more	16.49	123	23.0
HOUSEHOLD TYPE			
Average household	**13.41**	**100**	**100.0**
Married couples	16.95	126	61.4
Married couples, no children	12.41	93	19.3
Married couples with children	19.55	146	34.3
Oldest child under age 6	14.27	106	4.9
Oldest child aged 6 to 17	22.10	165	19.6
Oldest child aged 18 or older	18.59	139	9.8
Single parent with child under age 18	13.01	97	5.1
Single person	7.95	59	17.6
RACE AND HISPANIC ORIGIN			
Average household	**13.41**	**100**	**100.0**
Asian	13.74	102	4.4
Black	9.92	74	9.3
Hispanic	9.42	70	8.8
Non-Hispanic white and other	14.64	109	81.9
REGION			
Average household	**13.41**	**100**	**100.0**
Northeast	15.61	116	21.0
Midwest	12.83	96	21.2
South	12.70	95	35.3
West	13.39	100	22.5
EDUCATION			
Average household	**13.41**	**100**	**100.0**
Less than high school graduate	7.07	53	6.9
High school graduate	15.30	114	28.4
Some college	11.11	83	17.1
Associate's degree	15.43	115	11.4
Bachelor's degree or more	15.25	114	35.9
Bachelor's degree	14.02	105	20.8
Master's, professional, doctoral degree	17.34	129	15.0

Note: Market shares may not sum to 100.0 because of rounding and missing categories by household type. "Asian" and "black" include Hispanics and non-Hispanics who identify themselves as being of the respective race alone. "Hispanic" includes people of any race who identify themselves as Hispanic. "Other" includes people who identify themselves as non-Hispanic and as Alaska Native, American Indian, Asian (who are also included in the "Asian" row), or Native Hawaiian or other Pacific Islander, as well as non-Hispanics reporting more than one race.
Source: Calculations by New Strategist based on the Bureau of Labor Statistics' 2012 Consumer Expenditure Survey

Pork Chops

Best customers:	**Householders aged 35 to 54**
	Married couples with school-aged or older children at home
	Single parents
	Blacks
	Households in the South
	Householders without a high school diploma
Customer trends:	**Average household spending on pork chops is likely to resume its decline**
	as the baby-boom generation ages and household size shrinks.

Households with children and households headed by blacks are the biggest spenders on pork chops. Married couples with school-aged or older children at home spend 35 to 47 percent more than average on this item. Single parents, whose spending approaches average on only a few items, spend 28 percent more than average on pork chops. Householders aged 35 to 54, most with children, spend 12 to 23 percent more. Black households spend 39 percent more than average on pork chops. Households in the South, where many blacks reside, spend 23 percent more than average on this item. Householders with no more than a high school education spend 18 to 21 percent more than average on pork chops.

Average household spending on pork chops fell by a steep 54 percent between 2000 and 2010, after adjusting for inflation, then climbed 12 percent between 2010 and 2012. Spending on pork chops had been in decline as Americans substituted fast food and deli items for home-cooked meals. The recent rise could be a sign of economic recovery and may be short-lived. Average household spending on pork chops is likely to resume its decline as the baby-boom generation ages and household size shrinks.

Table 90. Pork chops

Total household spending	$3,488,624,640.00
Average household spends	28.04

	AVERAGE HOUSEHOLD SPENDING	BEST CUSTOMERS (index)	BIGGEST CUSTOMERS (market share)
AGE OF HOUSEHOLDER			
Average household	**$28.04**	**100**	**100.0%**
Under age 25	17.04	61	4.0
Aged 25 to 34	26.29	94	15.2
Aged 35 to 44	34.46	123	21.3
Aged 45 to 54	31.32	112	22.1
Aged 55 to 64	29.11	104	19.0
Aged 65 to 74	28.65	102	12.3
Aged 75 or older	17.45	62	6.1

	AVERAGE HOUSEHOLD SPENDING	BEST CUSTOMERS (index)	BIGGEST CUSTOMERS (market share)
HOUSEHOLD INCOME			
Average household	**$28.04**	**100**	**100.0%**
Under $20,000	20.67	74	15.5
$20,000 to $39,999	27.26	97	21.9
$40,000 to $49,999	25.06	89	7.9
$50,000 to $69,999	29.23	104	15.1
$70,000 to $79,999	35.73	127	7.1
$80,000 to $99,999	33.64	120	10.6
$100,000 or more	32.34	115	21.6
HOUSEHOLD TYPE			
Average household	**28.04**	**100**	**100.0**
Married couples	33.54	120	58.1
Married couples, no children	28.29	101	21.0
Married couples with children	37.37	133	31.3
Oldest child under age 6	26.10	93	4.2
Oldest child aged 6 to 17	41.20	147	17.5
Oldest child aged 18 or older	37.98	135	9.6
Single parent with child under age 18	35.99	128	6.7
Single person	13.85	49	14.7
RACE AND HISPANIC ORIGIN			
Average household	**28.04**	**100**	**100.0**
Asian	26.53	95	4.1
Black	39.00	139	17.5
Hispanic	29.51	105	13.2
Non-Hispanic white and other	25.95	93	69.5
REGION			
Average household	**28.04**	**100**	**100.0**
Northeast	28.75	103	18.5
Midwest	22.39	80	17.7
South	34.57	123	45.9
West	22.27	79	17.9
EDUCATION			
Average household	**28.04**	**100**	**100.0**
Less than high school graduate	32.96	118	15.3
High school graduate	34.03	121	30.3
Some college	24.56	88	18.0
Associate's degree	27.08	97	9.5
Bachelor's degree or more	24.21	86	27.2
Bachelor's degree	22.67	81	16.1
Master's, professional, doctoral degree	26.82	96	11.1

Note: Market shares may not sum to 100.0 because of rounding and missing categories by household type. "Asian" and "black" include Hispanics and non-Hispanics who identify themselves as being of the respective race alone. "Hispanic" includes people of any race who identify themselves as Hispanic. "Other" includes people who identify themselves as non-Hispanic and as Alaska Native, American Indian, Asian (who are also included in the "Asian" row), or Native Hawaiian or other Pacific Islander, as well as non-Hispanics reporting more than one race.
Source: Calculations by New Strategist based on the Bureau of Labor Statistics' 2012 Consumer Expenditure Survey

Potato Chips and Other Snacks

Best customers: Householders aged 35 to 54

Married couples with children at home

Single parents

Customer trends: Average household spending on potato chips and other snacks may decline

because the small generation X is in the best-customer lifestage.

The best customers of potato chips and other snacks are households with children. Married couples with children at home spend 72 percent more than the average household on this item, the figure peaking among those with school-aged children at 93 percent more. Single parents, whose spending approaches average on only a few items, spend 2 percent more than average on potato chips. Householders aged 35 to 54, most with children at home, spend 28 to 29 percent more than average on potato chips and other snacks and control 48 percent of the market.

Average household spending on potato chips and other snacks increased 17 percent between 2000 and 2012, after adjusting for inflation. Americans' penchant for snack food was behind the increase, as was the growing variety of snacks on grocery store shelves. Average household spending on potato chips and other snacks may decline in the years ahead because the small generation X is in the best-customer lifestage.

Table 91. Potato chips and other snacks

Total household spending $13,883,581,440.00
Average household spends   111.59

	AVERAGE HOUSEHOLD SPENDING	BEST CUSTOMERS (index)	BIGGEST CUSTOMERS (market share)
AGE OF HOUSEHOLDER			
Average household	**$111.59**	**100**	**100.0%**
Under age 25	71.79	64	4.2
Aged 25 to 34	116.07	104	16.8
Aged 35 to 44	144.29	129	22.4
Aged 45 to 54	142.52	128	25.3
Aged 55 to 64	107.56	96	17.6
Aged 65 to 74	84.13	75	9.1
Aged 75 or older	48.88	44	4.3

	AVERAGE HOUSEHOLD SPENDING	BEST CUSTOMERS (index)	BIGGEST CUSTOMERS (market share)
HOUSEHOLD INCOME			
Average household	**$111.59**	**100**	**100.0%**
Under $20,000	61.11	55	11.5
$20,000 to $39,999	78.84	71	15.9
$40,000 to $49,999	101.06	91	8.0
$50,000 to $69,999	115.60	104	15.0
$70,000 to $79,999	149.57	134	7.5
$80,000 to $99,999	147.79	132	11.7
$100,000 or more	181.87	163	30.5
HOUSEHOLD TYPE			
Average household	**111.59**	**100**	**100.0**
Married couples	150.71	135	65.6
Married couples, no children	106.62	96	19.9
Married couples with children	191.88	172	40.4
Oldest child under age 6	136.74	123	5.6
Oldest child aged 6 to 17	214.89	193	22.9
Oldest child aged 18 or older	187.84	168	11.9
Single parent with child under age 18	113.87	102	5.4
Single person	47.68	43	12.7
RACE AND HISPANIC ORIGIN			
Average household	**111.59**	**100**	**100.0**
Asian	92.40	83	3.6
Black	69.45	62	7.8
Hispanic	101.70	91	11.4
Non-Hispanic white and other	120.43	108	81.0
REGION			
Average household	**111.59**	**100**	**100.0**
Northeast	101.33	91	16.4
Midwest	120.20	108	23.9
South	105.94	95	35.4
West	120.67	108	24.4
EDUCATION			
Average household	**111.59**	**100**	**100.0**
Less than high school graduate	90.22	81	10.6
High school graduate	92.90	83	20.8
Some college	105.10	94	19.4
Associate's degree	126.05	113	11.2
Bachelor's degree or more	133.92	120	37.8
Bachelor's degree	129.20	116	23.1
Master's, professional, doctoral degree	141.88	127	14.8

Note: Market shares may not sum to 100.0 because of rounding and missing categories by household type. "Asian" and "black" include Hispanics and non-Hispanics who identify themselves as being of the respective race alone. "Hispanic" includes people of any race who identify themselves as Hispanic. "Other" includes people who identify themselves as non-Hispanic and as Alaska Native, American Indian, Asian (who are also included in the "Asian" row), or Native Hawaiian or other Pacific Islander, as well as non-Hispanics reporting more than one race.
Source: Calculations by New Strategist based on the Bureau of Labor Statistics' 2012 Consumer Expenditure Survey

Potatoes, Fresh

Best customers: Householders aged 35 to 74

Married couples with school-aged or older children at home

Asians

Households in the Northeast

Customer trends: Average household spending on fresh potatoes may resume its decline as home cooking becomes less common, but only if discretionary income grows.

Families that cook meals from scratch are the best customers of fresh potatoes. Married couples with school-aged or older children at home spend 47 to 48 percent more than average on potatoes. Householders ranging in age from 35 to 74 spend 5 to 18 percent more than average on this item. Asian households spend 37 percent more than average on potatoes. Households in the Northeast outspend the average by 15 percent.

After declining 5 percent between 2000 and 2006, average household spending on fresh potatoes grew 8 percent between 2006 and 2012, after adjusting for inflation. Behind the increase is the renewed surge of home cooking in an effort to control spending. Average household spending on potatoes may resume its decline as home cooking becomes less common, but only if discretionary income grows.

Table 92. Potatoes, fresh

Total household spending $4,782,551,040.00
Average household spends   38.44

	AVERAGE HOUSEHOLD SPENDING	BEST CUSTOMERS (index)	BIGGEST CUSTOMERS (market share)
AGE OF HOUSEHOLDER			
Average household	**$38.44**	**100**	**100.0%**
Under age 25	25.57	67	4.4
Aged 25 to 34	33.70	88	14.2
Aged 35 to 44	41.84	109	18.9
Aged 45 to 54	45.52	118	23.4
Aged 55 to 64	40.69	106	19.4
Aged 65 to 74	40.33	105	12.6
Aged 75 or older	28.20	73	7.2

	AVERAGE HOUSEHOLD SPENDING	BEST CUSTOMERS (index)	BIGGEST CUSTOMERS (market share)
HOUSEHOLD INCOME			
Average household	**$38.44**	**100**	**100.0%**
Under $20,000	26.09	68	14.3
$20,000 to $39,999	31.23	81	18.3
$40,000 to $49,999	37.51	98	8.6
$50,000 to $69,999	39.93	104	15.0
$70,000 to $79,999	45.03	117	6.5
$80,000 to $99,999	45.66	119	10.5
$100,000 or more	54.66	142	26.6
HOUSEHOLD TYPE			
Average household	**38.44**	**100**	**100.0**
Married couples	48.85	127	61.7
Married couples, no children	41.94	109	22.7
Married couples with children	53.59	139	32.8
Oldest child under age 6	40.51	105	4.8
Oldest child aged 6 to 17	56.38	147	17.4
Oldest child aged 18 or older	57.06	148	10.5
Single parent with child under age 18	37.56	98	5.1
Single person	18.44	48	14.2
RACE AND HISPANIC ORIGIN			
Average household	**38.44**	**100**	**100.0**
Asian	52.68	137	5.9
Black	30.29	79	9.9
Hispanic	39.60	103	12.9
Non-Hispanic white and other	39.55	103	77.2
REGION			
Average household	**38.44**	**100**	**100.0**
Northeast	44.38	115	20.8
Midwest	37.54	98	21.7
South	36.75	96	35.6
West	37.32	97	21.9
EDUCATION			
Average household	**38.44**	**100**	**100.0**
Less than high school graduate	39.84	104	13.5
High school graduate	37.28	97	24.2
Some college	32.93	86	17.6
Associate's degree	43.57	113	11.2
Bachelor's degree or more	40.92	106	33.6
Bachelor's degree	40.15	104	20.8
Master's, professional, doctoral degree	42.22	110	12.7

Note: Market shares may not sum to 100.0 because of rounding and missing categories by household type. "Asian" and "black" include Hispanics and non-Hispanics who identify themselves as being of the respective race alone. "Hispanic" includes people of any race who identify themselves as Hispanic. "Other" includes people who identify themselves as non-Hispanic and as Alaska Native, American Indian, Asian (who are also included in the "Asian" row), or Native Hawaiian or other Pacific Islander, as well as non-Hispanics reporting more than one race.
Source: Calculations by New Strategist based on the Bureau of Labor Statistics' 2012 Consumer Expenditure Survey

Poultry Other than Chicken

Best customers: **Householders aged 35 to 64**
                                          Married couples with children at home
                                          Single parents
                                          Blacks

Customer trends: **Average household spending on poultry other than chicken is likely to resume its decline as home cooking becomes less common, but only if discretionary income grows.**

Middle-aged married couples, many with children, spend the most on poultry other than chicken (primarily turkey). Married couples with children at home spend 41 percent more than the average household on this item. Couples without children at home, many of them empty-nesters, spend 19 percent more than average on this item. Poultry other than chicken is one of the relatively few items on which single parents, with their lower incomes, spend an average amount. Householders ranging in age from 35 to 64, many with children at home, spend more than average on this item. Blacks spend 17 percent more than the average household on other poultry.

Average household spending on poultry other than chicken tumbled 21 percent between 2000 and 2006, after adjusting for inflation, then climbed by a small 1 percent between 2006 and 2012. Behind the decline was Americans' waning interest in cooking from scratch, and behind the increase was the reluctant return to home cooking. Average household spending on poultry other than chicken is likely to resume its decline as home cooking becomes less common, but only if discretionary income grows.

Table 93. Poultry other than chicken

Total household spending $4,085,821,440.00
Average household spends   32.84

	AVERAGE HOUSEHOLD SPENDING	BEST CUSTOMERS (index)	BIGGEST CUSTOMERS (market share)
AGE OF HOUSEHOLDER			
Average household	**$32.84**	**100**	**100.0%**
Under age 25	18.97	58	3.8
Aged 25 to 34	30.32	92	14.9
Aged 35 to 44	34.29	104	18.1
Aged 45 to 54	43.69	133	26.3
Aged 55 to 64	37.26	113	20.8
Aged 65 to 74	25.30	77	9.3
Aged 75 or older	22.95	70	6.8

	AVERAGE HOUSEHOLD SPENDING	BEST CUSTOMERS (index)	BIGGEST CUSTOMERS (market share)
HOUSEHOLD INCOME			
Average household	**$32.84**	**100**	**100.0%**
Under $20,000	19.51	59	12.5
$20,000 to $39,999	21.07	64	14.5
$40,000 to $49,999	26.13	80	7.0
$50,000 to $69,999	32.73	100	14.4
$70,000 to $79,999	38.61	118	6.6
$80,000 to $99,999	45.96	140	12.3
$100,000 or more	57.42	175	32.7
HOUSEHOLD TYPE			
Average household	**32.84**	**100**	**100.0**
Married couples	41.97	128	62.1
Married couples, no children	39.24	119	24.9
Married couples with children	46.23	141	33.1
Oldest child under age 6	38.60	118	5.4
Oldest child aged 6 to 17	46.07	140	16.7
Oldest child aged 18 or older	51.26	156	11.0
Single parent with child under age 18	33.28	101	5.3
Single person	16.18	49	14.6
RACE AND HISPANIC ORIGIN			
Average household	**32.84**	**100**	**100.0**
Asian	24.54	75	3.2
Black	38.32	117	14.7
Hispanic	25.68	78	9.8
Non-Hispanic white and other	33.13	101	75.7
REGION			
Average household	**32.84**	**100**	**100.0**
Northeast	32.11	98	17.7
Midwest	28.77	88	19.4
South	33.84	103	38.4
West	35.84	109	24.6
EDUCATION			
Average household	**32.84**	**100**	**100.0**
Less than high school graduate	22.97	70	9.1
High school graduate	25.43	77	19.3
Some college	32.22	98	20.2
Associate's degree	30.36	92	9.1
Bachelor's degree or more	43.47	132	41.7
Bachelor's degree	38.36	117	23.3
Master's, professional, doctoral degree	52.11	159	18.4

Note: Market shares may not sum to 100.0 because of rounding and missing categories by household type. "Asian" and "black" include Hispanics and non-Hispanics who identify themselves as being of the respective race alone. "Hispanic" includes people of any race who identify themselves as Hispanic. "Other" includes people who identify themselves as non-Hispanic and as Alaska Native, American Indian, Asian (who are also included in the "Asian" row), or Native Hawaiian or other Pacific Islander, as well as non-Hispanics reporting more than one race.
Source: Calculations by New Strategist based on the Bureau of Labor Statistics' 2012 Consumer Expenditure Survey

Prepared Food (except Desserts, Frozen Meals, and Salads)

Best customers:	**Householders aged 35 to 64** **Married couples with school-aged or older children at home** **Asians and Hispanics** **Households in the West**
Customer trends:	**Average household spending on prepared foods should resume its growth in the years ahead as grocery stores compete with restaurants for customers.**

Grocery stores increasingly offer fresh prepared foods as they compete with fast-food restaurants for customers. Americans have responded, the average household spending $148 on prepared foods (not including desserts, frozen meals, or salads) in 2012. The biggest spenders on prepared foods are the busiest—households with children. Married couples with school-aged or older children at home spend 63 to 81 percent more than average on this item. Householders aged 35 to 64, many with children at home, spend 11 to 15 percent more than average on prepared foods. Hispanic households, which tend to include more children than average, spend 16 percent more on prepared food. Asian households spend 19 percent more than average on this item. Households in the West, where many Hispanics and Asians reside, spend 40 percent more than average on prepared food.

Average household spending on prepared food from grocery stores rose by a substantial 53 percent between 2000 and 2006, after adjusting for inflation, then fell 2 percent between 2006 and 2012. Behind the earlier increase were consumers looking for eat-and-run convenience and the growing variety of prepared food offered by grocery store delis. Behind the more recent decline is the shift to more meals cooked from scratch following the Great Recession. Average household spending on prepared foods should resume its growth in the years ahead as grocery stores continue to compete with restaurants for customers.

Table 94. Prepared food (except desserts, frozen meals, and salads)

Total household spending	$18,389,928,960.00
Average household spends	147.81

	AVERAGE HOUSEHOLD SPENDING	BEST CUSTOMERS (index)	BIGGEST CUSTOMERS (market share)
AGE OF HOUSEHOLDER			
Average household	**$147.81**	**100**	**100.0%**
Under age 25	82.31	56	3.7
Aged 25 to 34	152.41	103	16.7
Aged 35 to 44	163.54	111	19.2
Aged 45 to 54	163.81	111	21.9
Aged 55 to 64	170.26	115	21.1
Aged 65 to 74	142.81	97	11.6
Aged 75 or older	88.38	60	5.8

	AVERAGE HOUSEHOLD SPENDING	BEST CUSTOMERS (index)	BIGGEST CUSTOMERS (market share)
HOUSEHOLD INCOME			
Average household	**$147.81**	**100**	**100.0%**
Under $20,000	96.39	65	13.7
$20,000 to $39,999	107.96	73	16.5
$40,000 to $49,999	131.05	89	7.8
$50,000 to $69,999	137.25	93	13.4
$70,000 to $79,999	179.92	122	6.8
$80,000 to $99,999	188.87	128	11.3
$100,000 or more	241.24	163	30.6
HOUSEHOLD TYPE			
Average household	**147.81**	**100**	**100.0**
Married couples	192.16	130	63.1
Married couples, no children	149.81	101	21.1
Married couples with children	232.60	157	37.0
Oldest child under age 6	153.52	104	4.7
Oldest child aged 6 to 17	241.58	163	19.4
Oldest child aged 18 or older	266.89	181	12.7
Single parent with child under age 18	132.06	89	4.7
Single person	73.68	50	14.8
RACE AND HISPANIC ORIGIN			
Average household	**147.81**	**100**	**100.0**
Asian	175.55	119	5.1
Black	93.07	63	7.9
Hispanic	170.85	116	14.5
Non-Hispanic white and other	153.41	104	77.9
REGION			
Average household	**147.81**	**100**	**100.0**
Northeast	114.39	77	14.0
Midwest	130.55	88	19.6
South	138.57	94	34.9
West	207.62	140	31.7
EDUCATION			
Average household	**147.81**	**100**	**100.0**
Less than high school graduate	164.25	111	14.5
High school graduate	122.37	83	20.6
Some college	143.27	97	20.0
Associate's degree	139.20	94	9.3
Bachelor's degree or more	167.09	113	35.7
Bachelor's degree	171.23	116	23.1
Master's, professional, doctoral degree	160.08	108	12.6

Note: Market shares may not sum to 100.0 because of rounding and missing categories by household type. "Asian" and "black" include Hispanics and non-Hispanics who identify themselves as being of the respective race alone. "Hispanic" includes people of any race who identify themselves as Hispanic. "Other" includes people who identify themselves as non-Hispanic and as Alaska Native, American Indian, Asian (who are also included in the "Asian" row), or Native Hawaiian or other Pacific Islander, as well as non-Hispanics reporting more than one race.
Source: Calculations by New Strategist based on the Bureau of Labor Statistics' 2012 Consumer Expenditure Survey

Prepared Food, Frozen (Other than Meals)

Best customers: Householders aged 25 to 54
Married couples with school-aged or older children at home
Single parents
Households in the Midwest

Customer trends: Average household spending on frozen prepared food other than meals
will continue to fall because of the growing preference for fresh food.

The biggest spenders on frozen prepared food other than meals are the busiest households—parents with children. Married couples with school-aged children spend 85 percent more than average on this item, and those with adult children at home spend 45 percent more. Single parents spend 17 percent more than average on frozen prepared food other than meals. Householders ranging in age from 25 to 54, most with children, spend 12 to 23 percent more than average on frozen prepared food. Households in the Midwest outspend the average by 17 percent.

Average household spending on frozen prepared food fell by 15 percent between 2000 and 2012, after adjusting for inflation. One factor behind the decline is the growing availability of fresh rather than frozen prepared food. Average household spending on frozen prepared food will continue to fall because of consumers' preference for fresh food.

Table 95. Prepared food, frozen (other than meals)

Total household spending $8,736,491,520.00
Average household spends   70.22

	AVERAGE HOUSEHOLD SPENDING	BEST CUSTOMERS (index)	BIGGEST CUSTOMERS (market share)
AGE OF HOUSEHOLDER			
Average household	**$70.22**	**100**	**100.0%**
Under age 25	61.76	88	5.8
Aged 25 to 34	86.04	123	19.8
Aged 35 to 44	78.80	112	19.5
Aged 45 to 54	86.02	123	24.2
Aged 55 to 64	65.28	93	17.0
Aged 65 to 74	48.77	69	8.4
Aged 75 or older	35.96	51	5.0

	AVERAGE HOUSEHOLD SPENDING	BEST CUSTOMERS (index)	BIGGEST CUSTOMERS (market share)
HOUSEHOLD INCOME			
Average household	**$70.22**	**100**	**100.0%**
Under $20,000	45.31	65	13.6
$20,000 to $39,999	58.69	84	18.8
$40,000 to $49,999	76.82	109	9.7
$50,000 to $69,999	81.13	116	16.7
$70,000 to $79,999	85.86	122	6.8
$80,000 to $99,999	78.03	111	9.8
$100,000 or more	90.28	129	24.1
HOUSEHOLD TYPE			
Average household	**70.22**	**100**	**100.0**
Married couples	85.41	122	59.1
Married couples, no children	58.76	84	17.4
Married couples with children	111.48	159	37.3
Oldest child under age 6	77.92	111	5.1
Oldest child aged 6 to 17	129.73	185	22.0
Oldest child aged 18 or older	101.94	145	10.2
Single parent with child under age 18	82.22	117	6.1
Single person	34.23	49	14.5
RACE AND HISPANIC ORIGIN			
Average household	**70.22**	**100**	**100.0**
Asian	51.52	73	3.2
Black	59.79	85	10.7
Hispanic	59.23	84	10.6
Non-Hispanic white and other	73.90	105	79.0
REGION			
Average household	**70.22**	**100**	**100.0**
Northeast	62.54	89	16.1
Midwest	82.07	117	25.9
South	68.96	98	36.6
West	66.69	95	21.4
EDUCATION			
Average household	**70.22**	**100**	**100.0**
Less than high school graduate	59.90	85	11.1
High school graduate	63.25	90	22.5
Some college	75.60	108	22.2
Associate's degree	75.90	108	10.7
Bachelor's degree or more	74.09	106	33.3
Bachelor's degree	77.24	110	21.9
Master's, professional, doctoral degree	68.76	98	11.4

Note: Market shares may not sum to 100.0 because of rounding and missing categories by household type. "Asian" and "black" include Hispanics and non-Hispanics who identify themselves as being of the respective race alone. "Hispanic" includes people of any race who identify themselves as Hispanic. "Other" includes people who identify themselves as non-Hispanic and as Alaska Native, American Indian, Asian (who are also included in the "Asian" row), or Native Hawaiian or other Pacific Islander, as well as non-Hispanics reporting more than one race.
Source: Calculations by New Strategist based on the Bureau of Labor Statistics' 2012 Consumer Expenditure Survey

Prepared Meals, Frozen

Best customers: Householders aged 45 to 54
Married couples with school-aged or older children at home
Single parents

Customer trends: Average household spending on frozen meals is likely to continue to decline
as grocery stores offer more of the fresh variety.

The biggest spenders on frozen meals are householders who want the least bother. Some are buying low-fat or low-carb frozen meals as part of a dietary regimen. Others are on the go and do not want to take the time to cook or stop at a restaurant. Married couples with school-aged or older children at home spend the most on frozen meals, 21 to 43 percent more than the average household. Even single parents, whose spending on most items is well below average, spend 23 percent more on this item. Spending on frozen prepared meals is 30 percent above average among householders aged 45 to 54.

Average household spending on frozen meals more than doubled between 2000 and 2006, after adjusting for inflation. It then fell 23 percent from 2006 to 2012. The earlier increase occurred as consumers demanded greater convenience in meal preparation and as the variety of frozen meals—including many ethnic options—expanded. The decline occurred in part because of budget cutting in face of the Great Recession and because grocery stores were offering more fresh prepared meals. Average household spending on frozen meals is likely to continue to decline as grocery stores offer more of the fresh variety.

Table 96. Prepared meals, frozen

Total household spending $7,540,853,760.00
Average household spends   60.61

	AVERAGE HOUSEHOLD SPENDING	BEST CUSTOMERS (index)	BIGGEST CUSTOMERS (market share)
AGE OF HOUSEHOLDER			
Average household	**$60.61**	**100**	**100.0%**
Under age 25	37.28	62	4.0
Aged 25 to 34	60.48	100	16.1
Aged 35 to 44	59.38	98	17.0
Aged 45 to 54	79.08	130	25.8
Aged 55 to 64	58.72	97	17.7
Aged 65 to 74	58.06	96	11.5
Aged 75 or older	47.97	79	7.7

	AVERAGE HOUSEHOLD SPENDING	BEST CUSTOMERS (index)	BIGGEST CUSTOMERS (market share)
HOUSEHOLD INCOME			
Average household	**$60.61**	**100**	**100.0%**
Under $20,000	46.02	76	16.0
$20,000 to $39,999	46.60	77	17.3
$40,000 to $49,999	52.37	86	7.6
$50,000 to $69,999	63.59	105	15.2
$70,000 to $79,999	75.42	124	6.9
$80,000 to $99,999	65.91	109	9.6
$100,000 or more	88.98	147	27.5
HOUSEHOLD TYPE			
Average household	**60.61**	**100**	**100.0**
Married couples	70.15	116	56.2
Married couples, no children	61.49	101	21.1
Married couples with children	75.65	125	29.3
Oldest child under age 6	63.62	105	4.8
Oldest child aged 6 to 17	73.57	121	14.4
Oldest child aged 18 or older	86.63	143	10.1
Single parent with child under age 18	74.39	123	6.4
Single person	44.23	73	21.7
RACE AND HISPANIC ORIGIN			
Average household	**60.61**	**100**	**100.0**
Asian	51.55	85	3.7
Black	46.52	77	9.6
Hispanic	41.95	69	8.7
Non-Hispanic white and other	66.03	109	81.8
REGION			
Average household	**60.61**	**100**	**100.0**
Northeast	60.56	100	18.0
Midwest	67.52	111	24.7
South	57.58	95	35.4
West	58.75	97	21.8
EDUCATION			
Average household	**60.61**	**100**	**100.0**
Less than high school graduate	43.38	72	9.3
High school graduate	49.20	81	20.2
Some college	64.92	107	22.1
Associate's degree	58.12	96	9.5
Bachelor's degree or more	73.77	122	38.4
Bachelor's degree	64.89	107	21.3
Master's, professional, doctoral degree	88.78	146	17.0

Note: Market shares may not sum to 100.0 because of rounding and missing categories by household type. "Asian" and "black" include Hispanics and non-Hispanics who identify themselves as being of the respective race alone. "Hispanic" includes people of any race who identify themselves as Hispanic. "Other" includes people who identify themselves as non-Hispanic and as Alaska Native, American Indian, Asian (who are also included in the "Asian" row), or Native Hawaiian or other Pacific Islander, as well as non-Hispanics reporting more than one race.
Source: Calculations by New Strategist based on the Bureau of Labor Statistics' 2012 Consumer Expenditure Survey

Rice

Best customers: Householders aged 35 to 54
Married couples with school-aged or older children at home
Single parents
Asians, Hispanics, and blacks
Households in the Northeast
Householders without a high school diploma

Customer trends: Average household spending on rice should decline as prepared food claims
a bigger share of the food dollar, but growing minority populations
may limit the drop.

Asian households are the biggest spenders on rice by far—they spend three-and-three-quarter times the average. Hispanics, who tend to have large families, spend 65 percent more than average, and blacks spend 18 percent more. Together the three groups, which represent 29 percent of the population, account for 52 percent of the market for rice. Married couples with school-aged or older children at home spend 41 to 50 percent more than the average household on this item. Single parents, whose spending approaches average on only a few items, outspend the average on rice by a solid 24 percent. Householders aged 35 to 54, most with children, spend 28 to 34 percent more than average on rice. Households in the Northeast outspend the average by 26 percent. Householders who did not complete high school, many of them Hispanic, spend 24 percent more than average on this item.

Average household spending on rice fell 23 percent between 2000 and 2006, then grew 31 percent between 2006 and 2010, after adjusting for inflation. Between 2010 and 2012, average household spending on rice declined 5 percent. Behind the 2006-to-2010 spending increase were growing Asian and Hispanic populations, a renewed surge of home cooking in an effort to rein in household spending because of the Great Recession, and soaring prices for rice. Spending on rice should continue its decline as prepared food claims a growing share of the food dollar, but growing minority populations may limit the drop.

Table 97. Rice

Total household spending $3,066,854,400.00
Average household spends   24.65

	AVERAGE HOUSEHOLD SPENDING	BEST CUSTOMERS (index)	BIGGEST CUSTOMERS (market share)
AGE OF HOUSEHOLDER			
Average household	**$24.65**	**100**	**100.0%**
Under age 25	25.33	103	6.7
Aged 25 to 34	27.06	110	17.7
Aged 35 to 44	31.53	128	22.2
Aged 45 to 54	33.08	134	26.6
Aged 55 to 64	17.86	72	13.3
Aged 65 to 74	15.39	62	7.5
Aged 75 or older	13.88	56	5.5

	AVERAGE HOUSEHOLD SPENDING	BEST CUSTOMERS (index)	BIGGEST CUSTOMERS (market share)
HOUSEHOLD INCOME			
Average household	**$24.65**	**100**	**100.0%**
Under $20,000	19.26	78	16.4
$20,000 to $39,999	20.54	83	18.8
$40,000 to $49,999	23.51	95	8.4
$50,000 to $69,999	24.41	99	14.3
$70,000 to $79,999	28.31	115	6.4
$80,000 to $99,999	26.39	107	9.4
$100,000 or more	34.54	140	26.2
HOUSEHOLD TYPE			
Average household	**24.65**	**100**	**100.0**
Married couples	28.68	116	56.5
Married couples, no children	18.18	74	15.4
Married couples with children	33.42	136	31.9
Oldest child under age 6	21.79	88	4.0
Oldest child aged 6 to 17	36.94	150	17.8
Oldest child aged 18 or older	34.81	141	10.0
Single parent with child under age 18	30.62	124	6.5
Single person	11.64	47	14.0
RACE AND HISPANIC ORIGIN			
Average household	**24.65**	**100**	**100.0**
Asian	91.55	371	16.1
Black	29.04	118	14.8
Hispanic	40.74	165	20.7
Non-Hispanic white and other	21.20	86	64.6
REGION			
Average household	**24.65**	**100**	**100.0**
Northeast	31.17	126	22.8
Midwest	22.48	91	20.2
South	21.95	89	33.2
West	26.02	106	23.8
EDUCATION			
Average household	**24.65**	**100**	**100.0**
Less than high school graduate	30.45	124	16.1
High school graduate	24.63	100	24.9
Some college	19.59	79	16.4
Associate's degree	21.44	87	8.6
Bachelor's degree or more	26.92	109	34.4
Bachelor's degree	24.70	100	20.0
Master's, professional, doctoral degree	30.66	124	14.4

Note: Market shares may not sum to 100.0 because of rounding and missing categories by household type. "Asian" and "black" include Hispanics and non-Hispanics who identify themselves as being of the respective race alone. "Hispanic" includes people of any race who identify themselves as Hispanic. "Other" includes people who identify themselves as non-Hispanic and as Alaska Native, American Indian, Asian (who are also included in the "Asian" row), or Native Hawaiian or other Pacific Islander, as well as non-Hispanics reporting more than one race.
Source: Calculations by New Strategist based on the Bureau of Labor Statistics' 2012 Consumer Expenditure Survey

Salad Dressing

Best customers:
Householders aged 35 to 74
Married couples without children at home
Married couples with school-aged or older children at home

Customer trends:
Average household spending on salad dressing may resume its decline
as the economy continues to recover from the Great Recession and
eating out and prepared food regain their popularity.

Older married couples spend the most on salad dressing. Householders ranging in age from 35 to 74 spend more than average on this item. Married couples without children at home (most empty-nesters) outspend the average on salad dressing by 23 percent. Married couples with school-aged children spend 34 percent more than the average household on salad dressing, and those with adult children at home spend 54 percent more.

Average household spending on salad dressing fell 18 percent between 2000 and 2006, after adjusting for inflation, but stabilized since then with a 5 percent gain between 2006 and 2012. The earlier spending decline was due to the growing popularity of fast food as well as prepared salads from grocery stores. The more recent gain reflects the return to home cooking in the wake of the Great Recession. Average household spending on salad dressing may resume its decline as the economy continues to recover and eating out and prepared food regain their popularity.

Table 98. Salad dressing

Total household spending $3,892,976,640.00
Average household spends   31.29

	AVERAGE HOUSEHOLD SPENDING	BEST CUSTOMERS (index)	BIGGEST CUSTOMERS (market share)
AGE OF HOUSEHOLDER			
Average household	**$31.29**	**100**	**100.0%**
Under age 25	19.27	62	4.0
Aged 25 to 34	26.81	86	13.9
Aged 35 to 44	32.90	105	18.3
Aged 45 to 54	36.28	116	22.9
Aged 55 to 64	34.81	111	20.4
Aged 65 to 74	33.97	109	13.1
Aged 75 or older	24.33	78	7.6

	AVERAGE HOUSEHOLD SPENDING	BEST CUSTOMERS (index)	BIGGEST CUSTOMERS (market share)
HOUSEHOLD INCOME			
Average household	**$31.29**	**100**	**100.0%**
Under $20,000	20.70	66	13.9
$20,000 to $39,999	23.65	76	17.0
$40,000 to $49,999	32.66	104	9.2
$50,000 to $69,999	34.15	109	15.8
$70,000 to $79,999	37.20	119	6.6
$80,000 to $99,999	37.97	121	10.7
$100,000 or more	44.53	142	26.6
HOUSEHOLD TYPE			
Average household	**31.29**	**100**	**100.0**
Married couples	41.85	134	65.0
Married couples, no children	38.34	123	25.5
Married couples with children	42.94	137	32.3
Oldest child under age 6	36.80	118	5.4
Oldest child aged 6 to 17	42.04	134	16.0
Oldest child aged 18 or older	48.26	154	10.9
Single parent with child under age 18	24.14	77	4.0
Single person	16.01	51	15.2
RACE AND HISPANIC ORIGIN			
Average household	**31.29**	**100**	**100.0**
Asian	15.93	51	2.2
Black	22.27	71	8.9
Hispanic	29.27	94	11.7
Non-Hispanic white and other	33.22	106	79.7
REGION			
Average household	**31.29**	**100**	**100.0**
Northeast	28.52	91	16.5
Midwest	34.24	109	24.3
South	30.09	96	35.8
West	32.58	104	23.5
EDUCATION			
Average household	**31.29**	**100**	**100.0**
Less than high school graduate	23.23	74	9.7
High school graduate	31.42	100	25.0
Some college	31.65	101	20.8
Associate's degree	33.50	107	10.6
Bachelor's degree or more	33.28	106	33.5
Bachelor's degree	32.63	104	20.8
Master's, professional, doctoral degree	34.37	110	12.7

Note: Market shares may not sum to 100.0 because of rounding and missing categories by household type. "Asian" and "black" include Hispanics and non-Hispanics who identify themselves as being of the respective race alone. "Hispanic" includes people of any race who identify themselves as Hispanic. "Other" includes people who identify themselves as non-Hispanic and as Alaska Native, American Indian, Asian (who are also included in the "Asian" row), or Native Hawaiian or other Pacific Islander, as well as non-Hispanics reporting more than one race.
Source: Calculations by New Strategist based on the Bureau of Labor Statistics' 2012 Consumer Expenditure Survey

Salads, Prepared

Best customers:	**Householders aged 35 to 74**
	Married couples without children at home
	Married couples with school-aged or older children at home
Customer trends:	**Average household spending on prepared salads will continue to rise**
	as consumers look for healthy, convenient meal options.

The best customers of prepared salads are older married couples. Householders ranging in age from 35 to 74 spend 6 to 19 percent more than the average household on this item. Married couples with adult children at home spend 23 percent more than average on prepared salads. Those with school-aged children outspend the average by 28 percent. Couples without children at home (most of them empty-nesters) spend one-third more than average on prepared salads.

Average household spending on prepared salads rose by a stunning 49 percent between 2000 and 2006, after adjusting for inflation, then fell 5 percent between 2006 and 2012. Behind the gain was Americans' growing demand for the convenience and quality of fresh prepared food. Behind the more recent decline was the shift to more meals cooked from scratch at home in an attempt to save money. Average household spending on prepared salads may resume its rise in the years ahead as consumers look for healthy, convenient meal options.

Table 99. Salads, prepared

Total household spending	$4,365,757,440.00
Average household spends	35.09

	AVERAGE HOUSEHOLD SPENDING	BEST CUSTOMERS (index)	BIGGEST CUSTOMERS (market share)
AGE OF HOUSEHOLDER			
Average household	**$35.09**	**100**	**100.0%**
Under age 25	15.95	45	3.0
Aged 25 to 34	30.86	88	14.2
Aged 35 to 44	37.07	106	18.3
Aged 45 to 54	41.07	117	23.2
Aged 55 to 64	38.02	108	19.8
Aged 65 to 74	41.87	119	14.4
Aged 75 or older	25.99	74	7.2

	AVERAGE HOUSEHOLD SPENDING	BEST CUSTOMERS (index)	BIGGEST CUSTOMERS (market share)
HOUSEHOLD INCOME			
Average household	**$35.09**	**100**	**100.0%**
Under $20,000	20.16	57	12.1
$20,000 to $39,999	27.13	77	17.4
$40,000 to $49,999	29.97	85	7.6
$50,000 to $69,999	34.45	98	14.2
$70,000 to $79,999	41.64	119	6.6
$80,000 to $99,999	40.44	115	10.2
$100,000 or more	59.95	171	32.0
HOUSEHOLD TYPE			
Average household	**35.09**	**100**	**100.0**
Married couples	43.86	125	60.7
Married couples, no children	46.82	133	27.8
Married couples with children	42.24	120	28.3
Oldest child under age 6	33.37	95	4.3
Oldest child aged 6 to 17	45.00	128	15.3
Oldest child aged 18 or older	43.14	123	8.7
Single parent with child under age 18	30.15	86	4.5
Single person	22.79	65	19.3
RACE AND HISPANIC ORIGIN			
Average household	**35.09**	**100**	**100.0**
Asian	32.48	93	4.0
Black	21.63	62	7.7
Hispanic	22.64	65	8.1
Non-Hispanic white and other	39.50	113	84.5
REGION			
Average household	**35.09**	**100**	**100.0**
Northeast	38.37	109	19.7
Midwest	38.48	110	24.3
South	28.72	82	30.5
West	39.60	113	25.4
EDUCATION			
Average household	**35.09**	**100**	**100.0**
Less than high school graduate	20.86	59	7.8
High school graduate	28.08	80	20.0
Some college	35.40	101	20.8
Associate's degree	36.91	105	10.4
Bachelor's degree or more	45.07	128	40.5
Bachelor's degree	40.55	116	23.0
Master's, professional, doctoral degree	52.72	150	17.4

Note: Market shares may not sum to 100.0 because of rounding and missing categories by household type. "Asian" and "black" include Hispanics and non-Hispanics who identify themselves as being of the respective race alone. "Hispanic" includes people of any race who identify themselves as Hispanic. "Other" includes people who identify themselves as non-Hispanic and as Alaska Native, American Indian, Asian (who are also included in the "Asian" row), or Native Hawaiian or other Pacific Islander, as well as non-Hispanics reporting more than one race.
Source: Calculations by New Strategist based on the Bureau of Labor Statistics' 2012 Consumer Expenditure Survey

Salt, Spices, and Other Seasonings

Best customers: Householders aged 35 to 54
                       Married couples with school-aged or older children at home
                       Asians

Customer trends: Average household spending on salt, spices, and other seasonings may decline
                       as household size shrinks with the aging of the population.

The biggest spenders on salt, spices, and other seasonings are households most likely to cook from scratch—married couples with children. Married couples with children at home spend 45 percent more than average on this item. Householders aged 35 to 54, many with children, spend 15 to 25 percent more than average on salt and spices. Asians outspend the average by 59 percent.

Average household spending on salt, spices, and other seasonings grew 41 percent between 2000 and 2012, after adjusting for inflation—despite the growing propensity of Americans to substitute prepared food for home-cooked meals. Behind the increase were changing tastes, with specialty flavorings growing in popularity. Spending on salt, spices, and other seasonings may decline in the years ahead as household size shrinks along with the aging of the population.

Table 100. Salt, spices, and other seasonings

Total household spending $4,817,387,520.00
Average household spends   38.72

	AVERAGE HOUSEHOLD SPENDING	BEST CUSTOMERS (index)	BIGGEST CUSTOMERS (market share)
AGE OF HOUSEHOLDER			
Average household	**$38.72**	**100**	**100.0%**
Under age 25	27.05	70	4.6
Aged 25 to 34	36.62	95	15.3
Aged 35 to 44	44.68	115	20.0
Aged 45 to 54	48.40	125	24.7
Aged 55 to 64	38.58	100	18.2
Aged 65 to 74	36.27	94	11.3
Aged 75 or older	22.77	59	5.7

	AVERAGE HOUSEHOLD SPENDING	BEST CUSTOMERS (index)	BIGGEST CUSTOMERS (market share)
HOUSEHOLD INCOME			
Average household	**$38.72**	**100**	**100.0%**
Under $20,000	24.53	63	13.3
$20,000 to $39,999	29.16	75	17.0
$40,000 to $49,999	35.40	91	8.1
$50,000 to $69,999	34.21	88	12.8
$70,000 to $79,999	47.04	121	6.8
$80,000 to $99,999	47.57	123	10.8
$100,000 or more	64.84	167	31.4
HOUSEHOLD TYPE			
Average household	**38.72**	**100**	**100.0**
Married couples	51.60	133	64.7
Married couples, no children	44.13	114	23.8
Married couples with children	56.32	145	34.2
Oldest child under age 6	42.82	111	5.0
Oldest child aged 6 to 17	58.74	152	18.0
Oldest child aged 18 or older	60.68	157	11.1
Single parent with child under age 18	36.66	95	5.0
Single person	16.06	41	12.3
RACE AND HISPANIC ORIGIN			
Average household	**38.72**	**100**	**100.0**
Asian	61.41	159	6.9
Black	34.18	88	11.1
Hispanic	42.01	108	13.6
Non-Hispanic white and other	38.97	101	75.5
REGION			
Average household	**38.72**	**100**	**100.0**
Northeast	38.78	100	18.1
Midwest	38.40	99	22.0
South	36.21	94	34.8
West	43.17	111	25.1
EDUCATION			
Average household	**38.72**	**100**	**100.0**
Less than high school graduate	38.18	99	12.9
High school graduate	33.70	87	21.7
Some college	34.58	89	18.4
Associate's degree	38.22	99	9.7
Bachelor's degree or more	45.76	118	37.3
Bachelor's degree	46.78	121	24.1
Master's, professional, doctoral degree	44.04	114	13.2

Note: Market shares may not sum to 100.0 because of rounding and missing categories by household type. "Asian" and "black" include Hispanics and non-Hispanics who identify themselves as being of the respective race alone. "Hispanic" includes people of any race who identify themselves as Hispanic. "Other" includes people who identify themselves as non-Hispanic and as Alaska Native, American Indian, Asian (who are also included in the "Asian" row), or Native Hawaiian or other Pacific Islander, as well as non-Hispanics reporting more than one race.
Source: Calculations by New Strategist based on the Bureau of Labor Statistics' 2012 Consumer Expenditure Survey

Sauces and Gravies

Best customers:	**Householders aged 35 to 54**
	Married couples with school-aged or older children at home
Customer trends:	**Average household spending on sauces and gravies is likely to decline as the small generation X passes through the best-customer lifestage and prepared food claims a growing share of the food dollar.**

Married couples with children at home, the householders most likely to cook from scratch, are the best customers of sauces and gravies. They spend 55 percent more than average on this item, the figure peaking among those with school-aged children at 69 percent more. Householders aged 35 to 54, most with children, spend 20 to 25 percent more than average on sauces and gravies.

Average household spending on sauces and gravies increased 21 percent between 2000 and 2012, after adjusting for inflation. Behind the increase are changing tastes, with specialty sauces growing in popularity. Average household spending on this item is likely to decline in the years ahead as the small generation X passes through the best-customer lifestage and prepared food claims a growing share of the food dollar.

Table 101. Sauces and gravies

Total household spending	$7,498,552,320.00
Average household spends	60.27

	AVERAGE HOUSEHOLD SPENDING	BEST CUSTOMERS (index)	BIGGEST CUSTOMERS (market share)
AGE OF HOUSEHOLDER			
Average household	**$60.27**	**100**	**100.0%**
Under age 25	35.37	59	3.8
Aged 25 to 34	59.78	99	16.0
Aged 35 to 44	72.31	120	20.8
Aged 45 to 54	75.54	125	24.8
Aged 55 to 64	60.60	101	18.4
Aged 65 to 74	50.91	84	10.2
Aged 75 or older	35.78	59	5.8

	AVERAGE HOUSEHOLD SPENDING	BEST CUSTOMERS (index)	BIGGEST CUSTOMERS (market share)
HOUSEHOLD INCOME			
Average household	**$60.27**	**100**	**100.0%**
Under $20,000	33.43	55	11.7
$20,000 to $39,999	47.05	78	17.6
$40,000 to $49,999	51.82	86	7.6
$50,000 to $69,999	63.25	105	15.2
$70,000 to $79,999	80.16	133	7.4
$80,000 to $99,999	76.92	128	11.3
$100,000 or more	94.19	156	29.3
HOUSEHOLD TYPE			
Average household	**60.27**	**100**	**100.0**
Married couples	80.06	133	64.5
Married couples, no children	64.47	107	22.3
Married couples with children	93.37	155	36.4
Oldest child under age 6	69.58	115	5.3
Oldest child aged 6 to 17	101.97	169	20.1
Oldest child aged 18 or older	93.84	156	11.0
Single parent with child under age 18	56.56	94	4.9
Single person	27.60	46	13.6
RACE AND HISPANIC ORIGIN			
Average household	**60.27**	**100**	**100.0**
Asian	51.90	86	3.7
Black	48.38	80	10.1
Hispanic	50.76	84	10.6
Non-Hispanic white and other	63.85	106	79.5
REGION			
Average household	**60.27**	**100**	**100.0**
Northeast	62.62	104	18.8
Midwest	63.14	105	23.2
South	53.41	89	33.0
West	66.88	111	25.0
EDUCATION			
Average household	**60.27**	**100**	**100.0**
Less than high school graduate	45.47	75	9.9
High school graduate	53.39	89	22.1
Some college	56.75	94	19.4
Associate's degree	73.03	121	12.0
Bachelor's degree or more	69.53	115	36.4
Bachelor's degree	69.04	115	22.8
Master's, professional, doctoral degree	70.35	117	13.5

Note: Market shares may not sum to 100.0 because of rounding and missing categories by household type. "Asian" and "black" include Hispanics and non-Hispanics who identify themselves as being of the respective race alone. "Hispanic" includes people of any race who identify themselves as Hispanic. "Other" includes people who identify themselves as non-Hispanic and as Alaska Native, American Indian, Asian (who are also included in the "Asian" row), or Native Hawaiian or other Pacific Islander, as well as non-Hispanics reporting more than one race.
Source: Calculations by New Strategist based on the Bureau of Labor Statistics' 2012 Consumer Expenditure Survey

Sausage

Best customers: Householders aged 35 to 54
     Married couples with school-aged or older children at home
     Single parents
     Blacks

Customer trends: Average household spending on sausage is likely to resume its decline
     in the years ahead because the small generation X is in the
     best-customer lifestage.

Households with children are the biggest spenders on sausage. Married couples with school-aged or older children at home spend 47 to 54 percent more than average on this item, and single parents, whose spending approaches average on only a few items, spend 8 percent more than average on sausage. Householders aged 35 to 54, many with children at home, spend 19 to 23 percent more than average on sausage. Blacks spend 20 percent more than average on this item.

Average household spending on sausage declined 13 percent between 2000 and 2006, after adjusting for inflation, and then climbed 9 percent between 2006 and 2012. The growing popularity of fast-food breakfasts rather than home-cooked meals during the period leading up to the Great Recession was one factor behind the earlier drop in spending. More home cooking in an attempt to save money is the reason for the recent increase. Average household spending on sausage is likely to resume its decline in the years ahead because the small generation X is in the best-customer lifestage.

Table 102. Sausage

Total household spending $3,998,730,240.00
Average household spends   32.14

	AVERAGE HOUSEHOLD SPENDING	BEST CUSTOMERS (index)	BIGGEST CUSTOMERS (market share)
AGE OF HOUSEHOLDER			
Average household	**$32.14**	**100**	**100.0%**
Under age 25	24.19	75	4.9
Aged 25 to 34	26.89	84	13.5
Aged 35 to 44	38.36	119	20.7
Aged 45 to 54	39.67	123	24.4
Aged 55 to 64	30.27	94	17.2
Aged 65 to 74	35.54	111	13.3
Aged 75 or older	18.91	59	5.8

	AVERAGE HOUSEHOLD SPENDING	BEST CUSTOMERS (index)	BIGGEST CUSTOMERS (market share)
HOUSEHOLD INCOME			
Average household	**$32.14**	**100**	**100.0%**
Under $20,000	23.69	74	15.5
$20,000 to $39,999	25.34	79	17.8
$40,000 to $49,999	26.28	82	7.2
$50,000 to $69,999	34.27	107	15.4
$70,000 to $79,999	41.48	129	7.2
$80,000 to $99,999	40.21	125	11.0
$100,000 or more	45.24	141	26.4
HOUSEHOLD TYPE			
Average household	**32.14**	**100**	**100.0**
Married couples	40.82	127	61.7
Married couples, no children	34.61	108	22.4
Married couples with children	45.91	143	33.6
Oldest child under age 6	35.99	112	5.1
Oldest child aged 6 to 17	47.40	147	17.5
Oldest child aged 18 or older	49.59	154	10.9
Single parent with child under age 18	34.86	108	5.7
Single person	15.01	47	13.9
RACE AND HISPANIC ORIGIN			
Average household	**32.14**	**100**	**100.0**
Asian	35.21	110	4.7
Black	38.45	120	15.0
Hispanic	33.48	104	13.1
Non-Hispanic white and other	30.85	96	72.0
REGION			
Average household	**32.14**	**100**	**100.0**
Northeast	34.18	106	19.2
Midwest	28.65	89	19.8
South	33.93	106	39.3
West	31.00	96	21.7
EDUCATION			
Average household	**32.14**	**100**	**100.0**
Less than high school graduate	37.31	116	15.2
High school graduate	33.67	105	26.1
Some college	28.19	88	18.1
Associate's degree	33.65	105	10.3
Bachelor's degree or more	31.21	97	30.6
Bachelor's degree	31.01	96	19.2
Master's, professional, doctoral degree	31.54	98	11.4

Note: Market shares may not sum to 100.0 because of rounding and missing categories by household type. "Asian" and "black" include Hispanics and non-Hispanics who identify themselves as being of the respective race alone. "Hispanic" includes people of any race who identify themselves as Hispanic. "Other" includes people who identify themselves as non-Hispanic and as Alaska Native, American Indian, Asian (who are also included in the "Asian" row), or Native Hawaiian or other Pacific Islander, as well as non-Hispanics reporting more than one race.
Source: Calculations by New Strategist based on the Bureau of Labor Statistics' 2012 Consumer Expenditure Survey

Soups, Canned and Packaged

Best customers: **Married couples without children at home**
                        Married couples with school-aged or older children at home
                        Households in the West

Customer trends: **Average household spending on soup may rise if the product promotes**
                        itself as an inexpensive convenience food.

Families with children are the best customers of soup. Couples with school-aged or older children at home spend 40 to 51 percent more than average on soup. Married couples without children at home, many of them older empty-nesters, spend 28 percent more than average on this item. Households in the West outspend the average by one-fifth.

Average household spending on canned and packaged soup has been fairly stable since 2000, rising 1 percent between 2000 and 2006 and falling 4 percent between 2006 and 2012, after adjusting for inflation. Spending on soup may rise if the product promotes itself as an inexpensive convenience food.

Table 103. Soups, canned and packaged

Total household spending	$5,760,460,800.00
Average household spends	46.30

	AVERAGE HOUSEHOLD SPENDING	BEST CUSTOMERS (index)	BIGGEST CUSTOMERS (market share)
AGE OF HOUSEHOLDER			
Average household	**$46.30**	**100**	**100.0%**
Under age 25	29.63	64	4.2
Aged 25 to 34	38.40	83	13.4
Aged 35 to 44	47.59	103	17.8
Aged 45 to 54	56.21	121	24.0
Aged 55 to 64	45.27	98	17.9
Aged 65 to 74	54.07	117	14.1
Aged 75 or older	41.05	89	8.7

	AVERAGE HOUSEHOLD SPENDING	BEST CUSTOMERS (index)	BIGGEST CUSTOMERS (market share)
HOUSEHOLD INCOME			
Average household	**$46.30**	**100**	**100.0%**
Under $20,000	31.45	68	14.3
$20,000 to $39,999	38.13	82	18.6
$40,000 to $49,999	43.47	94	8.3
$50,000 to $69,999	46.27	100	14.4
$70,000 to $79,999	47.49	103	5.7
$80,000 to $99,999	58.13	126	11.1
$100,000 or more	68.17	147	27.6
HOUSEHOLD TYPE			
Average household	**46.30**	**100**	**100.0**
Married couples	60.48	131	63.4
Married couples, no children	59.16	128	26.6
Married couples with children	62.94	136	32.0
Oldest child under age 6	46.32	100	4.6
Oldest child aged 6 to 17	64.98	140	16.7
Oldest child aged 18 or older	69.89	151	10.7
Single parent with child under age 18	39.69	86	4.5
Single person	25.91	56	16.6
RACE AND HISPANIC ORIGIN			
Average household	**46.30**	**100**	**100.0**
Asian	46.13	100	4.3
Black	27.29	59	7.4
Hispanic	34.12	74	9.2
Non-Hispanic white and other	51.52	111	83.5
REGION			
Average household	**46.30**	**100**	**100.0**
Northeast	44.82	97	17.5
Midwest	47.31	102	22.7
South	40.72	88	32.8
West	55.75	120	27.1
EDUCATION			
Average household	**46.30**	**100**	**100.0**
Less than high school graduate	38.39	83	10.8
High school graduate	37.58	81	20.2
Some college	48.00	104	21.4
Associate's degree	48.53	105	10.4
Bachelor's degree or more	54.16	117	36.9
Bachelor's degree	53.71	116	23.1
Master's, professional, doctoral degree	54.94	119	13.8

Note: Market shares may not sum to 100.0 because of rounding and missing categories by household type. "Asian" and "black" include Hispanics and non-Hispanics who identify themselves as being of the respective race alone. "Hispanic" includes people of any race who identify themselves as Hispanic. "Other" includes people who identify themselves as non-Hispanic and as Alaska Native, American Indian, Asian (who are also included in the "Asian" row), or Native Hawaiian or other Pacific Islander, as well as non-Hispanics reporting more than one race.
Source: Calculations by New Strategist based on the Bureau of Labor Statistics' 2012 Consumer Expenditure Survey

Sports Drinks

Best customers:	**Householders aged 25 to 54**
	Married couples with school-aged or older children at home
	Single parents
	Hispanics
	Households in the Midwest
Customer trends:	**Average household spending on sports drinks may stabilize in the years ahead because they are being marketed as a healthy alternative to sodas.**

The biggest spenders on sports drinks are the largest households. Married couples with children at home spend 68 percent more than average on this item. Those with school-aged children spend nearly twice the average on this item. Householders aged 35 to 44, most of them parents, spend 57 percent more than average on sports drinks. Together with the adjacent younger and older age groups, which spend 11 to 12 percent more than average on sports drinks, they control two-thirds of the market. Single parents, whose spending approaches average on only a few items, spend 9 percent more than average on sports drinks. Hispanics, who have the largest families, outspend the average by 40 percent. Households in the Midwest spend 12 percent more than average on sports drinks.

Sports drinks is a recently added category in the Consumer Expenditure Survey, and there are no comparative spending data from 2000 or 2006. Between 2010 and 2012, however, average household spending on sports drinks declined by a substantial 25 percent. Spending on this item may stabilize in the years ahead because sports drinks are being marketed as a healthy alternative to sodas.

Table 104. Sports drinks

Total household spending $1,881,169,920.00
Average household spends   15.12

	AVERAGE HOUSEHOLD SPENDING	BEST CUSTOMERS (index)	BIGGEST CUSTOMERS (market share)
AGE OF HOUSEHOLDER			
Average household	**$15.12**	**100**	**100.0%**
Under age 25	11.13	74	4.8
Aged 25 to 34	16.96	112	18.1
Aged 35 to 44	23.78	157	27.3
Aged 45 to 54	16.84	111	22.0
Aged 55 to 64	12.35	82	14.9
Aged 65 to 74	10.00	66	8.0
Aged 75 or older	6.74	45	4.4

	AVERAGE HOUSEHOLD SPENDING	BEST CUSTOMERS (index)	BIGGEST CUSTOMERS (market share)
HOUSEHOLD INCOME			
Average household	**$15.12**	**100**	**100.0%**
Under $20,000	7.54	50	10.5
$20,000 to $39,999	10.92	72	16.3
$40,000 to $49,999	12.38	82	7.2
$50,000 to $69,999	16.81	111	16.1
$70,000 to $79,999	16.57	110	6.1
$80,000 to $99,999	16.46	109	9.6
$100,000 or more	27.65	183	34.2
HOUSEHOLD TYPE			
Average household	**15.12**	**100**	**100.0**
Married couples	19.12	126	61.4
Married couples, no children	11.64	77	16.0
Married couples with children	25.36	168	39.4
Oldest child under age 6	14.99	99	4.5
Oldest child aged 6 to 17	29.57	196	23.3
Oldest child aged 18 or older	24.79	164	11.6
Single parent with child under age 18	16.43	109	5.7
Single person	7.49	50	14.7
RACE AND HISPANIC ORIGIN			
Average household	**15.12**	**100**	**100.0**
Asian	7.18	47	2.1
Black	12.29	81	10.2
Hispanic	21.10	140	17.5
Non-Hispanic white and other	14.76	98	73.3
REGION			
Average household	**15.12**	**100**	**100.0**
Northeast	12.86	85	15.4
Midwest	16.96	112	24.9
South	14.81	98	36.5
West	15.64	103	23.3
EDUCATION			
Average household	**15.12**	**100**	**100.0**
Less than high school graduate	14.71	97	12.7
High school graduate	13.16	87	21.7
Some college	13.71	91	18.7
Associate's degree	21.46	142	14.0
Bachelor's degree or more	15.77	104	32.9
Bachelor's degree	17.01	113	22.4
Master's, professional, doctoral degree	13.67	90	10.5

Note: Market shares may not sum to 100.0 because of rounding and missing categories by household type. "Asian" and "black" include Hispanics and non-Hispanics who identify themselves as being of the respective race alone. "Hispanic" includes people of any race who identify themselves as Hispanic. "Other" includes people who identify themselves as non-Hispanic and as Alaska Native, American Indian, Asian (who are also included in the "Asian" row), or Native Hawaiian or other Pacific Islander, as well as non-Hispanics reporting more than one race.
Source: Calculations by New Strategist based on the Bureau of Labor Statistics' 2012 Consumer Expenditure Survey

Sugar

Best customers: Householders aged 35 to 54
Married couples with school-aged or older children at home
Single parents
Hispanics and blacks
Householders with no more than a high school diploma

Customer trends: Average household spending on sugar is likely to resume its decline as the small generation X passes through the best-customer lifestage.

The biggest spenders on sugar are households that do the most cooking from scratch, typically families with children. Couples with school-aged or older children at home spend 35 to 62 percent more than average on sugar. Single parents spend 15 percent more. Householders aged 35 to 54, most with children, spend 9 to 24 percent more than average on this item. Hispanics, who tend to have large families, spend 30 percent more than average on sugar, and blacks spend 20 percent more. Householders with no more than a high school diploma, many of them Hispanic, spend 26 percent more than average on sugar.

Average household spending on sugar fell 16 percent between 2000 and 2006, after adjusting for inflation, then grew 29 percent between 2006 and 2012. Behind the earlier decline was the rise in popularity of prepared food as busy families found less time to cook from scratch. The rise since 2006 is due in part to more home cooking in the aftermath of the Great Recession. Average household spending on sugar is likely to resume its decline as the small generation X passes through the best-customer lifestage.

Table 105. Sugar

Total household spending $3,033,262,080.00
Average household spends   24.38

	AVERAGE HOUSEHOLD SPENDING	BEST CUSTOMERS (index)	BIGGEST CUSTOMERS (market share)
AGE OF HOUSEHOLDER			
Average household	**$24.38**	**100**	**100.0%**
Under age 25	21.22	87	5.7
Aged 25 to 34	23.80	98	15.8
Aged 35 to 44	30.30	124	21.6
Aged 45 to 54	26.51	109	21.5
Aged 55 to 64	23.60	97	17.7
Aged 65 to 74	21.72	89	10.7
Aged 75 or older	17.07	70	6.8

	AVERAGE HOUSEHOLD SPENDING	BEST CUSTOMERS (index)	BIGGEST CUSTOMERS (market share)
HOUSEHOLD INCOME			
Average household	**$24.38**	**100**	**100.0%**
Under $20,000	20.53	84	17.7
$20,000 to $39,999	21.26	87	19.7
$40,000 to $49,999	26.56	109	9.6
$50,000 to $69,999	30.66	126	18.2
$70,000 to $79,999	26.68	109	6.1
$80,000 to $99,999	22.45	92	8.1
$100,000 or more	26.28	108	20.2
HOUSEHOLD TYPE			
Average household	**24.38**	**100**	**100.0**
Married couples	29.41	121	58.6
Married couples, no children	23.33	96	19.9
Married couples with children	33.35	137	32.2
Oldest child under age 6	24.72	101	4.6
Oldest child aged 6 to 17	32.95	135	16.1
Oldest child aged 18 or older	39.42	162	11.4
Single parent with child under age 18	28.15	115	6.1
Single person	11.56	47	14.1
RACE AND HISPANIC ORIGIN			
Average household	**24.38**	**100**	**100.0**
Asian	23.53	97	4.2
Black	29.23	120	15.1
Hispanic	31.75	130	16.3
Non-Hispanic white and other	22.37	92	68.9
REGION			
Average household	**24.38**	**100**	**100.0**
Northeast	24.04	99	17.8
Midwest	25.33	104	23.0
South	26.11	107	39.9
West	20.84	85	19.3
EDUCATION			
Average household	**24.38**	**100**	**100.0**
Less than high school graduate	30.70	126	16.4
High school graduate	30.61	126	31.3
Some college	22.70	93	19.2
Associate's degree	23.85	98	9.7
Bachelor's degree or more	18.51	76	23.9
Bachelor's degree	18.53	76	15.1
Master's, professional, doctoral degree	18.47	76	8.8

Note: Market shares may not sum to 100.0 because of rounding and missing categories by household type. "Asian" and "black" include Hispanics and non-Hispanics who identify themselves as being of the respective race alone. "Hispanic" includes people of any race who identify themselves as Hispanic. "Other" includes people who identify themselves as non-Hispanic and as Alaska Native, American Indian, Asian (who are also included in the "Asian" row), or Native Hawaiian or other Pacific Islander, as well as non-Hispanics reporting more than one race.
Source: Calculations by New Strategist based on the Bureau of Labor Statistics' 2012 Consumer Expenditure Survey

Sweetrolls, Coffee Cakes, and Doughnuts

Best customers: Married couples with school-aged or older children at home
Hispanics and Asians
Households in the West

Customer trends: Average household spending on sweetrolls, coffee cakes, and doughnuts
may decline in the years ahead because the small generation X is in the
best-customer lifestage.

The biggest spenders on sweetrolls, coffee cakes, and doughnuts are households with children. Married couples with school-aged or older children at home spend 42 to 46 percent more than average on this item. Hispanics and Asians outspend the average by 18 and 12 percent, respectively. Households in the West, where many Asians and Hispanics reside, spend 19 percent more than average on sweetrolls, coffee cakes, and doughnuts.

Average household spending on sweetrolls, coffee cakes, and doughnuts fell 22 percent between 2000 and 2006, after adjusting for inflation, and was essentially flat between 2006 and 2012. Behind the spending decline was the growing propensity of Americans to grab snacks from restaurants rather than grocery stores. Average household spending on sweetrolls, coffee cakes, and doughnuts may decline in the years ahead because the small generation X is in the best-customer lifestage.

Table 106. Sweetrolls, coffee cakes, and doughnuts

| Total household spending | $2,952,391,680.00 |
| Average household spends | 23.73 |

	AVERAGE HOUSEHOLD SPENDING	BEST CUSTOMERS (index)	BIGGEST CUSTOMERS (market share)
AGE OF HOUSEHOLDER			
Average household	**$23.73**	**100**	**100.0%**
Under age 25	13.82	58	3.8
Aged 25 to 34	17.24	73	11.7
Aged 35 to 44	25.89	109	18.9
Aged 45 to 54	26.69	112	22.3
Aged 55 to 64	25.65	108	19.8
Aged 65 to 74	25.10	106	12.7
Aged 75 or older	26.62	112	11.0

	AVERAGE HOUSEHOLD SPENDING	BEST CUSTOMERS (index)	BIGGEST CUSTOMERS (market share)
HOUSEHOLD INCOME			
Average household	**$23.73**	**100**	**100.0%**
Under $20,000	15.33	65	13.6
$20,000 to $39,999	18.26	77	17.3
$40,000 to $49,999	24.09	102	9.0
$50,000 to $69,999	31.33	132	19.1
$70,000 to $79,999	21.12	89	5.0
$80,000 to $99,999	24.79	104	9.2
$100,000 or more	33.85	143	26.7
HOUSEHOLD TYPE			
Average household	**23.73**	**100**	**100.0**
Married couples	30.18	127	61.8
Married couples, no children	25.57	108	22.5
Married couples with children	31.89	134	31.6
Oldest child under age 6	21.69	91	4.2
Oldest child aged 6 to 17	34.66	146	17.4
Oldest child aged 18 or older	33.63	142	10.0
Single parent with child under age 18	22.58	95	5.0
Single person	12.51	53	15.7
RACE AND HISPANIC ORIGIN			
Average household	**23.73**	**100**	**100.0**
Asian	26.52	112	4.8
Black	16.04	68	8.5
Hispanic	28.07	118	14.8
Non-Hispanic white and other	24.35	103	77.0
REGION			
Average household	**23.73**	**100**	**100.0**
Northeast	24.51	103	18.6
Midwest	24.50	103	22.9
South	20.21	85	31.7
West	28.18	119	26.8
EDUCATION			
Average household	**23.73**	**100**	**100.0**
Less than high school graduate	24.74	104	13.6
High school graduate	23.91	101	25.1
Some college	23.75	100	20.6
Associate's degree	24.50	103	10.2
Bachelor's degree or more	22.96	97	30.5
Bachelor's degree	21.67	91	18.2
Master's, professional, doctoral degree	25.15	106	12.3

Note: Market shares may not sum to 100.0 because of rounding and missing categories by household type. "Asian" and "black" include Hispanics and non-Hispanics who identify themselves as being of the respective race alone. "Hispanic" includes people of any race who identify themselves as Hispanic. "Other" includes people who identify themselves as non-Hispanic and as Alaska Native, American Indian, Asian (who are also included in the "Asian" row), or Native Hawaiian or other Pacific Islander, as well as non-Hispanics reporting more than one race.
Source: Calculations by New Strategist based on the Bureau of Labor Statistics' 2012 Consumer Expenditure Survey

Tea

Best customers: Householders aged 35 to 64
Married couples with school-aged or older children at home
Single parents
Asians
Households in the Northeast

Customer trends: Average household spending on tea may rise because of the introduction
of new products and tea's touted health benefits.

Although the media frequently tout the nutritional benefits of tea, Americans still spend far less on tea than on coffee. For some years tea was closing in. In 2010, the average household spent 48 percent as much on tea as on coffee, up from 37 percent in 2000. With the recent surge in coffee spending, however, the ratio declined again, to 35 percent in 2012. The middle aged are the best customers of tea, with householders ranging in age from 35 to 64 spending 8 to 17 percent more than average on this item. Married couples with school-aged or older children at home spend 49 to 50 percent more than average on tea. Single parents, whose spending approaches average on only a few items, spend 13 percent more than average on tea. Asian householders outspend the average by 54 percent. Households in the Northeast spend 22 percent more than average on tea.

Average household spending on tea purchased at grocery or convenience stores rose by a substantial 47 percent between 2000 and 2010, after adjusting for inflation, but declined slightly (down 1 percent) from 2010 to 2012. Behind the rise in spending on tea are the health and nutritional claims for green and black tea, as well as the greater variety of tea available in grocery stores. Average household spending on tea may resume its rise because of the introduction of new products and tea's touted health benefits.

Table 107. Tea

Total household spending $3,777,269,760.00
Average household spends   30.36

	AVERAGE HOUSEHOLD SPENDING	BEST CUSTOMERS (index)	BIGGEST CUSTOMERS (market share)
AGE OF HOUSEHOLDER			
Average household	**$30.36**	**100**	**100.0%**
Under age 25	19.86	65	4.3
Aged 25 to 34	28.98	95	15.4
Aged 35 to 44	32.82	108	18.8
Aged 45 to 54	35.48	117	23.1
Aged 55 to 64	33.73	111	20.3
Aged 65 to 74	29.98	99	11.9
Aged 75 or older	19.21	63	6.2

	AVERAGE HOUSEHOLD SPENDING	BEST CUSTOMERS (index)	BIGGEST CUSTOMERS (market share)
HOUSEHOLD INCOME			
Average household	**$30.36**	**100**	**100.0%**
Under $20,000	19.06	63	13.2
$20,000 to $39,999	22.02	73	16.3
$40,000 to $49,999	31.96	105	9.3
$50,000 to $69,999	33.76	111	16.1
$70,000 to $79,999	52.19	172	9.6
$80,000 to $99,999	33.02	109	9.6
$100,000 or more	41.28	136	25.5
HOUSEHOLD TYPE			
Average household	**30.36**	**100**	**100.0**
Married couples	38.76	128	62.0
Married couples, no children	34.07	112	23.4
Married couples with children	41.42	136	32.1
Oldest child under age 6	24.79	82	3.7
Oldest child aged 6 to 17	45.15	149	17.7
Oldest child aged 18 or older	45.54	150	10.6
Single parent with child under age 18	34.43	113	5.9
Single person	14.49	48	14.2
RACE AND HISPANIC ORIGIN			
Average household	**30.36**	**100**	**100.0**
Asian	46.79	154	6.7
Black	20.00	66	8.3
Hispanic	30.07	99	12.4
Non-Hispanic white and other	32.15	106	79.5
REGION			
Average household	**30.36**	**100**	**100.0**
Northeast	36.99	122	22.0
Midwest	29.72	98	21.7
South	27.79	92	34.1
West	29.88	98	22.2
EDUCATION			
Average household	**30.36**	**100**	**100.0**
Less than high school graduate	26.90	89	11.6
High school graduate	28.36	93	23.3
Some college	27.98	92	19.0
Associate's degree	38.43	127	12.5
Bachelor's degree or more	32.29	106	33.5
Bachelor's degree	31.24	103	20.5
Master's, professional, doctoral degree	34.07	112	13.0

Note: Market shares may not sum to 100.0 because of rounding and missing categories by household type. "Asian" and "black" include Hispanics and non-Hispanics who identify themselves as being of the respective race alone. "Hispanic" includes people of any race who identify themselves as Hispanic. "Other" includes people who identify themselves as non-Hispanic and as Alaska Native, American Indian, Asian (who are also included in the "Asian" row), or Native Hawaiian or other Pacific Islander, as well as non-Hispanics reporting more than one race.
Source: Calculations by New Strategist based on the Bureau of Labor Statistics' 2012 Consumer Expenditure Survey

Tomatoes

Best customers: Householders aged 35 to 54
Married couples with children at home
Asians and Hispanics
Households in the Northeast and West

Customer trends: Average household spending on fresh tomatoes may grow along
with the Asian and Hispanic populations.

The best customers of fresh tomatoes are the largest households. Married couples with children at home spend 40 percent more than average on tomatoes. Householders ranging in age from 35 to 54, many with children, spend 11 to 24 percent more than average on this item. Asians spend 48 percent more than average on tomatoes, and Hispanics—who have the largest families—spend 44 percent more. Households in the West, where many Asians and Hispanics live, spend 23 percent more than average on tomatoes. Households in the Northeast spend 10 percent more.

Average household spending on fresh tomatoes was essentially unchanged between 2000 and 2012, after adjusting for inflation. Although the small generation X is in the best-customer lifestage, average household spending on tomatoes may grow in the years ahead as the Asian and Hispanic populations grow.

Table 108. Tomatoes

Total household spending $4,895,769,600.00
Average household spends   39.35

	AVERAGE HOUSEHOLD SPENDING	BEST CUSTOMERS (index)	BIGGEST CUSTOMERS (market share)
AGE OF HOUSEHOLDER			
Average household	**$39.35**	**100**	**100.0%**
Under age 25	25.26	64	4.2
Aged 25 to 34	38.04	97	15.6
Aged 35 to 44	43.71	111	19.3
Aged 45 to 54	48.87	124	24.6
Aged 55 to 64	37.92	96	17.6
Aged 65 to 74	37.09	94	11.4
Aged 75 or older	29.30	74	7.3

	AVERAGE HOUSEHOLD SPENDING	BEST CUSTOMERS (index)	BIGGEST CUSTOMERS (market share)
HOUSEHOLD INCOME			
Average household	**$39.35**	**100**	**100.0%**
Under $20,000	24.11	61	12.9
$20,000 to $39,999	33.15	84	19.0
$40,000 to $49,999	38.41	98	8.6
$50,000 to $69,999	36.83	94	13.5
$70,000 to $79,999	45.89	117	6.5
$80,000 to $99,999	43.83	111	9.8
$100,000 or more	61.51	156	29.3
HOUSEHOLD TYPE			
Average household	**39.35**	**100**	**100.0**
Married couples	51.36	131	63.4
Married couples, no children	43.33	110	23.0
Married couples with children	55.27	140	33.0
Oldest child under age 6	44.65	113	5.2
Oldest child aged 6 to 17	54.81	139	16.6
Oldest child aged 18 or older	62.65	159	11.2
Single parent with child under age 18	30.66	78	4.1
Single person	21.58	55	16.3
RACE AND HISPANIC ORIGIN			
Average household	**39.35**	**100**	**100.0**
Asian	58.16	148	6.4
Black	24.92	63	8.0
Hispanic	56.70	144	18.1
Non-Hispanic white and other	38.89	99	74.2
REGION			
Average household	**39.35**	**100**	**100.0**
Northeast	43.37	110	19.9
Midwest	38.39	98	21.6
South	32.57	83	30.8
West	48.34	123	27.7
EDUCATION			
Average household	**39.35**	**100**	**100.0**
Less than high school graduate	42.72	109	14.2
High school graduate	34.83	89	22.1
Some college	32.92	84	17.2
Associate's degree	38.92	99	9.8
Bachelor's degree or more	46.07	117	36.9
Bachelor's degree	43.23	110	21.9
Master's, professional, doctoral degree	50.86	129	15.0

Note: Market shares may not sum to 100.0 because of rounding and missing categories by household type. "Asian" and "black" include Hispanics and non-Hispanics who identify themselves as being of the respective race alone. "Hispanic" includes people of any race who identify themselves as Hispanic. "Other" includes people who identify themselves as non-Hispanic and as Alaska Native, American Indian, Asian (who are also included in the "Asian" row), or Native Hawaiian or other Pacific Islander, as well as non-Hispanics reporting more than one race.
Source: Calculations by New Strategist based on the Bureau of Labor Statistics' 2012 Consumer Expenditure Survey

Vegetables, Canned

Best customers:
Householders aged 35 to 64
Married couples with school-aged or older children at home
Households in the Midwest

Customer trends:
Average household spending on canned vegetables is likely to decline in the years ahead as the large baby-boom generation ages and household size shrinks.

The largest households spend the most on canned vegetables. Married couples with school-aged or older children at home spend 39 to 46 percent more than average on canned vegetables. Householders aged 35 to 64, many with children, spend 7 to 14 percent more than average on this item. Households in the Midwest outspend the average by 12 percent.

Average household spending on canned vegetables fell 12 percent between 2000 and 2006, after adjusting for inflation, then climbed 25 percent between 2006 and 2012. Behind the decline in the earlier part of the decade was the greater propensity to eat out. The increase in spending during the later part of the decade was due to more home cooking in the aftermath of the Great Recession. Average household spending on canned vegetables is likely to decline in the years ahead as the large baby-boom generation ages and household size shrinks.

Table 109. Vegetables, canned

Total household spending $6,791,869,440.00
Average household spends   54.59

	AVERAGE HOUSEHOLD SPENDING	BEST CUSTOMERS (index)	BIGGEST CUSTOMERS (market share)
AGE OF HOUSEHOLDER			
Average household	**$54.59**	**100**	**100.0%**
Under age 25	43.97	81	5.3
Aged 25 to 34	50.31	92	14.9
Aged 35 to 44	59.42	109	18.9
Aged 45 to 54	62.30	114	22.6
Aged 55 to 64	58.39	107	19.6
Aged 65 to 74	53.57	98	11.8
Aged 75 or older	38.78	71	6.9

	AVERAGE HOUSEHOLD SPENDING	BEST CUSTOMERS (index)	BIGGEST CUSTOMERS (market share)
HOUSEHOLD INCOME			
Average household	**$54.59**	**100**	**100.0%**
Under $20,000	36.02	66	13.9
$20,000 to $39,999	45.84	84	18.9
$40,000 to $49,999	51.82	95	8.4
$50,000 to $69,999	53.91	99	14.3
$70,000 to $79,999	63.31	116	6.5
$80,000 to $99,999	64.30	118	10.4
$100,000 or more	80.13	147	27.5
HOUSEHOLD TYPE			
Average household	**54.59**	**100**	**100.0**
Married couples	68.11	125	60.6
Married couples, no children	60.47	111	23.1
Married couples with children	73.08	134	31.5
Oldest child under age 6	55.65	102	4.7
Oldest child aged 6 to 17	75.67	139	16.5
Oldest child aged 18 or older	79.62	146	10.3
Single parent with child under age 18	52.86	97	5.1
Single person	28.68	53	15.6
RACE AND HISPANIC ORIGIN			
Average household	**54.59**	**100**	**100.0**
Asian	42.40	78	3.4
Black	45.91	84	10.6
Hispanic	55.14	101	12.7
Non-Hispanic white and other	56.00	103	77.0
REGION			
Average household	**54.59**	**100**	**100.0**
Northeast	54.28	99	17.9
Midwest	61.15	112	24.8
South	54.12	99	36.9
West	49.08	90	20.3
EDUCATION			
Average household	**54.59**	**100**	**100.0**
Less than high school graduate	50.56	93	12.1
High school graduate	54.77	100	25.0
Some college	52.49	96	19.8
Associate's degree	61.57	113	11.1
Bachelor's degree or more	55.20	101	31.9
Bachelor's degree	56.40	103	20.6
Master's, professional, doctoral degree	53.18	97	11.3

Note: Market shares may not sum to 100.0 because of rounding and missing categories by household type. "Asian" and "black" include Hispanics and non-Hispanics who identify themselves as being of the respective race alone. "Hispanic" includes people of any race who identify themselves as Hispanic. "Other" includes people who identify themselves as non-Hispanic and as Alaska Native, American Indian, Asian (who are also included in the "Asian" row), or Native Hawaiian or other Pacific Islander, as well as non-Hispanics reporting more than one race.
Source: Calculations by New Strategist based on the Bureau of Labor Statistics' 2012 Consumer Expenditure Survey

Vegetables, Dried

Best customers: **Householders aged 45 to 54**

                                 Married couples with school-aged or older children at home

                                 Single parents

                                 Asians and Hispanics

                                 Householders without a high school diploma

Customer trends: **Average household spending on dried vegetables may continue to increase along with the Asian and Hispanic populations.**

The biggest spenders on dried vegetables are Asian and Hispanic households, which spend 84 and 70 percent, respectively, more than the average household on this item and account for 29 percent of the market. Householders aged 45 to 54 outspend the average by 44 percent. Married couples with school-aged children spend 33 percent more than average on dried vegetables and those with adult children at home spend 63 percent more. Single parents, whose spending approaches average on only a few items, spend 4 percent more than average on dried vegetables. Householders without a high school diploma, many of them Hispanic, spend 37 percent more than average on dried vegetables.

Average household spending on dried vegetables increased 30 percent between 2000 and 2012, after adjusting for inflation. Behind this increase was growth of the Asian and Hispanic populations. Spending on dried vegetables may continue to increase along with the Asian and Hispanic populations.

Table 110. Vegetables, dried

Total household spending	$2,266,859,520.00
Average household spends	18.22

	AVERAGE HOUSEHOLD SPENDING	BEST CUSTOMERS (index)	BIGGEST CUSTOMERS (market share)
AGE OF HOUSEHOLDER			
Average household	**$18.22**	**100**	**100.0%**
Under age 25	10.44	57	3.8
Aged 25 to 34	16.34	90	14.5
Aged 35 to 44	19.43	107	18.5
Aged 45 to 54	26.16	144	28.4
Aged 55 to 64	16.95	93	17.0
Aged 65 to 74	18.86	104	12.5
Aged 75 or older	9.88	54	5.3

	AVERAGE HOUSEHOLD SPENDING	BEST CUSTOMERS (index)	BIGGEST CUSTOMERS (market share)
HOUSEHOLD INCOME			
Average household	**$18.22**	**100**	**100.0%**
Under $20,000	–	–	–
$20,000 to $39,999	17.07	94	21.1
$40,000 to $49,999	16.86	93	8.2
$50,000 to $69,999	18.37	101	14.6
$70,000 to $79,999	21.11	116	6.5
$80,000 to $99,999	17.95	99	8.7
$100,000 or more	22.23	122	22.8
HOUSEHOLD TYPE			
Average household	**18.22**	**100**	**100.0**
Married couples	21.84	120	58.2
Married couples, no children	16.40	90	18.8
Married couples with children	24.27	133	31.3
Oldest child under age 6	15.53	85	3.9
Oldest child aged 6 to 17	24.31	133	15.9
Oldest child aged 18 or older	29.68	163	11.5
Single parent with child under age 18	18.86	104	5.4
Single person	8.79	48	14.3
RACE AND HISPANIC ORIGIN			
Average household	**18.22**	**100**	**100.0**
Asian	33.52	184	8.0
Black	16.92	93	11.7
Hispanic	31.00	170	21.3
Non-Hispanic white and other	16.30	89	67.1
REGION			
Average household	**18.22**	**100**	**100.0**
Northeast	15.29	84	15.1
Midwest	19.27	106	23.4
South	17.58	96	35.9
West	20.63	113	25.5
EDUCATION			
Average household	**18.22**	**100**	**100.0**
Less than high school graduate	24.89	137	17.8
High school graduate	19.48	107	26.7
Some college	17.64	97	19.9
Associate's degree	18.21	100	9.9
Bachelor's degree or more	15.16	83	26.2
Bachelor's degree	13.43	74	14.7
Master's, professional, doctoral degree	18.07	99	11.5

Note: Market shares may not sum to 100.0 because of rounding and missing categories by household type. "Asian" and "black" include Hispanics and non-Hispanics who identify themselves as being of the respective race alone. "Hispanic" includes people of any race who identify themselves as Hispanic. "Other" includes people who identify themselves as non-Hispanic and as Alaska Native, American Indian, Asian (who are also included in the "Asian" row), or Native Hawaiian or other Pacific Islander, as well as non-Hispanics reporting more than one race. "–" means sample is too small to make a reliable estimate. Source: Calculations by New Strategist based on the Bureau of Labor Statistics' 2012 Consumer Expenditure Survey

Vegetables, Fresh, Total

Best customers:	**Householders aged 35 to 74**
	Married couples
	Asians and Hispanics
	Households in the West
Customer trends:	**Average household spending on fresh vegetables may continue to rise as consumers opt for fresh vegetables over frozen and canned, but prepared meals may limit the increase.**

Fresh vegetables are the second-largest grocery category in terms of household spending. The best customers of fresh vegetables are middle-aged and older married couples. Householders ranging in age from 35 to 74 spend more than average on this item. Married couples spend 32 percent more, the figure peaking at 47 percent among couples with adult children at home. Asians spend 71 percent more than average on fresh vegetables, and Hispanics spend 15 percent more. Households in the West, where many Asians and Hispanics reside and where high-quality fresh vegetables are available in abundance, spend 22 percent more than average on fresh vegetables.

Average household spending on fresh vegetables rose slowly but steadily over the entire 2000-to-2012 time period, after adjusting for inflation, gaining 7 percent overall. Average household spending on fresh vegetables may continue to rise as consumers opt for fresh vegetables over frozen and canned, but prepared meals may limit the increase.

Table 111. Vegetables, fresh, total

Total household spending	$28,135,434,240.00
Average household spends	226.14

	AVERAGE HOUSEHOLD SPENDING	BEST CUSTOMERS (index)	BIGGEST CUSTOMERS (market share)
AGE OF HOUSEHOLDER			
Average household	**$226.14**	**100**	**100.0%**
Under age 25	128.49	57	3.7
Aged 25 to 34	208.36	92	14.9
Aged 35 to 44	243.26	108	18.7
Aged 45 to 54	269.33	119	23.6
Aged 55 to 64	234.43	104	19.0
Aged 65 to 74	242.22	107	12.9
Aged 75 or older	169.44	75	7.3

	AVERAGE HOUSEHOLD SPENDING	BEST CUSTOMERS (index)	BIGGEST CUSTOMERS (market share)
HOUSEHOLD INCOME			
Average household	**$226.14**	**100**	**100.0%**
Under $20,000	135.71	60	12.6
$20,000 to $39,999	176.11	78	17.6
$40,000 to $49,999	209.28	93	8.2
$50,000 to $69,999	216.96	96	13.9
$70,000 to $79,999	267.51	118	6.6
$80,000 to $99,999	272.62	121	10.6
$100,000 or more	367.96	163	30.5
HOUSEHOLD TYPE			
Average household	**226.14**	**100**	**100.0**
Married couples	298.36	132	64.1
Married couples, no children	272.08	120	25.1
Married couples with children	317.32	140	33.0
Oldest child under age 6	260.26	115	5.3
Oldest child aged 6 to 17	329.64	146	17.3
Oldest child aged 18 or older	332.34	147	10.4
Single parent with child under age 18	176.69	78	4.1
Single person	118.25	52	15.5
RACE AND HISPANIC ORIGIN			
Average household	**226.14**	**100**	**100.0**
Asian	385.62	171	7.4
Black	148.65	66	8.3
Hispanic	259.06	115	14.4
Non-Hispanic white and other	233.73	103	77.6
REGION			
Average household	**226.14**	**100**	**100.0**
Northeast	249.49	110	19.9
Midwest	205.63	91	20.2
South	197.55	87	32.5
West	275.23	122	27.4
EDUCATION			
Average household	**226.14**	**100**	**100.0**
Less than high school graduate	212.98	94	12.3
High school graduate	191.57	85	21.1
Some college	185.27	82	16.9
Associate's degree	227.44	101	9.9
Bachelor's degree or more	284.97	126	39.7
Bachelor's degree	271.17	120	23.9
Master's, professional, doctoral degree	308.31	136	15.8

Note: Market shares may not sum to 100.0 because of rounding and missing categories by household type. "Asian" and "black" include Hispanics and non-Hispanics who identify themselves as being of the respective race alone. "Hispanic" includes people of any race who identify themselves as Hispanic. "Other" includes people who identify themselves as non-Hispanic and as Alaska Native, American Indian, Asian (who are also included in the "Asian" row), or Native Hawaiian or other Pacific Islander, as well as non-Hispanics reporting more than one race.
Source: Calculations by New Strategist based on the Bureau of Labor Statistics' 2012 Consumer Expenditure Survey

Vegetables, Frozen

Best customers: Householders aged 35 to 54
Married couples with school-aged or older children at home
Single parents
Households in the Northeast

Customer trends: Average household spending on frozen vegetables is likely to decline in the years ahead as Americans opt for the fresh variety and prepared food claims a growing share of the food dollar.

The largest households are the best customers of frozen vegetables. Married couples with school-aged children spend 49 percent more than average on this item and those with adult children at home spend 73 percent more. Householders aged 35 to 54, most with children, spend 15 to 19 percent more than average on frozen vegetables. Single parents, whose spending approaches average on only a few items, spend 12 percent more than average on frozen vegetables. Households in the Northeast spend 18 percent more.

Average household spending on frozen vegetables fell by 1 percent between 2000 and 2006, after adjusting for inflation, as fewer households cooked meals at home. Then the trend reversed and spending on frozen vegetables grew 8 percent between 2006 and 2012 as household belt tightening caused a renewed interest in home cooking. Average household spending on frozen vegetables is likely to decline in the years ahead as Americans opt for the fresh variety and prepared food claims a growing share of the food dollar.

Table 112. Vegetables, frozen

Total household spending $4,665,600,000.00
Average household spends   37.50

	AVERAGE HOUSEHOLD SPENDING	BEST CUSTOMERS (index)	BIGGEST CUSTOMERS (market share)
AGE OF HOUSEHOLDER			
Average household	**$37.50**	**100**	**100.0%**
Under age 25	18.91	50	3.3
Aged 25 to 34	39.02	104	16.8
Aged 35 to 44	43.03	115	19.9
Aged 45 to 54	44.50	119	23.5
Aged 55 to 64	37.42	100	18.3
Aged 65 to 74	35.27	94	11.3
Aged 75 or older	26.22	70	6.8

	AVERAGE HOUSEHOLD SPENDING	BEST CUSTOMERS (index)	BIGGEST CUSTOMERS (market share)
HOUSEHOLD INCOME			
Average household	**$37.50**	**100**	**100.0%**
Under $20,000	26.03	69	14.6
$20,000 to $39,999	28.85	77	17.3
$40,000 to $49,999	28.07	75	6.6
$50,000 to $69,999	38.32	102	14.8
$70,000 to $79,999	47.20	126	7.0
$80,000 to $99,999	53.59	143	12.6
$100,000 or more	54.59	146	27.3
HOUSEHOLD TYPE			
Average household	**37.50**	**100**	**100.0**
Married couples	47.95	128	62.1
Married couples, no children	39.99	107	22.2
Married couples with children	54.74	146	34.3
Oldest child under age 6	34.83	93	4.2
Oldest child aged 6 to 17	55.99	149	17.8
Oldest child aged 18 or older	65.06	173	12.2
Single parent with child under age 18	42.01	112	5.9
Single person	19.54	52	15.5
RACE AND HISPANIC ORIGIN			
Average household	**37.50**	**100**	**100.0**
Asian	26.13	70	3.0
Black	39.32	105	13.2
Hispanic	24.87	66	8.3
Non-Hispanic white and other	39.25	105	78.6
REGION			
Average household	**37.50**	**100**	**100.0**
Northeast	44.28	118	21.3
Midwest	38.50	103	22.8
South	37.68	100	37.4
West	30.70	82	18.4
EDUCATION			
Average household	**37.50**	**100**	**100.0**
Less than high school graduate	31.78	85	11.1
High school graduate	35.28	94	23.5
Some college	39.61	106	21.8
Associate's degree	38.19	102	10.1
Bachelor's degree or more	39.73	106	33.4
Bachelor's degree	39.86	106	21.2
Master's, professional, doctoral degree	39.51	105	12.2

Note: Market shares may not sum to 100.0 because of rounding and missing categories by household type. "Asian" and "black" include Hispanics and non-Hispanics who identify themselves as being of the respective race alone. "Hispanic" includes people of any race who identify themselves as Hispanic. "Other" includes people who identify themselves as non-Hispanic and as Alaska Native, American Indian, Asian (who are also included in the "Asian" row), or Native Hawaiian or other Pacific Islander, as well as non-Hispanics reporting more than one race.
Source: Calculations by New Strategist based on the Bureau of Labor Statistics' 2012 Consumer Expenditure Survey

Vegetable Juice, Fresh and Canned

Best customers:	**Householders aged 35 to 54**
	Married couples with children at home
	Single parents
	Asians
Customer trends:	**Average household spending on vegetable juice may continue to rise**
	in the years ahead as the large millennial generation has children.

The biggest spenders on vegetable juice are households with children. Married couples with school-aged children spend 53 percent more than average on vegetable juice, and those with adult children at home spend 52 percent more. Householders aged 35 to 54, most of them parents, spend 12 to 35 percent more than average on vegetable juice. Single parents, whose spending approaches average on only a few items, spend 21 percent more than the average household on vegetable juice. Asians outspend the average by 23 percent.

Average household spending on vegetable juice purchased at grocery or convenience stores has risen steadily. It grew 12 percent between 2000 and 2006, after adjusting for inflation, and 37 percent between 2006 and 2012. Spending on vegetable juice may continue to increase in the years ahead as the large millennial generation has children.

Table 113. Vegetable juice, fresh and canned

Total household spending	$2,361,415,680.00
Average household spends	18.98

	AVERAGE HOUSEHOLD SPENDING	BEST CUSTOMERS (index)	BIGGEST CUSTOMERS (market share)
AGE OF HOUSEHOLDER			
Average household	**$18.98**	**100**	**100.0%**
Under age 25	15.50	82	5.4
Aged 25 to 34	19.99	105	17.0
Aged 35 to 44	21.26	112	19.4
Aged 45 to 54	25.58	135	26.7
Aged 55 to 64	16.47	87	15.9
Aged 65 to 74	13.40	71	8.5
Aged 75 or older	13.33	70	6.9

	AVERAGE HOUSEHOLD SPENDING	BEST CUSTOMERS (index)	BIGGEST CUSTOMERS (market share)
HOUSEHOLD INCOME			
Average household	**$18.98**	**100**	**100.0%**
Under $20,000	12.90	68	14.3
$20,000 to $39,999	16.36	86	19.4
$40,000 to $49,999	20.87	110	9.7
$50,000 to $69,999	16.46	87	12.5
$70,000 to $79,999	22.09	116	6.5
$80,000 to $99,999	23.72	125	11.0
$100,000 or more	26.72	141	26.4
HOUSEHOLD TYPE			
Average household	**18.98**	**100**	**100.0**
Married couples	22.84	120	58.4
Married couples, no children	16.09	85	17.7
Married couples with children	27.97	147	34.6
Oldest child under age 6	23.83	126	5.7
Oldest child aged 6 to 17	28.99	153	18.2
Oldest child aged 18 or older	28.84	152	10.7
Single parent with child under age 18	23.01	121	6.4
Single person	10.06	53	15.7
RACE AND HISPANIC ORIGIN			
Average household	**18.98**	**100**	**100.0**
Asian	23.29	123	5.3
Black	16.29	86	10.8
Hispanic	20.00	105	13.2
Non-Hispanic white and other	19.24	101	76.1
REGION			
Average household	**18.98**	**100**	**100.0**
Northeast	21.78	115	20.7
Midwest	20.78	109	24.3
South	14.65	77	28.7
West	22.08	116	26.2
EDUCATION			
Average household	**18.98**	**100**	**100.0**
Less than high school graduate	16.02	84	11.0
High school graduate	17.93	94	23.6
Some college	16.87	89	18.3
Associate's degree	25.61	135	13.3
Bachelor's degree or more	20.24	107	33.6
Bachelor's degree	19.63	103	20.6
Master's, professional, doctoral degree	21.26	112	13.0

Note: Market shares may not sum to 100.0 because of rounding and missing categories by household type. "Asian" and "black" include Hispanics and non-Hispanics who identify themselves as being of the respective race alone. "Hispanic" includes people of any race who identify themselves as Hispanic. "Other" includes people who identify themselves as non-Hispanic and as Alaska Native, American Indian, Asian (who are also included in the "Asian" row), or Native Hawaiian or other Pacific Islander, as well as non-Hispanics reporting more than one race.
Source: Calculations by New Strategist based on the Bureau of Labor Statistics' 2012 Consumer Expenditure Survey

Water, Bottled

Best customers: Householders aged 35 to 54

Married couples with school-aged or older children at home

Single parents

Hispanics and Asians

Customer trends: Average household spending on bottled water may climb in the years ahead

as Americans question the quality of tap water and search for alternatives

to calorie-laden colas and fruit drinks.

The biggest spenders on bottled water are the largest households. Householders aged 35 to 54, many with children, spend 19 to 29 percent more than average on bottled water and control 46 percent of spending on this item. Married couples with school-aged or older children at home spend one-half more than average on this item, and single parents, whose spending is below average on most items, spend 14 percent more than average on bottled water. Asians spend 22 percent more than average on bottled water, and Hispanics, who have the largest families, spend 33 percent more. Bottled water is one of the relatively few items in the Consumer Expenditure Survey on which non-Hispanic whites spend (slightly) less than average.

Bottled water is a relatively new category in the Consumer Expenditure Survey, and there are no comparative spending data from 2000. Between 2006 and 2010, spending on bottled water declined 13 percent, in part because less expensive alternatives entered the market. Spending rebounded with a 4 percent increase between 2010 and 2012. Average household spending on bottled water may climb in the years ahead as Americans question the quality of tap water and search for alternatives to calorie-laden colas and fruit drinks.

Table 114. Water, bottled

Total household spending	$7,066,828,800.00		
Average household spends	56.80		

	AVERAGE HOUSEHOLD SPENDING	BEST CUSTOMERS (index)	BIGGEST CUSTOMERS (market share)
AGE OF HOUSEHOLDER			
Average household	**$56.80**	**100**	**100.0%**
Under age 25	42.01	74	4.9
Aged 25 to 34	54.25	96	15.4
Aged 35 to 44	67.82	119	20.7
Aged 45 to 54	73.49	129	25.6
Aged 55 to 64	55.05	97	17.7
Aged 65 to 74	49.54	87	10.5
Aged 75 or older	28.87	51	5.0

	AVERAGE HOUSEHOLD SPENDING	BEST CUSTOMERS (index)	BIGGEST CUSTOMERS (market share)
HOUSEHOLD INCOME			
Average household	**$56.80**	**100**	**100.0%**
Under $20,000	37.34	66	13.8
$20,000 to $39,999	44.69	79	17.7
$40,000 to $49,999	54.20	95	8.4
$50,000 to $69,999	56.22	99	14.3
$70,000 to $79,999	69.45	122	6.8
$80,000 to $99,999	75.20	132	11.7
$100,000 or more	82.32	145	27.1
HOUSEHOLD TYPE			
Average household	**56.80**	**100**	**100.0**
Married couples	67.37	119	57.6
Married couples, no children	52.49	92	19.3
Married couples with children	77.56	137	32.1
Oldest child under age 6	41.22	73	3.3
Oldest child aged 6 to 17	86.44	152	18.1
Oldest child aged 18 or older	85.38	150	10.6
Single parent with child under age 18	65.03	114	6.0
Single person	35.30	62	18.5
RACE AND HISPANIC ORIGIN			
Average household	**56.80**	**100**	**100.0**
Asian	69.52	122	5.3
Black	53.84	95	11.9
Hispanic	75.45	133	16.7
Non-Hispanic white and other	54.39	96	71.9
REGION			
Average household	**56.80**	**100**	**100.0**
Northeast	60.98	107	19.4
Midwest	49.99	88	19.5
South	58.06	102	38.1
West	58.14	102	23.1
EDUCATION			
Average household	**56.80**	**100**	**100.0**
Less than high school graduate	58.10	102	13.4
High school graduate	55.22	97	24.2
Some college	53.13	94	19.3
Associate's degree	62.15	109	10.8
Bachelor's degree or more	58.33	103	32.4
Bachelor's degree	55.61	98	19.5
Master's, professional, doctoral degree	62.92	111	12.9

Note: Market shares may not sum to 100.0 because of rounding and missing categories by household type. "Asian" and "black" include Hispanics and non-Hispanics who identify themselves as being of the respective race alone. "Hispanic" includes people of any race who identify themselves as Hispanic. "Other" includes people who identify themselves as non-Hispanic and as Alaska Native, American Indian, Asian (who are also included in the "Asian" row), or Native Hawaiian or other Pacific Islander, as well as non-Hispanics reporting more than one race.
Source: Calculations by New Strategist based on the Bureau of Labor Statistics' 2012 Consumer Expenditure Survey

Spending by Product and Service Ranked by Amount Spent, 2012

(average annual spending of consumer units on products and services, ranked by amount spent, 2012)

1.	Deductions for Social Security	$4,040.62
2.	Groceries (also shown by individual category)	3,920.65
3.	Vehicle purchases (net outlay)	3,210.49
4.	Mortgage interest (or rent, $3,064.09)	2,926.47
5.	Gasoline and motor oil	2,755.78
6.	Restaurants (also shown by meal category)	2,225.50
7.	Health insurance	2,060.78
8.	Property taxes	1,835.60
9.	Federal income taxes	1,568.33
10.	Electricity	1,387.83
11.	Dinner at restaurants	1,082.12
12.	Vehicle insurance	1,017.94
13.	Cellular phone service	861.97
14.	College tuition	824.99
15.	Vehicle maintenance and repairs	814.27
16.	Lunch at restaurants	746.81
17.	Cash contributions to church, religious organizations	734.30
18.	Cable and satellite television services	661.76
19.	Nonpayroll deposit to retirement plans	582.46
20.	Maintenance and repair services, owner	578.78
21.	Women's apparel	572.53
22.	State and local income taxes	526.08
23.	Deductions for private pensions	511.80
24.	Cash gifts to members of other households	464.50
25.	Alcoholic beverages	451.16
26.	Water and sewerage maintenance	398.56
27.	Prescription drugs	366.40
28.	Natural gas	359.35
29.	Residential telephone service and pay phones	358.54
30.	Homeowner's insurance	353.80
31.	Life and other personal insurance	352.61
32.	Airline fares	352.53
33.	Lodging on trips	341.61
34.	Computer information services	336.30
35.	Men's apparel	319.73
36.	Cigarettes	298.75
37.	Personal care services	292.83
38.	Dental services	268.32
39.	Fresh fruits	261.29
40.	Restaurant meals on trips	257.15
41.	Day care centers, nurseries, and preschools	236.56
42.	Cash contributions to charities	233.63
43.	Owned vacation homes	230.28
44.	Breakfast at restaurants	227.60
45.	Beef	226.32
46.	Fresh vegetables	226.14
47.	Vehicle finance charges	223.36
48.	Child support expenditures	208.46
49.	Physician's services	204.16
50.	Pet food	194.70

51.	Finance charges, except mortgage and vehicles	$181.53
52.	Elementary and high school tuition	169.04
53.	Snacks at restaurants	168.97
54.	Movie, theater, amusement park, and other admissions	168.75
55.	Pork	165.77
56.	Computers and computer hardware for nonbusiness use	162.71
57.	Hospital room and services	161.48
58.	Poultry	159.36
59.	Women's footwear	158.87
60.	Leased vehicles	158.68
61.	Cosmetics, perfume, and bath products	157.04
62.	Laundry and cleaning supplies	155.39
63.	Veterinarian services	149.95
64.	Expenses for other properties	149.93
65.	Prepared foods except frozen, salads, and desserts	147.81
66.	Interest paid, home equity loan/line of credit	140.37
67.	Carbonated drinks	139.74
68.	Legal fees	138.71
69.	Pet purchase, supplies, and medicines	135.69
70.	Other taxes	131.96
71.	Housekeeping services	131.93
72.	Cheese	131.47
73.	Fresh milk, all types	128.28
74.	Social, recreation, health club membership	127.44
75.	Household decorative items	126.84
76.	Fish and seafood	125.74
77.	Gardening, lawn care service	125.40
78.	Miscellaneous household products	125.00
79.	Trash and garbage collection	123.44
80.	Fees for participant sports	118.19
81.	Cleansing and toilet tissue, paper towels, and napkins	117.50
82.	Girls' (aged 2 to 15) apparel	115.92
83.	Toys, games, hobbies, and tricycles	114.59
84.	Beer and ale at home	112.49
85.	Men's footwear	111.75
86.	Potato chips and other snacks	111.59
87.	Vehicle registration	111.25
88.	Support for college students	104.82
89.	Wine at home	102.62
90.	Television sets	102.24
91.	Sofas	101.36
92.	Deductions for government retirement	100.54
93.	Nonprescription drugs	97.49
94.	Ready-to-eat and cooked cereals	94.82
95.	Jewelry	94.38
96.	Fees for recreational lessons	92.55
97.	Boys' (aged 2 to 15) apparel	87.96
98.	Candy and chewing gum	87.86
99.	Lunch meats (cold cuts)	87.23
100.	Coffee	86.50
101.	Maintenance and repair materials, owner	86.31
102.	Alimony expenditures	86.01
103.	Babysitting and child care	84.86
104.	Rent as pay	84.60
105.	Fuel oil	80.77
106.	Housing while attending school	76.65
107.	Mattresses and springs	76.43
108.	Lawn and garden supplies	76.04
109.	Beer and ale at bars, restaurants	75.94
110.	Stationery, stationery supplies, giftwrap	75.07

111.	Accounting fees	$75.03
112.	Funeral expenses	72.17
113.	Intracity mass transit fares	71.99
114.	Lawn and garden equipment	71.11
115.	Frozen prepared foods, except meals	70.22
116.	Bedroom linens	67.43
117.	Eyeglasses and contact lenses	66.52
118.	Motorized recreational vehicles	65.66
119.	Admission to sports events	65.45
120.	Books and supplies for college	65.30
121.	Children's (under age 2) apparel	63.31
122.	Bedroom furniture except mattresses and springs	63.24
123.	Service by professionals other than physician	62.38
124.	Hair care products	61.69
125.	Bread, other than white	61.60
126.	Athletic gear, game tables, exercise equipment	60.99
127.	Frozen meals	60.61
128.	Sauces and gravies	60.27
129.	Catered affairs	60.19
130.	Refrigerators and freezers	59.80
131.	School lunches	59.56
132.	Ground rent	58.68
133.	Lottery and gambling losses	57.93
134.	Postage	57.44
135.	Ice cream and related products	57.37
136.	Moving, storage, and freight express	56.88
137.	Bottled water	56.80
138.	Ship fares	56.53
139.	School tuition, books, and supplies other than college, vocational/technical, elementary, high school	55.30
140.	Canned and bottled fruit juice	54.92
141.	Canned vegetables	54.59
142.	Indoor plants and fresh flowers	53.57
143.	Property management, owner	53.28
144.	Eggs	53.08
145.	Other dairy (yogurt, etc.)	52.67
146.	Professional laundry, dry cleaning	52.24
147.	Biscuits and rolls	51.85
148.	Nonprescription vitamins	50.76
149.	Cookies	50.56
150.	Food prepared by consumer unit on trips	50.23
151.	Occupational expenses	48.41
152.	Bottled gas	47.44
153.	Other alcoholic beverages at bars, restaurants	47.43
154.	Lab tests, X-rays	46.91
155.	Canned and packaged soups	46.30
156.	Books	45.30
157.	Board (including at school)	44.93
158.	Alcoholic beverages purchased on trips	43.80
159.	White bread	43.52
160.	Care for elderly, invalids, handicapped, etc.	43.36
161.	Wall units, cabinets, and other furniture	42.39
162.	Nuts	42.35
163.	Parking fees	42.29
164.	Unmotored recreational vehicles	42.12
165.	Eye care services	41.86
166.	Pet services	41.70
167.	Topicals and dressings	40.99
168.	Oral hygiene products	40.82
169.	Coin-operated apparel laundry and dry cleaning	40.21

170.	Newspaper and magazine subscriptions	$39.58
171.	Power tools	39.34
172.	Boys' footwear	39.09
173.	Miscellaneous personal services	38.97
174.	Cash contributions to educational institutions	38.77
175.	Salt, spices, and other seasonings	38.72
176.	Cakes and cupcakes	37.94
177.	Frozen vegetables	37.50
178.	Crackers	37.17
179.	Girls' footwear	37.12
180.	Video game hardware and accessories	37.03
181.	Pasta, cornmeal, and other cereal products	36.98
182.	Fats and oils	36.79
183.	Rented vehicles	36.23
184.	Tolls	35.63
185.	Prepared salads	35.09
186.	Living room chairs	34.57
187.	Care in convalescent or nursing home	34.56
188.	Wine at bars, restaurants	34.54
189.	Deodorants, feminine hygiene, miscellaneous products	34.51
190.	Washing machines	34.12
191.	Sound components, equipment, and accessories	32.07
192.	Kitchen and dining room furniture	31.62
193.	Salad dressings	31.29
194.	Photographic equipment	31.17
195.	Meals as pay	30.79
196.	Tea	30.36
197.	Tobacco products other than cigarettes	30.30
198.	Video cassettes, tapes, and discs	29.70
199.	Jams, preserves, other sweets	29.61
200.	Hunting and fishing equipment	29.06
201.	Frozen and refrigerated bakery products	28.77
202.	Telephones and accessories	27.33
203.	Home security system service fee	27.23
204.	Lamps and lighting fixtures	26.83
205.	Small electric kitchen appliances	25.90
206.	Noncarbonated fruit-flavored drinks	25.83
207.	Butter	25.56
208.	Baby food	25.05
209.	Baking needs	24.95
210.	Cash contributions to political organizations	24.90
211.	Frankfurters	24.71
212.	Rice	24.65
213.	Termite and pest control products and services	24.58
214.	Outdoor equipment	24.51
215.	Sugar	24.38
216.	Clothes dryers	23.95
217.	Bathroom linens	23.90
218.	Sweetrolls, coffee cakes, doughnuts	23.73
219.	Cooking stoves, ovens	23.67
220.	Cream	23.58
221.	Checking accounts, other bank service charges	23.10
222.	Bicycles	21.69
223.	Other alcoholic beverages at home	21.40
224.	Hearing aids	21.23
225.	Photographer fees	21.12
226.	Nonclothing laundry and dry cleaning, sent out	21.09
227.	Recreation expenses on trips	20.99
228.	Canned fruits	20.35
229.	Automobile service clubs	20.09

230.	Laundry and cleaning equipment	$19.59
231.	Outdoor furniture	19.36
232.	Shaving products	19.18
233.	Vegetable juices	18.98
234.	Tableware, nonelectric kitchenware	18.89
235.	Intercity train fares	18.88
236.	Nonelectric cookware	18.86
237.	Peanut butter	18.68
238.	Nondairy cream and imitation milk	18.59
239.	Dried vegetables	18.22
240.	Local transportation on trips	17.81
241.	Olives, pickles, relishes	17.46
242.	Gifts of stocks, bonds, and mutual funds to members of other households	17.16
243.	Fresh fruit juice	17.06
244.	Musical instruments and accessories	16.80
245.	Dishwashers (built-in), garbage disposals, range hoods	16.61
246.	Books and supplies for elementary and high school	16.25
247.	Floor coverings	16.22
248.	Prepared flour mixes	16.18
249.	Electric floor-cleaning equipment	16.07
250.	Test preparation, tutoring services	15.86
251.	Computer accessories	15.85
252.	Rental of video cassettes, tapes, discs, films	15.72
253.	Maintenance and repair services, renter	15.71
254.	Nonalcoholic beverages (except carbonated, coffee, fruit-flavored drinks, and tea) and ice	15.36
255.	Appliance repair, including at service center	15.36
256.	Sports drinks	15.12
257.	Watches	15.09
258.	Computer software	15.04
259.	Satellite radio service	14.83
260.	Tenant's insurance	14.74
261.	Window coverings	14.64
262.	Prepared desserts	14.29
263.	Luggage	13.79
264.	Digital book readers	13.62
265.	Security services, owner	13.56
266.	Infants' equipment	13.42
267.	Pies, tarts, turnovers	13.41
268.	Cemetery lots, vaults, and maintenance fees	13.16
269.	Whiskey at home	12.93
270.	Living room tables	12.92
271.	Rental of party supplies for catered affairs	12.63
272.	Closet and storage items	12.60
273.	Intercity bus fares	11.96
274.	Vehicle inspection	11.85
275.	Hand tools	11.79
276.	Compact discs, records, and audio tapes	11.78
277.	Driver's license	11.64
278.	Taxi fares and limousine service	11.36
279.	Camping equipment	11.06
280.	Newspapers and magazines, nonsubscription	10.88
281.	Microwave ovens	10.55
282.	Streamed and downloaded audio	10.39
283.	Electric personal care appliances	10.39
284.	Lamb, organ meats, and others	10.19
285.	Shopping club membership fees	10.16
286.	Curtains and draperies	9.88
287.	Voice over IP	9.64

288.	Infants' furniture	$9.59
289.	Flour	9.36
290.	Photo processing	9.15
291.	Phone cards	9.00
292.	Hair accessories	8.92
293.	Parking at owned home	8.87
294.	Portable heating and cooling equipment	8.84
295.	Stamp and coin collecting	8.80
296.	China and other dinnerware	8.76
297.	Margarine	8.74
298.	Material for making clothes	8.74
299.	Coal, wood, and other fuels	8.72
300.	Dried fruits	8.71
301.	Sewing materials for household items	8.48
302.	Internet services away from home	8.25
303.	Kitchen and dining room linens	8.15
304.	Miscellaneous video equipment	8.08
305.	Glassware	7.94
306.	Repairs and rentals of lawn and garden equipment, hand and power tools, etc.	7.90
307.	Vocational and technical school tuition	7.66
308.	Docking and landing fees	7.45
309.	Personal digital audio players	7.41
310.	Vacation clubs	7.38
311.	VCRs and video disc players	7.35
312.	Bread and cracker products	7.31
313.	Frozen fruits	7.16
314.	Maintenance and repair materials, renter	7.12
315.	Live entertainment for catered affairs	6.48
316.	Rental of recreational vehicles	6.11
317.	Apparel alteration, repair, and tailoring services	6.03
318.	Office furniture for home use	6.02
319.	Global positioning system devices	5.66
320.	Frozen fruit juices	5.55
321.	Repair of computer systems for nonbusiness use	5.52
322.	Streamed and downloaded video	5.35
323.	Medical equipment for general use	5.16
324.	Window air conditioners	4.95
325.	Artificial sweeteners	4.91
326.	Nonclothing laundry and dry cleaning, coin-operated	4.79
327.	Watch and jewelry repair	4.72
328.	Personal digital assistants	4.70
329.	Water sports equipment	4.45
330.	Rental of furniture	4.44
331.	Towing charges	4.37
332.	Water-softening service	4.30
333.	Sewing patterns and notions	4.20
334.	Winter sports equipment	4.19
335.	Slipcovers and decorative pillows	3.94
336.	Applications, games, ringtones for handheld devices	3.86
337.	Portable memory	3.76
338.	Business equipment for home use	3.63
339.	Online gaming services	3.51
340.	Supportive and convalescent medical equipment	3.48
341.	Delivery services	3.43
342.	Safe deposit box rental	3.36
343.	Video game software	3.26
344.	Reupholstering and furniture repair	3.21
345.	Repair of TV, radio, and sound equipment	3.09
346.	Septic tank cleaning	2.95

347.	Flatware	$2.93
348.	Credit card memberships	2.92
349.	Deductions for railroad retirement	2.89
350.	Adult diapers	2.86
351.	Playground equipment	2.84
352.	Wigs and hairpieces	2.82
353.	Plastic dinnerware	2.68
354.	Smoking accessories	2.68
355.	Sewing machines	2.54
356.	Fireworks	2.46
357.	Global positioning services	2.06
358.	Silver serving pieces	2.04
359.	Rental and repair of miscellaneous sports equipment	1.86
360.	Pinball, electronic video games	1.78
361.	Smoke alarms	1.75
362.	Rental and repair of musical instruments	1.70
363.	Clothing rental	1.69
364.	Rental of medical equipment	1.53
365.	Shoe repair and other shoe services	1.52
366.	Appliance rental	1.50
367.	Satellite dishes	1.24
368.	School bus	1.15
369.	Other serving pieces	1.04
370.	Installation of television sets	0.74
371.	Books and supplies for vocational and technical schools	0.71
372.	Clothing storage	0.70
373.	Rental of office equipment for nonbusiness use	0.68
374.	Rental of supportive and convalescent medical equipment	0.68
375.	Telephone answering devices	0.59
376.	Dating services	0.50
377.	Installation of computer	0.44
378.	Repair and rental of photographic equipment	0.39
379.	Books and supplies for day care and nursery	0.38

Source: Calculations by New Strategist based on the Bureau of Labor Statistics' 2012 Consumer Expenditure Survey